THE FIRST ENGLISH DETECTIVES

The First English Detectives

The Bow Street Runners and the Policing of London, 1750–1840

J. M. BEATTIE

OXFORD
UNIVERSITY PRESS

OXFORD
UNIVERSITY PRESS

Great Clarendon Street, Oxford OX2 6DP

Oxford University Press is a department of the University of Oxford.
It furthers the University's objective of excellence in research, scholarship,
and education by publishing worldwide in

Oxford New York

Auckland Cape Town Dar es Salaam Hong Kong Karachi
Kuala Lumpur Madrid Melbourne Mexico City Nairobi
New Delhi Shanghai Taipei Toronto

With offices in

Argentina Austria Brazil Chile Czech Republic France Greece
Guatemala Hungary Italy Japan Poland Portugal Singapore
South Korea Switzerland Thailand Turkey Ukraine Vietnam

Oxford is a registered trade mark of Oxford University Press
in the UK and in certain other countries

Published in the United States
by Oxford University Press Inc., New York

British Library Cataloguing in Publication Data

Data available

Library of Congress Cataloging in Publication Data
Library of Congress Control Number: 2011939890

Typeset by SPI Publisher Services, Pondicherry, India
Printed in Great Britain
on acid-free paper by
MPG Books Group, Bodmin and King's Lynn

ISBN 978-0-19-969516-4

1 3 5 7 9 10 8 6 4 2

For
Natalie, Nicholas, Sarah, Chloe, and Kazuo

Preface and Acknowledgements

The main concern of this book is to study a group of men in eighteenth and early nineteenth-century London who were important in shaping the way policing developed in the metropolis over several decades, but whose place in the history of that crucial period has been largely neglected. The Bow Street runners, as they came to be called, were established on the initiative of Henry Fielding, the novelist and an active magistrate living in Bow Street, and with the support of a government searching for ways to deal with a sharp increase in serious crime at the conclusion in 1748 of what had been a major war. The runners were established to confront violent offenders on the streets and highways in and around London, men who were beyond the capacities of the existing forces of nightwatchmen and constables to control.

Henry Fielding died soon after the government agreed to support his efforts to create a group of what he called honest thief-takers, and the project was taken up by his half-brother, John, who developed the office into the leading centre of policing and prosecution in the metropolis over the next quarter century, and the runners into a group of officers committed to the investigation of criminal offences who established, within a few years, stability of membership. That longevity was made possible by the government's continuing financial support, never more than modest in John Fielding's years, but sufficient to provide the runners with the foundation of an income that could be increased by work undertaken on behalf of government departments and other institutions, and by providing policing services for victims of crimes willing to pay to have their stolen property found or at least to have the men who robbed or stole from them brought to justice. Stability of membership and experience enabled the runners to acquire skill and expertise in carrying out investigations, and a sense of how to collect evidence to be presented before the judges and juries at the Old Bailey, the leading criminal court in London. The runners acquired a reputation (at least among the propertied classes) for being good at their work—at discovering and tracking down offenders, and having the courage when that was called for to make arrests. They were, I will argue, detectives in all but name.

These themes—the establishment and early years of the runners under Henry Fielding, the development of the Bow Street office, and the work of the runners under John Fielding—form the subject of the first half of the book. Fielding's achievement was to make his Bow Street house not just a magistrate's office in his own lifetime, but, because the government provided stipends for two other justices besides himself, an institution that would survive him. His legacy can be seen in the government's decisions to support a new force of patrolmen at Bow Street in 1783, something that Fielding had long advocated, and, in 1792, to create seven other 'public', or 'police offices' in the metropolis, on the Bow Street model.

The second half of the book, in which I continue to follow the work of the runners as a main concern, also takes up a second theme that carried inevitable consequences for that work, and indeed for the place of the runners in the policing of London: ideas and proposals for further reform of policing institutions in the metropolis. There was little sustained concern about the policing of London during the more than two decades of war that began in 1793 against the new republic in France and was only finally concluded with the defeat of Napoleon in 1815. But as that war drew to an end, and the common experience of the eighteenth century was repeated in a sharp rise of criminal prosecutions with the coming of the peace, anxiety about crime drew criticism of policing and the other elements of the criminal justice system as it had at the end of every war in the eighteenth century. And, again, as in the past, the government was eventually forced to act.

It is important for an understanding of the attempts to control what appeared to be a rising level of crime that what was understood as 'the police' in 1815 was Bow Street and the seven offices that dated from 1792—not the long-established parochial institutions of the night watch and local constables, whose duties did not extend beyond their own parishes. The intention of the reform effort undertaken in the last years of Lord Sidmouth's term as Home Secretary between 1818 and 1822 was to make the existing police offices more effective and to increase their patrolling capacities in the interest of reducing crime by preventive means rather than by detection and prosecution. Robert Peel inserted a new idea when he succeeded Sidmouth in 1822 in favouring a unified police for the metropolis, but he too concentrated in his early years on further improvements in the existing police offices.

Peel proposed the idea of a unified police in a more radical way than he initially intended when, in the last years of the 1820s, prosecutions for crimes against property rose even more strongly than earlier, and now not just within the boundaries of the metropolis, but in areas on the borders of the urban world, in parishes that had virtually no policing institutions at all. It was that new concern as much as anything that Peel responded to in establishing a committee in 1828 to investigate the state of crime and policing, and that led a year later to legislation that created the Metropolitan Police. This was to be a new force in a unified police district that encompassed the metropolis and new areas on its borders, though not the City of London. It represented a fundamental re-thinking in the Home Office, and an entirely new idea since it created a police not by expanding and imposing central leadership on the personnel at the police offices, but by replacing the night watch. It was to be led by two commissioners under the Home Office. Where the old structure of police was rigid and uncoordinated, the new force could be enlarged at will, and expanded in geographical range as necessary. The ease of passage of this legislation was as surprising as its substance, given the attitudes and ideas that had characterized previous debates about the police.

The public offices of the stipendiary magistrates remained as sites of summary justice, and as the crucial link between reported offences and the criminal courts. The runners did not, however, survive the formation of the New Police. Within a decade of its establishment, the stipendiary magistrates lost the administrative powers that had made them leaders of the police, and the runners were quietly disbanded. They went without fanfare and without complaint from any quarter, though, as I shall suggest in a brief Epilogue, without being entirely forgotten.

It is a pleasure to acknowledge the help I have received in the course of writing this book. I am grateful for financial support from the Social Science and Humanities Research Council of Canada and the Centre for Criminology and Sociolegal Studies at the University of Toronto. The Centre has been my academic home since my retirement, and I am grateful to my colleagues there for their friendship and their support and encouragement of my work. I owe thanks to Rita Donelan and Lori Wells, to the librarians, Andrea Shier and Tom Finlay, the Director, Mariana Valverde, and especially to Rosemary Gartner and Tony Doob, for their help on numerous occasions.

I am grateful to a succession of graduate students for research assistance over the last decade: Elaine Breckenridge; Erica Charters; Kelly De Luca; Sandra Herber; Karen Macfarlane; Sheena Sommers; Yen Tran. I have also benefitted from the research skills of Louise Falcini. I owe thanks to Natalie Simpson for sorting out and making legible my photographs of documents, and to Katherine Beattie for the Tables and Figures, and a great deal more.

I owe special thanks to several colleagues and friends for reading parts or all of the text of the book and giving me the benefit of their advice, particularly Donna Andrew, David Cox, Simon Devereaux, Randall McGowen, Ruth Paley, Elaine Reynolds, Allyson May, and Chris Williams. And to several who have sent me documents and in other ways shared their research with me. I am particularly grateful in this respect to Donna Andrew, Simon Devereaux, Rachael Griffin, Joanna Innes, Peter King, Norma Landau, Randall McGowen, Andrea McKenzie, and Greg Smith.

I wish to thank Jim Phillips and my colleagues in the Legal History Group at the University of Toronto for the opportunity to talk about Bow Street on several occasions and for their helpful responses.

I am grateful to the editors and publishers of the journals *Crime, Histoire & Sociétés/Crime, History & Societies* and *Law and History Review*, for permission to draw on material that appeared originally in their pages. And to the National Portrait Gallery, the Archives Centre of the City of Westminster, and the Fisher Library, University of Toronto, for permission to reproduce images from their collections.

I am also very grateful to my editors at Oxford University Press, particularly to Emma Barber for her skillful and generous help as the book went through the production process.

I owe my greatest debt to my wife, Susan, for her loving support and encouragement of my work over many years. I am grateful to her, as I have been many times, for reading every draft and giving me the great benefit of her editorial skills. We both take great pleasure in dedicating the book to our grandchildren.

Contents

List of Tables and Figures

Tables

Figures

List of Illustrations

List of Abbreviations

Add Mss	Additional Manuscripts
BL	British Library
HO	Home Office papers
JHC	Journals of the House of Commons
LMA	London Metropolitan Archives
MEPO	Metropolitan Police papers
MINT	Royal Mint papers
NLI	National Library of Ireland
OBP	Old Bailey Proceedings
ODNB	Oxford Dictionary of National Biography
Parl. Debates	[W. Cobbett], *The Parliamentary History of England, from the Earliest Period to the year 1803* (36 vols.); [T. C. Hansard], *The Parliamentary Debates, from the Year 1803 to the Present Time* (1st–2nd series)
PC	Privy Council papers
SP	Secretary of State Papers
T	Treasury papers
TNA	The National Archives
TNA/PRO	Gifts and deposits at The National Archives

1

Introduction

On the evening of 30 March 1767, John Griffiths and three other men were returning by hackney coach from a race meeting in Holloway when they were stopped on the outskirts of London by a gang of armed men who demanded their money. One of the men in the coach jumped out in an effort to escape, and was knocked down and badly beaten. Griffiths refused to give up his purse and was shot dead. The others did not resist. Within hours, seven men from the Bow Street magistrates' office went in search of the robbers, gathering information from pubs and from a variety of informers. Two days later they arrested five men, though not before another coach had been held up by some of the gang, and another passenger badly wounded. At the trials that followed, the evidence provided by the Bow Street men helped to convict four of the robbers. The man who had killed Griffiths was sentenced to death under the Murder Act of 1752. As that statute directed, he was hanged three days later and his body was dissected by surgeons. Three others were capitally convicted, though two were reprieved and probably transported. A fifth man turned king's evidence and was granted immunity.[1]

The seven men who scoured East London in search of these robbers and arrested them after a bloody fight, were working under the direction of Sir John Fielding, a magistrate living at number 4, Bow Street, near Covent Garden. They had been brought together in the early 1750s by his predecessor at Bow Street, his half-brother, Henry Fielding, the novelist, who had persuaded the government to provide funds to support men capable of confronting highwaymen and footpads at a time when violence on the streets of London and on the main roads carrying traffic in and out of the metropolis was a source of considerable anxiety. Henry Fielding died within months of receiving this subvention, leaving Bow Street to John, who, although he had been blind since he was nineteen, turned out to be the most innovative magistrate of the eighteenth century. With the government's financial support over the next quarter century, John Fielding created an office staffed by three justices in receipt of government stipends, who joined with him to enable the public for the first time to report offences or to get a magistrate's help at stated times every day of the week, except Sunday (and even then in an emergency). The public were encouraged to attend the examinations of suspected offenders at

---

[1] OBP, April 1767 (Francis Gorman and Henry Johnson) t17670429-51; OBP, April 1767 (Lawrence Sweetman and Samuel Collins) t17670429-54; LMA: OB/SP/91, April 1767 (indictments 65, 67, 70–2); T 1/454, f. 84. For a fuller account of this case, see ch. 4, text at n. 102. The Murder Act is 25 Geo II, c. 27 (1752).

Bow Street, and the press to report the proceedings, which, as we will see, they did with regularity by the 1770s.

The government's annual grant also enabled Fielding to provide support for the men who went after the gang of robbers in 1767. They formed by then a stable group of half a dozen men whose main mission was to investigate offences and to seek to arrest and prosecute serious offenders, and who I believe are best thought of as detectives—though anachronistically, since the word was not used before the nineteenth century. They were an entirely new element in the policing forces in the metropolis. Their rapid engagement in the effort to apprehend suspected felons distinguished them fundamentally from the existing peace-keeping forces of night watchmen and parish constables, who had no such duties.

The nightwatch was a paid force by the middle of the eighteenth century and almost certainly more effective at preventing crime during the hours of darkness than its critics were fond of saying. They walked established beats at set times, checked that doors and windows were locked, and called out the time through the night—enabling intending burglars to keep track of them, it was always said. They made occasional arrests when they came upon offences, and they were without a doubt helpful to the inhabitants they served. But they were not expected to search out offenders.[2]

The parish constables were for the most part private citizens serving for a year as part of their civic duty, or in some cases as paid replacements for men who could afford to engage a substitute. Constables had heavy administrative duties, and they were expected to help keep the streets clear of vagrants and prostitutes, to arrest petty offenders, and to control crowds on days of celebration or when crowds assembled for some unlawful purpose.[3] They were certainly important to the well being of the metropolis. But they were parish or ward officers. They were not obliged to do anything that might take them beyond the boundaries of the jurisdiction they served. With respect to criminal offences that rose to the level of felonies they were expected to obey a magistrate's warrant to conduct a search or make an arrest. But there was no expectation that they would investigate offences or make an effort to find and apprehend offenders.

Very occasionally, a magistrate or a high constable would develop an interest in a particular case and go out of his way to follow it up; some became more regularly active in these ways.[4] But that was unusual. Magistrates and constables mainly responded to information; they did not develop it. The established process of prosecution of felonies depended fundamentally on private initiative. It had always

---

[2] Elaine A. Reynolds, *Before the Bobbies: the Night Watch and Police Reform in Metropolitan London, 1720–1830* (London, 1998); J. M. Beattie, *Policing and Punishment in London, 1660–1750: Urban Crime and the Limits of Terror* (Oxford, 2001), ch. 4.

[3] Joan R. Kent, *The English Village Constable 1580–1642: A Social and Administrative Study* (Oxford, 1986); Paul Griffiths, *Lost Londons: Change, Crime, and Control in the Capital City, 1550–1660* (Cambridge, 2008); Beattie, *Policing and Punishment in London*, ch. 3.

[4] John Styles, 'An Eighteenth-Century Magistrate as Detective: Samuel Lister of Little Horton', *Bradford Antiquary*, 47, new series (1982), 98–117; Ruth Paley, 'Thief-takers in London in the Age of the McDaniel Gang, c. 1745–54' in Douglas Hay and Francis Snyder (eds.), *Policing and Prosecution in Britain, 1750–1850* (Oxford, 1989), 301–42.

been left to the victim to find perpetrators or to pay someone to do so, and then to pay all the costs that would follow as the criminal process wound its way from the magistrate's hearing to the trial court. We will see that in the early eighteenth century it would have been possible to engage a private thief-taker. But the Bow Street men were the first quasi-official thief-takers—men who were available to victims to be hired, but also available to Fielding to be sent at no cost to the victim to find and arrest offenders when he judged it in the public interest.

Fielding's officers had no official title because the office had no official standing. The government's financial support came initially in the form of a payment through the office of the secretary of state, renewed annually but without guarantee of permanence. The half dozen men who agreed to work essentially for fees by the job were known at first simply as 'Fielding's men', or 'Sir John's men', after he was knighted in 1761. By the early 1770s they were being called 'runners', a term that was almost certainly intended as derogatory since it associated them with men who worked as assistants to bailiffs in the disreputable job of arresting debtors, or who escorted men to gaol who had been committed for trial. It was not a name the Bow Street men ever used of themselves. By the nineteenth century they preferred to be called 'principal officers', as a way of distinguishing themselves from the more junior patrolmen who had become by then an important part of the Bow Street office policing forces. But the nickname 'runners' became more respectable over time, and it was the name by which they were remembered long after their disbandment in 1839. It is as Bow Street runners that they remain known in popular memory, and, in the absence of an alternative that would be appropriate over their 90-year history, it is the name I will use for them.

Not a great deal has been known in detail about the runners until the recent publication of David Cox's analysis of the work they undertook in the provinces after 1792. Cox has useful things to say about the runners in general, but his book is focussed largely on an aspect of their work that has not been examined at length in any previous study, that is, their engagement in effect as a form of 'national' police, investigating difficult cases on behalf of provincial clients who could afford to pay for their services—private prosecutors, as well as magistrates and other local officials. It is extremely valuable to have this side of their policing uncovered so effectively by Cox's painstaking research.[5] Our books are complementary, since my central concern here is on the runners' policing activity in London and from their establishment in the early 1750s.

Other than that book, there has been no extended scholarly work on the runners. They have been the subject of several popular studies which are mainly episodic and anecdotal and provide little in the way of systematic analysis of the runners' work or of the developments in prosecution at the Bow Street office.[6] The runners are

---

[5] David J. Cox, *A Certain Share of Low Cunning. A History of the Bow Street Runners, 1792–1839* (Cullompton, Devon, 2010). Patrick Pringle wrote briefly about the runners' work in the provinces in his introduction to Henry Goddard, *Memoirs of a Bow Street Runner* (London, 1956).

[6] Gilbert Armitage, *The History of the Bow Street Runners* (London, 1932); Patrick Pringle, *Hue and Cry. The Story of Henry and John Fielding and their Bow Street Runners* (London, 1955); Anthony Babington, *A House in Bow Street. Crime and the Magistracy, London 1740–1881* (London, 1969).

invariably mentioned in general accounts of London policing. For 'traditional' historians of the police they were part of the ineffective, fragmented, and largely corrupt policing that was replaced by Sir Robert Peel's Metropolitan Police Force in 1829.[7] Sir Leon Radzinowicz's magisterial account of criminal administration after 1750, based on wide-ranging research into printed and some manuscript sources, is on an entirely different level from all earlier work. He devoted parts of three volumes to the reform of the police which together provide a rich analysis of plans and proposals for improvements in the police over the late eighteenth and early nineteenth centuries. Radzinowicz says relatively little, however, about policing practices, including the work of the magistrates at Bow Street and even less about the runners. Although he recognized Bow Street's leading position among other police offices, he was largely dismissive of their importance since they appeared to contribute little to the achievement of a centralized and hierarchical force of the kind that Peel established in 1829 and that Radzinowicz regarded as the only rational solution to the policing problems he so fully exposed.[8]

More recent work has introduced balance to the study of London policing by revealing the many ways that changes in eighteenth-century practices anticipated elements in Peel's New Police, diminishing to some extent the sense of 1829 as a fundamental watershed in policing history.[9] Two monographs in particular have

---

[7] W. L. Melville Lee, *A History of Police in England* (London, 1901; repr. Montclair, NJ, 1971); Charles Reith, *The Police Idea. Its History and Evolution in England in the eighteenth century and after* (Oxford, 1938); *Idem, The Blind Eye of History: a study of the present police era* (London, 1952); *Idem, A New Study of Police History* (London 1956); T. A. Critchley, *A History of Police in England and Wales* (London 1967; 2nd edn. 1978). For a categorization of historians of the police as 'traditional,' 'revisionist,' and 'post-revisionist', see Robert Reiner, *The Politics of the Police* (Hemel Hempstead, 1992; 4th edn. Oxford, 2010), 39–66.

[8] Leon Radzinowicz, *A History of the English Criminal Law and its Administration from 1750*. Vol. 2: *The Clash between Private Initiative and Public Interest in the Enforcement of the Law* (London, 1956); Vol. 3: *Cross Currents in the Movement for the Reform of the Police* (London, 1956); Vol. 4: *Grappling for Control* (London, 1968). References to Bow Street are scattered through these volumes, but see in particular, vol. 2, part 2, and 263 ff.

[9] Particularly important is the unpublished thesis of Ruth Paley, 'The Middlesex Justices Act of 1792: its origins and effects', Ph.D. thesis (University of Reading, 1983); and see her '"An Imperfect. Inadequate, and Wretched System?" Policing London before Peel', *Criminal Justice History* (10, 1989), 95–130. Other important recent work includes Douglas Hay and Francis Snyder, 'Using the Criminal Law, 1750–1850' in *Idem* (eds.), *Policing and Prosecution in Britain 1750–1850* (Oxford, 1989); Andrew T. Harris, *Policing the City. Crime and Legal Authority in London, 1780–1840* (Columbus, 2004); David Philips, 'A New Engine of Power and Authority: the Institutionalisation of Law Enforcement in England 1780–1830' in V. A. C. Gatrell, Bruce Lenman, and Geoffrey Parker (eds.), *Crime and the Law. The Social History of Crime in Western Europe since 1500* (London, 1980); John Styles, 'Sir John Fielding and the problem of criminal investigation in 18th century England' *Transactions of the Royal Historical Society* (33, 1983); *Idem*, 'The Emergence of the Police: Explaining Police Reform in Eighteenth- and Nineteenth-Century England', *British Journal of Criminology* (27/1, 1987): 15–22. Simon Devereaux, 'Convicts and the State: The Administration of Criminal Justice in Great Britain during the Reign of George III', Ph.D. Thesis (University of Toronto, 1997). Bruce P. Smith has provided a superb analysis of recent work in 'English Criminal Justice Administration, 1650–1850', *Law and History Review*, 25 (3, 2007): 593–634—a follow-up in essence to the important assessment by Joanna Innes and John Styles, 'The Crime Wave: Recent Writing on Crime and Criminal Justice in Eighteenth-Century England', *Journal of British Studies*, 25 (1986): 380–435, reprinted in Adrian Wilson (ed.), *Rethinking Social History: English Society 1570–1920 and its Interpretation* (Manchester, 1993), 201–65.

extended our knowledge of the nature of London policing in the eighteenth and early nineteenth centuries. Stanley Palmer has provided the most detailed general account yet published of the subject in his study of policing developments in England and Ireland between 1780 and 1850. With respect to Bow Street and the runners, Palmer takes the view that the forces under the control of the magistrates there—which by the 1820s included foot and horse patrols—were not numerous enough to make a great deal of difference to the policing of London. He has little to say about the runners themselves, in large part perhaps because his starting point in 1780 meant that he overlooked the years in which they were at their most active in the metropolis.[10] In her study of the night watch in Westminster, Elaine Reynolds does not have much reason to refer to the runners, but her work is an important and significant contribution to policing in this period. Reynolds provides a fine account of the efforts of local authorities in Westminster to strengthen the preventive policing of the watch across the eighteenth and into the nineteenth centuries. She also provides in her final chapter a valuable analysis of the making of the 1829 Act, in which she shows that the acceptance of the legislation by local authorities helps to explain the ease with which Peel was able to steer his 1829 Metropolitan Police bill through parliament.[11]

Finally, two general studies of English policing by Clive Emsley and Philip Rawlings provide valuable accounts of the way policing changed in the eighteenth and nineteenth centuries.[12] They are valuable from my point of view because instead of presenting the story of this period as a single narrative of movement towards the Act that created the Metropolitan Police in 1829—a narrative into which it has always proved impossible to fit the Bow Street office and the runners—they favour a framework that recognizes the existence in this period of two broad forms of policing that can be summarized as preventive and detective. It is useful to think of these, as developing in parallel, though independently, as each responded differently to a mix of ideas and sentiments as to what policing ought to be and to the immediate pressure of changing circumstances and conditions.

I find that a useful way to think about the policing of London over the eighteenth and early nineteenth centuries, and to conceive of it, in addition, as falling into two overlapping phases. I see the first of these beginning (earlier than most accounts have allowed) in the late seventeenth and early eighteenth centuries with decisions made at the level of local policing, in parliament, and by initiatives taken by the central government. Some of the responses at the local level could be characterized as measures to prevent offences taking place; others were clearly intended to encourage the detection, apprehension, and effective punishment of offenders. No one then spoke of preventive and detective policing, but improvements in both were clearly being urged and practised.

---

[10] Stanley H. Palmer, *Police and Protest in England and Ireland 1780–1850* (Cambridge, 1988).

[11] Reynolds, *Before the Bobbies.*

[12] Clive Emsley, *The English Police. A Political and Social History* (Hemel Hempstead, 1991; 2nd edn. London, 1996); Philip Rawlings, *Policing. A Short History* (Cullompton, Devon, 2002).

There may have been several reasons why concerns about policing were raised in the late seventeenth century, but there is no reason to doubt the signal importance of sharp increases in crimes against property, some very threatening, many less serious but deeply annoying to the property-owning citizens of London, all of concern to those anxious about the moral health of the society.[13] Whether changes in prosecutions signified a change in the actual number of offences or merely a greater determination on the part of victims to prosecute is an issue that cannot be settled with certainty. But contemporaries had no doubts at all that it was the former, and I would argue that there is good reason to think that the sharp increases in the number of cases coming before the courts in the last decade of the century bore some relationship to the level of offending and were a consequences of several factors. One was a difficulty in the labour market caused by sustained immigration into the capital of young men and women looking for work, many of whom found it difficult at the best of times to patch together a living in the metropolis. In the 1690s those difficulties were made all the more serious by several years of poor harvests and thus higher bread prices, and by further inflationary pressures from the issuing of new coinage. But what made the crime issue a matter of urgency, particularly perhaps for members of parliament and for everyone who had to travel into and out of London, was a serious increase in violent offences on the London streets and on the major roads around the capital. Some of that violence may have stemmed from demobilizations of armed forces in the early years of the decade and after 1697 at the conclusion of the war that William III had taken the country into on his accession in 1689. Whatever the cause, violence on the roads was a serious problem in the last years of the seventeenth century, as it was to be from time to time through the eighteenth.

One can see responses of various kinds in the late seventeenth century to a perceived increase in crime in London. One was at the local level, among the authorities responsible for mounting the night watch and choosing parish constables. In the City of London, for example, and elsewhere in the metropolis, the men who managed the wards moved to increase the numbers of night watchmen and to organize their patrolling in more effective ways. At the same time, they began a process that was to transform the lighting of the streets over the coming decades. These improvements in the watch and in street lighting were sufficiently extensive to require the replacement in the 1730s of the customary system of citizen participation by Acts of Parliament that enabled local authorities to collect a new rate, replacing the requirement to serve with a requirement to pay. Watchmen were thereafter hired men, paid a weekly wage. Parishes increasingly engaged contractors to provide oil lamps on more than just the major streets.[14]

The response in parliament to the various crime problems in the 1690s also carried significant long-term consequences. On the one hand there were sustained

---

[13] The following paragraphs on the response of local authorities, parliament, and the central government to the crime problems of London in the 1690s and first half of the eighteenth century summarize the argument in Beattie, *Policing and Punishment in London*, chs. 7–8.

[14] Reynolds, *Before the Bobbies*, chs. 2–3; Beattie, *Policing and Punishment in London*, chs. 3–4.

moves sponsored by backbench members to enlarge the scope of the death penalty for the minor property offences that were common in the large urban world—in particular, shoplifting and theft by servants. These were offences commonly committed by women and were apparently at unusually high levels in the 1690s and the early years of the eighteenth century when—perhaps for the only time in the history of London crime—women accounted for more than half of all property offenders at many sessions of the Old Bailey, the principal criminal court in London.[15] Making those essentially minor offences punishable by hanging was clearly an effort to frighten women from giving in to the temptation to steal from shops or from their employers.

That had been the intention of the sheaf of capital statutes already on the books. At the same time, an entirely new kind of response was taken up in parliament, also beginning in the 1690s, against offences that threatened harm to their victims as well as the loss of valuable property—highway and street robbery and burglary. These offences were already capital. The new legislation, sponsored by backbench members of parliament, introduced inducements in the form of rewards guaranteed by parliament to encourage the arrest, prosecution, conviction and punishment of the most serious offenders. The first such statute, in 1692, offered £40 for the conviction of a highwayman; others followed over the next several years aimed at burglars, coiners, and other offenders. Inducements to prosecute were to be hugely increased in 1720, when, in the midst of another wave of violent crime following another cycle of war and peace—the war of Spanish Succession (1702–1713) having been concluded by the Treaty of Utrecht in 1713—the central government offered the extraordinary sum of £100 for the conviction of a highwayman, making it clear at the same time by designating the streets of London as 'highways' that they also had street muggers in the metropolis very much in their sights.[16]

These efforts in parliament and in the king's government to encourage prosecutions were no doubt aimed at victims of offences, hoping to encourage them to make an effort to find their attackers and bring them to justice. The result, however, was much more clearly to encourage the enterprise of private thief-takers. Such men had been known since the early seventeenth century, but the rewards that became available through statute and proclamation multiplied their numbers in the first half of the eighteenth century. They became notorious, not so much for catching and prosecuting genuine offenders (though they did some of that), as for setting themselves up as intermediaries between victims and their attackers, extracting payments for the return of stolen goods and using the threat of prosecution to keep offenders in thrall. Much more seriously, some encouraged or even staged robberies, and procured perjured evidence to ensure convictions.[17]

---

[15] Beattie, *Policing and Punishment in London*, 63–71; Peter King, *Crime and Law in England, 1750–1840: Remaking Justice from the Margins* (Cambridge, 2006), ch. 6.

[16] Beattie, *Policing and Punishment in London*, ch. 7.

[17] Timothy Wales, 'Thief-takers and their Clients' in Paul Griffiths and Mark S. R. Jenner (eds.), *Londinopolis: essays in the cultural and social history of early modern London* (Manchester, 2000), 67–85; Beattie, *Policing and Punishment in London*, ch. 5.

The government's large supplementary rewards remained available for most of the second quarter of the century, with the consequence that gang activity in London and corrupt prosecutions became increasingly common. Indeed, false charges and perjured evidence became such a problem at the Old Bailey that the judges were moved in the 1730s to allow accused felons to engage counsel for the first time, against a long-standing rule of court, and to begin to define laws of evidence to protect defendants against blatant abuse.[18] The £100 reward was discontinued in 1745 in the middle of another war because violent offences fell away, as they usually did in wartime, but the government was forced to reinstate it when the peace in 1748 brought soldiers and sailors back to be discharged near London, and robbery on the streets and highways spiked once more. The result was a bill for reward payments much larger than the government cared to pay— determined as it was to reduce the debt incurred during the war—and at the same time renewed corrupt thief-taker activity.[19]

It was in these circumstances, that the secretary of state mainly in charge of domestic affairs, the duke of Newcastle, turned in desperation to Henry Fielding. And it is at this point that my account of Bow Street and the runners begins, with a government subvention to Fielding that enabled him to maintain a group of paid officers, to engage a clerical staff, and to establish a new form of magistrates' office. As we will see in chapter two, Henry Fielding was well prepared to offer a new strategy—or, at least, to offer a version of the detection and prosecution strategy that had seemed essential since the 1690s, but one, he claimed, that would encourage real thief-takers actually to confront violent offenders. The annual government grant established in 1754 provided the resources with which Henry's successor, his half-brother, John, created an active magistrates' office and a group of 'real' thief-takers. I set out in chapter three John Fielding's establishment of the office in his first dozen years, during which the government provided financial support for other magistrates besides Fielding, and increased the subvention for policing from £200 to £600. Chapter four is devoted to the work—detective work as I shall claim—that the runners carried out under John Fielding's direction to his death in 1780 and in the following decade. And in chapter five, I set out the innovative prosecution process that Fielding created at Bow Street, and examine the extent to which the runners contributed to the building of prosecution cases both in the pretrial examinations before the magistrates and at the felony trials in which they gave evidence at the Old Bailey.

Bow Street policing under John Fielding was not simply aimed at catching and prosecuting offenders. He believed as strongly as anyone in preventive policing; and from time to time, when his resources allowed it, he put preventive measures into practice. As we will see, he strove throughout his time at Bow Street to develop a system of patrolling without ever succeeding in getting the necessary financial commitment from the government. He also encouraged the strengthening of the

---

[18] John H. Langbein, *The Origins of Adversary Criminal Trial* (Oxford, 2003), ch. 3.
[19] Ruth Paley, 'Thief-takers in London in the age of the McDaniel gang, c. 1745–1754' in Hay and Snyder (eds.), *Policing and Prosecution in Britain*, 301–41.

watch and supported reformative social institutions. But there is no doubt that in his quarter century at Bow Street Fielding's policing practice was principally focussed on investigating and prosecuting felonies. It was an outgrowth and extension of the culture of prosecution created by the reward system—less corrupt, more effective, more acceptable to the public, but a culmination nonetheless of attempts to deal with the periodic violence that characterized London crime in the eighteenth century. Bow Street practised a form of policing that had been encouraged by parliament and the government because violence touched not only the poor and working population, but also the wealthy, indeed everyone who used the highways, including merchants, parliamentarians, aristocrats, and their families. When danger on the roads was difficult to avoid, as it was from time to time until the very end of the eighteenth century, policing that promised vigorous detection, arrest, prosecution and serious punishment had seemed the only available answer. That was what Fielding had promised and delivered.

An obvious need for a detective police in London did not, however, long outlast him. For reasons I take up in chapter six, this phase of policing, virtually a century long, in which there was a strong impulse to encourage the seeking out of dangerous offenders was coming to an end by the 1780s. That decade—the immediate post-Fielding years—forms something of a transition in London policing. A new phase was emerging in which there came to be more emphasis on a different form of policing from that exemplified by the runners and John Fielding's Bow Street office. It was based essentially on an old assumption—that the way to fight crime was to prevent the bad habits that led the young to commit minor infractions that were the gateway to ever more serious offences and inevitably to a painful death on the gallows. We will explore in chapter six the way in which these ideas were articulated in the 1770s, to some extent in opposition to what some were coming to regard as the brutality of Fielding's catch-and-punish policing. By the next decade, the idea of prevention appeared more directly in various guises in the writings of a wide range of writers, the first period in which policing of any kind was discussed extensively in print.

The decade of the 1780s was also notable for the extent to which the government became directly involved in attempts to deal with the crime wave that had followed the end of the American war in 1782. For the first time, the government agreed to pay for something that Fielding had proposed several times—an armed patrol to guard the highways. And the administration also took up another of Fielding's ideas when in 1792 (after an abortive attempt at something much grander in 1785) it established seven new magistrates' offices in London on the model of Bow Street, each staffed by three stipendiary magistrates and six paid constables.

These various shifts in ideas and institutional developments in the 1780s had consequences for the runners, since it became clear that the patrolmen and to some extent the constables at the new magistrates' offices—or what came quickly to be called police offices—engaged in the kinds of investigations of property offences that had been at the heart of the runners' work for 40 years. An increasing number of full-time officers reduced the runners' opportunities to conduct the kind of investigations they had carried out under John Fielding, and indeed it was the case that from 1792 the runners' engagement in criminal investigations in London gradually diminished. On the other hand, as Cox has shown and as I shall report briefly in chapters seven and eight, they took the lead in the early decades of the nineteenth century in investigations into serious offences in the provinces.

Apart from the increasing numbers of police officers, the runners' work was to be changed in the late eighteenth and early nineteenth centuries by two more fundamental conditions. One was a long-term shift in the nature of crime in the metropolis, principally a remarkable falling away of violent offences, beginning in the last years of the eighteenth century and continuing well into the nineteenth, a subject I shall take up mainly in chapter seven. More immediately, after 1792 the runners' work was affected by some of the domestic consequences of the French Revolution, and of the war that began in February 1793 between Britain (as part of a broader coalition) and the new revolutionary government. Among those consequences were concerns about sedition and the possibility of an insurrection by radical elements in Britain supported by French arms. Dealing with such threats was the responsibility of the Home Secretary, who had long depended on the chief magistrate of Bow Street for advice. The inevitable result was that during the war, Bow Street was drawn even closer to the Home Department than ever before, and the runners were presented with new tasks, including the protection of the royal family, and to some extent efforts to investigate and prevent sedition. I take up these issues in chapter seven.

The subject of police reform was largely in abeyance during the wars against Revolutionary and Napoleonic France. In the interest of advancing his career as one of the new police magistrates, Patrick Colquhoun made an effort in 1795 to interest the government in his ideas about crime and policing by publishing a *Treatise on the Police of the Metropolis*, with six further editions over the next decade. His ideas interested Jeremy Bentham and some members of parliament, but he got little response from the government, even when the war ended in 1815 and the expected increase in property offences put policing matters back on the public agenda.

I take up in chapter eight the greatly expanded interest in police reform after 1815, including the investigations conducted by parliament into policing in 1816 and the following two years, and the efforts by the government to respond to the obvious need for measures to counter levels of property offences that had increased sharply through the postwar years, and after a brief pause, even more strongly in the second half of the 1820s. Bow Street and the police offices were central to much of the discussion of the policing of the metropolis in the postwar years. They *were* the police of the metropolis, and the first ideas about reforming the police centred on them—on how they might be better coordinated and encouraged to take up prevention rather than detection, how the constables in the police offices might be increased in number, and patrolling improved.

The arrival of Robert Peel at the Home Office in 1822 introduced a new proposal into the discussion, an idea that derived from his experience in Ireland, where he had recently served as Chief Secretary, and particularly from his intimate knowledge of the policing of Dublin. This was an emphasis on the need for more unity in the London police, for central control over a single force, not merely more effective coordination and cooperation among the police offices. There was little appetite for this when Peel proposed it in 1822. But, as is well known, a mere seven years later he was able to persuade parliament to accept such a unified police under two commissioners who reported directly to the secretary of state for the Home Department.

Why Peel was able to overcome what had long seemed to be powerful resistance to a unified police under the control of the government and to create the Metropolitan Police Force in 1829 has been much discussed, most often in terms of his political skill, the distraction of other important issues in that parliamentary session, and the obvious need for a strong police in a period of riots and protests in favour of radical political change. I offer a number of suggestions that have not been in my opinion sufficiently emphasized, principally focussing on the state of crime in the late 1820s. Beyond the sharp increase in number of offences in the last years of the 1820s, as striking as that was, I would point to a problem that was clearly very much on Robert Peel's mind by 1829: that is, the emerging difficulty of protecting parishes that had once been well outside the boundaries of the capital and had never had the forms of peace-keeping by night watch and multiple parish constables that had developed in the urban world, that were now being drawn within the metropolis by its enlarging population and geographical expansion. This was not of course the only issue at play in 1829, but I will argue that is an important part of the explanation of the form the Metropolitan Police took and the ease with which it was accepted in parliament.

It is an important point that, as part of the solution to the problem of those unpoliced areas, the new force created in 1829 replaced the night watch—not the police offices or Bow Street or the parish contables. The various patrols based at Bow Street were transferred over time to the new force. But the runners and the constables at the police offices went on as before, a parallel group of police. The runners conducted few investigations in London after 1829 because there was little call for detection there or for brave men to confront violent offenders, though there was more of both in the provinces where they continued to find a good deal of business.[20]

Bow Street's relations with the commissioners of the New Police turned out to be not entirely amicable, as we will see. But it was not that that caused the disbandment of the runners a decade after the establishment of the Met. Rather, it was a long-overdue change in the authority of the magistrates under whose control they worked. For several decades it had been becoming clear that a difficulty was emerging around the dual roles the police magistrates were increasingly called upon to play: on the one hand, acting as policemen by sending men out to solve crime and bring in suspects, and then, on the other, acting as judges by conducting an examination to decide whether the evidence was strong enough to warrant those suspects being sent to trial. If a magistrate then attended a quarter sessions court he might serve as a judge in a case involving a defendant he had committed to trial. But even without that, it was becoming obvious that their duty to act

---

[20] Cox, *A Certain Share of Low Cunning*, ch. 7.

judicially at the pretrial hearing was compromised by their engagement in the policing work of the office. This had not been clear in the eighteenth century. It was, by the 1830s. A statute of 1839 deprived magistrates of their executive or ministerial authority, under which they had acted essentially as policemen, and confined them to a judicial role. That spelled the end of the runners. Without an institutional base, the runners and police office constables were disbanded and, as we will see, given pensions or other jobs.

* * * * * * *

In writing a study of the Bow Street court and the work of the runners between the mid- eighteenth century and 1839 one confronts a fundamental problem: none of the records compiled in the office over those years has survived. One serious loss is the record of the day-to-day work of the magistrates dealing with crimes and misdemeanours and the variety of other issues that confronted urban magistrates. Such records exist in substantial runs in the City of London archives relating to the work of the City magistrates.[21] But nothing from Bow Street has survived. Such evidence would have been of immense value in helping to construct the changing pattern of the magistrates' work over time, and thus of the detective work of the runners that is my central concern.

There have been other serious losses. John Fielding believed strongly in the importance of what one might call 'criminal intelligence', and he supported a sizeable clerical staff to keep records of a variety of matters concerning crime in the capital as an aid to the detective work of his runners. No one before had thought to keep an account of reported offences or descriptions of suspected offenders, records of prisoners acquitted at the Old Bailey, lists of stolen property, addresses of pawn-brokers and of known receivers. Dozens of volumes of such material must have piled up in the office over the years, and as we will see, from time to time they were useful in underpinning a prosecution case at the Old Bailey, identifying a repeat offender or a convict returned from transportation before his sentence had been served. Alas, not a scrap remains. Everything in the house was destroyed in the Gordon riots in June 1780 (three months before Fielding died) when Bow Street became one of the rioters' targets. According to Sampson Wright, Fielding's successor as chief magistrate, 'all [the] Books and Papers . . . were burnt.'[22] What was not lost then, was apparently abandoned a century later, along with all subsequent records, when a new court was built across Bow Street in 1880.[23]

On the plus side, we are fortunate to have eight of the annual financial accounts that Fielding was obliged to submit to the Treasury, dating from the 1750s and 1760s.[24] They provide useful information about the structure of the office and the work of the runners in the early years. Beyond that, we have to rely on three main

---

[21] Greg T. Smith (ed.), *Summary Justice in the City: A Selection of Cases heard at the Guildhall Justice Rooms, 1752–1781*, London Record Society, forthcoming.

[22] BL: Add Mss 35621, 229.

[23] Henry Goddard, *Memoirs of a Bow Street Runner*, ed. Patrick Pringle (London, 1956), ix.

[24] A ninth, dating from 1784–85, also survives. For the accounts, see ch. 3, n.7.

sources of evidence for the work of the office before 1792: a scattering of material in the state papers in the National Archives; the London newspaper press; and the printed reports of trials at the Old Bailey—the *Proceedings* of the court, or as contemporaries tended to call them, the 'Sessions Paper'. We are fortunate that the London newspapers become more informative in John Fielding's years than they had been earlier about criminal matters, including pretrial proceedings at Bow Street and the work of the runners. This was no accident, but rather a consequence of Fielding's determination to open his magisterial work to the public and his encouragement of the press to attend and report on his work.[25] It is helpful that the main collection of eighteenth-century newspapers and the Old Bailey *Proceedings* have both recently been digitized and are available on fully-searchable websites.[26]

By the 1780s, and especially after 1792, other useful sources become available. Some resulted from the creation of the Home Office in 1782, when the two secretaries of state who had hitherto shared responsibilities for foreign and domestic affairs divided those duties. In the Home Department, as it was first called, a section devoted to overseeing criminal matters began to keep records of correspondence between the secretary and under-secretary with magistrates in London and elsewhere, most particularly with the chief magistrate at Bow Street, the government's main contact with respect to crime in the metropolis. Of more specific value for the work of the runners are financial accounts that became available as the result of a statute in 1792 that established seven new public offices in the metropolis on the model of Bow Street. That Act also created a receiver of police who reported every quarter on the expenditures in those offices and who was instructed to take Bow Street under his care. The financial affairs of the office were then regularly reported to the Treasury and those records survive in sufficiently complete runs to provide useful information about its structure and work.[27] In following the work of the runners in the late eighteenth and early nineteenth centuries, I continue to rely on newspapers—including *The Times*, which has also been digitized[28]—and on the reports of trials at the Old Bailey, though, as we will see, the runners were not as prominent in the court after 1815 as they had been under John Fielding.

---

[25] See ch. 5, section 2.

[26] *17th–18th Century Burney Collection Newspapers* (Gale Group); <http://www.oldbaileyonline. org>. The Old Bailey website was created by Tim Hitchcock and Robert Shoemaker. They have recently created a much expanded digitized record—<http://www.londonlives.org>—that adds Old Bailey manuscripts records and other sources relating to crime in London, along with records of poverty and poor relief in several metropolitan parishes.

[27] For the Home Office records and the quarterly financial accounts of the receiver of police, see chs. 6–7.

[28] <http://archive.timesonline.co.uk>.

2

Henry Fielding at Bow Street

When Henry Fielding became a Westminster magistrate at the end of 1748 he made the house he occupied in Bow Street, Covent Garden, a centre of magisterial work that was different from anything that had gone before. He built on the work of his predecessor, Sir Thomas DeVeil, who in his 10 years in Bow Street had made his residence well known as a place where the public would be able to find a justice of the peace with some regularity. But Fielding also began a process that was to give the room in which examinations were conducted much more of a court-like setting. In addition, he gathered together the first body of officers dedicated to catching and prosecuting offenders. In his five-and-a-half years as the chief magistrate of Westminster—before ill-health forced his withdrawal in 1754, and indeed caused his death soon thereafter—Fielding initiated practices and won government approval for a plan that was to make Bow Street the leading centre of policing in the metropolis.[1]

Fielding had been called to the bar in 1740 and was thus unusually well prepared for a place on the commission of the peace when—through an old school-friend, George Lyttelton—he was named as a Westminster magistrate in October 1748 and became chairman of the Westminster Sessions in the following March. In January 1749 he successfully sought inclusion on the Middlesex commission too, an appointment that was only made possible by the patronage of the duke of Bedford who transferred leases of sufficient value to Fielding to enable him to meet the property qualification of £100 a year required of a county justice of the peace.[2] Though he received an annual stipend of £400 from the government, he may have been disappointed by the income that came his way merely as a Westminster magistrate, particularly since he claimed not to have milked the post in the way DeVeil had done.[3] But there was more to his ambition to join the Middlesex bench than that. As an active and reform-minded magistrate, he also wanted the greater scope and the added authority that membership on the county bench provided, for just as he came into office at the end of 1748 London was engulfed by a considerable increase in crime, particularly robberies and other violent offences. Bow Street felt the effects of this crime wave immediately, situated as it was in Covent Garden, at the centre of a densely populated area that drew large numbers of pleasure seekers

---

[1] For Henry Fielding as a magistrate, see Lance Bertelsen, *Henry Fielding at Work: Magistrate, Businessman, Writer* (London, 2000).

[2] Martin C. Battestin with Ruthe R. Battestin, *Henry Fielding: A Life* (London, 1989), 446–50.

[3] Henry Fielding, *The Journal of a Voyage to Lisbon*, ed. Martin C Battestin (Oxford, 2008), 558.

to its theatres, its brothels, and its drinking and gambling places. It was also an area in which the problems of policing were complicated by its being at the intersection of several jurisdictions, where the City of Westminster met the crowded western suburbs of the City of London as well as several large Middlesex parishes under the jurisdiction of the county magistrates—parishes like St Andrew, Holborn, St Giles in the Fields, and St James Clerkenwell, all dangerous places. Fielding's move to the Middlesex bench was almost certainly to make it easier for him to deal with the increasing business that came his way from the wider environs of Covent Garden, a well-known sink of iniquity that extended well beyond Westminster.[4]

The peace that brought the war of Austrian Succession to a conclusion in 1748 was no exception to the common experience in the eighteenth century that the end of a long war abroad meant an increase in prosecutions for property crime at home, much of it conducted with violence. Indeed the coming of peace had been anticipated with some apprehension. The *Gentleman's Magazine* noted in July 1748 that

> The approach of peace has raised terror in many private gentlemen . . . [as a] consequence of discharging so many men from their occupations in the army, the fleet, and the yards for building and repairing the navy. As one half of these men will not be able to get employment, there is a great, and just apprehension, that necessity will compel them to seize by violence, what they can see no method to attain by honest labour.[5]

Within months of the peace treaty being signed those predictions were proving to be all too true. Over the next several years the newspapers and monthly magazines were full of reports of robberies and other violent offences in and around the capital, frequently involving wealthy, even aristocratic, victims, which made them all the more newsworthy and made the crime wave seem all the more serious to the opinion-makers and men of property who sat in parliament.[6] After being held up himself one night in Hyde Park, Horace Walpole wrote in the winter of 1749–50 of there being 'little news from England, but of robberies.'[7]

It was a measure of the seriousness with which the government came to regard the crime problem in London—and a measure too of the growing importance of

---

[4] Tony Henderson, *Disorderly Women in Eighteenth-Century London: Prostitution and Control in the Metropolis, 1730–1830* (London, 1999).

[5] TNA: SP 36/101, 1; *Gentleman's Magazine*, 18 (July 1748), 293.

[6] And not just violent offences, though they inevitably attracted public attention. The merchants of London also felt the effects in the increase in theft from ships and warehouses on the river—and sufficiently strongly to encourage them to form societies to encourage the apprehension and prosecution of such thieves in 1749 and 1751 (Sir Leon Radzinowicz, *A History of English Criminal Law and its Administration Since 1750*. 4 Vols (London, 1948–68) I, ch. 12.). Peter D'Sena, 'Perquisites and Pilfering in the London Docks, 1700–1795', M. Phil thesis (Open University, 1986), 107, 131. For the response to anxieties about crime in this period see Nicholas Rogers, 'Confronting the Crime Wave: The Debate Over Social Reform and Regulation, 1749–1753' in Lee Davison et al. (eds.), *Stilling the Grumbling Hive: The Response to Social and Economic Problems in England, 1689–1750* (Stroud, 1992), 76–81; *Idem, Confronting the Crime Wave: Demobilization and Disorder in Mid-Eighteenth Century Britain* (New Haven, 2012).

[7] Horace Walpole, *Correspondence with Sir Horace Mann*, ed. W. S. Lewis, Warren Hunting Smith, and George S. Lam, 6 vols. (New Haven, 1960), 4, 111.

parliament in the shaping of domestic social policy by the middle of the eighteenth century[8]—that the administration included in the king's speech opening parliament in November 1751 a request that the members take into their consideration the crime wave in and around London and 'consider seriously of some effectual provisions to suppress those audacious crimes of robbery and violence which are now become so frequent, especially about this great capital.'[9] Within weeks, a committee was established to 'revise and consider the laws in being, which relate to felonies,' authorizing thereby a much more general investigation into the criminal law and its institutions than had ever been undertaken by parliament.[10] The committee, which included the prime minister, Henry Pelham, William Pitt, and other leading members of the house, obviously took the task to heart, and within a few months produced three batches of resolutions that set out ways in which the administration of justice might be strengthened. Fourteen bills were introduced over the next two years to give effect to these suggestions, though in the end only two major pieces of legislation reached the statute book as a result of the committee's work. One was a compilation of unrelated measures in a statute that came to be known as the Disorderly Houses Act because it imposed new controls over places of public entertainment and aimed to make it easier to prosecute the keepers of brothels and gaming houses. The statute also introduced the first scheme to pay some of the costs of prosecution, imposed a stiff fine for advertising a willingness to pay for the return of stolen goods, no questions asked, and strengthened the magistrates' powers to hold persons picked up on suspicion of theft for up to six days to enable victims of robberies to attend their re-examination—authority that was to be crucial to the way the Bow Street magistrates' court worked under John Fielding.[11] The second statute was simple and brutal. The so-called Murder Act ordered that murderers be executed two days after conviction and that their bodies either be hanged in chains or given to surgeons to be 'dissected and anatomized'—a response not to an outbreak of ordinary homicide (though there were some murder cases that attracted serious public attention in this period), but to robbery. As the preamble revealed, the intention was to add 'some further terror and peculiar mark of infamy to the punishment of death' in the hope that it would deter robbers from using excessive violence.[12]

For his part, Henry Fielding had been preoccupied from the beginning of the crisis by the consequences of the crime wave and had developed strong views about its causes and how it might be diminished. Soon after arriving at Bow Street he had

---

[8] Joanna Innes; *Inferior Politics: Social Problems and Social Policies in Eighteenth-Century Britain* (Oxford, 2009), chs. 1–2; Richard Connors, '"The Grand Inquest of the Nation": Parliamentary Committees and Social Policy in Mid-Eighteenth-Century England', *Parliamentary History*, 14 (3, 1995): 285–313.

[9] *JHC* 26 (1750–54), 298.

[10] Ibid, 27. For the committee and its work, see Nicholas Rogers, 'Confronting the Crime Wave', 77–98; J. M. Beattie, *Crime and the Courts in England, 1660–1800* (Princeton and Oxford, 1986), 520–5, 551–2; Radzinowicz, *History of English Criminal Law*, vol. 1, ch. 12; and Connors, '"The Grand Inquest of the Nation"', 301–13.

[11] 25 Geo II, c. 36 (1752).

[12] 25 Geo II, c. 37 (1752).

sent proposals to Lord Hardwicke, the lord chancellor, for a bill to reform the night watch in Westminster and neighbouring Middlesex parishes by creating better-organized patrols, manned by a larger number of younger and more effective watchmen.[13] Nothing came of that. Fielding made a much more substantial contribution to the mid-century debate about crime and the criminal law in the form of his *Enquiry into the Causes of the Late Increase of Robbers*, published just as the parliamentary committee was forming in January 1751.[14] Much of the analysis in this long pamphlet was conventional wisdom. Like the parliamentary committee, he placed a good deal of the blame for the increase in crime on the deteriorating behaviour and growing insubordination of the poor, a problem he saw in historical terms as a consequence of the growth of luxury and the social effects of enlarging commerce. Luxury, as Fielding saw it, had given rise to diversions and bad habits that wasted the time and the money of those who could least afford to be deflected from their labour; it encouraged drinking and gambling, and in general had turned the working population away from following an honest and upright course of life.[15] He also laid blame for the growth of crime on the weaknesses of the poor law and the law relating to vagrancy, as well as on the lack of controls over pawnbrokers, most of whom, he thought, were willing to take in goods without enquiring into their ownership and thus provided outlets for the disposal of stolen property that encouraged theft.[16]

Fielding thus put much of the blame for the increase in crime on the deterioration of controls over the poorest sections of society. But he also criticized the way the criminal law was administered, including what he thought was the indulgent tenderness of juries when dealing with men and women accused of capital offences, and the tendency of the king and his ministers to grant too many pardons. The ease, as he saw it, with which offenders escaped the gallows convinced robbers and other violent men that they need have no fear of serious punishment. He also thought that the carnival atmosphere in which executions were carried out at Tyburn had become more of an encouragement than a deterrent to crime.[17]

Fielding's analysis of the causes of violent crime was wide-ranging. But perhaps the most original sections in his *Enquiry* were those in which he raised policing issues of the kind that were arising from his practice at Bow Street. For in the winter of 1749–50, with reports increasing of violence in the streets of London, Fielding had taken what was to turn out to be an important initiative by organizing a group of men to devote themselves to seeking out and apprehending serious offenders and bringing them to Bow Street for examination and commitment to trial. The need

---

[13] Martin Battestin is surely right to think that a document in the Newcastle Mss is the bill in question (BL: Add Mss 33054, 406–13). He transcribes it as Appendix I in *Henry Fielding*, 706–11.

[14] Henry Fielding, *An Enquiry into the Causes of the late Increase of Robbers* (1751) in Malvin R. Zirker (ed.) *Henry Fielding. An Enquiry into the Causes of the Late Increase of Robbers and Related Writings* (Oxford, 1988), 61–172.

[15] *Ibid*, 75–98.

[16] *Ibid*, 98–130.

[17] *Ibid*, 158–72. For the procession to Tyburn, see Andrea McKenzie, *Tyburn's Martyrs: Execution in England, 1675–1775* (London, 2007), ch. 1.

for such a body, as he saw it, sprang from the reluctance of victims to undertake prosecutions and the difficulties they faced if they chose to do so, particularly the difficulties of apprehending members of gangs who were frequently armed and prepared to use violence to rescue any of their associates in danger of being taken. Victims got little help, Fielding confirmed, from the existing policing forces. The impunity with which London robbers acted and the indifference they showed to the consequences of their actions, exposed the serious weakness and incapacity of the civil authorities. A more vigorous response was required—indeed the kind of response that Fielding was organizing at Bow Street, the success of which would depend on public support of men willing to undertake the dangerous task of finding and apprehending violent offenders. And because the force that he was assembling included men who were not sworn peace officers, it also required a proper understanding of the powers available under the law to ordinary citizens to bring felons to justice. The two long passages of the *Enquiry* in which Fielding discusses these issues bear fundamentally on his efforts to establish a police presence and police authority at Bow Street.

On the one hand Fielding set out to defend the activities of men known as 'thief-takers', private men who had made it their business to apprehend and prosecute felons whose conviction would bring a reward, about whom there were at best feelings of ambivalence in the popular mind, feelings that could easily tip over into serious hostility when they were perceived as acting corruptly. Thief-takers were generally despised because they dealt in blood: the rewards they sought were earned for the conviction of defendants threatened with execution. But such men had been known in London since at least the early seventeenth century, and, as we have seen, they had been particularly common since the 1690s when parliament had insti-tuted rewards of £40 for the conviction of several kinds of offenders, and especially when the administration added the princely sum of £100 for the conviction of highwaymen and street robbers in London.[18] That huge reward had been with-drawn in 1745, but when violent crime once again escalated it was reinstated in February 1749 to run for a year, and again, in December 1750, for a further 15 months. Thief-taking gangs were active in these years as a consequence, and the negative side of their detective activity—the corruption and malicious charges that had always been encouraged by rewards—was even more in evidence then.[19]

In organizing a group of thief-catchers as a way of confronting gangs of offenders and reducing crime in the capital, Henry Fielding found it essential to justify thief-taking as an activity. He did so in a section of his 1751 pamphlet in which he dealt

---

[18] For thief-takers and thief-taking in the first half of the eighteenth century, see J. M. Beattie, *Policing and Punishment in London, 1660–1750: Urban Crime and the Limits of Terror* (Oxford, 2001), ch. 5 and 401–23; Tim Wales, 'Thief-takers and their Clients in Later Stuart London' in Paul Griffiths and Mark S. R. Jenner (eds), *Londinopolis: essays in the social and cultural history of early modern London* (Manchester, 2001), 67–85; Ruth Paley, 'Thief-takers in London in the Age of the McDaniel Gang, c. 1745–54' in Douglas Hay and Francis Snyder (eds), *Policing and Prosecution in Britain, 1750–1850* (Oxford, 1989), 301–41.

[19] Paley, 'Thief-takers in London in the Age of the McDaniel Gang, c. 1745–54'.

with the law concerning the arrest of felons.[20] The widespread hostility against those who successfully prosecuted felons, he argued, was misplaced. Great confusion had been caused by the evil deeds of a few and by the popular tendency to think of them simply as informers—men and women who turned in those who broke petty laws for the sake of a share of fines. Thief-takers were different, he argued. They risked their lives and, given the weakness of the civil authorities, carried out an essential activity by bringing violent men to justice. They did 'Good to Society.' And he went on: 'if to do Good at the extreme Hazard of your Life be honourable, then is this Office honourable.' To the argument that thief-takers were motivated only by rewards, Fielding replied 'doth not the Soldier and the Sailor venture his Life with the same View?'[21] Thief-takers performed a public duty and should be honoured for it.

Fielding had preceded this defence of thief-taking with a long passage on a subject that was equally crucial to the work of the men at the Bow Street office, and a subject, he said, equally misunderstood by the public: the powers available not only to sworn officers of justice to make arrests, but to ordinary citizens too. His analysis was based largely on two widely-quoted seventeenth-century authorities, Michael Dalton's *Country Justice* and Matthew Hale's *History of the Pleas of the Crown*, supported by references to several statutes. Fielding's intention in this section was to remind constables that they had authority by virtue of their office to arrest suspected felons. But he was also anxious to make it clear that under certain circumstances a 'private person' could also effect lawful arrests. He set out what those circumstances were and the limits of those powers. But the central point of his detailed discussion of that subject was to confirm that an ordinary man could act against suspected felons, especially if he had a magistrate's warrant to do so, 'for though he is not bound to execute such Warrant, yet if he doth, it is good and justifiable.'[22] He surely had his own men in mind here and the authority those among them who were not sworn constables could exercise simply by virtue of his warrants. As we will see, over the coming decades some of the active men around the Bow Street office were Westminster constables. But most were not, and the issue of the authority under which they could act—to make arrests and conduct searches—was clearly a matter of the greatest importance. It was very much in Fielding's mind as he composed the detailed and closely-argued passages in his *Enquiry into the Causes of the late Increase of Robbers* dealing with policing matters, particularly the section on the 'apprehending the Persons of Felons.'[23]

These issues around the popular conception of thief-taking and the law of arrest were of more than just general interest to Fielding since he was attempting to gather a group of men at the Bow Street magistrates' court to pursue and apprehend suspected offenders. One other issue turned out to be crucial: how were these men to be supported? If they were going to devote time to the business of thief-catching,

---

[20] Fielding, *Enquiry into the Causes of the late Increase of Robbers*, 145–54.
[21] *Ibid*, 153.
[22] *Ibid*, 149.
[23] *Ibid*, 145–54.

Fielding argued, they would have to be paid in some way.[24] Parliamentary rewards provided one obvious source of funds, supplemented when they were available by the royal proclamation reward. Fielding supported the efforts of his men to raise as much as possible from those rewards by signing the affidavits they submitted to trial judges who distributed the reward money. But state rewards were not as lucrative as they might have seemed on paper. The judges had developed the habit by the middle of the century of distributing them as widely as possible, almost certainly to prevent thief-takers (who had a well-deserved reputation for corruption) from acquiring the lion's share. By the 1750s, the victim of the offence was usually awarded a significant portion of the total and other, often numerous, claimants were given sums that in some cases amounted to little more than a token payment. In the early years, judges seem to have perceived the Bow Street men as no better than other thief-takers and to have been reluctant to reward them too lavishly.[25] Fielding revealed his annoyance in his *Enquiry* at what he thought was a bad policy when he complained that even when a felon is convicted, 'I have been told that the Money does not come so easily and fully to the Pockets of those who are entitled to as it ought.'[26] He had been told, and told often, there can be little doubt, by his own men.

Other financial support for the Bow Street men might have come from private rewards, advertised by a victim seeking the return of stolen goods. But neither form of reward was likely to provide sufficient and sufficiently reliable support over the long term to sustain a group of men devoted full-time to the work of seeking out and apprehending offenders, and who might in any case be called upon to do other policing work for which there would be no prospect of reward payments. One consequence, as we will see, was that several of the earliest Bow Street officers either had jobs in other areas of the criminal justice apparatus or were found such jobs.[27] But not all of the Bow Street men could be supported that way, especially those who were Westminster constables. From the beginning, some of the leading Bow Street officers were serving constables, typically men who were willing to serve as constables for those whose turn it was, but who chose to avoid the duty by paying a

---

[24] Battestin, *Henry Fielding*, 577–8.

[25] When, in January 1754, William Palmer Hind and five others of his officers petitioned against the Recorder of London's interpretation of the statutes that established the £40 rewards, Fielding supported them by delivering the petition himself directly to John Sharpe, the under-secretary of state, underlining its central point. Their petition argued that although the Acts establishing the rewards in question directed that they were to be paid to those who apprehended the offender, the Recorder of London (who made out the conviction certificates at the Old Bailey) and the high court judges had chosen to distribute them so broadly that those who risked their lives to capture dangerous men were never adequately rewarded (TNA: SP 36/125, ff. 23, 91). Asked for his advice, the attorney general found against that narrow reading of the statutes and supported the practice that had developed over the first half of the century by which those who provided information or who played any role at all in the taking, prosecution, and conviction of the offender had some entitlement to a share in the reward. The case, and attorney general Ryder's answers are at TNA: SP 36/153, ff. 10–11 (misdated 12 January 1753 for 1754).

[26] Fielding, *Enquiry into the Causes of the Late Increase of Robbers*, 152. For the distribution of rewards, see Beattie, *Policing and Punishment*, 401–4.

[27] Below, ch. 3, text at nn. 30–3.

substitute. Experienced, long-serving, parish constables had become common in London by the middle of the eighteenth century.[28] It was clearly not as big a step for men who had been in the office for some years and who were in effect paid and permanent constables as it would have been for householders serving for a year to attach themselves to the Bow Street office and to devote most of their time to police work.

Men who brought the authority of the constable's office were very valuable indeed. For, despite Fielding's insistence that the private citizen could enforce a magistrate's warrant, there were clearly many policing situations that required much greater authority than the ordinary citizen possessed. When it came to breaking down doors, it was essential to have a constable present if any arrest made was to withstand legal challenge.[29] The private thief-takers in the reigns of William III and Queen Anne had found it useful to forge alliances with constables for that reason,[30] and the situation at Bow Street was no different. The continuing appointment as constables of Westminster of men willing to remain attached to the Bow Street office was relatively straightforward to arrange because they were appointed directly by the magistrates rather than (as in the City of London) being elected by their neighbours to serve in a precinct. And it was further simplified when in 1756 their numbers were increased to 80 by Act of Parliament.[31]

The need to attract constables to work at Bow Street made the issue of how these men were to be supported all the more crucial for Henry Fielding. Apart from the problematic nature of thief-taking and the issues surrounding the authority of ordinary citizens to carry out magistrates' orders, the financial question came to be fundamental as it became clear that public and private rewards could not be counted on to sustain a stable force of half a dozen men, along with the administrative and other miscellaneous staff that the Bow Street office required. When he published his *Enquiry* in 1751, Fielding had not as yet devised a way of financing his group of thief-catchers. As a consequence his experiment came close to failing. In the fall of 1753, Fielding reported to the Treasury that for some time his men had 'desisted from their undertaking' because they were not adequately compensated under a system in which the judges gave no more than a small share of reward money to those who actually faced the greatest danger in bringing robbers to trial.[32] When the opportunity arose in 1753 he was thus eager to suggest to the government an alternative way of supporting his officers and a much cheaper way of encouraging effective prosecutions than through massive proclamation rewards.

---

[28] In the City of London, eg, 40% of the constabulary were substitutes by 1750: Beattie, *Policing and Prosecution*, 144–50.

[29] The essential character of the constable's authority was underlined—to take just one case—when two of John Fielding's men, investigating a theft of tools, found their way barred, and had to send for a Westminster constable before forcing a door (OBP, February 1759 (William Wilson and Mary Harris, als Wilson) t17590228-13.

[30] Beattie, *Policing and Punishment*, 244–7.

[31] 29 Geo II, c. 25 (1756). For constables in the City of London, see Beattie, *Policing and Punishment*, ch. 3.

[32] Fielding's 'Memorial': Huntington Library: HM 11617, quoted by Battestin, *Fielding*, 578.

The solution he offered was to change the character of London policing over the next 80 years.

The decisive initiative came from the government in the fall of 1753 as crime in London continued to be as serious as ever and as winter approached—'the Season of the year,' John Fielding was later to say, 'when Thieves and Robbers take the Advantage of the long Evenings and dark Nights to execute their obnoxious Schemes'.[33] The Pelham administration was clearly reluctant to renew the £100 supplementary reward for the conviction of robbers in London, almost certainly for the reasons that had led them to bring it to a temporary end in 1745: the corruption it encouraged, and the significant and unpredictable costs involved. During the two years in which it had recently been in force, the proclamation reward had cost the Treasury £4,600 in 1750 and £6,500 in 1751 and the first half of 1752 at a time when the government was striving to reduce the massive national debt that had been incurred in the recent war.[34] In any case, the drain on the Treasury had done little to stem the violence, and by the fall of 1753 ministers were desperate for new ideas and a new response that might do something to control the streets of the capital. They were willing to pay, but they wanted the costs to be more modest and to be known, not open-ended as they were under the system of proclamation rewards.

It was in these circumstances in August 1753, at the end of a week in which five victims were reported to have been killed by robbers in London,[35] that the duke of Newcastle, the secretary of state most concerned with domestic matters, asked Henry Fielding for advice, indeed for a new plan of policing. By his own account, Fielding was seriously ill when he received Newcastle's request, but he nonetheless produced a 14-page document within four days. It provided the central ideas that gave permanence to the group that would become known as the Bow Street runners.[36]

The document itself has not survived, but, as Battestin has said, its main intentions can be reconstructed from other sources. At its heart was a plan to encourage and support the Bow Street officers. As an alternative to supplementary rewards by proclamation, Fielding proposed that he be given a sum of money beyond his own stipend to be used for two purposes. One was to encourage rapid reporting of London offences to Bow Street by offering to pay for their immediate advertising, with descriptions of the offenders and of the goods taken; the advertisement would also include the offer of a reward, if the victim was willing to pay, as

---

[33] TNA: T 38/671, f. 1.

[34] TNA: SP 36/153, f. 16: 'An Account of what Sums have been paid by the Treasury in Rewards for Apprehending Highwaymen and Street Robbers for the Six last Years, Viz From the Year 1748 to the Year 1753, both inclusive.' This is undated, but internal evidence suggests late January or early February 1754. It seems to have been drawn up in support of Fielding's plan—to emphasize its value to the Treasury compared to the cost of the royal proclamation reward—since it notes that the £6,500 paid in 1751 and 1752 was up to June in the latter year, the point at which 'the last Proclamation ended' and appears to contrast this with the £600 given to Fielding in 1753 (his personal stipend of £400 and £200 to support his police).

[35] This was Fielding's recollection—in his *Voyage to Lisbon*, 555.

[36] Battestin, *Henry Fielding*, 574–8.

a way of encouraging information from pawnbrokers and others with knowledge of the offenders. Soon after coming to Bow Street Fielding had used the press to encourage victims and witnesses of crime to report their losses to Bow Street.[37] With government funding, he intended to enlarge on that by offering to pay for the advertisement and to reward the messenger who brought the information. The advertisement would appear the following day in the *Public Advertiser*—in which, it was frequently pointed out by their critics, Henry Fielding and his half-brother John had a financial interest.[38]

Fielding's principal intention, however, was to use the government subvention to support his officers with fees for services—with payments at his discretion for their expenses and their 'trouble' in bringing offenders to justice and carrying out other policing tasks for which no state or even private rewards would be available. This was at the heart of the Bow Street system. Without a staff of officers prepared to seek out and apprehend accused offenders, the house in Bow Street would have remained simply a place where an active and engaged magistrate could be found, to whom the public would be able to register their complaints and obtain warrants at most hours of the day. That would have been useful, but it was not what Fielding had in mind. He might have continued to encourage constables to investigate offences, but without the government subvention they would have remained simply thief-takers for whom even state rewards would not have been sufficient to encourage continuity and permanence of service. The government's financial support, he argued, would encourage his men not only to catch robbers and other serious offenders, but to engage in more general policing efforts too. In the first year, Fielding was given £200 for these purposes above his own £400 stipend.[39] His men began for the first time to earn income from the office for their efforts and trouble, not a great deal at first, but sufficient to enable them to remain active and to earn other income from rewards, public and private, and payments for work for government departments.[40]

The government's annual subvention also enabled the Fieldings to maintain a staff of clerks who kept detailed records, and to build up contacts with magistrates around the country. In these ways, Bow Street developed an institutional memory and a culture, and in time a group of officers who made that service their career. Henry Fielding's plan of 1753 and the government's support gave permanence to a new kind of magistrates' office emerging in Bow Street and to the new kind of

---

[37] *Covent Garden Journal*, 28 January 1752.

[38] Battestin, *Henry Fielding*, 561. The Fieldings' financial interest was well known: *The Public Advertiser* was occasionally referred to at the Old Bailey as 'justice Fielding's paper.' OBP, February 1755 (William Banks) t17550226-7; December 1755 (Christopher Wade) t17551204-44.

[39] TNA: SP 36/153, f. 16.

[40] Fielding also continued to argue that the basic state rewards—those established by parliament—were not distributed in a way that was fair to his men. In supporting his officers' petition against the judges' practice in distributing rewards widely (above, n. 23), Fielding said that 'the scheme he was now upon would be entirely frustrated' if the Recorder was not directed to distribute rewards according to the strict letter of the law or the government did not make up their losses to his officers (TNA: SP 36/125, f. 91).

policing operation it supported. As was so often the case in the eighteenth-century criminal justice system, resources were the key to change.

Fielding's proposals were accepted by the cabinet in late 1753 and he received £200 from the Treasury to put his 'plan of police' into action. By then he was seriously ill. He remained in London long enough to see what he thought were the first fruits of this new plan of police: indeed he was later to claim that it was so successful that there were no robberies at all on London streets in the months following its introduction.[41] He and his wife sailed to Portugal in the summer of 1754 in the vain hope that a warmer climate might restore his health. He died in Lisbon six weeks after their arrival.

In London, John Fielding had overseen the establishment of the new plan and had succeeded his brother as the chief magistrate for Westminster. Over the next quarter century he was to expand and develop the police that Henry had put in place. One decisive change was the public acknowledgement of the existence of the Bow Street officers. Henry Fielding had thought it prudent not to disclose the names of his officers, fearing public resentment against them. John took a different view. A notice in the *Public Advertiser* of 20 December 1754 announced that not only would advertisements be published following the reporting of crimes to Bow Street, but, for the first time, a 'Set of brave Fellows' would be immediately dispatched in pursuit of the offenders, and not only to any part of London, but any part of the kingdom, and that on a quarter of an hour's notice.[42] 'Quick notice and sudden pursuit' was to be the essence of the plan.[43] It was clear to the public by then, if it had not been before, that these men were to be regularly available and that new initiatives were to be introduced into official policing. As a consequence of the post-war crime wave and the inadequacy of the existing means for dealing with it, the policing forces at Bow Street had been established on a foundation that made the detection and apprehension of offenders a central task and changed the face of official policing in London.

---

[41] Fielding, *Voyage to Lisbon*, 557.

[42] Battestin, *Henry Fielding*, 578–9.

[43] John Fielding, *A Plan for Preventing Robberies within Twenty Miles of London, with an Account of the Rise and Establishment of the real Thieftakers* (London, 1755), 1.

3

Sir John Fielding and the Making of the Bow Street Runners, 1754–1765

The government's support of the Bow Street office continued after Henry Fielding's ill health forced him to leave England in the summer of 1754. His half-brother, John, who had been a member of the Westminster bench since 1751 and who assumed the leadership of the office even before Henry left the country, was given a personal stipend of £400 from the Secret Service accounts and remained as chief magistrate of Westminster until his death in 1780. He set out his policing ideas in a pamphlet in 1755 that examined the establishment of the Bow Street office and the problems of crime that needed to be addressed. The emphasis, inevitably, given the government's subvention, was on the need to tackle violence, highway robbery in particular.[1] For a while, Fielding shared the duties of the office (and the stipend) with Saunders Welch, who, as chief constable of Holborn and a close friend and associate of Henry Fielding, had led the first group of constables organized as thief-catchers in the winter of 1749. Welch was appointed to the Westminster bench in 1755, having been strongly recommended by Henry Fielding, and he came into the magistracy thinking that the work he had done over the past several years entitled him to share the duties of chief magistrate at Bow Street and to share the stipend equally with John Fielding. The latter's view was that he was the natural successor to his half-brother and that Welch should be content with a secondary role and a stipend of £100. After a couple of years of squabbling, Welch was given his own stipend of £200 by the government and agreed to set up a separate magistrates' office, though he continued for some time to annoy Fielding by insisting on establishing himself near Bow Street and thus 'dividing the Civil Power round my House, where it ought to be the strongest,' as Fielding complained to the Treasury in December 1757.[2]

Fielding encouraged other (unpaid) Middlesex justices to share the magisterial duties at Bow Street, but he remained the dominant presence there. Even when, as we will see, the government provided stipends for two other magistrates in the late 1760s and something of a rotation system emerged, Fielding remained the leading

---

[1] John Fielding, *A Plan for Preventing Robberies within Twenty Miles of London, with an Account of the Rise and Establishment of the real Thieftakers* (London,1755).

[2] TNA: T 1/372/109, T 38/671; BL: Add Mss 32862, f. 375, Add Mss 32874, f. 379; Fielding, *A Plan for Preventing Robberies*, 1. For Fielding's stipend, paid from the Secret Service Accounts, 1754–62, see Sir Lewis Namier, *The Structure of Politics at the Accession of George III*, 2nd edn. (London, 1963), 228, 430ff.

figure. Bow Street was widely known as 'Mr Fielding's office' or, 'Sir John's' after his knighthood in 1761.

The government's subvention for the costs of policing—'to defray the Expences of executing Mr Fielding's Plan for apprehending Thieves and Robbers and for preventing other Disorders in and near this Metropolis'—remained at first at £200. John Fielding got it increased within a few years by overspending his budget and persuading the duke of Newcastle, now first lord of the Treasury, to accept the increasing costs of more active policing, as well as the further costs of advertising crimes in London newspapers and of recruiting a permanent clerical staff for the office. By 1757 such charges had doubled the initial budget to £400; it was to be increased again by 1765 to £600.[3]

What Fielding did with the money—what policing activities would be undertaken, how many men would be engaged and how they would be rewarded—was left largely to him. Henry Fielding's plan seems to have called for the support of six officers,[4] and in most years payments for searching out and attempting to apprehend serious offenders (along with other work) went mainly to that number of men, with occasional payments to a few assistants. Fielding had to request a renewal of the stipend every year and that required him to account for the previous year's expenditures. But since the subvention had been set up in an informal way, without guarantee of continuity, the accounting system remained similarly informal. Fielding sent his account of the year's expenditures and a request for the renewal of the stipend to the secretary of state, who sent it on to the Treasury. But since the funds did not come from an established account that would be subject to regular accounting procedures, the records of Fielding's annual expenses were simply kept among the massive bulk of the Treasury's general papers. This explains why the costs of Bow Street remained unknown to the public—even to men in London who knew that the subvention existed.[5] It also no doubt explains why so many of the accounts can no longer be found. As we will see, an Act of Parliament of 1792 setting up seven similar offices in the metropolis resulted in a more formal accounting system that was also applied to Bow Street. A receiver of police submitted quarterly accounts to the Treasury which have been more carefully preserved.[6] Before 1792, however, only nine annual Bow Street accounts appear to have survived—a complete run for the four years 1756–59, and those

---

[3] See below, ch. 4, text at nn. 1–3.

[4] In forwarding the petition of the Bow Street men with respect to the distribution of the parliamentary rewards in January 1754 (noted above, ch. 2, text at n. 25), John Sharpe referred to Fielding's 'Six Mirmidons, who are the instruments by which he proposes to destroy that Hydra of Villains with which our Streets and Roads have been of late so terribly invested . . .' (TNA: SP 36/125, f. 23).

[5] Edward Sayer, the deputy high steward of Westminster, complained in 1784 that such support of a magistrate's office was 'unknown to the laws of this country', and that with respect to the costs of salaries, fees, and other emoluments at Bow Street 'the mystery of office has thrown a cautious veil.' *Observations on the Police or Civil Government of Westminster, with a proposal for reform* (London, 1784), 10.

[6] See below, ch. 7, text at n. 11.

for 1761–62, 1766–67, and 1785.[7] We are fortunate to have even these few documents. They enable us to glimpse the broad structure of the office in these early years and something of the work of the men who would become known as the runners, matters that would be otherwise impenetrable given the absence of other manuscript material concerning the Bow Street court, its personnel and activities. The office accounts are inevitably clearer on some matters than others, but it is possible to get a sense from them of the kinds of activities that Fielding thought necessary in carrying out the plan of police agreed to by the government and the way in which he built on and expanded his brother's initial establishment.

1. THE EARLY YEARS OF THE OFFICE: STRUCTURE, PERSONNEL, WORK

John Fielding's work as a magistrate was recorded by his clerk, Joshua Brogden, who had worked for Henry before him, and who presumably continued to receive an annual salary of about £300 from the fees collected in the office, as he had previously, since no such payment appears in the accounts submitted to the Treasury.[8] Fielding was almost certainly the busiest Westminster magistrate. The Bow Street office seems to have been open for magisterial business for long hours most days of the week, well into the evening. As we will see, a so-called 'ordinary' man had been engaged by 1756 to be on duty in the office every day; when he was not available—for he was also often an active officer—someone was hired to wait in his stead.[9] It may even have been possible to report serious offences through the night.[10] There are numerous indications in the press and in trial accounts that people assumed they could go to Bow Street at any time of the day and well into the evening with the expectation of seeing a magistrate or at least someone who would be able to receive and act on their complaint. Occasionally, offenders apprehended by Bow Street men were taken to a public house across the street from the office, the Brown Bear, which served as a temporary lock-up and a place where suspects could be interrogated before being taken before the magistrate.[11] But more often Fielding seems to have dealt with business as it appeared. He took some of his meals at the Brown Bear and could be interrupted there too if the need was urgent.[12]

---

[7] They ran in each case from roughly 1 October or 1 November of one year to the end of the following September or October, and were described as being the account for the second of those years, a convention I have followed. They are to be found at TNA: T 38/671 (a bound volume containing the accounts for 1756, 1757, 1759); T 1/387 (1758); T 1/413 (1761); T 1/414 (1762); T 1/449 (1766); T 1/454 (1767); T 1/626 (1785).

[8] Henry Fielding, *The Journal of a Voyage to Lisbon*, ed. Martin Battestin (Oxford, 2008), 558.

[9] T 38/671, ff. 10, 30.

[10] In giving evidence at the trial of two mail robbers at the Old Bailey in 1753, Henry Peal said that he had received the first news of the crime, having been 'at Mr Fielding's over night.' OBP, July 1753 (John Stockdale and Christopher Johnson) t17530718-33.

[11] For the importance of the Brown Bear, see below, ch. 6, section 3. In the early years the officers also used another nearby public house, the Barley Mow, but, as we will see, the Brown Bear came to serve as their main base and a form of police station from the mid 1750s into the nineteenth century.

[12] OBP, December 1766 (Samuel Pointon) t17661217-44.

The records of Fielding's work as a magistrate were kept by Brogden and a clerical staff—that is, his decisions with respect to the criminal suspects brought by his own men, by parish constables and victims of offences, and of his responses to the great jumble of charges and complaints that came the way of any urban magistrate willing to receive them. They would have recorded the business conducted in the parlour in Bow Street dedicated to magisterial work or in what came later to be a purpose-built courtroom, recording decisions in particular cases, taking depositions from victims and examinations of the accused, keeping a note of recognizances and warrants issued, of fines collected and commitments to await trial or to the Bridewell.[13] The records of John Fielding's daily business as a magistrate must have been similar to the books kept on behalf of the lord mayor of London when he conducted magisterial business at the Mansion House and on behalf of the aldermen of the City when they sat daily in turn as magistrates in the rotation court in the Guildhall. Indeed, such records must have been kept by every active justice of the peace in the country.[14]

The unique policing activities conducted by the Bow Street office meant, however, that John Fielding's clerical requirements went well beyond those of ordinary magistrates. He used the government funds to hire extra clerical staff— not just Joshua Brogden, who, as chief clerk, was in charge of the routine work of the office, but also a number of assistants, whose main tasks grew out of Fielding's ambitions to collect information about offenders and offences. The office accounts for 1756 record payments to a stationer for 'Alphabets and other Books necessary for Informations of Robberies.' At the same time, he appointed one of his officers as a so-called 'Register Clerk to the Police' whose duty it was 'to take all Informations and Descriptions of suspicious Persons, Robbers, and things stolen' and whose salary was part of the doubling of the office budget at the end of that year.[15] Subsequent accounts make it clear that the 'informations' referred to here were not the formal statements required in the pretrial process when a magistrate dealt with a suspect accused of a felony, but rather gossip and rumours picked up from a variety of sources about men and women suspected of committing offences. All went into Fielding's books for possible future reference. By the following year, as the systematic collection of such information developed, large books were being regularly purchased for the office, one devoted exclusively to robberies, and another to 'a Description of [suspicious] Persons,' both alphabetically arranged. Within a few years, Fielding hired another clerk to record the outcomes of trials at the Old

---

[13] For pretrial process at Bow Street, see ch. 5, section 2.

[14] For the City magistrates' courts, see Drew D. Gray, *Crime, Prosecution, and Social Relations: summary courts of he City of London in the late eighteenth century* (London, 2009); J. M. Beattie, *Policing and Punishment in London, 1660–1750: Urban Crime and the Limits of Terror* (Oxford, 2001), ch. 2; Greg T. Smith (ed.), *Summary Justice in the City: A Selection of Cases heard at the Guildhall Justice Rooms,1752–1781* (London Record Society, forthcoming). For magistrates' notebooks in general see Norma Landau, *The Justices of the Peace, 1679–1760* (Berkeley, 1984), 175–6, 191–3; and for a skilfully-edited example of an eighteenth-century urban magistrate's record, see Ruth Paley (ed.), *Justice in Eighteenth-Century Hackney: The Justicing Notebook of Henry Norris and the Hackney Petty Sessions Book* (London Record Society, 1991).

[15] TNA: T 38/671, ff. 4, 10.

Bailey, paying particular attention to the sentences imposed on those convicted 'in order to detect returned Transports'—that is, to enable the Bow Street office to keep track of convicts who had been ordered to be transported to America so that those who returned before the expiration of their terms of seven or fourteen years could be tracked and apprehended.[16] Fielding also required his clerks to keep an account of descriptions and makers' numbers of watches reported stolen, and the addresses of pawnbrokers so they could be contacted as soon as news of a robbery or theft was received in the office.[17]

All of this information was in support of the activity at the heart of Fielding's Bow Street operations—investigating offences, catching and prosecuting felons—and in some circumstances preventing felonies from occurring. This is what he meant when he used the word 'police' to describe the forces he assembled at Bow Street and the activities in which they engaged. Such usage had not been common in England. The word was disliked for its association with what was thought to be the oppression and despotism of the French system of government, so different from the freedom and liberty enjoyed by the British under their constitution in church and state. For the most part, the word police connoted general civil administration: Samuel Johnson was reporting its established meaning when, in his *Dictionary* (1755), he defined police as 'the regulation and government of a city or country, so far as regards the inhabitants.' That is the meaning it continued to have for many writers, as in Edward Sayer's *Observations on the Police, or Civil Government, of Westminster* (1784).[18] Fielding meant something much more specific, something much closer to the modern sense of the word, when he described the origins of the Bow Street office under his brother as *An Account . . . of a Police set on foot by His Grace the Duke of Newcastle* (1758), or when, as we will see, he pressed the government to accept and fund a variety of 'policing plans,' or published advertisements under the heading *From the Police*, or appointed a 'Register Clerk to the Police.' It was not that he thought that broader forms of peace-keeping and regulation were unimportant—indeed, as we will see, he occasionally engaged his men in efforts to deal with immorality or to eliminate the forms of popular behaviour that moralists disparaged, and practised other means of establishing an orderly and disciplined society that Fielding's critics thought should be his main concern. But he saw his task—and his duty, having accepted the government subvention for the purpose—as mainly more focussed than that. The idea of police as a professional group of men carrying out peace-keeping duties under the control of magistrates entered the language with Fielding and, as we will see, continued to carry that meaning in the early decades of the nineteenth century when the forms and purpose of the 'police of the metropolis' became pressing issues.[19]

---

[16] TNA: T 1/454, f. 90, no. 56; and see T 1/449, f. 31, no. 8.

[17] For the usefulness of the watch book, see below, n. 23; ch. 4, text at n 38; ch. 5, text at nn. 114–15.

[18] On the continuing broad meaning of police, see Sir Leon Radzinowicz, *A History of the English Criminal Law and its Administration from 1750*, 4 vols, (London 1948–68), vol. 3, 1–8.

[19] See ch. 8.

The man whom Fielding appointed as register clerk to oversee the collection of information about offenders and suspects, William Marsden, was more than a mere clerk. Indeed, he became in effect Fielding's deputy with respect to policing matters. He was the leader of the policing forces.[20] He may well have been in charge of the compilation of criminal 'intelligence' to increase his effectiveness in that role, though the actual work of recording the masses of information that Fielding required almost certainly fell to assistant clerks. It may also have been a way of increasing the income of a man, and a role, he valued highly. In 1757, Marsden was living at Bow Street. Five years later Fielding had increased his initial salary as 'register clerk' of £30 a year by paying him an additional sum for each report of a robbery and each conviction entered into the books 'duly Alphabetted with the Names and descriptions.'[21]

Nicholas Bond, who succeeded Marsden as 'register clerk' continued the collection of criminal intelligence that was a compilation of reasonably accurate information, along with rumours and suspicions since he was charged with 'completing the Register of Robberies, Informations, Examinations, Convictions, suspicious Book, and Newgate Calendars.'[22] Such detailed material about crime and suspected offenders was fundamental to Fielding's policing ambitions. It proved on occasion to be helpful to the prosecution in trials at the Old Bailey that a Bow Street clerk could produce a record of a description of a suspect or of a decision to undertake an investigation or an entry in the 'watch book' of the number of a stolen watch.[23] But what Fielding mainly valued was the way such information enabled the Bow Street men to respond rapidly when crimes were reported to the office.[24]

Bow Street's involvement in a case—in a robbery or any other criminal offence—generally began with the arrival of the victim in the office or a messenger bringing news of an event or occasionally a pawnbroker bringing in goods recently reported as stolen. The allegations made and, if possible, descriptions of the offenders, were recorded by the Bow Street clerks. One of the elements of the police plan devised in 1753 was intended to encourage the reporting of crime by rewarding the messenger (a shilling became a standard amount) and paying for the advertisement that would appear in the following day's newspapers, sometimes in

---

[20] The chief clerk of the office—Joshua Brogden in the 1750s—also played a role in the policing work of the office. In 1761 Brogden was given a portion of the budget with which to pay minor day-to-day costs like the hiring of coaches and horses, sums for the immediate support of witnesses, payments to informers, and the like, while Fielding handed out the more occasional, and larger sums to the runners for the work they undertook on behalf of the office. When Marsden succeeded Brogden as chief clerk, he continued that work. (No account has survived for the years 1763–65.) In the 1766 and 1767 accounts Marsden is recorded as making those payments. He remained an active officer, even as chief clerk.

[21] OBP, September 1757 (Brent Coleman, et al) t17570914-29; TNA: T 1/414, f. 127, no. 10.

[22] T 1/449, f. 33, no. 15.

[23] For examples, see OBP, April 1761 (William Darwell (*sic*) and William Pentelow (*sic*)) t17610401-28; OBP, September 1783 (Thomas Booker) t17830910-38.

[24] See the notice addressed 'To the Public' in the *Public Advertiser*, 19 February 1757 (repeated 20, 21, and 23 February).

more than one paper, but most often in the *Public Advertiser*.[25] Frequently a handbill would be printed even ahead of advertisements and be distributed to pawnbrokers and other likely places by some of the Bow Street men. Fielding believed strongly in the importance of the rapid dispersal of information if goods were going to be found and offenders apprehended. Advertising was fundamental to his policing strategy. In 1757, as part of his campaign to increase the government's subvention, he included in his annual statement of expenses an itemized list of the advertisements printed in the *Public Advertiser* in the previous year—401 in all, at a cost of almost £64. Not all these advertisements, by any means, had concerned recent offences. About a third contained warnings or general advice or exhortations about criminal matters, 20 per cent repeated a general explanation of the Fieldings' Plan of Police and encouraged victims to report offences, and others announced that Fielding had committed particular offenders to trial or provided the dates of his upcoming re-examinations of other offenders as an encouragement to victims to attend in the hope of identifying their assailants. But 162 advertisements printed in the *Public Advertiser* that year (40 per cent of the total) did report recent offences, described the goods taken and the offenders involved, and in most cases offered a reward for evidence leading to their apprehension and conviction. Many such advertisements ran more than once so fewer than 162 offences were involved.[26]

Apart from encouraging anyone with information to come forward, the advertisements were intended to alert pawnbrokers and anyone else inclined to buy second-hand goods, in the hopes that they would hold them, and if possible the seller until Fielding's men could be summoned or they could otherwise get the suspect before the justice. They were effective in some straightforward cases, as when a lodger stole a cloak and textiles from her landlady, the latter reported the theft to Fielding and the pawnbroker who had given her a guinea and a half on the goods 'took her up' some days later and brought her before the justice in Bow Street, responding no doubt to the advertisement and the reward offered.[27]

In cases of robbery or other serious offences, Bow Street men commonly became involved immediately. The financial accounts that John Fielding submitted to the Treasury bear witness to the frequency and to some extent the zeal with which they did so. The accounts also provide some clues as to the identity of the first officers recruited by the Fieldings.

The Bow Street force had been formed initially when Henry Fielding persuaded half a dozen men to join together to attack the gangs of robbers who were giving cause for anxiety in London in the years following the peace of 1748. These men, Fielding claimed, were constables or ex-constables, clearly in an effort to give them respectability and distinguish them from private thief-takers. That this was not entirely true—certainly not after the first year—may explain why Henry Fielding

[25] For the Fieldings' interest in that paper, see Martin C. Battestin with Ruthe R. Battestin, *Henry Fielding: A Life* (London, 1989), 561.
[26] TNA: T 38/671, ff. 18–19.
[27] OBP, April 1758 (Margaret Cameron) t17580405-21.

made an effort to keep their names secret, though he said that he did so to protect them from the hostility of the public. The most prominent of the early recruits was William Pentlow, who was a constable—a headborough of St George's parish, Bloomsbury. He quickly distinguished himself for his bravery in going after highwaymen. In March 1750 he arrested two notorious robbers, Thomas Lewis and Thomas May, who had committed a series of violent assaults on the highways around London, jamming a pistol into the mouth of one of their victims, and holding it to the ear of another while they stripped them of their valuables. Pentlow said at their trial that he knew them from descriptions given by their victims and knew where they were to be found. He took Lewis 'in bed in Newtoner's Lane'; and, with others, arrested May 'at an infamous house, the Crown and Cannon, in St Giles's.' When Lewis and May attempted to undermine Pentlow's credibility at the Old Bailey by associating him with the private thief-takers and as a man who 'would swear away any person's life for a trifle', Henry Fielding was in court to support him. There was not, he said, 'an honester, or a braver man than he in the king's dominion;' and he told the duke of Newcastle that Pentlow was 'a man of whose Courage and Integrity I have seen the highest Proofs.'[28] This was clearly the kind of man that Fielding wanted for the band of 'real' thief-takers he was attempting to establish in the winter of 1749–50 and that no doubt explains why he recommended him to the Middlesex bench in 1751 as keeper of the New Prison.[29] The point was surely not simply to reward him, but in the absence of other sources of support, to ensure that he could continue as a Bow Street officer, which he did through the 1750s.

Pentlow was by no means the first gaoler to be involved in thief-taking and other areas of law-enforcement.[30] Prison staff were well-placed to gather intelligence about offences and offenders. It had long been common for gaolers to be engaged by victims of thefts and robberies to help find and arrest their attackers. They were in many ways ideal recruits for Fielding's thief-taking corps, not only because they could pick up useful information about the criminal world, but also because they were used to dealing with tough men, guarding them in gaol, and occasionally taking them to magistrates' offices or to Newgate from the Middlesex prisons on the eve of their trials at the Old Bailey. Several of the early Bow Street men, besides Pentlow, were prison officers—or were given such posts to provide them with a means of support when they proved to be useful to the work of the office. Among the men 'attached', as they would have said, to Bow Street in its early years were three of Pentlow's turnkeys at the New Prison: Robert Saunders, Thomas Street,

[28] OBP, April 1750 (Thomas Lewis and Thomas May) t17500425-14; BL: Add Mss 32685, f. 59. In his account of the origins of Bow Street policing, John Fielding said that Pentlow's arrest of Lewis and May was the means by which a large gang of street robbers was broken, and he adds several other instances of his bravery and skill over several years (Fielding, *Plan for Preventing Robberies*, 2). Pentlow's reputation was such, another man said at the Old Bailey, that the mere mention of his name caused the men who were about to rob him to desist and run (OBP, July 1750 (Thomas Dunkin and Edward Brasby) t17500711-59).

[29] Battestin, *Henry Fielding*, 511–12.

[30] Joanna Innes, 'Gaolers as officeholders: the early modern English experience' (unpublished paper, 1996).

and Edward Gaul.[31] Henry Wright was an under-keeper at Tothill Fields Bridewell (from about 1764) while he was attached to Bow Street, c.1766–74.[32] One of the officers of the Palace Court, William Norden, was also an active Bow Street man.[33]

The men attached to the Bow Street office in the early years were a mixed group, to say the least. Edward Wright, was said in 1755 to be 'a runner at Mr Fielding's office to carry persons backwards and forwards'—that is, not one of the front-line officers but an assistant to take people from the office to one of the Westminster or Middlesex gaols and if necessary to bring them back for re-examinations. At the same time he was charged with receiving stolen goods and with keeping a disorderly house in the notorious Black Boy Alley, a house described as 'nothing but a den of thieves.'[34] He maintained his connection with Bow Street into the late 1760s. Leonard Yates, who was an active Bow Street officer at the end of 1757, had been closely enough associated with pickpockets to have given evidence in four cases at the Old Bailey earlier that year.[35] In two he had not taken part but knew those involved and what had happened; in the others he had helped to set up the victim or had acted as a shield to enable the thief to escape. Three of those he testified against were acquitted; but his evidence helped to convict the fourth defendant of picking pockets in the crowd that had gathered outside St James's Palace on the king's birthday. One cannot be absolutely certain that this Leonard Yates is the man who began to work at Bow Street later in 1757, but the name is distinctive and he seems all along to have been willing to work on both sides of the law. At Bow Street he was first employed to distribute handbills, and particularly to watch for pickpockets—a job for which he was peculiarly suited. Within a few months he was chasing highwaymen and footpads.[36] Yates was not the only man involved in felony who turned out to be a useful recruit: one of the active officers in the late 1750s, William Darvall, had been a highwayman who was taken into the office after giving the evidence that condemned his accomplice.[37] It is clear that not every man attached to the office in its early years was as respectable as the Fieldings claimed.[38] But, as we will see, within a few years the magistrates were able to attract men to

---

[31] OBP, April 1755 (Bridget Golden, et al) t17550409-40; May 1758 (George Albeat) t17580510-9; May 1764 (Solomon Solomons, et al) t17640502-55.

[32] OBP, September 1784 (Henry Morgan) t17840915-1.

[33] OBP, December 1755 (Unnamed) t17551222-24.

[34] OBP, April 1755 (Francis Pryer, et al) t17550409-25.

[35] OBP, February–March 1757 (Lawrence Gorman and Thomas Walker) 717570223-11; February–March 1757 (Mary Jones) t17570223-28; February–March 1757 (Catherine Walker) t17570223-12; April 1757 (Catherine Walker) t17570420-23.

[36] TNA: T 1/387, ff.1–5.

[37] See below, text at nn. 59–64.

[38] At the same time not everyone who claimed an attachment to Bow Street because they brought suspected offenders before the magistrates there had been recruited by the Fieldings. The well-known thief-taker Stephen McDaniel—who would become notorious within a few years for serious corruption—called himself an 'officer' at an Old Bailey trial in 1750, e.g., but there is no other evidence that he was actually employed by the Fieldings (OBP, February–March, 1750 (John Bowen et al) t17500228-41). For McDaniel, see Ruth Paley, 'Thief-takers in London in the Age of the McDaniel Gang' in Douglas Hay and Francis Snyder (eds.), *Policing and Prosecution in Britain*, 301–41.

Bow Street who were not as obviously tainted by connections with known or suspected offenders.

The government's subvention was crucial to the creation of the policing side of the Bow Street magistrates' work. The duke of Newcastle provided resources to support that policing because of the perceived threats from robbers and highwaymen. John Fielding's first surviving annual account, for the year beginning October 1755, makes it clear that the £200 annual stipend went in large part for payments of expenses and small fees to men involved in detecting and prosecuting such offenders. In October and November 1755, for example, Bow Street men were paid for pursuing a highwayman who robbed near Hackney (17/6d), for 'sitting up in an Hospital with a Highwayman that was wounded till fit to be examined' (£1/11/6d), for 'finding Evidence for a Murder' (1/3d), for 'two Days Horse hire to inquire into a Robbery' (6/0d), for 'pursuing and apprehending Jonathan Wigmore', a highwayman (£8/8/0d), for 'patrolling the Squares' (19/6d), and for going to Barnet 'to inquire into a Murder.' In addition, Fielding paid more than £10 for pistols and hangers—short swords—to arm 'the pursuers of Robbers'.[39] Over the following 11 months the account includes further payments to the runners for apprehending highwaymen, street robbers, shoplifters, and pickpockets; for collecting evidence against some of those suspects; investigating three other murders, one of which involved 'opening a Pavement' and another 'dragging a Pond' in pursuit of evidence; further patrolling of Westminster squares; and, in September 1756, for 'two Men and two Horses patrolling the great Roads to prevent Robberies'.[40]

Fielding's decision to send men to patrol the squares in Westminster and the 'great Roads', the highways leading into the city, was a response to numerous reports in the press of attacks by footpads and highwaymen. These included assaults on travellers of all kinds, on the poor as well as the rich, on stage-coaches as well as private conveyances. But inevitably the wealthy provided the most tempting targets and attacks on them no doubt increased demands that something be done. An obvious sense of vulnerability was caused by reports of assaults like that on Alexander Thompson, Esq., who was travelling by coach from York to London, accompanied by several servants, when he was stopped just north of the capital by two highwayman. They first threatened to shoot him if he did not order his servants to ride on, which he did; they then attacked him when he attempted to draw his sword, striking him with a pistol and knocking out 'several of his Teeth' before taking his watch and purse, and a pocket book containing 'Bank-bills to a very

---

[39] TNA: T 38/671, ff. 1–2.

[40] TNA: T 38/671, f. 4. The evidence that Fielding sent officers to investigate murders is both interesting and puzzling. It was rare for magistrates to conduct pretrial hearings into murder allegations. That was left to coroners whose duty it was to investigate all suspicious or unexplained deaths, to convene a jury, hold hearings in which they took evidence, and, if the jury returned a verdict that the death was felonious, to send the results of their inquests to an appropriate court where they would form the basis of indictments. For coroners, see Ian A. Burney, *Bodies of evidence: medicine and the politics of the English Inquest, 1830–1926* (Baltimore, 2000); Thomas Rogers Forbes, *Crowner's Quest* (American Philosophical Association, 28 (January 1978).

considerable amount.'[41] Or by the report that 'a gentleman was robbed of a silver Watch and some Money in the Fields behind St Giles's, by a Gang of Footpads, consisting of four, who have infested those Fields for some time past.' When this latter attack was reported to Bow Street, Fielding sent out a patrol who 'met the whole gang, attacked and disarmed them, and seized three of them.' Several others were apprehended when one of the arrested men turned King's evidence. In the end, four were examined at Bow Street and committed to trial.[42]

Patrolling the squares and in particular patrolling and guarding the highways on the outskirts of London reveals an aspect of Bow Street policing that was to be increasingly one of its most important characteristics: its geographical range. Because the men attached to the office were not part of the parochial constabulary they were free to operate across the metropolis as a whole and, indeed, well beyond. To facilitate the broadening reach of the office, Fielding was named over the next few years in the commissions of the peace of Kent, Essex, and Surrey, in addition to those of Middlesex and Westminster. This meant that his men did not have to seek the assistance of local magistrates in the counties surrounding the metropolis to get Bow Street warrants 'backed' in order to make an arrest or carry out a search. Otherwise they might have had to seek out such help, though in practice there did not appear to be serious impediments to their working wherever their enquiries took them. Fielding's announcements in the newspapers at the end of 1754 about his 'plan of police' had included the promise that reports of serious offences would bring an instant response by men willing to go anywhere to apprehend an offender. The Bow Street accounts for 1756 make it clear that Fielding set no limits to tasks they might undertake. They conducted enquiries into robberies on Hounslow Heath and offences at several places in Surrey; they pursued men into Hertfordshire and Bedfordshire, and a housebreaker to Bristol—hiring horses and post-chaises as they did so.[43]

In the previous year Fielding had published a pamphlet to encourage men of property to subscribe to a prosecution fund 'to prevent robberies within twenty miles of London' by agreeing to pay messengers to send him immediate notice of offences. Turnpike gatekeepers and publicans were also encouraged to act as agents in a communication network that would result in early news of all highway robberies being received in Bow Street so that Fielding's men could seek out and

---

[41] *Public Advertiser*, 28 January 1757. Similar attacks by highwaymen were reported in the same paper on 31 January and through February; on 15 March a gang of seven robbers were committed to Newgate by Fielding when one of their number turned King's evidence and gave an account of 37 robberies they had committed 'in the Fields near Town.'

[42] *Public Advertiser*, 30 August 1757. A 'private patrol' seems to have been a group of men not attached to the office, but recruited for the purpose. The accounts record a payment of £1.5.0 on September 30 to '5 Persons for patrolling the Fields when the Footpads were apprehended'—i.e. five persons unnamed, in a year in which Fielding more often than not named his officers when accounting for payments to them for patrolling and other work. The accounts also include the payment of a guinea for coaches on 8 September, the day on which four street robbers were brought from various prisons to be examined in public at Bow Street. (TNA: T 38/671, f. 17).

[43] TNA: T38/671, *passim*.

apprehend the offenders.[44] Bow Street's sphere of operations broadened over time beyond the counties near London because Fielding was anxious to see it develop as a central resource, and because magistrates across the country came to value the expertise of its officers and formed the habit of calling for their help when faced with difficult cases.[45] In this as in other respects Bow Street was to become the Scotland Yard of its day, the acknowledged centre of policing skill and experience, largely because of John Fielding's ambition and determination, and because the financial base provided by the government supported a stable clerical staff and in time a stable group of long-serving officers.

The financial resources were in fact to increase in the early years as a result of Fielding's ambitions. In the course of 1757 he overspent his budget of £200 by more than 50 per cent—justifying the expanded policing retrospectively by claiming that 'almost every Highwayman, Street Robber, House Breaker, and Mail Robber that has make his Appearance has been apprehended, executed, transported, or is now in Custody.'[46] In requesting an increase in the subvention to £400 at the end of 1757, he laid out new plans that further expanded Bow Street's policing activities. Such an increase was required, Fielding reported to the Treasury, to enable him to support four 'Pursuers, all Peace Officers, who are to subject themselves to be call'd at any Hour of the day or Night to pursue to any Part of the Kingdom it shall be thought necessary' and the maintenance of two 'pursuit Horses' to avoid the inevitable delays that hiring such horses incurred.[47] The request was granted.

The consequences of these increasing resources are to be seen in the number and variety of policing activities reported in the annual accounts. Compared to about 10 entries in 1756, Fielding made about 60 payments to his officers in the following year for patrolling areas in which robberies had been reported and for pursuing and apprehending suspects. In 1758, he made more than eighty.[48] In 1757, six men appear to have taken up most of the chasing of serious offenders, including William Marsden, William Pentlow, his deputy at the New Prison, Robert Saunders, and Joseph Street, another New Prison turnkey. These men, along with Samuel Phillipson and Stephen Scott, carried the burden of pursuing highwaymen and street robbers in 1757, though a number of other men were occasionally rewarded for similar work. In some cases, these men worked alone, most often with a partner, very occasionally in larger groups.

---

[44] Fielding, *A Plan for Preventing Robberies*, 12–14.

[45] For the runners' work outside the metropolis after 1792, see David J. Cox, *A Certain Share of Low Cunning. A History of the Bow Street Runners, 1792–1839* (Cullompton, 2010).

[46] TNA: T 38/671, f. 9.

[47] TNA: T 38/671, f. 10. The 'pursuers' were to be given an annual fee of £10, along with payments from Fielding's discretionary fund and shares of any public and private rewards that might be earned. The government provided the extra money, but there is little evidence that henceforth only four men were designated as the pursuers, or that men who undertook these tasks were Westminster constables, which is what I take 'peace officer' to mean, or that they were each given £10 a year to encourage them in this work. Fielding's purpose in promising that these men would be 'peace officers' was surely to reassure the cabinet that his men would be respectable.

[48] TNA: T38/671.

In February 1757, for example, Scott and Phillipson received payments for riding the turnpikes around London to give notice to the keepers along the way that two known highwaymen were active, one of whom, William Page, had robbed Lord Ferrers—who was himself to become infamous some years later when he murdered his steward and was executed at Tyburn.[49] Saunders took up the chase when information was received in the office that these highwaymen had been seen in the White Horse tavern in Fetter Lane. He went there three times without finding them and soon after, no doubt following another tip, Scott chased them to Coney Hatch, also without success. Pentlow, Saunders, Street, and Scott (occasionally with assistants) went after other robbers around the metropolis—when offences were reported in residential areas or in Chelsea Fields or St George's Fields across the river.[50]

The Bow Street financial accounts document the kind of work that the Bow Street men were undertaking in these years, but not its extent. A budget of £200 or even £400 did not enable Fielding to compensate them for every job he sent them on. To take one example of many, in August 1757 Fielding sent Marsden and other officers to apprehend four robbers who had stopped William Saunders at Highgate on his way into the city and taken his money, shoe buckles, and watch and cut his breeches at the waistband so he could not easily run after them. Saunders had gone to Bow Street the next morning, a Sunday, and had given Fielding a description of the robbers and their clothes. That evening Marsden and others went to Highgate. When they got to the fields where Saunders had been robbed, Marsden went ahead, pretending to be a lone traveller. He came upon the four men and, with the help of his companions, took three of them. Marsden took the fourth man the following day when one of the robbers turned king's evidence and revealed where he could be found. All of this was described by George Grace and Marsden at some length at the Old Bailey trial that followed. They would have been eligible for reward money, but there is no entry in the Bow Street accounts of their having received anything from Fielding's funds.[51]

The accounts provide an incomplete picture of the policing activities carried on through Bow Street. But they reveal some of the character of that policing, and they make it clear that Fielding fulfilled his early pledge that his officers were ready to go anywhere in the country in search of offenders. They include, for example. payments to Pentlow for pursuing a man to Deptford and Doggers Bar in December 1756, and soon thereafter more than £14 for chasing two others to Portsmouth, bringing one of them back in a post-chaise. In the winter of 1756–57, among other investigations, Marsden pursued highwaymen to Windsor, Saunders and Street followed others to Henley, and Scott and Phillipson chased a man who had held up the Norwich mail.[52] In this work the Bow Street men rode the two 'pursuit horses' that had been acquired 'for the use of the police', or they hired horses as necessary.

---

[49] Radzinowicz, *History of English Criminal Law*, vol. 1, 170, 172.
[50] TNA: T 38/671, ff. 11–13.
[51] OBP, September 1757 (Brent Coleman and John Roberts) t17570914-29.
[52] TNA: T 38/671, ff. 12–15.

They were also armed—with pistols, swords, and, in 1757, at least one blunder-buss.[53]

In the course of 1757, Bow Street men also took on an increasing amount of night-time patrolling. In January the press reported that 'Mr Fielding's armed Patrole' were going around all the squares in Westminster from time to time.[54] Bow Street men regularly guarded the highways leading into London. In the course of the year and into the following winter patrolling became a major activity, conducted particularly by Marsden, Saunders, Street, and Pentlow. The group of active officers was, however, far from stable at this stage. Scott and Phillipson, for example, ceased to be involved in 1758 and their places were taken by several new men. One, John Spensley was a constable and had acted in various ways in the previous year but not frequently as either a member of the patrol or a pursuer. He now took on a more central role, and was joined by five others: William Parsons (who was also a constable), James Porter, Richard Peers, Leonard Yates, and William Darvall—the latter two of whom had been recruited because of their first-hand knowledge of active offenders.[55]

There was a good deal of activity to report in 1757 and 1758. But looked at closely it becomes clear that much of the effort to catch and prosecute highwaymen was becoming increasingly concentrated on a handful of targets. For just as robberies and other serious offences had increased in the years of peace after 1748, they had fallen away as sharply as the effects of the onset of what was to be the Seven Years War became felt in 1757. Many fewer violent offences were tried at the Old Bailey in the course of that war and many fewer offenders were hanged at Tyburn by the last years of the 1750s compared to the early years of the decade.[56]

As John Fielding's budget increased, then, what had been the primary target of Bow Street policing—violence on the streets of London and the highways surrounding the capital—was becoming less threatening. Fielding no doubt found the diminishing levels of violence cause for celebration. On the other hand, he was not prepared to declare the war against the robbers entirely over. In requesting renewal of his policing stipend at the end of 1758 he was careful to say that new gangs were giving trouble and needed to be dealt with.[57] But like any administrator with a budget to spend—especially a budget that had just been increased—he must have given some thought to the possibility that his small force of officers might not be as fully occupied in tackling problems that had been their primary *raison d'être* and to have considered ways of refocusing and adjusting their work. One result was a more concentrated and persistent effort to catch a highwayman named William Page and another pair of robbers and to ensure their effective prosecution than had ever been possible when the office budget had been stretched to the limit.

---

[53] TNA: T 38/671, ff. 13–15; T 1/387, 1.

[54] *Public Advertiser*, 20 January 1757.

[55] For Darvall as a highwayman, see below, text at n. 59. For Yates, the associate of pickpockets, see above, text at nn. 35–6.

[56] J. M. Beattie, *Crime and the Courts 1660–1800* (Oxford, 1986), 531–4; Table 10.1.

[57] TNA: T 1/387, covering letter.

William Page first appeared in the Bow Street accounts in February and March 1757, when Saunders, Street, Marsden, Pentlow, and John Barnes, the high constable of Westminster, all pursued him or waited for him at various places— Henley, Hounslow, and Moorfields on the edge of the City of London—until towards the end of March when he was said to have gone to Scotland.[58] He was back by the summer and committing highway robberies in the Maidenhead area in Kent. The Bow Street men took up the chase once again, for some time without success. Things perhaps heated up for him and his accomplice, William Darvall (or Darwell) when at the end of July they robbed the Bishop of Bath and Wells near Maidenhead. Darvall was apprehended soon thereafter[59] and Fielding went to the county gaol in Maidstone to learn what he could from him about Page's movements and to persuade him to turn king's evidence. He helped that cause along by giving Darvall a guinea to provide a slightly more comfortable stay in gaol than he would have otherwise experienced. A second visit to Darvall by a Bow Street officer produced crucial intelligence about Page's contacts in London and elsewhere. That information enabled Scott and Phillipson to track Page through Kent, Buckinghamshire, Middlesex and Berkshire, and on 8 August to apprehend him. He was examined at Bow Street and committed to Newgate, guarded by soldiers.[60]

That was not the end of Fielding's engagement in the case. Perhaps because the budget allowed it and because he feared that the evidence gathered so far was weak, Fielding set about gathering further evidence and organizing the prosecution. He engaged a solicitor, wrote to the Lord Provost of Edinburgh to get help locating a witness (and urged Secretary of State Holdernesse to support that request), sent Parsons to find someone able to identify Page's horse, and then Parsons and Marsden to find the man in Essex who had tried to change the numbers and in other ways alter watches Page had taken from his victims before pawning them. Fielding issued subpoenas to compel the attendance of other witnesses, at least one of whom (Henry Harvey) was paid his expenses for agreeing to give evidence, though he turned out to be a dud.[61]

In the meantime, Darvall, Page's accomplice, had been moved to London in September, and continued to be supported in gaol. In January 1758, Page was brought from Newgate to Bow Street to be 'further examined', that is to be questioned again in a public setting to fill out whatever statement he had made at his initial pretrial examination about the charges against him, the intention being to encourage any other victims who suspected that he had robbed them to come forward. His trial at the Old Bailey followed soon thereafter.[62] It was conducted by lawyers at Bow Street's expense. Fielding's accounts record a payment of £14 to a solicitor—George Box 'the Attorney'—and five guineas to a barrister, John Aylett

---

[58] For Page as a 'gentleman highwayman', see Andrea McKenzie, *Tyburn's Martyrs. Execution in England, 1675–1775* (London, 2007), 118–19.

[59] *Public Advertiser*, 26 July 1757.

[60] TNA: T 1/671, ff. 13–17, *passim*; *Public Advertiser*, 10 August 1757.

[61] TNA: T 1/671, ff. 13–17; Fielding's correspondence with Secretary Holdernesse is at BL: Egerton Mss 3438, f. 194.

[62] OBP, February, 1758 (William Page, *alias* Willams, *alias* Gage) t17580222-28.

Stow,[63] though the brief printed trial account does not disclose any part he may have played. The evidence turned out to be weak in any case. Darvall's detailed accomplice evidence was insufficiently corroborated by vague and hesitant testimony from the other witnesses Fielding had been able to find—including Harvey. Lord Ferrers not only refused to pay the prosecution costs, he also refused to attend the trial. Page played on the concern that the notorious McDaniel case had created some years earlier about the reliability of thief-takers' evidence by denying any connection with Darvall (apart from having known him in school) and hinting darkly at the possibility that Darvall had been induced to perjure himself, following his 'long conection with Mr Fielding.' The jury found Page not guilty, perhaps with the judge's encouragement, given the judiciary's concern in this period about accomplice evidence and the need for corroboration.[64]

The Old Bailey trial was far from being the end of Bow Street's engagement in the case, however. There were to be further trials at the Hertfordshire and Kent assizes. Fielding went in person to Hertfordshire 'as Committing magistrate to Conduct the Prosecution', and persuaded Ferrers to go with him to give evidence, paying his expenses. With the help of a barrister—'Mr Cox the Council,' to whom he paid four guineas—and with the accomplices' evidence corroborated by Ferrers, Fielding secured Page's conviction. Not content with that, he sent Marsden to the subsequent Kent assizes where Page was also convicted of committing highway robbery in that county and sentenced to death. Fielding continued to pursue him even then by instructing one of his clerks to collect 'out of the News Papers all the Robberys' Page had been accused of committing, obviously preparing to defeat any attempt to get him pardoned. It was unnecessary. Page was hanged in March 1758.[65] If evidence were required to confirm that eighteenth-century magistrates continued to wield policing powers even as their role as judges in pretrial proceedings became more obvious, Fielding's determined pursuit of William Page provides it.

Over the same period that the Page saga was playing out, the Bow Street men were also chasing two other highwaymen who had stopped coaches and robbed other travellers on the main Essex roads and occasionally in Kent. What appears to have been an intense effort began in December 1757 when Marsden and a constable named Bowcher were paid 9s.9d. (nine shillings and nine pence) for going to Stamford Hill in what must have seemed a routine search. It turned out to be far from routine because the two highwaymen involved, Nixon and Darkin, proved to be difficult to find and impossible to discourage. The first pursuit having

---

[63] TNA: T 1/387/43 ff. 10, 11. Stow was one of a small number of barristers who attended at the Old Bailey in the third quarter of the eighteenth century. See Allyson N. May, *The Bar and the Old Bailey, 1750–1850* (Chapel Hill, 2003), 30, 95. Box was paid for acting 'in two prosecutions against Page the Highwayman, one at the Old Bailey for robbing John Webb, Esqr. on the Highway, and the other at Hertford for robbing the Right Honble the Earl of Ferrers, Mr Webb and Lord Ferrers refusing to be at any Expence.' He was also employed by the office to manage a case in King's Bench in 1765 (T 1/449, f. 31).

[64] For the McDaniel case, see above, n. 38. For the strict application of a corroboration rule in this period, see John H. Langbein, *The Origins of Adversary Criminal Trial* (Oxford, 2003), 203–13.

[65] *London Evening Post*, 23 March 1758.

failed, Marsden and Pentlow resumed the investigation after a robbery in Stratford a few days later; Spensley subsequently pursued Nixon and Darkin in Epping Forest; and in the last week of December, Street, Saunders, Marsden, Spensley, Leonard Yates and James Porter were all paid for their efforts to catch them by patrolling and searching in the Stratford area.[66]

And so it went on into the New Year, with payments through January for the support of the 'pursuit horses' in Essex and for the cost of hiring extra horses for the new men who joined the chase. Yates, Porter, and William Parsons were all new to the office and had mainly been doing routine administrative work for a few months, distributing handbills and the like. They were now pressed into the pursuit of Nixon and Darkin and particularly into a new level of sustained patrolling on the Essex roads at night. Spensley, Marsden, Saunders and Street also continued to receive payments through January for going out several nights—the latter two for nine nights at one stretch and Street another tour of eight—and now into Kent as well as Essex. More arms were bought for the patrollers in the course of the month: three pair of pistols and a musquetoon. The accounts also record two payments for 'Disguise habitts for the pursuers,' the nature of which was undisclosed. Perhaps the more promising stratagem brought to bear was the £6 expended to hire a post-chaise for 'carrying Armed Men to patroll the Roads' in Essex and Kent. When Darkin was finally taken at the end of the month, the policing effort had involved eight of the most active Bow Street men, some of them for many days and nights in December and January, and had cost about £50.

Sending armed men in coaches remained unusual. But night patrolling, both on foot and horseback, became a more established element in Bow Street policing in 1758 and into the following winter. In October, Pentlow, Marsden, Darvall, Peers and a number of unnamed Westminster constables were paid to patrol the London streets for eight nights 'to apprehend and suppress' two gangs of footpads, 13 in all, six of whom they arrested. The fact that one of the constables was badly wounded in making those arrests and that three Bow Street men were sent to bring in 'Scampey the Jew', one of their receivers, suggests that that confrontation had not been without difficulty and danger. Its timing, not much more than a week before the annual accounts were to be sent to the Treasury, enabled Fielding (perhaps not altogether fortuitously) to justify the heavy expenditures that year on patrolling the streets and highways. Since several members of the London gangs 'remain untaken, tho' known', he said in submitting his accounts and requesting speedy renewal of the government's subvention, 'it makes the continuation of [the] Night Patrol absolutely necessary'.[67] Over the next few months a mounted patrol was sent out on 22 occasions, most often involving one or two men (though in one case as many as seven), and on stints that averaged just under six nights.[68]

---

[66] This and the following paragraph are based on the Bow Street accounts for December. 1757–February. 1758: TNA: T 1/387, ff. 4–10.

[67] TNA: T 1/387, cover page.

[68] TNA: T 1/387, *passim*.

2. WARTIME: POLICING THE POOR

The increase of the Bow Street policing budget to £400 in 1758 and the reduced volume of serious crime in the war years made it possible for John Fielding to commit his men to much more thorough and expensive policing, including new forms of patrolling, than could have been contemplated in the busy years at the beginning of the decade. The surviving financial accounts for these years also reveal that he engaged in another set of policing measures during the war that were equally preventive in intent, that is, sending his officers to shut down forms of popular entertainment that he and other middle class men believed led working men into crime, like drinking and gambling, because they cost time and money and encouraged laziness and bad habits that led inevitably to bad companions and bad life choices.

Fielding had not previously seen his duty at Bow Street as requiring him to deal with the bawdy houses, unlicensed alehouses and gambling houses that made the Covent Garden area a notorious centre of immorality of the kind that drew men into crime. He was to be criticized for thinking that that was largely the business of other magistrates in the area and of the parish constables they could command.[69] Generally, he took the view that his charge was of a higher order. But in the 1750s he did indeed send his men to engage in work of this kind. He may have been encouraged to do so in these years by a Reformation of Manners campaign and a movement of ideas and social action that had seen the formation of charitable societies to confront some of the most visible social problems in the metropolis, including the crowds of young boys living on the streets, and the large numbers of prostitutes, many of them very young girls.[70] Fielding was active in several of these charitable societies. He published a pamphlet advocating an asylum for girls in danger of being drawn into prostitution out of necessity and by the temptations of pimps and bawdy-house keepers, and a hospital for the rescue and rehabilitation of older prostitutes.[71] He not only contributed, but joined the boards of directors when such institutions were established as the Lambeth Asylum and the Magdalen Hospital.[72] Fielding was also motivated in these engagements by a view, shared with many others in the 1750s, that the country was losing population just at a time when, with the renewal of warfare against France in Europe and overseas, it was in need of young, healthy men to serve in the army and navy. These were the convictions that had led Fielding in 1756 (in response to a request from a naval captain) to gather a group of 30 boys from the streets, to feed them and equip them

---

[69] Below, ch. 4, text at nn. 14–21.

[70] For the Reformation of Manners campaign in the metropolis in this period, see Joanna Innes, *Inferior Politics. Social Problems and Social policies in Eighteenth-Century Britain* (Oxford, 2009), 292–9.

[71] John Fielding, *A Plan for a Preservatory and Reformatory, for the Benefit of Deserted Girls and Penitent Prostitutes* (London, 1758).

[72] Donna T. Andrew, *Philanthropy and Police. London Charity in the Eighteenth Century* (Princeton, 1989), chs. 3–4.

with a Bible and clean clothes, and to send them to sea on board ships of the royal navy—an initiative that led in the same year to Fielding and Jonas Hanway establishing a charity—the Marine Society—that would prove to be immensely successful at equipping boys for service on merchant ships and in the navy.[73]

It was in this climate of social reform that Fielding sent his runners to help regulate some of what he believed to be the obvious temptations that drew unwary members of the working population into activities that wasted both their time and money. He was particularly hostile to gambling which was also closely linked in his mind with cheating and fraud and with the kind of dishonesty that threatened trust and the well-being of a commercial society. The dangers of being cheated by wily men was clearly close to his heart—perhaps because before coming to Bow Street he had managed the Fieldings' advertising and employment office (the Universal Register Office), an experience that made him conscious of the importance of honesty in business dealings and the dangers of misrepresentation.[74] Perhaps, too, as a blind man he was keenly aware of the ease with which sharpers could take advantage of the unwary. He was concerned enough about the need for honesty and about the corrosive effects of gaming that he drew up legislation in 1757, sponsored in the house of commons by the lord mayor and the Recorder of London, that resulted in a statute prohibiting gaming in public houses by journeymen, labourers and servants, and that aimed to control the fraudulent obtaining of goods and to prohibit unlawful pawning.[75] He was to return to these subjects several times in the future.[76]

Presented with the opportunity provided by the reduced levels of violent offences during the war to focus some of his policing resources on the harmful aspects of popular culture and what he considered the real causes of crime, Fielding set out to suppress gaming houses and other places where unlawful games were being played, and to prosecute other activities that wasted the time and money of the working population. He must have thought that this use of the Bow Street policing resources required some justification, for in 1758 he published a second account of the establishment of the Bow Street office that differed considerably from that he had given three years earlier. In writing about his plans for the Bow Street office in 1755, Fielding had focussed on robbery and the war against the gangs.[77] Three years later, he was concerned to emphasize the broader objectives of Henry

---

[73] Jonas Hanway, *An account of the Marine Society* (London, 1758); J. S. Taylor, *Jonas Hanway, founder of the Marine Society: charity and policy in eighteenth-century Britain* (London, 1985).

[74] Battestin, *Henry Fielding*, 498, 526–7, 543, 556, 595.

[75] 30 Geo II, c. 24 (1757). Radzinowicz found no evidence for his authorship of this statute (*History of English Criminal Law*, vol. 3, 69), but Fielding disclosed it in a letter to the duke of Newcastle (Add Mss 32876, f. 274) and his Bow Street accounts include payments that make his authorship clear, including his expenses in attending the house of commons and a reference with respect to the printing costs of 'Mr Fielding's Bill.' (TNA: T 1/671, ff. 13, 15, 17).

[76] Fraud, deceit and gambling are linked at several points in the pamphlet Fielding was to publish in 1761 entitled *Extracts from such of the penal laws, as particularly related to the peace and good order of the Metropolis: to which are added, the felonies made so by statute, . . . and a short treatise on the office of constable.* See, e.g., the section entitled 'Cautions to Shopkeepers and Tradesmen. . . .' 250–63, which he subsequently published as a separate pamphlet in 1776.

[77] Fielding, *A Plan for Preventing Robberies*. See above, n. 1.

Fielding's policing ideas and plans.[78] The bulk of his 1758 pamphlet emphasized the need for policing that would eliminate 'disorders' in the metropolis, curb the activities of gamblers and cheats, suppress illegal music meetings and dances that attracted servants and apprentices, and clear the streets of nuisances like beggars and prostitutes.[79] The difference between the two accounts is so striking as to be inexplicable without consideration of the way in which the beginning of the Seven Years War had affected the character of crime, and shifted the balance in Bow Street policing.

The theme was established at the outset. 'In large and populous Cities,' Fielding wrote, 'especially in the Metropolis of a flourishing Kingdom, Artificers, Servants, and Labourers, compose the Bulk of the People, and keeping them in good Order is the Object of the Police, the Care of the Legislature, and the Duty of the magistrates, and all other Peace-Officers'.[80] What followed was a version of the commonplace notion that serious crime was the consequence of moral failing, of the unwillingness of men and women to work to support themselves and their families, and, in addition, of the ease with which apprentices and working men could be tempted into the bad habits that would lead them eventually to stealing, then to worse offences until they committed a crime that would take them to an early death on the gallows at Tyburn.[81] The judges had been reminded by Lord Chancellor Hardwicke in 1754 as they set out on circuit that the laws should be 'carefully executed against Crimes of a lower kind with which Young Offenders are apt to begin and from thence to proceed to Crimes of a more enormous nature'.[82] Fielding's version of these widely-held assumptions stressed the bad effects of gambling and of the numerous diversions and amusements in the city. He was no doubt right to say that diminishing such activities was included in Henry Fielding's policing plan. But there had not been sufficient resources to put those ideas into effect. It was the new circumstances created by the war that explain the emphasis on crime prevention in this pamphlet of 1758 and that led John Fielding to say that it was 'much better to prevent even one Man from being a Rogue, than from apprehending and bringing forty to Justice.'[83] That had not been uppermost in his mind when the gangs were pressing or in his brother's when he persuaded Newcastle to support his Bow Street men in 1753; nor was it a notion that would have been likely to attract government financial support. The truth of that became clear when the Seven Years War came to an end, when, as we will see, serious crime once again became Bow Street's principal target.

During the war, however, Fielding was able to mount something of a campaign against social evils—a shift in the balance of policing that the pamphlet of 1758 was written to explain and justify. He made gambling one of his central targets—not

---

[78] John Fielding, *An Account of the Origin and Effects of a Police set on foot by His Grace the Duke of Newcastle* (1758).

[79] Fielding, *Account of the Origin*, 16–18.

[80] *Ibid*, vii.

[81] McKenzie, *Tyburn's Martyrs*, 59–67; Beattie, *Policing and Punishment*, 51–62.

[82] TNA: SP 36/147, f. 226.

[83] Fielding, *Account of the Origin*, 35.

the private clubs of the upper classes, but the places in which tradesmen and men of similar standing might be tempted to venture their small capital and where they could easily become victims of men who were certain to cheat them. Fielding made an effort to close gaming houses, particularly in the summer of 1758 when at least 32 payments for information about the location of such places and payments to his men for raiding them were recorded in the office accounts.[84] Gambling came in many forms. Fielding was also concerned to curb the gaming that had for long been embedded in the culture and recreations of the working population, very commonly enjoyed in alehouses in such games as skittles and shuffleboard as well as cards. Fielding's efforts to eradicate these forms of popular recreation were conducted by means of summonses, warnings, and cautions to publicans. In some cases he ordered that the hardware involved in such games be destroyed—that skittles be burned, for example, or that shuffleboard equipment, or as on one occasion a billiard table, be destroyed; even more damaging to the owners because they were in many cases elaborate, finely decorated, and expensive, Fielding also paid his men on a few occasions for finding and destroying E.O. (even and odd) tables.[85] But his policing relied principally on warnings and threats of the removal of licences—relying on the authority conferred on magistrates by the Disorderly Houses Act passed in 1752.[86] He paid a standard fee of 2s.6d per establishment to informers who reported evidence of gaming in pubs, and he acted on the information by having his officers investigate and deliver a summons that presumably—the evidence of that would be in the lost magistrates' books—led to a fine, possibly a threatened loss of licence. The Bow Street accounts submitted to the Treasury in the late 1750s make it clear that Fielding took these activities seriously, particularly in 1758, when dozens of informations and summonses are recorded in his account for that year.[87]

Another target of Fielding's moral policing was dancing—popular dancing, not, of course, the balls and other entertainments of the rich. In November 1756, a Westminster constable was paid 2s.6d. 'for suppressing an illegal Meeting of Servants and Apprentices at a Dance at the Golden Lyon near Gros[venor] Square', and thereafter other entries record payments for evidence about 'hops', many of them held in pubs—dances, no doubt led by a fiddler and a couple of other musicians.[88] Fielding was clearly persuaded that such pleasures wasted the time and the money of young men and women who could ill afford to mis-spend either. He may also have thought they provided far too many opportunities for them to come into more than casual contact, that in fact some of the women were

[84] TNA: T 1/387, ff.12–17, and *passim*.

[85] In March 1758, Fielding paid a man called Higginson ten guineas for 'the Intrinsical Value of two fine E'.O' Tables which cost at least £70 and which were publickly burnt to prevent Gaming.' (TNA: T 1/387, f.10). That there was some danger involved in seeking out these tables is suggested by the unusually generous fees paid to informers and the payment on one occasion for 'a disguise' for one of them. (Ibid, ff. 9–11). Burning the tables in public was aggressive and unpopular, and required Fielding to hire constables 'to keep the peace.' (*Ibid*, f.17).

[86] 25 Geo II, c. 36 (1752).

[87] TNA: T 1/387, *passim*.

[88] TNA: T 1/387, ff. 3, 4, 10; T 38/671, f. 3;

prostitutes. At any event, Fielding put a good deal of effort into suppressing these urban offspring of county dances by paying informers and sending his runners to observe and report—on one occasion paying for tickets to make this possible as well as to serve as evidence, and on another paying his men to hire nine coaches to bring to Bow Street for examination 'a great Number of disorderly Persons assembled at an illegal Hop at the Angel in Bunhill Fields'.[89] He was later to say that 'nine out of ten of these irregular Meetings have been suppressed merely by the magistrates sending to the Parties, and making them acquainted with the Nature of the Offence, and the Penalties which the Laws in such Cases prescribe'—having in mind here, no doubt, the large fines possible under the Disorderly Houses Act of 1752.[90]

For the same purpose of discouraging time-wasting and harmful self-indulgence, Fielding sent men to Marylebone at one point in 1758 'to prevent a Play being acted by Journeymen Apprentices etc.' and in the following year to suppress 'some illegal Performances at the little Theatre by desire of the Lord Chamberlain.'[91] He took so broad a view of the lord chamberlian's powers to regulate theatrical performances under the Theatre Licencing Act of 1735 that he thought the increasingly common and popular debating societies in London in which political and social subjects were discussed and competing points of view put to a vote— 'spouting clubs' as he called them—came within the intent and meaning of the act and ought to be prohibited.[92]

Not surprisingly, Fielding stirred up considerable hostility by his campaign against some of the most innocuous elements in the culture of the working population of London. He had become 'obnoxious to many Bodies of People,' he told the duke of Newcastle, including 'Sharpers and Gamesters of all kinds and all the Publicans within the Bills of Mortality,' not to speak of thieves and robbers.[93] His point in complaining to the secretary of state in 1757 was to ask him to arrange that he be knighted by the king (as De Veil had been) as a way of adding to his authority at a difficult time. A knighthood would signal the king's approbation and strengthen his power and influence, Fielding concluded, but he was clearly vain enough to have sought a knighthood for its own sake. This effort at any event was unsuccessful, though he was to get his reward four years later.

Fielding's turn towards preventive policing—for this surely is what he had engaged in during the war—culminated in his publishing in 1761 *Extracts from such of the penal laws, as particularly relate to the peace and good order of the*

---

[89] TNA: T 38/671, ff. 28, 29. The targets may have been suspected prostitutes on this occasion.

[90] Fielding, *Extracts from such of the penal laws, as particularly relate to the peace and good order of the Metropolis* (new edition, 1762), 6–7, 181–3. Another edition was published in 1769.

[91] TNA: T 1/387, f.14; T 38/671, f. 27.

[92] Fielding, *Extracts from such of the penal laws* (1762), 183–4. For the debating societies, see Donna T. Andrew (ed.), *London Debating Societies, 1776–1799* (London, 1994).

[93] BL: Add Mss 32876, f. 274. Further evidence of the hostility to Fielding's activities in these years was to come in the summer of 1758 when rumours were spread that he had been suspended as a magistrate and committed to Newgate—rumours about which he was sufficiently touchy that he tried to get the government to deny them in the *Gazette* or in some other formal way. BL: Add Mss, 32882, ff. 58–9.

Metropolis. There is little reason to doubt that Fielding's main point in compiling this long and detailed account of dozens of statutes was to make known the myriad laws that supported the good government and order of the metropolis, particularly to the parish constables of Westminster and Middlesex, so they could be enforced.[94] But Fielding may also have anticipated that dealing with the petty offences and misdemeanours that are the subject of the book may have become a larger part of his work than he had earlier anticipated. He may have seen this publication as a way of establishing his office—with its £400 subvention for clerks and runners, not to speak of his salary—as the leader in that effort. In attempting to suppress gaming and dancing and in general to police the morals of the working population that is so evident in the accounts of 1757–59, the Bow Street office was taking on work that the parish constables were expected to do. As we will see, Fielding was already by 1761 anticipating the end of the Seven Years War and the likelihood that peace would bring its usual harvest of violent offences and danger on the roads. But as he prepared his treatise on the laws regulating everyday life in the metropolis in the middle years of the war, he could not be certain that the reasons why he had been given a privileged position among the magistrates of Middlesex and Westminster would necessarily continue. Preventing crime, he was prepared to say and to act on in 1761, was better than having to prosecute and punish it.

3. POSTWAR: A NEW PLAN OF POLICE

As it turned out, Fielding's anticipation of a renewal of serious offences and danger with the conclusion of the war was all too accurate. The demobilization of what had been a very large army and the discharge of thousands of sailors again created anxieties about crime and violence in the streets of London and on the highways leading into the city.[95] Fielding had been thinking about a renewal and extensions of the 'Plan of Police' in 1761 and sought the government's support for them through the duke of Newcastle.[96] No copy of his new plan seems to have survived, but an abstract among the papers of Charles Jenkinson, an under-secretary of state, reveals the far-reaching character of Fielding's thinking about policing London as the war drew to a close.[97] Anticipating some aspects of the Westminster Justices Act of 1792, even of the 1829 Act that created the Metropolitan police, Fielding proposed the creation of five or six paid 'magistrates of police' who would head offices like his in Bow Street. The fees they collected would go to paying the wages

[94] Fielding charged £30 to his accounts in May 1762 to pay for 150 copies of his *Extracts*, a signed copy of which he intended to give to every Westminster constable (TNA: T 1/414, f.131). One of those copies is in the Fisher Library, University of Toronto.
[95] For the size of the armies demobilized after wars in the eighteenth century, see Douglas Hay, 'War, Dearth and Theft in the Eighteenth Century: The Record of the English Courts', *Past and Present* 95 (May, 1982), 138–9.
[96] BL: Add Mss 32921, f. 404.
[97] BL: Add Mss 38334, ff. 75–9 – reproduced in Radzinowicz, *History of English Criminal Law*, vol. 3, Appendix I, 477–9.

of a clerical staff and 'Rewards to Police Officers, and Persons who assist them.' The magistrates would meet once a month as a commission of police for the metropolis, under the leadership (of course) of Fielding at the 'Center Office' in Bow Street, where information of the work of all the offices would be collected into a 'general Register.' The plan included proposals for foot patrols to be organized from each office, the more careful licencing of public houses, improvements in street lighting, and a strengthened night watch. Fielding also proposed that 'a Paper be established by Law, in which every Thing, relative to the Discovery of Offenders, should be advertised'—an anticipation of the paper later known as the *Hue and Cry*.[98]

These measures, Fielding argued, would bolster the civil power in London and serve to remove the causes of crime by imposing greater controls over the population. But that was only one side of his plan. In addition to strengthening what he called the 'Interior Force' of the capital, he proposed that a regiment of light horse be quartered in the environs to act as sentinels and pursuers on the highways to deal with robbers—with the commanding officer reporting regularly to Fielding at the 'Center Office of Police'. He betrayed some sense of the controversial character of such a proposal by arguing that this 'Exterior Force' would be gradually eliminated as the civil power in the metropolis 'recovers its Dignity.' But he felt no need to meet directly what would certainly have been strong constitutional objections to the use of troops as policemen. In a passage that is an interesting comment on the authority of the officers attached to Bow Street, he anticipated what he clearly considered to be the only legitimate objection to employing the military by emphasizing the right of *any* citizen to pursue and apprehend felons.[99]

Nothing came of that plan, but the idea and the value of a mounted patrol of some kind obviously struck home as the roads became increasingly dangerous. Fielding had already by the spring of 1761 instituted patrols conducted by his own men and paid from his budget, as we learn from a trial at the Old Bailey in April 1761 in which two of his men were accused of mistakenly killing a passenger in a coach they thought was being attacked by a highwayman. Asked about his patrols in general, Fielding said that 'when informations are brought to me of a road being infested, it is my constant practice to send out four, or five, or more persons, to patroll those roads all night, and they are paid accordingly.' On this occasion, he had sent William Pentlow and William Darvall, the ex-highwayman who had been taken into the office after giving evidence against Page. They were sent not to patrol the highway generally, but to guard the Leeds coach that had several times been stopped along a particular stretch of road near Barnet by a single highwayman whose description (reported by victims and recorded by Marsden) they were given. They went for that reason in a hired post-chaise driven by a young postilion. This venture did not turn out well, which is why we know about it. They set out at three in the morning, made contact with the coach they were to guard at the Islington turnpike house, and were following after it when, near Holloway, they were

---

[98] BL: Add Mss 38334, ff. 75–9 – reproduced in Radzinowicz, *History of English Criminal Law*, vol. 3, Appendix I, 478.
[99] BL: Add Mss 38334, ff. 78–9.

themselves stopped by a highwayman who threatened to 'blow [their] brains out' if they did not turn over their money. They had a blunderbuss and 'let fly', but for reasons unexplained, it merely 'drove him back' and he made off. On they went, and as they came upon the coach they were meant to be guarding they saw a man nearby on horseback who—in the murky dawn light (it was by then about five a.m.)—they thought had a pistol and who they took to be the highwayman they had just encountered. No doubt still in a highly nervous state, Darvall shot at him with a pistol, hitting one of the passengers, who subsequently died. The man on horseback turned out to be a guard hired by the coach company. Fielding and Marsden were both in court to confirm that Darvall and Pentlow had been given orders to guard the coach and, by entries in the office books, to confirm that a highwayman had been active on that stretch of road for some time. Marsden also denied that it was known that the Leeds coach travelled with a mounted guard. Indeed he claimed that when coaches had guards they rode 'in the basket' at the back; he 'never knew them to have pistols in their hands on horseback.' Darvall was convicted of manslaughter, granted benefit of clergy, burned in the hand, and discharged. Pentlow was acquitted.[100]

Most of the patrolling in the winter of 1761–62, as we learn from the account Fielding submitted to Newcastle at the end of 1762, was less specifically focussed than that ill-fated undertaking. The first payments (in November and December, 1761), for example, were for a total of 56 nights patrolling by six men: two along the Western road for 16 nights riding the office's 'pursuit horses'; two for a total of 24 nights on hired horses along the main roads in Kent and Surrey leading into the city; and two others for 16 nights also on hired horses riding the Hampstead, Highgate and Islington roads.[101] There were to be further patrols in January and February 1762 and through the rest of the year.

It was presumably the success of that effort rather than Fielding's exotic scheme to involve the cavalry in policing the highways (as well as the serious danger on the roads) that encouraged the government to provide support for a horse patrol in the winter of 1763–64. It was instituted in October 1763 with the support of George Grenville, the new first lord of the Treasury, and operated under Fielding's control, presumably as an addition to the patrolling activities of his own officers. It consisted of eight men who rode in pairs every night along four of the five major highways entering the city.[102] Fielding urged Grenville, without success, to increase

[100] OBP, April 1761 (William Darwell (*sic*) and William Pentelow (*sic*)) t17610401-28. For benefit of clergy, see Beattie, *Crime and the Courts*, 141–6.

[101] TNA: T 1/414, f. 126.

[102] Within a few weeks Grenville received an anonymous letter from Whitechapel criticizing the new horse patrol on the grounds that Fielding was personally profiting from its establishment and that its officers were little better than thieves. In his defence, Fielding justified the costs (four shillings a night to hire each horse and four shillings to each man, plus their expenses and the cost of their arms) and provided a list of the eight patrolmen. They were William Smith, the court keeper at the Westminster Guildhall; Richard Higgins, a baker and a Westminster constable; William Langrid, a chandler and a Middlesex constable; Thomas Adams, a Westminster constable; Thomas Street, 'a publican who keeps the tap at the New Prison in Clerkenwell'; William Pentlow, the son of the keeper of the New Prison and late in Hale's Light Horse; Mr Partridge, late a constable of Middlesex; William

the government's support so that all five could be patrolled every night, but nonetheless reported through Jenkinson in March 1764 that the horse patrol had had 'very good effects' over the winter. Within a few months, however, Grenville became concerned at the expence, which by then had amounted to close to £1,000, and—struggling as he was with the debt burden inherited from the war—took the view that the counties that were mainly benefiting from the protection provided by the patrol should pay for it, rather than the king's Civil List. Despite Fielding's urging and his reports of large number of robberies on the highways, the government's support for a horse patrol had been withdrawn by October 1764.[103]

Whether Fielding's own horse patrols continued and for how long is more difficult to discern since his financial accounts for 1763–65 have not survived. When we get another view of the policing activities of Bow Street, in accounts for 1766 and 1767, mounted patrolling by the Bow Street officers had been sharply curtailed, no doubt because of the significant costs involved, even though the annual subvention had been increased by then to £600. Two 'pursuit horses' were still being maintained, and officers were sent from time to time to patrol roads, and on one occasion in 1767 to guard coaches over a two-week period.[104] But mounted patrols were much less common then than they had been earlier in the decade.

Despite the reduction in patrolling, the Bow Street office remained focussed on robbery and other violence. The principal officers were never confined to any one line of work: as well as working under the direction of the magistrates, they undertook investigations on behalf of private citizens and government departments, and those might or might not have involved the pursuit of dangerous men. But much of their activity on behalf of the office continued to be concerned with robbers and other offenders who threatened to harm their victims as well as taking their property and a significant portion of the office's expenditures went to support their apprehension and prosecution.

The increase in the Bow Street budget to £600, along with increasing opportunities to earn other rewards as the reputation of the office grew, perhaps explain why by the late 1760s the six principal officers were tending to remain attached to the office for longer periods than had been the case earlier. Nor was it any longer apparently necessary to recruit gaolers to act as runners, or to reward Bow Street men with jobs in the prisons. The runners were becoming better known to the public through their regular appearances in the printed reports of Old Bailey trials as witnesses for the prosecution. My sense then is that within a decade of John

---

Wright, 'a person formerly employed by me, who has been at sea during the war'; Jonathan Fordsan, 'my own coachman'; and Richard Fuller, 'the person who was the means of discovering the whole Coventry gang.' 'None of these', Fielding added, 'were ever charged with murder or felony...' (Radzinowicz, *History of English Criminal Law*, vol. 3, 61, n. 9).

[103] BL: Add Mss 38201, f. 328; Add Mss 38202, f. 202; Add Mss 57809, ff. 111, 113–14; Add Mss 57821, f. 118; William James Smith (ed.), *The Grenville Papers*, 2 vols. (1852), II, 369, 385–6; John R. G. Tomlinson (ed.), *Additional Grenville Papers, 1763–1765* (Manchester, 1962), 147, 151; Radzinowicz, *History of English Criminal Law*, vol. 3, 58–62.

[104] TNA: T 1/449, f. 34; T 1/454, ff. 83, 84.

Fielding's assuming the leadership of the Bow Street office, the men who made up the main strike force in his policing system were regarded as perhaps more respectable than they had been earlier, and that they were committed to the work and ready to remain involved over a number of years. In these ways as in others the office was becoming increasingly 'professional'. What that meant for the policing of the capital and for the system of criminal justice in the following decades is the subject of the next chapter.

4

Detection: The Runners at Work, 1765–1792

1. A 'TRANSPORTING AND HANGING POLICE'?

The policing activities conducted by the Bow Street office settled into a stable pattern by the mid 1760s. The runners continued to be dispatched by the magistrates or to be engaged privately to investigate offences of all kinds, but the balance of their work over the next quarter century was to be decidedly towards the investigation and prosecution of felons, largely involving crimes against property, with particular attention being paid to those in which offenders used violence or the threat of violence against their victims. We are fortunate to be able to get a sense of the central core of the runners' work in the financial accounts that survive for the two years, 1765–67. The payments made from the office funds, which these accounts record, by no means represent the full range of the runners' activities, since they also undertook tasks for private prosecutors, for some government departments, and for other magistrates. They do, however, provide us with a valuable snapshot of the jobs they took on at the request of John Fielding and the other Bow Street magistrates—money for their 'trouble,' as well as their expenses when they were sent to investigate reported offences, apprehend suspects, or to patrol the streets. They did this work under the direction of Fielding himself or of his chief clerk, William Marsden, with Fielding managing the payments for the important work and Marsden distributing payments for more minor jobs.

As an aid to analysing these accounts, I have arranged the 257 entries for 1767 into the three broad categories shown in Table 4.1.[1] This confirms that from John Fielding's point of view, the public work of the runners continued to focus on serious offenders—highwaymen, footpads, to a lesser extent shoplifters, gangs who stole from coaches, and the like. More than half of the budget was spent directly on efforts to catch and arrest such offenders. Typical of the brief entries in the accounts under this head are the following:

8 Nov. 1766: £2.16.0 to John Noakes and William Haliburton 'for the execution of a Plan for six nights successively to remove a Gang of Thieves dangerous to the Neighbourhood of St Martins Lane and Chairing Cross'. (f. 78).

---

[1] TNA: T 1/454, ff. 76–93. The account for November 1766 to October 1767 is more complete than that for the previous year (TNA: T 1/449, ff.30-) and provides a fuller picture of the range of the officers' work.

Table 4.1. Bow Street office expenses, 1767[1]

A. Policing Costs (direct)	£	%
1. Investigations and arrests	198.15.0	
2. Patrolling	13.90	
3. Maintenance of 'pursuit horses'	67.0.0	
4. Rewards to shopkeepers	13.2.0	
5. Arms	2.0.0	
6. Support of witnesses, payments to informers	17.18.0	
7. Salary of the 'register clerk'	33.13.0	
8. Maintenance of the criminal records	18.2.0	
9. Transport of prisoners	1.6.0	
Sub-total	365.5.0	61.3
B. Policing Costs (partial)	£	%
10. Coach hire	13.1.0	
11. Printing and distributing of hand bills	6.0.6	
12. Advertisements	46.9.0	
13. Books and newspapers for the office	16.12.0	
Sub-total	82.2.0	13.8
C. Other Costs	£	%
14. Fielding's attendance at assizes and quarter sessions	12.16.0	
15. Correspondence with country magistrates	15.18.0	
16. Runners' arrest of prostitutes, gamblers, beggars	23.4.0	
17. Office expenses	54.7.0	
18. Miscellaneous	42.12.0	
Sub-total	148.17.0	25.0
Total	596.4.0	100.1

[1] Source: TNA: T 1/454.

29 Nov. 1766: £12.12.0 to Noakes, Haliburton, Richard Bond, John Heley, Henry Wright and his brother, Edward Wright: 'for apprehending Webb and Donnally two Notorious Shop-Lifters, for going in the Night to stop the Turnpikes on Information of a Mail being stopt on Hounslow Heath, for trouble in apprehending the Persons charged with Murdering a Woman in the Borough, for going to Kingston in pursuit of Goatley, a Foot Pad and dispensing Hand Bills there; for apprehending Crawford, Bowdon, Mallett, Stephens and Valentine Shop-Lifters and Thieves'. (f. 79).

12 Jan. 1767: £6.13.6 to Haliburton, Heley, Bond, Noakes and Henry Wright for 'attending two nights in the Streets with a Coach and Post Chaise in order to apprehend a Gang of Portmanteau Stealers and for apprehending Johnson, Strode, Smith and Marston, Persons concerned in those Robberies and also Doyle and Lloyd Shop-Lifters'. (f. 82).

13 Mar. 1767. £2.5.0 to Haliburton, Heley, and Noakes for 'delivering Hand Bills in Surry to detect the Footpad supposed to be wounded ... for going to all the Stable Keepers in the Borough [of Southwark] and Westminster to find out Tremble the Highwayman's Horse and watching three Nights at Tremble's Lodgings and other places to apprehend him.' (f. 84).

The account contains 46 entries of this kind, totalling payments of close to £200, most of which went to the six most active officers. Although they were on occasion helped by parish constables or by assistants in the office who mainly delivered messages or distributed handbills and the like, the bulk of the work of investigating offences and making arrests was carried out by the runners, occasionally on their own, but, as in the examples quoted above, more often with a partner or in groups of three or four, particularly when they went after large numbers of offenders. If the danger were serious enough, all six might respond together, led by William Marsden. This happened on several occasions in 1767, including one in which a gang had killed one of their victims and badly beaten another and seemed prepared to go on robbing violently. Their activities brought out the full force of Fielding's men in their pursuit.[2]

A significant proportion of the office expenditures went on this work of detection, apprehension, and prosecution. The direct costs of that work included the payments to the runners for their expenses and 'trouble,' including patrolling, along with payments for the maintenance of 'pursuit horses,' firearms, record-keeping, and the like. I estimate that such direct costs of detection and prosecution accounted for just over 60 per cent of expenditures in the financial year, 1766–67. Additional costs for that work were included in more general sums spent for coach hire, advertisements, and stationery, and the printing of hand bills. Even on the conservative assumption that only half of those expenditures were incurred in the policing of serious offences, it seems clear that something in the region of 70 per cent of the budget of the Bow Street magistrate's office was devoted to the central task of searching out and arresting felons and to ensuring that at least some cases would be prosecuted.

How much each of the runners earned from the office funds is impossible to calculate exactly, since the money for each undertaking was paid to the group of officers who had played some part in the investigation and arrest involved and it is more than likely that that sum was divided up unequally among them. Payments came in two forms. For major undertakings—investigations or patrolling that might last several days and take them far from the office—the men involved put in a total bill which Fielding checked and paid himself. For smaller sums—coach hire, for example, or collecting a witness required in the office or fetching a prisoner from a gaol—they were paid directly and immediately by the chief clerk (Marsden in 1767), who was given a lump sum by Fielding and accounted for it quarterly. Fielding's and Marsden's disbursements made up the annual account sent in at the end of the financial year. In 1767, Fielding made a dozen group payments to the six runners in various combinations, ranging from a few shillings to more than £26, and from one or two men to all six. If the money had been divided equally among the claimants (though it almost certainly was not), the runners would have received between £12 and £18 each from that source. Numerous smaller payments from Marsden for other work, would have raised most of their incomes from the office to

---

[2] See below, text at nn. 102–3.

more than £20, with John Noakes in the lead at more than £25. The others earned around £20, except Stephenson, whose £5 was a much smaller sum than he had earned in the previous year when he had been more active.[3]

The money from the office funds provided the runners with the foundation of an income which they could supplement from several other sources. The main additions were payments from victims of offences of all kinds, men and women who reported thefts or burglaries to the magistrates at Bow Street and requested help, but whose cases were not sufficiently serious to move Fielding to send one or more of his men at public expense. The office might pay for an advertisement, but any reward offered for the discovery and conviction of the offenders (which Fielding recommended) and the immediate help of the runners would be at the victim's expense. It is impossible to learn how many private prosecutors engaged the help of the runners. Of the 18 trials at the Old Bailey in 1767 in which one or more runners gave evidence for the prosecution, six were cases in which John Fielding had paid them to investigate and apprehend the accused. In the other 12, they had been engaged by the victim.[4] They would have been paid both for their expenses and 'trouble' and in addition would have been eligible to receive some portion of any private rewards offered by the victims and in at least eight of the 18 cases part of a parliamentary reward. Beyond investigations carried out at Fielding's order or at the behest of a private prosecutor, the runners also worked occasionally for the secretaries of state and other government departments—the Mint and Admiralty, for example—for the Bank of England, and for provincial magistrates.

How much they were making from all these sources by the 1770s, it will never be possible to know. In an account of the structure and work of the office written in the spring of 1783 by Sampson Wright, chief magistrate following Fielding's death in 1780, he said of the runners that they had been 'enabled to procure a very comfortable Livelihood with Reputation to themselves and Benefit to the Public.'[5] He also revealed that some of the less onerous work of the office was being done by then by half a dozen assistants, some of whom were regularly on duty at the theatres—at the Theatre Royal in the Haymarket during the summer, and at the 'winter theatres,' stationed at the doors and in the neighbourhood streets to keep them clear of pickpockets. Together with these assistants, Wright said, the runners had

---

[3] TNA: T 1/454. Noakes' stipend is at f. 78.

[4] Based on the Bow Street accounts for that year (TNA: T 1/454) and the printed accounts of the trials at the Old Bailey at <http://www.oldbaileyonline.org>.

[5] NLI 15930 (1). 'An Account of the Plan and Establishment of the Public Office in Bow Street London.' The document is undated and unsigned, but internal evidence indicates that it was written by Sampson Wright in 1783. He had submitted a similar plan 'for protecting the Roads round London,' to Lord Sydney in August 1782, then secretary of state for the new Home Department (TNA: HO 42/1, ff. 290–3). Wright's description seems to have been written for Lord North who succeeded Sydney briefly in April 1783. For the establishment of the Home Department in 1782, see Simon Devereaux, 'The Criminal Branch of the Home Office, 1782–1830' in Greg T. Smith, Allyson N. May, and Simon Devereaux (eds.), *Criminal Justice in the Old World and the New* (Toronto, 1998). It was common after 1782 for new home secretaries to be presented with an account of the Bow Street office, written by the chief magistrate. I am grateful to Simon Devereaux for providing me with a copy of this document from the National Library of Ireland, and another description of the office, dated 1777 (NLI: 15929 (3)).

'formed themselves into a sort of Society . . . [and] attend the office constantly.' Certainly, there is every indication that the runners had developed under John Fielding a degree of comradeship and mutual support in carrying out work that was occasionally dangerous, and in which reliance on a partner or two was obviously necessary from time to time. It is possible too, that an attachment to Bow Street was beginning to carry a certain prestige, as Wright seemed to suggest.

That emerging sense of solidarity at Bow Street is also reflected in the stability of tenure that is evident by the 1770s. Several of the runners whose activities can be documented in the financial accounts of 1766 and 1767 remained active in the 1770s and some into the 1780s, including John Noakes, who retired in 1775, John Heley (1778), and William Haliburton (1783). They were joined and gradually replaced in the 1770s and 1780s by a new group of active men, some of whom were to serve well into the next century. They included most notably Nicholas Bond (1768–86), who began as a runner, became the chief clerk and leader of the runners, and was named one of the three Bow Street magistrates in 1786. The group of active runners in the late eighteenth century also included John Clarke (c.1771–93), Charles Jealous (1773–94), Moses Morant (1776–92), Thomas Carpmeal (1778–1808), Patrick Macmanus or McManus (1780–1816), John Atkins (1783–91), and John Townsend, who became the best known of them all, and who began as a member of the patrol in 1784, became a runner in the following year and died in office in 1832, almost 50 years later.[6]

From Henry Fielding's day on, some runners were or had been Westminster constables—the authority the post conferred making them useful to the work of the office, and their activity as constables no doubt bringing them to Fielding's notice. Noakes, Heley, Haliburton, and Joseph Stephenson (1765–74) joined as constables and continued to serve as parish officers while being attached to Bow Street. After describing himself at the Old Bailey in 1772 as a constable of the Liberty of Westminster, Noakes went on to say 'I go with Sir John Fielding's people.'[7] That pattern of constables continuing to serve their parishes while making themselves available to take part in investigations and the other work undertaken by the Bow Street men seems to have changed in the 1770s, perhaps as the office became better known and the work of the runners more onerous. Several men who were constables when they became associated with Fielding's office abandoned their parish posts after a year or two, including John Clarke and Patrick Macmanus; Charles Jealous was a constable attached to Saunders Welch's office in Litchfield Street before becoming identified with Bow Street.

In the early years, as we have seen, many of the runners had been recruited from among the turnkeys at the main gaols of the metropolis—Newgate, the New Prison

---

[6] There are no lists of Bow Street officers before the post of receiver of police was established by the Middlesex Justices Act of 1792 and the Bow Street men began to receive a retainer (see below, ch. 7). Before that, the dates given in the text are based on evidence in the financial reports 1754–67, the material gathered in the immensely useful websites <http://www.londonlives.org>, and <http://www. oldbaileyonline.org>, depositions and informations taken at Bow Street, London newspapers, and occasional mentions elsewhere.

[7] OBP, June 1772 (Joseph Guyant *et al*) t17720603–44.

in Clerkenwell, and Tothill Fields Bridewell. They brought perhaps some useful knowledge of habitual offenders, but that source of recruits was no longer being exploited by the 1770s. Townsend was a gaoler at Newgate before joining the new Bow Street patrol in 1784,[8] and John Atkins worked first at the New Prison before he also joined the patrol in 1783 and later the runners. But that was unusual by then.

John Clarke became a runner around 1771, recruited perhaps because, having been apprenticed to a button-maker, he had considerable knowledge of the metal trades and brought expertise with respect to the processes involved in the counter-feiting of silver and copper coins. Clarke was to be one of the most important runners over the following two decades, particularly in the detection and prosecu-tion of coiners, for which he received supplementary rewards from time to time from the solicitor of the Mint.[9] Few runners brought that kind of useful skill to the job or much in the way of specialized training in any field. Several had served apprenticeships and perhaps had worked at their trades for some time before joining the office: in depositions given at the office, John Heley was described as a shoemaker; Charles Jealous a sadler; John Shallard a pastry-cook; and Patrick Macmanus a hatter. For the most part the runners assumed the all-purpose addition of 'labourer' when signing Bow Street documents, though it is an interesting comment on their growing sense of their status and respectability that Macmanus was described as a 'gentleman' by 1779, as was Carpmeal, a few years later. Few of them may have been skilled men, but all but two of the runners in the 1770s and 1780s (Henry Wright and David Prothero) signed the informations they gave before the magistrates. John Sayer marked some and signed others.[10]

As for their work after 1767, the runners continued to investigate and prosecute a wide range of offences, concentrating inevitably on felonies rather than on the more minor offences that neither the government nor private prosecutors were interested in paying for. The accounts for 1767 reveal that Fielding occasionally sent officers to pick up beggars and prostitutes, cheats and gamblers. But that remained in most years a minor part of their work. As Ruth Paley has shown, the Bow Street magistrates were clearly not as active in committing minor offenders for punishment or trial as other magistrates in the capital.[11] Indeed, if anything, the Bow Street office became more, not less, focussed on the prosecution of felons after 1767, a consequence in part of a period of heightened anxiety about the level and character of crime in London. Concern about what were thought to be increasing levels of burglary and housebreaking was sufficiently general to encourage the house of commons to establish a committee in 1770 to look into causes and possible responses. It came at a time when serious questions were also being asked about penal issues, in particular about the effectiveness of transportation to the American

---

[8] For the patrol, see ch. 6, section 2.
[9] For Clarke's role as an investigator and prosecutor of coining cases, see ch. 5, text at nn. 126–39.
[10] LMA: OB/SP.
[11] Ruth Paley, 'The Middlesex Justices Act of 1792: its origins and effects', Ph.D. thesis (University of Reading, 1983), appendix.

colonies, a sanction that had been the mainstay of the criminal courts for 50 years, but that had started to seem less of a deterrent than it was supposed to be, given the rapid economic and social development of the American colonies in recent years. Doubts had been expressed about transportation in the 1750s. They were renewed in the late 1760s, not only because crime was a persistent problem in London, but also because of the increasingly tense relations between Britain and the colonies over taxation and other matters and the fundamental questions of governance that those issues had raised.[12]

It was in these circumstances of concern about policing, prosecution, and deterrence, that Fielding entered into a period of significant creativity and invention in which he made Bow Street into a public office even more prominent than it had been, and with new elements in the system of pretrial process designed to improve the effectiveness of the policing and prosecution of serious offenders.[13] It is possible that the innovations that Fielding introduced at Bow Street in the early 1770s were sparked by criticisms in the press about the failures of Bow Street, particularly from those who thought that policing ought to be devoted to preventing crime by attacking immorality in all its forms, not to punishing offenders after the fact. Fielding was himself chastized for ignoring the wider social and moral contexts of crime and for emphasizing detection and prosecution rather than making an effort to prevent criminal offences in the first place. A series of articles on 'The Police' that ran in *The Oxford Magazine* between 1769 to 1772 were critical of him and his Bow Street men on these grounds. A proper police—such as the anonymous author or authors of these essays thought was to be found in major European cities like Vienna and Berlin—would be as much concerned with public discipline, with gambling and vice, with nuisances in the streets and the regulation of the environment in general as with the effort to bring major offenders to justice. Anticipating some nineteenth-century and more modern ideas about the interconnectedness of civility and crime, the writer insisted that the police should be as concerned 'to prevent the throwing a peascod or an orange-peel . . . as to send a man and horse, upon the first information given at the Bow Street Office, in pursuit of a highwayman.'[14] Without vice and debauchery, an essayist said, there would be no highway robbery. What was required was a religiously-based reformation and a police that would support it.[15]

---

[12] A. Roger Ekirch, *Bound for America: The Transportation of British Convicts to the Colonies, 1718–1775* (Oxford, 1987); J. M. Beattie, *Crime and the Courts in England, 1660–1800* (Oxford, 1986), ch. 9; Gwenda Morgan and Peter Rushton, *Eighteenth-century criminal transportation: the formation of the criminal Atlantic* (Basingstoke, 2004).

[13] For Fielding's innovations at Bow Street, see ch. 5, section 2.

[14] *Oxford Magazine*, vol. 3, 4 July 1769; for the European comparisons, vol 8, February 1772, 41–2.

[15] Ibid, vol. 3, September 1769, 82; and see, on this theme, vol. 4, May 1770, 161–5; vol 5., December 1770, 201–4. When Fielding and other Middlesex magistrates attempted to prevent masquerades, widely believed to be both immoral and so expensive as to lead to the ruin of numerous tradesmen, a London newspaper commented that this regard for the morals of the metropolis proves them to be 'a worthy police.' *General Evening Post*, 14–16 December 1773.

As for Fielding himself, though the lead author of the *Oxford Magazine* articles found much about his work and his writings to praise (especially his analysis of the criminal law published in 1761), his fundamental criticism remained unchanged: Bow Street concentrated far too much on catching the most serious offenders. 'Sir John Fielding's is a transporting and hanging system of Police', he concluded in his final essay; 'mine is meant to prevent those severe acts of public justice.'[16] Fielding revealed his sensitivity to this charge in an advertisement in the press in 1771 in which he reminded the public that several magistrates sat every Wednesday morning at Bow Street 'to hear complaints relating to public nuisances,' adding somewhat testily that 'if, instead of unjustly traducing the characters of Magistrates in the public papers, for neglecting their duty in suppressing bawdy-houses, gaming-houses, disorderly-houses, and other nuisances...persons would cooperate with the Magistrates by furnishing them with such informations as might enable them to do their duty effectually, the public would be more benefited, and subordination better supported.'[17]

There was truth nonetheless to the charge. Not that—as the critic seemed to suggest—Fielding was particularly punitive in outlook. He was not an outspoken opponent of the death penalty, but he certainly thought that it should be reserved for the most serious offenders.[18] However, his critics were right about the emphases in the policing system he was building at Bow Street. With respect to preventive measures, while he agreed they were important,[19] he also thought they should be implemented by other magistrates. His mission was different. He was in receipt of government funds to do something that no other magistrate—no other agency— was prepared to do: to mount a policing effort to bring serious offenders to justice who would otherwise go unprosecuted. That was his principal task, particularly at times when robbers, burglars, and housebreakers were causing anxiety among the propertied classes in London. The years in which he was being criticized by the *Oxford Magazine* writers were just such a period of anxiety—as the establishment of the parliamentary committee in 1770 to enquire into the reasons for a recent increase in burglary and housebreaking suggests.[20] In these years, Fielding was heavily engaged in devising ways to expand across the country the gathering and distributing of information about offences as yet unsolved and offenders being sought.[21] He was also constructing a more intensive and more public form of

---

[16] *Oxford Magazine*, vol. 8, February 1772, 43.

[17] *Gazetteer*, 5 January 1771. For these Wednesday morning sessions, see ch. 5.

[18] In writing to the earl of Suffolk in 1773 about the value of the criminal records kept at Bow Street, Fielding confirmed his belief that there were occasions when it was necessary to make 'public Examples by Executions.' In those cases, he continued, 'Wisdom, Policy and Humanity dictate that the most abandoned, dangerous and incorrigible Offenders should be pointed out for this melancholy Purpose.' His main point in writing was to argue that there was no better source of information about the character of such offenders than the store of evidence that had been collected at Bow Street over many years. TNA: SP 37/10, f. 11.

[19] Apart from his policing practices in 1757–58, and the arguments presented in his treatise on the penal law (1761) discussed in ch. 3, section 2), see the evidence he gave before a parliamentary committee in 1770 (ch. 5, text at nn. 1–3).

[20] See ch. 5, text at nn. 1–3.

[21] See ch. 5, text at n. 4.

pretrial process at Bow Street designed to enhance the collection of prosecution evidence against the accused felons he committed to trial at the Old Bailey. His critics were right. He was heavily engaged in prosecution, though—he would have added—in the interest of preventing crime in the future. The runners played a crucial role in this work—in the investigation of offences, the apprehension of suspects, and the gathering of evidence. We turn now to examine in more detail how they went about their business.

2. DETECTION

The runners commonly acted as soon as the report of an offence reached the office, especially if a victim could supply descriptions of the suspects and clues as to where they might be found. A quick response to such news was one of the Fieldings' principal aims. It was possible in part because many of the runners—perhaps all—lived close to the office and were available to be called out at any time of the day or night. Marsden, a leader of the runners, lived in the house.[22] Most of the others in the early years generally lived in the immediate neighbourhood, within a few hundred yards of the office—in Russell Street (Heley), Stanhope Street (Macmanus), Brownlow Street (Jealous), the Strand (Clarke), Broad Court, off Bow Street (Carpmeal).[23]

When reports of offences came to the office and the runners were to be sent out to investigate and perhaps to pursue the suspects, the information collected at Bow Street about previous offences and descriptions of suspects might provide a lead. The runners would also often broadcast information about the offence and tap their most promising sources. In replying to Lord Hardwicke's enquiry in 1783 about how the office was trying to discover who had broken into and stolen from Lord Grantham's house in Whitehall, Sampson Wright, Fielding's successor as chief magistrate, made it clear that their efforts to detect and apprehend such offenders depended on the collection and organizing of information. He told Hardwicke that

> Hand Bills, containing a Description of the several things stolen, have been delivered at all the Pawnbrokers, Silversmiths, and other Shops, where the Property taken is, from the Nature of it, likely to be disposed of; and Advertisements, offering His majesty's pardon to any One of the Offenders who will surrender and give an Account of his Accomplices, have been published in the Gazette and Daily Papers, and every other Step taken that appeared likely to produce Information; but, I am sorry to say, without Success.
>
> Some Persons who were violently suspected of the Robbery have been taken up and examined in hopes of their making Discovery, and have been committed and kept in Prison as long as the Law would justify, and for want of sufficient Evidence to authorize their further Confinement have been set at large ...[24]

---

[22] OBP, September 1757 (Brent Coleman *et al*) t17570914-29.
[23] Revealed in depositions in the sessions papers (LMA: OB/SP).
[24] BL: Add Mss 35621, f. 229.

To make their appeal for information as speedy as possible, the office kept up-to-date lists of pawnbrokers, silversmiths, and 'Cloaths Shops' in order to deliver handbills to them.[25] Beyond that, the runners had a good deal of information in their records about people they suspected of committing offences and of those who had been charged but escaped conviction and punishment. Keeping track of the 'Night-houses and disorderly Houses to which Offenders generally resort', was one of the jobs of the office clerks, along with lists of known and suspected offenders,[26] and in the Grantham case they had rounded up some of these men, committed them for the six days the law allowed, hoping that one of them might confess. What Wright did not say in his letter to Hardwicke was that the runners were almost certainly hoping to get a lead from some of the people they paid to pass on information and rumours about recent offences.

Much of the successful detection and apprehension of suspected offenders by Bow Street officers depended on the rapid collection and communication of information about the offence and, if possible, descriptions of the perpetrators. Runners were on duty every day in the office or waiting in the more congenial surroundings of the Brown Bear public house across the street, which was used into the early years of the nineteenth century as a lock-up as well as a hangout. They might respond to news of an offence by immediately going out on their own initiative, essentially hired by the victim to give them help, or they might be dispatched by Fielding or another magistrate or by the man who emerged in the early years of the office as the leader of the runners, the 'register clerk to the police', later known as the 'conductor of pursuits and patroles.' Most often, two of the runners would go out together—they seemed to work commonly in pairs—to examine the scene of a crime, to take up leads, give chase, visit likely receivers, or to look for witnesses. Most victims seeking help would have been expected to pay the expenses of an investigation and, in addition, to offer a reward of a few pounds for information. They would also face the costs of a trial, if one were to follow, though in the event of a conviction, the victim and his or her witnesses might receive financial compensation from the court to cover some of their costs.[27] As in the rest of the criminal justice system, Bow Street served those best who could afford to bear the charges. But it did fully support some investigations, and it was a source of help to all victims who could afford to pay, where little help had existed previously.

That help was often rapid and (in cases we know about) sometimes decisive. When a report was received at Bow Street late one evening in January 1773 of a robbery on the Kentish Town road, three runners were sent in a coach 'in hopes of being stopt.' They were not disappointed. Two highwaymen held up their coach and the runners jumped out and pursued them across the fields, taking them near

---

[25] NLI 15929 (3).

[26] NLI 15929 (3); 15930 (1).

[27] For the costs of prosecution, and the statutes of 1752, 1754, and 1778 that established and expanded the awarding of costs to prosecutors and witnesses, see J.M. Beattie, *Crime and the Courts in England, 1660–1800* (Princeton and Oxford, 1986), 41–8.

St Pancras.[28] A break-in at 2 a.m. at the house of a pawnbroker in Piccadilly, in which four men armed with cutlasses had confined and threatened the family and their servants and plundered the house of plate, diamond rings, and other goods to the value of £800, was reported to Bow Street, and Nicholas Bond 'immediately sent proper persons in search of the offenders.' One of the four—by means not reported—was apprehended.[29] Similarly, following a violent robbery by mounted men in the fields near Lamb's Conduit Street in Bloomsbury on a Sunday night in 1780, the press reported that 'An immediate information being given to the office in Bow-street, Jealous and others were dispatched to the different stable-keepers in and about Holborn, and from their prosecuting the enquiry with great spirit and vigour, the two offenders were secured within hours in a house in Eagle-street.'[30]

In some cases the officers knew who to look for because the suspect was known to the victim—a lodger, for example, accused by a fellow lodger of breaking into his or her room, stealing goods and absconding; or a servant or apprentice accused by an employer. Such suspected thieves might not be immediately easy to find, but a distribution of handbills or an advertisement might bring news from a pawnbroker or other receiver and provide some clue as to where they had gone. It might take a search around previous known addresses or places of employment, but when they were found, identification was at least straightforward.

The Bow Street officers were frequently engaged in this kind of search, evidence-gathering, and arrest, and in identifying and assembling the witnesses who would provide the strongest evidence against the accused. In a case in 1778 that was well reported in the press and (because of the violence involved) drew a large crowd to the pretrial hearing at Bow Street, Thomas Hughes, a servant who had been recently dismissed by Lady Morton, returned to her house in Chiswick, broke into the room of her gardener where he must have known he would find the 48 guineas and various items of clothing that he stole, and then viciously attacked a maid with a hatchet when she interrupted him as he made his escape. The maid was able to tell what had happened and, as the newspapers reported, 'application was immediately made to Justice Addington in Bow Street, and . . . proper steps' were taken to catch and arrest Hughes. Those steps involved considerable activity on the part of two officers, Richard Bond (Nicholas Bond's brother) and David Prothero, who rode all night to get to Oxford and the next day to Worcester, finally tracking Hughes into Wales and arresting him at his mother's house. They brought him to London, and, within a week of the offence being committed, assembled eight witnesses for the pretrial hearing into his case at Bow Street—including the

---

[28] OBP, January 1775 (Samuel Male and James Wilson) t17750113–19. It is an interesting reflection on the frequency of highway robbery in this period that Mary Grignion, the victim of the robbery, said at the trial that she had not been at all frightened. 'No,' she replied to the judge's question, 'I had been robbed so often lately that I was not frightened at the time. I flung my money into my hat; I cannot tell how much; there was another man just at the side of the person, that put a pistol into the coach; I said take your pistol away and I will give you my money.' For a similar arrest, see OBP, October 1768 (Patrick Hanlon *et al*) t17681019–29.

[29] *London Evening Post*, 5–7 February 1778.

[30] *British Mercury and Evening Advertiser*, 5 December 1780.

second-hand clothes dealer who had bought Hughes's clothes from him, the shopkeepers who had sold him a new hat and coat, his landlady, other witnesses who could corroborate aspects of the evidence, and three of Lady Morton's servants.[31]

Some of the arrests made by Bow Street officers resulted from previous encounters with suspects and often as a result of chance meetings. The evidence given by John Heley and Nicholas Bond at the trial of William Wiggins and John Savage in 1772 made it clear that they had known them for some time, possibly had been looking for them, and that when they each, separately, saw them on the roads to the west of London one Sunday morning, along with a third man, David Evans, they suspected they were out for a purpose. Heley said in court that he 'knew them very well.' They were obviously anxious to catch them, yet on their own they would not have tried it. When Bond and Heley met later that day at Bow Street, Bond organized and led a substantial force of eight men to try to find them. At a subsequent trial he described how they had arrested Wiggins:

> I got some men together, and I stationed four of them at Buckingham Gate Turnpike; two and myself at Hyde Park Corner, and two others at Tyburn Turnpike; the turnpike men informed me, that two gentlemen that had just passed by in a post chaise, had informed them they had been robbed; after staying near an hour, I saw three men on the left, coming from Paddington Turnpike, and going towards Park-lane; I and the two men who were with me followed them for about a hundred yards; when I was within about five yards of them, I knew Wiggins to be one of the three, by his back. . . .

After a chase and struggle Bond arrested Wiggins. The other two were Savage and David Evans. They got away, but the Bow Street men knew how to find Savage or were told by Wiggins, and the next morning they took him in a house in St Giles's in bed with two other men—sharing a bed in this way (at a shilling a night each) was common—who were also arrested and taken to be examined before Fielding. Under Savage's pillow they found a watch.[32] They were later to catch Evans who they persuaded to turn king's evidence.

It was later revealed that just before they were arrested on the Sunday evening Wiggins, Savage, and Evans had robbed two men in a post-chaise in Shepherd's Bush, taking their hats and a watch. Evans testified at the trial of his accomplices that they had all set out from St Giles's to make their way to Richmond, 'in order to rob.' Having arrived at Richmond, he said,

> we walked round the Green, but there were so many watch boxes and lamps, we thought that place would not do for us; we crossed Kew Bridge: we drank at an alehouse or two, in order to make us almost drunk to raise our spirits; then we went to a place I have since heard is called Shepherd's Bush

[31] *London Evening Post*, 20–2, 24–7, and 27–9 January 1778; *Morning Chronicle*, 29 January 1778.
[32] OBP, October 1772 (William Wiggins and John Savage) t17721021-24.

and stopped the chaise carrying the two men. The victims reached town as Bond and his assistants were chasing Wiggins and the other suspects down Park Lane and into Grosvenor Square. They went immediately to Bow Street to report the robbery to Sir John Fielding and were called back two days later, on the Tuesday, to identify Wiggins as one of the robbers and the watch found under Savage's pillow as the one taken from them.

For his part, the third of the robbers, David Evans, an 18-year-old apprentice glazier and painter, had not been immediately arrested and was keeping himself 'out of the way', as we learn from another case tried at the same session.[33] By Wednesday, however, he was ready to try the roads once more and went to the Nag's Head public house in Tothill Street, Westminster—a house, he said, 'for whores and thieves,' commonly known as a 'flash house'—to find some likely companions. He found William Griffiths and Timothy Johnson, the former 'just come from sea', the latter a gold and silver coat button-maker. They set off to walk towards Hampstead, though not before Evans recovered a pistol that he had hidden after the Sunday robbery. As it turned dark, they came upon two women and two children in a single-horse chaise in Tottenham Court Road, which they stopped. Evans drew out the pistol which went off inadvertently—it had a defective spring— and the stone button with which it was loaded hit one of the women and fell into her apron pocket. She was not injured, but no doubt sufficiently frightened that when Evans stood on the step of the chaise she willingly gave him her money. Since he was having such trouble with his pistol, Evans said that 'had it been two men, I should have been taken, but as it was two women, I robbed one.' A few days later, by means entirely unclear, Evans was apprehended and taken to Bow Street, where the runners persuaded him (by the threat of the gallows because he had fired the pistol) to turn king's evidence against not only Griffiths and Johnson, but also Wiggins and Savage.[34]

The apprehension of Wiggins and Savage (and perhaps of Evans too) depended on the runners' knowledge of them. They were down as suspects to be watched, if not actually in the records collected at Bow Street, then in the officers' shared memory and experience. The runners were often prepared to say that they recognized an offender from the description given by the victim of a robbery. They turned out to be correct in some cases—as when a hackney coachman and his two passengers described a footpad who had stopped and robbed them of a watch in Soho just after midnight one evening in September 1783 and Jealous found the watch early the next morning at the lodgings of the man he recognized from the description.[35] Other Bow Street arrests were made when the runners came upon

[33] OBP, October 1772 (William Griffiths and Timothy Johnson) t17721021–23.

[34] Having agreed to give evidence against Griffiths and Johnson before Fielding at Bow Street, Evans went back on that promise (for a reason impossible to discern) and declared at their trial that they had nothing to do with the robbery. They were acquitted, though Griffiths himself was subsequently convicted of highway robbery and sentenced to death. OBP, December 1772 (William Griffiths) t17721209–46.

[35] LMA: OB/SP/1783/September/62. When one man 'known' to the Bow Street officers was seen leaving a shop that was subsequently broken into during the following night, Jealous waited for several

someone in the streets acting suspiciously—running away when the runners spotted them, for example, in the case of William Lee, who Jealous and Macmanus caught and searched and discovered several silver spoons and pick-lock keys in his pockets on the very day on which a theft of silver was reported to the office.[36]

After years of investigating and record-keeping, Bow Street had a store of information about suspects, their lodgings and hangouts, the whereabouts of known receivers, and descriptions of stolen goods, that led to arrests and supported numbers of prosecutions. It was reported in the press in 1775, for example, that a landlady had called in the Bow Street men when a woman who had agreed to take lodgings, left a large box and failed to return. The runners opened the box and found a quantity of plate, clothing, eight pistols, picklocks, and other tools. Examining 'the books of the Office,' the paper went on, the runners discovered that many of the items had been taken in burglaries and robberies. The woman was traced and her male accomplices were apprehended.[37] The lists of stolen watches kept in the office, with the makers' names and numbers, proved to be particularly useful in tracing suspects who sold or pawned such items.[38]

Equally important to the effort to detect and apprehend suspected offenders was the information that the office broadcast through advertisements in the press, in handbills, or, after 1772, in the *Hue and Cry*. One of the effects of that distribution of information about recent offences and the goods that had been taken (allied with the offer of rewards) was the encouragement it appears to have given well-established and well-known pawnbrokers to act in some senses as agents of the police by agreeing to number their shops so that the runners could keep a list and find them easily[39] and being willing to call in Bow Street officers on at least some occasions when a customer offered suspicious goods for sale or pawn. How many pawnbrokers cooperated in Fielding's policing effort or how often, it is of course impossible to say, but it is clear that the runners cultivated the larger pawnbrokers, ensured that they had copies of the *Hue and Cry*, and that they received handbills describing recent thefts with descriptions of offenders and stolen goods. Newspapers regularly carried advertisements from the 'PUBLIC OFFICE, Bow-Street,'

hours outside his lodgings to arrest him at 9 a.m. In his room Jealous found a crow bar, a cutlass, and pick-lock keys. None of the stolen items taken from the shop was found, but he was nonetheless taken to Bow Street and examined (LMA: OB/SP/1784/April/39). There is a suspicion in some other cases, as we will see when we examine the trial of John Roberts (below, text at nn. 59–60), that the description of a robber may have sufficiently resembled someone they were keen to charge that the runners made arrests in the hope that the victim would be prepared to identify them in court.

[36] OBP, September 1784 (William Lee and Richard Ridout) t17840915-26. John Heley and John Clarke—possibly out on patrol—came upon a man carrying a large bundle on the day several thefts were reported to the office, followed him into the house where he lodged, and found the goods that had been reported stolen (*General Evening Post*, 23–5 August 1774).

[37] *London Evening Post* 14–17 January 1775.

[38] For cases in which the Bow Street 'watch book' established a connection between the accused and the stolen goods at issue, see OBP, January 1775 (Edward Batsford) t17750111-65; February 1775 (Daniel Angus) t17750218-29; January 1790 (Thomas Newton *et al*) t17900113-4.

[39] John Heley, giving evidence in court in 1775 said that having found 'duplicates' at the prisoner's lodgings, he found the pawnbroker who had issued them by referring to 'our list of the pawnbrokers' who had agreed 'to number their shops.' OBP, February 1775 (John Armer) t17750218-19.

describing goods lost, and concluding, like this example on 1 January 1780 in the *Gazetteer*, 'If offered to be pawned or sold, stop them and the party, and give notice to Sir John Fielding, and you shall receive one guinea from the owner'. Others offered more—five or 10 guineas being not uncommon.

At least occasionally, pawnbrokers found it in their best interests to 'stop' people offering to sell or pawn goods that they suspected might be stolen. John Fielding was no doubt overly sanguine when he told the house of commons committee in 1770 that the large dealers cooperated so fully with his runners that thieves had been driven to change the way they disposed of stolen goods,[40] but there is abundant evidence in the press and in the accounts of Old Bailey trials that pawnbrokers regularly reported suspicious cases to Bow Street and responded after the fact when they recognized from the handbills the runners circulated or advertisements in the press or the *Hue and Cry* that they had taken in stolen goods. The story of John Hambleton's arrest for stealing a large quantity of plate and other things from an apartment in Somerset House in 1772 was a commonplace of crime news in the press. He was arrested when a pawnbroker, offered the goods for purchase, 'pretended to go for scales and weights' but instead went to the Bow Street office. The pawnbroker received three guineas reward, as offered in a handbill by the owner, 'and Sir John Fielding ordered him a guinea more for his honesty.'[41] 'Anne Henings brought this gold ring to my house to pawn,' Nicholas Simonds, said in giving evidence in a burglary case in 1768; 'it occurred to me there had been handbills from Sir John Fielding, in which was a ring mentioned.... I found the bill which described it; I went with the ring to Sir John Fielding, he advised me to wait till the woman came again; she came again and brought a sattin gown; I stopped her, and took her to Sir John Fielding; there she gave information of James Manning the prisoner,' who was arrested.[42] Another pawnbroker took in a watch on a Saturday evening from a man who seemed well dressed and gave a plausible story about needing money. On the following Monday morning the pawnbroker received a handbill from Bow Street that made it clear the watch had been stolen in a highway robbery two hours before he had taken it in. He went to Bow Street, described the man who had been in his shop, and David Prothero, a runner, tracked him down.[43] The notorious John Rann, 'Sixteen-string Jack,' was also convicted after a career on the road because a pawnbroker was suspicious of two women Rann and his accomplice had sent to pawn a stolen watch and turned them in to Bow Street.[44] Pawnbrokers' duplicates—the receipt they gave to customers—were very often the crucial link that tied a suspect to stolen property

---

[40] See ch. 5, text at n. 3.

[41] *General Evening Post*, 29–31 December 1772.

[42] OBP, May 1768 (James Manning) t17680518–17.

[43] OBP, December 1781 (Richard Isaacs) t17811205–33.

[44] OBP, October 1774 (John Rann et al) t17741019–50). For other cases (of many) in which pawnbrokers' notices to Bow Street led to arrests, see *General Evening Post*, 28–30 July 1772; OBP April 1776 (William Cockin and William Miles) t17760417–6; January 1772 (William Brown) t17720109–21; June 1772 (Thomas Adams et al) t17720603–10.

when the Bow Street men found them in carrying out searches in lodgings or on the suspects themselves.[45]

Thieves could dispose of stolen goods in many other ways besides dealing with established pawnbrokers. The runners became familiar with the most active receivers and from time to time they made arrests after visiting some of the likely dealers. Asked at the Old Bailey in 1780 why he had chosen to go to the house in which he found stolen clothes an hour after they had been taken from a chaise in Piccadilly, Carpmeal replied that 'When we have an information we go to the house of the people who receive these things; we know pretty well who are concerned together.'[46] We go, John Clarke said on the same subject, to 'all the noted houses.'[47]

The most useful information, however, from which the Bow Street officers built up their knowledge of offenders and criminal associations came from informers— men (and some women) in a position to overhear talk about offences committed or planned. That kind of information must have come their way with respect to particular offences from people looking to benefit from a potential reward, though perhaps more commonly from those willing regularly to cooperate with police officers for a price, passing on gossip and their more direct knowledge of offences. Time and again at the Old Bailey the runners began their testimony, as did Patrick Macmanus at a trial in 1783, by saying 'We had information at Bow-street . . . that there was a man lay at such a house, and that they suspected he was a highway-man'.[48] Or, John Noakes in 1768: 'I had information that the prisoner . . . bought stolen goods' in explaining why three runners watched his house for several hours before arresting him and several of his customers.[49] Or Macmanus, again, asked why the runners had searched the prisoner's house: 'There was an information at the office, that such sort of people lived there, that stole trunks.'[50] Informers (along with advertisements and handbills offering rewards for information) provided the Bow Street officers with an important weapon, especially against highwaymen, street robbers, burglars, and coiners—indeed perhaps their most important weapon. After a series of highway robberies by three young men on Hounslow Heath, Nicholas Bond 'received intelligence' on a Monday evening that one of them was William Sampson, a clerk to a lace merchant. Immediately seeking out the merchant, Bond learned that Sampson had left London that morning, taking the Portsmouth road. Bond pursued him that same evening in a hired post-chaise, and arrested him at 3 a.m. at an inn in Farnham. One of the watches taken in

---

[45] OBP, June 1772 (Francis Mascado) t17720503–6.

[46] OBP, February 1780 (Henry Barnett) t17800223–3.

[47] OBP, September 1776 (William Wood) t17760911–1.

[48] OBP, September 1783 (Thomas Booker) t17830910–38.

[49] OBP, October. 1768 (Thomas Lloyd *et al*) t17681021–41. For the runners conducting similar stake-outs, some of them through the night, see OBP, December 1769 (Peter Graham *et al*) t17691206–10; December1769 (Thomas Cave *et al*) t17691206–3.

[50] OBP, February 1783 (Thomas Dudfield and Hart Levy) t17830226–3.

the robberies was found in his 'apartment' in London, and he was committed for trial.[51]

How many informers—snitches, or 'noses,' as they were occasionally called—like the man who gave Bond this lead were in the pay of Bow Street officers and how precisely these contacts were maintained is impossible to document. But that they were crucial to their work of detecting and apprehending the most serious offenders, indeed offenders of all kinds, is certain. When more than £1,000 worth of lace was stolen from an auction house, the Bow Street officers knew the main receivers in London well enough to be certain that there were only four 'capable of making so large a purchase', but they only learned which one of them had in fact bought the lace when they received 'private information' from an informer. John Fielding, who directed the operation to catch these burglars, advised the victim to have his servants keep watch on that receiver and to follow him when he left home—thinking perhaps that the runners were too well known to be able to do it themselves. He did so, reported the suspected receiver's movements to the runners, and the Bow Street men found the lace in the house he had visited. Jealous disclosed at the pretrial hearing and at the trial at the Old Bailey that they also discovered a set of pick-lock keys which they took to the building in which the lace had been stored and found that they opened the doors.[52]

Informers also made it possible for Patrick Macmanus, Archibald Ruthvin, Jealous, and John Shallard (an assistant) to trace four horses stolen from an estate in Chesham, Buckinghamshire, and brought to London for sale in various parts of the metropolis.[53] In another case in 1781, Jealous and Carpmeal arrested four men at the Falcon public house in Clerkenwell on suspicion of stopping a heavily-laden wagon on a highway just outside London and stealing a large quantity of goods three days earlier. They 'went after [the four men] on purpose,' Carpmeal said in court, presumably having been tipped off that they had committed the offence and that they could be found in that pub.[54]

Connections between police officers and informers were largely established and maintained in the alehouses and taverns in the crowded and dangerous sections of town, especially in the flash houses like the Nag's Head in Tothill Street that were the common resort of men who engaged in theft and robbery and who were likely to talk about it, even to brag and boast about their exploits, in the only centres of sociability available to them. Some of the officers active in the 1780s gave evidence about their use of informers to the 1816 and 1817 commons committees investigating the police of the metropolis. They all agreed that informers and flash houses were crucial to their work. A visit to a notorious house, they said, might turn up someone they had been looking for, or they might pick up a scrap of intelligence over a drink and a chat with the publican or a group of patrons. Such houses

---

[51] *General Evening Post*, 15–17 November 1774.
[52] LMA: OB/SP/May 1781/32; OBP, May 1781 (John M'Neil and William John Ridgely, alias Richley) t17810530-55.
[53] LMA: OB/SP/April 1786/11.
[54] OBP, July 1781 (Abraham Abrahams, James Parker, Moses Robus, and Arthur Levy) t17810711-3.

were indispensable to their maintaining contact with men willing to earn a little by passing information. One of the Bow Street men, Samuel Taunton, told the committee that 'thieves are a set of men who are apt to talk and open their minds a little to each other; and if we have any body that we can obtain information from, it is from conversations at those times.'[55] Such talk, passed on to runners who could match it to reports of offences recently committed, made robbers vulnerable, and perhaps helps to explain why, not infrequently, arrests were made within days, even hours, of a complaint received at Bow Street. Some contemporaries complained that John Fielding connived at the preservation of flash houses—and the dissolute character of the Covent Garden area in which the office was located—because of the usefulness of places where information against the most dangerous offenders could be gathered.[56]

It was in the officers' as well as the informers' interests that the identity of these men or even the fact that information had been passed to the police not be disclosed at preliminary hearings at Bow Street or in trials at the Old Bailey. The principal exception was in the case of victimless crimes, such as coining, in which it was necessary for the runners to explain why they had targeted a particular house.[57] For the most part the involvement of informers in the prosecution of felonies was not disclosed in detail, but the fact that 'evidence received' had enabled the runners to identify and apprehend a suspect within hours of offences being reported to the office is clear in many trials. In some cases the runners went after men and women on their lists of 'known offenders' who seemed to fit the descriptions given by the victims. More often, one can only suspect that an informer had passed on a tip—and perhaps information about where a suspect lodged or could be found—and the runners' main task was to find the evidence that might tie that suspect to that offence and if possible get him or her to confess.

For obvious reasons the use of informants and the gathering of such information remains largely hidden: as Townsend told the house of commons committee in 1816, 'in most cases we never bring our informer forward.'[58] Occasionally, however, the involvement of an informer was revealed in court, as it was in the prosecution of James Roberts, alias James Yark, at the Old Bailey in December 1783, who was charged with an accomplice (not yet arrested) of stopping a small open carriage on the western edge of the metropolis of London at 4 p.m. on a Saturday afternoon

---

[55] *Parliamentary Papers*, 1817 (484) vol. 7: *Second Report from the Committee on the State of the Police of the Metropolis*, 393.

[56] For criticism of Fielding's failure to close the numerous bawdy houses and unlawful drinking places that give the Covent Garden area the reputation for being an 'abominable . . . sink of iniquity,' see *Oxford Magazine*, vol. 3 (1769), 81–2; William Augustus Miles, *Letter to Sir John Fielding, Knt. Occasioned, by his extraordinary request to Mr Garrick for the suppression of The Beggars Opera* (1773), 8–9, 12–17; Joseph Cawthorne, *Considerations on the Authority of the Magistrate, commonly called the Police* (London, 1788), 17–18.

[57] See ch. 5, text at n. 125.

[58] *Committee on the Police of the Metropolis* (1816), 141. If it was necessary to get a conviction, they might 'bring all the parties forward, face to face', as Townsend on one occasion advised a fellow officer to do in order to prove his case—though in reporting this to the committee, he also emphasized that it was unusual.

in November, presenting pistols and robbing its two occupants, Mrs Susannah Bond and Mary, her daughter.

Roberts and his accomplice were alleged to have taken a purse and five pieces of Spanish silver—one dollar and four 'bits', or pieces of eight—and 10 shillings in English money, all the property of John Bond, Susannah's husband. When the women arrived home some minutes after the attack, John Bond wrote immediately to Bow Street to report the case, describing the robbers, their horses, the purse and money, and sent the letter with three of his servants who were armed and whom he expected then to go on the look-out for the robbers.[59] We learn from the trial before Mr Justice Willes that this information was received on the Saturday evening at Bow Street by Charles Jealous and Thomas Carpmeal. They arrested Roberts at 8 a.m. the following day in the lodgings of Ruth Mercer, a prostitute, where they found them both in bed. His accomplice was never found. Why did they go after Roberts? The case is unusual in that Jealous volunteered this information. 'We went to him', he said, 'from a particular information, which I hope your lordship will not enquire into'—in other words from an informer. Jealous also revealed that they got the tip-off through another 'officer of justice', one Dennis McDonald, who was attached to the Rotation Office in Lichfield Street. McDonald testified that on the Saturday evening one of his informers who knew where Roberts was currently living got word of the robbery and 'called upon me and told me.' McDonald then went to Bow Street to enlist the help of Jealous and Carpmeal.

Why McDonald did that was not disclosed. But it is clear from questions posed by Roberts' attorney, Sheridan, and McDonald's aggressive replies that there was something very suspicious about the speed of the arrest. The evidence linking Roberts to the crime was not particularly strong, since the victims were hesitant in court about his identity and were only willing to swear that he was their attacker after being pressed to do so by Willes—just one of the judge's numerous interventions and rulings that make it clear that he was pushing very hard for a guilty verdict. Even more problematic was the inevitable lack of certainty in the identification of the money and the purse that had been found in Mercer's room. Jealous was reduced to emphasizing that he had found riding boots and a whip, all still wet (it had been raining the previous evening), and that Mercer had tried to hide Roberts' spurs.

It was also revealed by the judge's questions that Jealous, Carpmeal and McDonald were all familiar with Roberts, and he with them. The Bow Street men claimed in court that they had recognized Roberts and his accomplice from the description given by the victims, that they were 'well acquainted' with them and 'suspected' them of committing this offence. The point of Willes's enquiry about their acquaintance with him was almost certainly to signal to the jury that the prisoner was an 'old offender'. It also suggests that the judge had been given information about the case ahead of the trial and had been persuaded that Roberts was a dangerous offender who should not be allowed to escape conviction and

---

[59] OBP, December 1783 (James Roberts, alias Yark) t17831210–2.

execution because of weaknesses in the evidence. There is indeed a strong suggestion—implied by some of defence counsel Sheridan's questions, but not stated explicitly—that, knowing him and suspecting him of committing robberies, the Bow Street men and McDonald had been waiting for an opportunity to fit Roberts to a robbery that would elicit jury disgust, as this attack on two women might be expected to do. The introduction of 'evidence' of an informer that pointed to Roberts' guilt may have been disclosed as a way of supporting a weak case. It was certainly unusual for the prosecution to bring in such evidence. It must have been a prosecution decision to disclose his role at the Roberts trial, suggested perhaps by a solicitor who drew the brief, or by William Garrow, counsel for the prosecution, who was appearing in his very first trial, at the beginning of what was to prove a remarkably successful decade as the leading Old Bailey counsel.[60]

Whether or not this particular informer provided evidence crucial to the arrest and to the verdict in the Roberts case, the importance to the work of the Bow Street men and other officers of the information provided by such sources could hardly be exaggerated. It was clearly accepted by magistrates and judges.[61] It is hardly a surprise that the magistrates at Bow Street or other police offices would not be inclined to enquire too closely into the evidence their own officers brought against the suspects they charged. Jealous said at the Roberts trial that he hoped Mr Justice Willes would not enquire into the identity of their informer; McDonald told Sheridan in response to a question that he would 'not tell you who told me' that Roberts had committed the offence and where he lived. When Sheridan told him that he would have to disclose his source, he replied that he would do so only if the judge asked him to, but that he thought it would be 'unfair.' Willes agreed, and ruled against disclosure. 'They should not discover [his name]', he said to Sheridan; 'you should ask him [McDonald] what kind of intelligence he received, without mentioning the person.' The report in the *Proceedings* does not reveal whether Sheridan complained about the receipt of this evidence, which he was surely entitled to have done.[62]

Another long trial at the Old Bailey in 1786 provides further evidence of the usefulness to the police of the contacts that could be made in drinking establishments in certain parts of town. This involved a street robbery by two young apprentices (James Cowdery and James Wood) who, armed with pistols, stopped James Chilcott on the City Road between Islington and Shoreditch and took his watch and money. Townsend said in court that he 'received an information' about the robbery, information that led him to believe that the men he wanted

---

[60] J. M. Beattie, 'Scales of Justice: Defense Counsel and the English Criminal Trial in the Eighteenth and Nineteenth Centuries,' *Law and History Review*, 8 (2, 1991) 236–47.

[61] For the unsettled status of hearsay evidence in the eighteenth century, see John H. Langbein, *The Origins of Adversary Criminal Trial* (Oxford, 2003), 233–47.

[62] The jury found Roberts guilty. Willes capped his partisanship by announcing that, despite a recommendation from the Bonds that Roberts be shown mercy, he would not recommend that the king grant him the pardon that would save him from the gallows because 'these are times which require a degree of severity, or else our lives and properties cannot be protected'. Despite that, he was pardoned, though on condition of his being transported to Africa. OBP, December 1783 (James Roberts, alias Yark) t17831210–2.

would be found at the Lord Rodney's Head in Chequers Alley, off Whitecross Street. 'I called in to see who was there', Townsend testified in court; 'I looked around the tap-room and saw nobody there that I wanted.' He did, however, know a great deal about the landlord, Joseph Chant, and he got him to admit (using threats he did not disclose in court) that he had bought Chilcott's watch from the two young men and had in turn sold it to one Robert East, another shady character who operated as both a receiver and (when it suited him) thief-taker, and who had been called 'a hardened villain' by a judge in a trial earlier that very day—a point that Garrow, defending, made sure the jury remembered. East was almost certainly the man who had alerted Townsend to the robbery, in the hope of earning some part of the £80 reward money that would be forthcoming. Townsend got the names of the robbers from Chant and the information that enabled him to apprehend them after some days of tracking. In his defence, one of the apprentices claimed that Chant often asked him 'to go out a thieving, and that he would find me in pistols and cutlasses', but Chilcott's identification of them as the robbers at Bow Street and at the Old Bailey trial, as well as his identification of his watch, brought the inevitable guilty verdict and death sentence. The judge did however say that he would recommend their pardon 'on account of their youth.'[63]

The Cowdery and Wood case underlines the importance, indeed the indispens-ability for Bow Street policing practices of the 'flash houses', especially the places where highwaymen and street robbers and other major offenders sought sociability, told their tales, recounted their successes, gathered their courage, and where they very often lived with prostitutes. These houses provided them with a place to recruit accomplices, to bring together a gang, to generate strength in numbers. But it also made them vulnerable to the informer who might be listening and to the police who might be watching, or who might turn up at any time.

In his effort to discredit the evidence given by the principal witnesses for the prosecution in the Cowdery and Wood case, Garrow probed Townsend in cross-examination on his familiarity with and use of the Lord Rodney's Head public house, as well as his knowledge of the suspected informer, East's, line of work:

Garrow: Have you frequent occasions to go to [Chant's] house?
Townsend: Several times . . . because people, which I am very sorry to say, under the description of that kind of people, used to use that house.
Garrow: Have you occasionally found any people there that you have wanted?
Townsend: We have found people there that we have wanted, but it has turned out that the evidence would not bring them to public justice.[64]

---

[63] OBP, October 1786 (James Cowdery and James Wood) t17861025–5.

[64] That is, unlike the present case, they were not able to get evidence that would stand up in court. Garrow also tried to persuade the jury that East's evidence was not to be trusted by labelling him a thief-taker, or what he called a 'private trap.' Townsend denied all knowledge of that term. 'I know a good many things', he said; 'I know I am a public trap, but I really do not know what a private trap is.' OBP, October 1786 (Cowdery and Wood) t17861025–5.

The importance for the police of places like Chant's public house is revealed in other Old Bailey trials. Though he was not apparently a snitch by habit, Willliam Alvey gave the evidence that convicted a man for burglary in 1784, having heard the offence being planned at another notorious public house, the Hind, in Redcross Street (and having then followed them at a distance to a currier's where they poisoned his dog, broke in, and took some skins). Judge Willes observed that it did Alvey no good to be in a place like the Hind, two years after being released from Newgate, but his evidence held up.[65]

The most direct and revealing evidence about flash houses and their usefulness to Bow Street was provided, as we have seen, by the officers who gave evidence to the house of commons committees that investigated the 'State of the Police of the Metropolis' in 1816 and 1817, committees before which several Bow Street men testified who could look back to the last quarter of the eighteenth century—including Townsend, 30 years on and still far from the end of his career as a runner.[66] The Bow Street magistrates who gave evidence were reluctant to admit that there were such establishments within their jurisdiction, perhaps because they licensed some of them and had done nothing to suppress the others. In the course of insistent questioning they came around to acknowledging that there might just be such places, particularly when a member of the committee provided a handy definition—'inferior public houses which are the resort of bad people of both sexes.'[67] The chief magistrate at Bow Street in 1816, Sir Nathaniel Conant was reluctant to confirm that it was 'an established known fact in the Police Office, that there are houses such as have been described, which are frequented by thieves, and people of the worst description, and to which resort the Police officers go just as regularly as a gentleman goes to his preserve, in his manor, to find game'. He waffled around a great deal but finally managed to say that 'I do not much understand their art; but I think one mode of it would be, if [the runners] wanted to know the offences of one offender, as applicable to the particular object in view, they would be very glad to get themselves into company with another who was likely to be in his confidence.' In plain words, they would seek out one of their informers. He hastened to add that all of this was 'part of the mystery, or of the art, or of the policy, which I can neither understand or explain.'[68]

The Bow Street officers, on the other hand, were quite open about their reliance on evidence gathered at such places. They were not only entirely familiar with the most notorious of the flash houses across the metropolis, they were willing to explain to the committee why they were essential to their policing practices. Townsend and other officers with years of service behind them, including John Vickery and John Sayer, made it clear to the committee that as far back as they could remember flash houses had been indispensable to the work of detection.

---

[65] OBP, December 1784 (William Astill and John Ellis) t17841218–10.

[66] *Committee on the Police of the Metropolis* (1816); *First and Second Reports of the Committee on the Police of the Metropolis* (1817).

[67] *Committee on the Police of the Metropolis: Second Report* (1817), 424.

[68] *Committee on the Police of the Metropolis* (1816), 21.

Vickery told the committee that they were becoming more benign, much less threatening to the police than they once had been—a reflection, if true, of a change in the character of crime in London in the early nineteenth century, and in particular of a sharp decline then in the levels of highway and street robberies and of gang violence in general.[69] It was not as dangerous now for the police to enter the places where thieves might congregate, Vickery told the committee in 1816, as it had been a few decades earlier when they might have expected to be insulted, even molested.[70] But dangerous or not, the officers all confirmed that the flash houses had always been an indispensable means of finding suspects and gathering evidence. Asked if they assisted 'in the detection of thieves', Townsend recalled that in his earlier days in the office (in the 1780s) he and other officers, hearing of an offence, would go 'to some of the flash–houses' and look for suspects.[71] John Vickery and John Sayer, both long-experienced Bow Street officers, spoke about their habit of dropping in for a drink from time to time at some of them, sending spies to others, each making the point that if such places were closed the police would have a much more difficult job finding those they suspected of committing offences.[72]

The police witnesses also agreed on the crucial importance of informers and the costs of maintaining their relationships with them. It obviously took some time and patience to establish a relationship with a man in a position to hear useful criminal intelligence. John Nelson Lavender, an officer at Queen Street in 1816 but who had once been a Bow Street man, as had his father before him, was questioned about informers. 'When you go to the flash-houses,' a member of the committee asked him, 'is it your custom to associate with the persons there?' 'Yes,' he replied, 'and a man must do that for a good while before he will be able to gain any information.' And, he might have added, pay for a good many drinks and much besides. In the nature of the case it is impossible to know how much the officers paid for information, but it is clear that the Bow Street runners were in a much better position to meet these expenses than their counterparts at the Rotation offices, or the constables at the public offices created in 1792. The Bow Street men—better treated in every way, as we will see—were able to include some such payments in their expenses,[73] whereas the magistrates elsewhere in the metropolis had no funds from which to reward their officers or pay their expences. A Queen's Square officer told the 1816 committee that he spent a 'good deal of money in obtaining information'—all of which had to come from his salary, though some presumably came from rewards, both the statutory and more private rewards.[74]

---

[69] For the changing character of London crime in the early nineteenth century, see ch. 8, section 1.
[70] *Committee on the Police of the Metropolis* (1816), 178.
[71] Ibid, 142.
[72] Ibid, 40, 48–9, 147–8, 173, 176, 178–80, 216; *Committee on the Police of the Metropolis: Second Report* (1817), 374, 392–3.
[73] TNA: T 38/671, f. 13; T 1/387, 9.
[74] *Committee on the Police of the Metropolis* (1816), 364–5.

Important as they were, informers must have been responsible for the detection and apprehension of only a portion of the offenders prosecuted by the Bow Street police officers. Robbery and other offences like housebreaking that threatened violence and were thought to be especially serious for this reason loomed large in the work of the runners, but they also went after shoplifters and pickpockets and minor thieves of all kinds, few of whom are likely to have talked about their offences in the way robbers were prone to do or to have fallen under the gaze of the sorts of informers with whom the Bow Street men had regular contact. Indeed, that must have been true of the wide range of other offences that they were sent to look into by the magistrates or for which they were engaged by private prosecutors. With experience, the runners developed useful detective skills, rudimentary no doubt in modern terms, but much more effective than those possessed by anyone charged with policing duties had ever brought to bear on London crime. Most seem to have been available full-time for the work of the office. By the late eighteenth century they had as a group decades of experience of investigating crimes and chasing suspects across the metropolis and indeed across the country. They must have acquired a considerable knowledge of the topography of crime in the capital as well as of the forms and characteristics of the offences they dealt with day in and day out. Cases about which no inside information was forthcoming and in which advertisements produced no leads were occasionally solved by the runners' investigations of crime scenes—investigations in which experience and common sense were their most important aids in turning up useful forensic evidence. Several runners developed expertise in some areas. William Garrow remarked in court about Charles Jealous's ability to tell the difference between city and country dirt on a highwayman's boots and to remember faces and also conversations at long remove.[75] Certainly Jealous seems to have been the most likely of the runners to stop and search men on dubious grounds in the streets, claiming to know them as suspicious characters.[76] He also revealed his skill at gathering forensic evidence when he traced an accused highwayman, who had shot and wounded his victim, to a stable near the Middlesex hospital, where he found the goods allegedly stolen in the robbery hidden in the hay. He also found a case of pistols, one of which was loaded with a ball that exactly matched one extracted from the victim's wound.[77] It could have been said of Jealous and of other runners that 'he understands his business well,' as a prosecutor said about Macmanus when he helped him make an arrest.[78]

Being frequently in the witness box and having to deal with the aggressive questioning of defence counsel must have developed the runners' sense of the kind of evidence that was useful in court and thus taught them what to look for in investigations of crime scenes. I presume that this is what Sampson Wright meant

[75] OBP, December 1783 (James Roberts, alias Yark) t17831210–2.
[76] OBP, April 1781 (Peter Boyce) t17810425–25; OBP, October 1783 (William Hatchman) t17831029–52.
[77] *London Evening Post*, 21–3 July 1778.
[78] OBP, December 1784 (Wood and Brown) t17841208–2.

when he said in 1783 that the runners' 'Experience and Knowledge of the Law of Evidence' made them 'ten times more useful than the [parish] Constable ever can be' when it came to prosecuting felons.[79] Undoubtedly he had in mind not only the kind of specialized expertise that Clarke brought to coining cases, but his and the runners' more general skills in examining crime locations, finding and interviewing witnesses, and checking alibis more carefully and systematically than had been done in the past. After a major burglary in 1778 in which about £200 worth of silver, jewellery, and clothes were taken, the press reported that the culprit had been uncovered by 'the vigilance of the active Mr Clarke, one of Sir John's people.' Clarke and Jealous both gave evidence at the subsequent trial, the former describing how his examination of the physical evidence around the doors and windows of the house undermined the story provided by a servant who had claimed that three men had broken in, tied him up and made off with the goods. Clarke was convinced that no one could have entered through the window: one pane was broken in a way that left part of the glass intact and jutting out in a sharp point; and 'on the inside of the other, a cobweb was still intire, which must have been broke before anyone could have entered.' Suspicion thus fell on the servant. Learning that he had a wife in lodgings, Clarke sent Jealous and Morant to search them, where they found more than £200 worth of plate and other goods.[80]

In a similar case, a newspaper reported that an investigation by Macmanus and Townsend of a door that a servant claimed had been forced by housebreakers, revealed them as 'too knowing for the servant,' who under their questioning confessed that he had staged the break-in himself.[81] Such successful investigations were a result of a commitment to solving crimes and a willingness to devote time to it that was new in the second half of the eighteenth century. The runners underwent no training, but they learned the value of material forensic evidence and the need to ensure that anything collected in the course of an investigation was documented and could be produced in court. This was a product of experience, but it could also be passed on. New recruits, Sampson Wright observed, learned on the job 'by acting and conversing with those [runners] of long Practice.'[82]

We shall take up in the following chapter the question of the possible effect on the character of trials at the Old Bailey of the presentation of prosecution evidence by these more professional witnesses. But here we might note that juries may have come to respect the evidence presented by men who appeared in the witness box in several trials at virtually every session. Many of the jurymen at the Old Bailey were themselves experienced. Two juries of 12 men heard all the trials of the accused from Middlesex, and another group of 12 typically sat on all the cases from the City of London. Each juror not only heard dozens of cases in a matter of a few days, but many of them returned to serve again at future sessions several times over. About a

---

[79] NLI 15930 (1).

[80] *London Evening Post*, 17–19 March 1778; OBP, April 1778 (Francis Lewis, al. Grimison) t17780429-7.

[81] *World*, 30 December 1789.

[82] NLI 15930 (1).

third of the Middlesex trial juries in the 1780s had had prior experience of jury service. The grand jurors at the Old Bailey, who heard the evidence of prosecution witnesses and either marked a bill of indictment for trial or threw it out, were also experienced in this period.[83] A significant number of jurors must have become familiar with the runners. Whether they trusted their evidence more than say that of a parish constable making a very occasional appearance is impossible to say. In many cases they helped to prosecute, the runners were vulnerable to a charge of self-interest because of the reward money they would earn from a defendant's conviction.[84] But their growing respectability enhanced their credibility. The jurors knew that they were active and knowledgeable investigators—as a foreman revealed when, at a burglary trial, he asked one of the runners if he had examined the crowbar they had taken from a defendant's house to see if it matched marks on the door frame of the house that had been broken into.[85] That kind of investigation was expected of them, part of the persuasion that they possessed skill and special knowledge. It was presumably those assumed qualities and their experience—and perhaps their courage—that made the runners attractive to the dozens of provincial magistrates, government departments, and private victims who called on them to investigate crimes in order to get their stolen property returned and to deter future offenders.[86]

3. APPREHENSION

Whether by means of an informer, a pawnbroker, an accomplice, a useful witness responding to an advertisement, their hard work at interviewing or chasing, from clues left at the scene of a crime, or their guessing at a possible candidate, the runners identified some of the suspects (though an unknown proportion) in the cases in which they became involved. Having done so they had to apprehend them and get them to Bow Street to bring them before the magistrates who were required by law to take depositions of victims and their witnesses and to examine the accused as the first stage of the process of prosecution. For the most part the business of taking suspects in charge appears to have been straightforward in the sense of not

[83] A total of 1,336 men served on Middlesex trial juries between 1780 and 1789; 964 served once only, 228 served twice, 82 three times, 46 four times, and 14 five times. Two men served on six and seven juries respectively during that decade. These data are based on the jurors named on the first page of the printed *Proceedings* for each session. For the level of experience of trial jurors and the makeup of the Old Bailey grand jury, see J. M. Beattie, 'London Jurors in the 1690s' in J. S. Cockburn and T. A. Green (eds.), *Twelve good men and true: the English criminal trial jury, 1200–1800* (Princeton, 1988), 214–53. For Essex and Staffordshire jurors in the late eighteenth century, see Peter King, 'Illiterate plebeians, easily misled: Jury composition, experience and behaviour in Essex, 1735–1815' in ibid, 254–304, and Douglas Hay, 'The class composition of the palladium of liberty: Trial jurors in the eighteenth century' in ibid, 305–57.

[84] See ch. 5, text at nn.156–8.

[85] He had not. OBP, April 1785 (William Harding) t17851406–27.

[86] For the runners' work outside London, see David J. Cox, *A Certain Share of Low Cunning. A history of the Bow Street Runners, 1792–1839* (Cullompton, Devon, 2010).

commonly requiring much force on the part of the arresting officer or to have been much resisted by those apprehended. Did he come 'without being in custody?', a runner was asked in court, without, I take it, being compelled in some way.[87] The authority of an officer, as of a constable, was sufficiently recognized that an arrest could be effected without a formal charge being made. Asked if a constable had attempted to arrest him, a man accused of shooting at him said, 'No, if he had touched me, I would have gone with him.'[88] Nonetheless, the runners reported often enough that they had 'got hold' of a suspect or got them into a coach to take them to Bow Street, and that must often have involved various degrees of persuasion. They must often have been in situations in which their strength was tested— as when, for example, Moses Morant came upon a man in an alehouse whom he was seeking for stealing and pawning a coat, and, searching his pockets, found the pawnshop ticket and 'by force got it from him.'[89] Occasionally the runners used restraints of some kind: handcuffs most commonly, occasionally ropes, though the latter mainly in coining cases and perhaps then as a way of immobilizing the accused completely to prevent them hiding or destroying evidence.

Complaints from suspects about having been roughed up were rarely reported in the press, in the statements they gave to the magistrates in the course of the pretrial process, or in trial accounts, though that is not perhaps a surprise. A certain amount of force would not perhaps have seemed out of the way in a period in which the use of violence in the imposition of authority—in the family, in schools or the workplace, in the armed forces—was not unusual or unexpected. It is clear that some arrests did involve physical conflict and carried the threat of injury to both offenders and policemen. Highwaymen and street robbers generally carried weapons of some kind. In going after them, the runners were themselves usually armed with cutlasses and pistols and used them when necessary.[90] I do not know whether stature and strength were required of runners coming into the job, but they must have developed a certain toughness with experience—that may be putting it mildly—and a willingness and ability to use it, especially when they thought themselves in danger. John Atkins described in court how he had tried to recruit a hostler to help him apprehend three men who were wanted for robbery. Coming upon them on the road where the robbery had taken place, the hostler wanted to turn tail, seeing that one of them had a knife. 'I said, oh! damn it, never fear,' he told the court. 'I ran, and the first man I came to made a blow at me. I hollood out as loud as I could, says I, *Charles Gealous* [sic]: he was not with me, but I thought his name would terrify them.' Whether or not that subdued them, Atkins and the reluctant hostler, caught two of the robbers, who were convicted, sentenced to

---

[87] OBP, January 1787 (Richard Notely *et al*) t17870110–53.

[88] OBP, October 1787 (William Whiteway) t17871024–19.

[89] LMA: OB/SP/April 1783/49.

[90] OBP, September 1779 (Edward Steward) t17790915–51; OBP, April 1781 (John Jones) t17810425–1; OBP, April 1782 (Job Wilkinson and Joseph Clark) t17820410–53; OBP, February 1784 (William Newland) t17840225–13. For a footpad shot by a Bow Street officer, see *General Evening Post*, 30 January–2 February 1773.

death, and subsequently pardoned, probably to await transportation.[91] Jealous had manhandled and perhaps terrified many other suspects. Fielding and his successors no doubt looked for men with some strength and size. As one man said in court when testifying that he overheard the defendant talking in a public house with an accomplice about a robbery: 'I took them to be two officers, come to arrest some man; but seeing the prisoner so little a man, I thought he was rather under size for that.'[92]

Certainly, the runners sometimes faced stout resistance from men who had used violence in carrying out their offences and must have known they faced almost certain execution if they were apprehended. Many of the footpads and highwaymen they confronted carried arms and were willing to use them. Four men sent from the office to apprehend two active street robbers in 1772 were fired at when they came upon them and one of the Bow Street men—unnamed in the press, but almost certainly one of the assistants in the office—was wounded and subsequently died.[93] Other Bow Street men were injured on the job and at least one other assistant— William Barnett—was killed when he helped David Prothero to arrest a man who had assaulted and badly beaten a woman. In the course of the altercation that ensued when the Bow Street men broke into their lodgings, Barnett was stabbed by the woman the suspect lived with and the reported victim of his violence. At that point Prothero, seeing the man with a long rasp in his hand, 'struck him as hard as I could with my hand . . . catched him by the collar, and got hold of the woman' and with the help of the two other men present, secured them. Barnett died the following day.[94] Some arrests obviously required a good deal of bravery. 'At the hazard of his life', Fielding said, Nicholas Bond secured three members of the so-called Finchley gang of housebreakers when he broke into a room in a public house 'and found them armed with a blunderbuss loaded to the muzzle, and several pistols and hangers.' The leader of the gang was taken by the runners after what was described as 'a stout resistance.' Bond may have had others with him, but he led the assault and caught the suspects unprepared.[95] John Heley was praised in the press for his 'activity in pursuit of offenders, and [his] intrepidity and bravery in seizing them.'[96] And Noakes and Clarke among others were similarly commended, the latter for arresting two men, one of whom attacked him with a knife.[97]

Giving evidence before the house of commons committee on the police of the metropolis in 1816, John Vickery was in no doubt that making arrests was dangerous, though perhaps becoming a little less so than it had been some decades earlier as crime seemed to be losing some of its most violent aspects. One

[91] OBP, September 1783 (John Barker and William Glanville) t17830910–36.
[92] OBP, December 1766 (Samuel Pointon) t17661217–44.
[93] *General Evening Post*, 12–14 May 1772.
[94] OBP, September 1779 (Mary Adey) t17790915–74.
[95] *London Evening Post*, 31 March–2 April, 2–4 April 1778. Bond was frequently praised for his bravery. He had earlier arrested two highwaymen in Chelsea who were suspected of killing one of their victims on the previous day. *General Evening Post*, 14–16 May 1776.
[96] *General Evening Post*, 28–30 April 1772.
[97] Ibid, 8–10 December 1772.

consequence of the lower levels of highway and street robbery in recent years, he said, and in particular of the milder administration of the law and reduction in capital punishment, was that officers had been 'much protected . . . in the apprehension of offenders.'[98] Nonetheless, he thought that officers continued to face dangerous situations from time to time and there was a need, he told the committee, for compensation for men injured on the job, provision for officers who received 'severe bodily injuries in the performance of their duty.' He spoke at length about the need for a settled retirement scheme for men 'worn out in the service.' It was, he said, 'a weary life, and wears men out very fast.' He himself had been wounded in 1814 attempting to take two men who had committed a murder.[99] John Sayer, testifying before the same committee, said that in his younger days, in the 1780s, the Bow Street men had faced some difficult opponents just patrolling the streets, let alone trying to make arrests. 'An officer could not walk in Duck-lane, Gravel-lane, or Cock-lane, without a party of five or six men along with him,' he told the committee; the gangs in these notorious places 'would have cut him to pieces if he was alone.'[100]

It is perhaps a measure of the danger of the job that no matter where they went in the metropolis the runners worked together, in pairs or larger groups. Payments from the office accounts in 1766 and 1767 reveal that only a quarter of the total were made to men acting alone, and in most cases those were for the least demanding work, such as collecting witnesses or distributing handbills. For the serious business of investigating crimes, going after and arresting offenders, patrolling, or observing crowds that had assembled on a ceremonial occasion when they expected pickpockets to be active, they most often went with a partner, usually the same partner. In total, close to 40 per cent of the payments made by Fielding and Marsden in those years went to pairs of officers. But almost as often they went out in larger groups, suggesting that they regularly expected to face difficulties in bringing in suspects, because of the number to be taken or because they anticipated having to face violent resistance. They also frequently went armed, with pistols and swords, and from time to time wounded or killed those they sought to arrest. When Sir Rowland Wynne was robbed by two footpads on the main road through Islington where several robberies had been reported in recent days, four runners were sent in a coach to find and arrest them; they were themselves attacked and, in firing back, killed one of the footpads.[101]

On some occasions, particularly when gangs of robbers had treated their victims with brutality, the runners went out in full force, all of them together, with

---

[98] *Committee on the Police of the Metropolis* (1816), 174.

[99] Ibid, 177, 179. Vickery's assailant had been charged with cutting and stabbing him, a capital offence, whether or not it caused death. At trial the weapon was identified as a poker and not capable of cutting or stabbing and the defendant was discharged, and then charged with assault. OBP, February 1814 (James King and William Evans) t18140216–40; *Times,* 18 January 1814.

[100] *Committee on the Police of the Metropolis* (1816), 212.

[101] *General Evening Post,* 12–14 May 1772. When a coach containing several officers and Fielding was stopped by footpads on the Chelsea road on a Saturday evening in 1773, the Bow Street men were all armed with pistols and shot and seriously wounded one of their attackers (*General Evening Post,* 30 January–2 February 1773).

assistants from the office and sometimes Westminster constables. They did so, for example, in March 1767 when a street gang injured several of their victims and killed one in the case with which I began this book. We learn from the account of the trial at the Old Bailey that John Griffiths and three other men had gone to Holloway to see a race of some kind. On their way back into the city, at about nine o'clock in the evening, it began to rain and they agreed to take a hackney coach the rest of the way. Within a few minutes the coach was stopped by a group of armed men. These were four sailors, shipmates who had been paid off some weeks before (according to their captain who gave evidence at their trial), several of them, perhaps all, Irishmen. They had spent the day drinking, at first at the Angel and Crown in Hornsey, north of Islington, an Irish pub where they knew the landlord's son, Thomas Fitzpatrick, who had been their shipmate. They drank a great deal and quarrelled among themselves and with the customers, and in the course of one argument one of them, Thomas Brown, had pulled out a pistol and threatened to blow a man's brains out. They had moved on to another alehouse until, in the evening and perhaps out of money, Brown proposed that they stop a coach. They were disappointed at their first attempt—the post-chaise was empty and they could only get two shillings and his shirt from the boy who was driving it—and were in no mood to be trifled with when they stopped the hackney coach carrying the four men from Holloway into the city. When one of the passengers tried to escape by jumping from the coach, he was knocked down and beaten. John Griffiths was even less fortunate. One of the sailors, Francis Gorman, came to his side of the coach, presented a pistol and said that there were 12 in the gang, that they wanted money, and that resistance was useless. There were in fact four, but they were drunk and clearly dangerous, and when Griffiths refused to give them money, Gorman put a pistol to his head and shot him. He died instantly. The robbers stayed long enough to collect £15 from the others in the coach before moving off. Nor was the killing of Griffiths sufficient to deter them from further violence. The next evening, Brown again urged them to take to the road and three from the previous night and two more of their shipmates did so, this time attacking the Newington stage coach, abusing the passengers and cutting one with a sword before stripping them of a watch, clothes, and money.

Bow Street became involved soon after news of the first robbery and murder reached the office. The chronology and much else about the subsequent investigation and arrests remains cloudy, but soon after the second robbery John Noakes and the other active Bow Street officers were searching for Gorman and his companions. That they knew to search in Whitechapel was almost certainly due to Thomas Fitzpatrick who must have reported his suspicions because he not only led Fielding's men to the East End, he was there with them to identify two of the robbers, Brown and Jeremiah Ryan, when they were spotted in the street. Brown got away, but Ryan was taken, and he provided the information that led to the arrest of Gorman and three others. Ryan knew where they lodged and where they were likely to be. When he was taken to Bow Street by Noakes, 'Sir John told him that if he was not the man who actually did the murder . . . he might be admitted [king's] evidence.' He sang to save his life, and the information enabled the Bow

Street men to find and arrest all of those involved in both robberies, except Brown. The search was led by Marsden, who later reported that they had gone to several public houses, including 'the Angel at St Agnes le Clear [Clare] where [the robbers] had been seen, at one Bath's where Sweetman had lodged, at the 3 Goats in White Chapel where one of them was known, at the White Lyon at Shadwell where they were taken.' They had also gone to a boxing match, where an informer (who was given 5s 3d.) said 'it was probable they might be'. The sailors had not been taken without a struggle because Marsden also reported that he had paid '10s 6d to Mr Brown Surgeon for Dressing [a] Wounded Man's head.'[102]

The accounts of the two trials in the *Sessions Papers* makes it seem that the only officer involved in the investigation and arrest was John Noakes, but the indictments reveal that Haliburton was also sworn as a witness before the grand jury, and Fielding's financial records make it clear that it had been in fact a very broad operation. Besides Noakes and Haliburton, Heley, Stephenson, Bond, and Henry Wright shared in the reward of £26.5.0 that Fielding paid from office funds, along with four other men who received some portion of that sum for their help, mainly, perhaps, for information. Fielding also awarded Marsden 10 guineas 'as a gratuity for Tracing and Conducting the Apprehension' of the robbers, as well as the £4.3.0 he claimed for expenses. Everyone involved would also have been eligible to receive some part of the parliamentary reward, £40 for each of the four men who were eventually convicted.[103]

In moving around the city quickly and in numbers, the runners relied on hiring coaches, another advantage made possible by the modest subvention from the government. They kept two horses for rapid pursuits, and hired others. But for making arrests or conducting the accused back and forth between Bow Street and Newgate and the other metropolitan gaols where they were held for trial or the pretrial process, hackney coaches were the most useful means of transport. The runners' frequent use of hired coaches is rarely revealed in newspaper reports or in trial accounts, except when the accused have complaints to make about the way they were treated on such journeys. But the office accounts in the 1750s and 1760s do make it clear how commonly the runners relied on coaches, picked up in the street perhaps, more often from one of the established waiting places near Bow Street. They had a list of such places at hand as well as a note of 'the Houses where Hackney Coachmen water their Horses in the Day time.'[104] The accounts for 1767

---

[102] TNA: T 1/454, f. 85. In the trials that followed, Gorman was convicted, sentenced to death on a Friday, executed (and his body dissected) the following Monday. Johnson who was tried with him as an accessory was also convicted but reprieved by the judge (OBP, April 1767 (Francis Gorman and Henry Johnson) t176704). Sweetman and Collins were convicted for the second robbery and sentenced to death (OBP, April 1767 (Lawrence Sweetman and Samuel Collins) t17670429–54). Ryan, who had turned king's evidence, was released. Brown was never taken.

[103] LMA: OB/SP/91, April 1767 (inds. 65, 67, 70–2); TNA: T 1/454, f. 84.

[104] NLI 15929 (3). These lists were helpful when the runners needed a coach quickly. They were also useful because hackney coachmen were thought to be an important source of information when thefts had involved trunks or other large objects. Knowing where they might be found made it possible to get handbills to them quickly, generally offering a reward for their cooperation.

show that Marsden paid £13 over the year for the hire of coaches for the runners.[105] This was not a great deal of money, but at a shilling or two a time, it supported the hiring of coaches three or more times a week on average. They were required for several purposes, but they were particularly important in investigations and making arrests.

Whether offenders were apprehended by the runners or brought in by the victims of alleged offences, the law required that they be brought before a magistrate if charges were to be laid. The runners took virtually all of the suspected felons they arrested to Bow Street where they would be examined by a magistrate and either committed to gaol to await trial at the next session of the Old Bailey or be granted bail—rare in felony cases in the eighteenth century—or have the charges against them dismissed, in which case they would be given their immediate freedom. With respect to the cases in which they had been in some way involved, the runners played an important role in the construction and presentation of the evidence for the prosecution at this pretrial hearing at Bow Street. They were also likely to be bound over to testify at the Old Bailey if the defendant they had given evidence against was committed for trial before judge and jury. This is our next subject, along with the innovations that John Fielding introduced into the pretrial procedures at Bow Street.

---

[105] TNA: T 1/454, *passim*.

5

Prosecution: The Runners in Court, 1765–1792

1. INTRODUCTION

In 1770, Sir John Fielding was one of three witnesses called before a house of commons committee enquiring into what was thought to have been a recent serious increase of offences in London, particularly of burglary and robbery. Fielding was able to tell the committee how many such offences had been reported to Bow Street in the previous four years—the only person in the country who could have given any estimate of the levels of reported offences—because, as he told the members, such felonies 'with the circumstances attending them, and particulars of goods stolen, are registered at his office.' His records revealed an increase in reported burglaries in the late 1760s, from 13 in a six-month peri:od over the winter of 1766–67 (with a total value of £280 in stolen goods) to 104, with a value of £4,241, in the six months before March 1770. Most had been the work of young men who were known in the Bow Street office, many of whom had been pickpockets as children and who had gone on to become burglars and housebreakers when they got older, Fielding thought, 'in order to procure a greater income to supply their increased expenses.'[1]

Asked for his advice about burglary and crime in general, Fielding's rather fragmentary evidence amounted in part to a plea for better preventive policing—for improvements in the night watch of Westminster by the engagement of more and younger men, increasing their pay, and removing the various parish watches from the control of watch committees that failed to communicate one with the other, putting them instead under a central commission of magistrates.[2] He expanded on familiar arguments about the need to attack the roots of crime by imposing stricter controls over the behaviour of the poor. He urged the committee to legislate changes in the licensing laws, for example, in order to close down many of the taverns and night-houses (especially the many dozens in the vicinity of Covent Garden) that shielded and supported thieves and encouraged men and women who could ill afford it to waste their time and money. And he suggested that prostitutes be labelled as vagrants so they could be subjected to the stern penalties of the Vagrancy Act of 1744.

---

[1] *JHC*, 32, 878–82; *Parl. Debates*, 16 (1770), 929–43.
[2] For Fielding's testimony to this parliamentary committee with respect to the Westminster watch, see Elaine A. Reynolds, *Before the Bobbies: the Night Watch and Police Reform in Metropolitan London, 1720–1830* (London, 1998), 48–50.

In addition to those measures, Fielding went on to say that it was essential to enforce the law if crime was to be prevented. In this respect, he continued, burglary and housebreaking presented problems. Because of the Bow Street system of rapid distribution of information about offences in the press and via handbills, and his success in persuading large and well-established pawnbrokers, silversmiths, and other similar dealers to cooperate with his office by reporting or stopping suspicious clients, Fielding thought that most minor offenders were seeking new outlets for stolen goods. As they saw the danger in using what had once been their main outlets, offenders were increasingly turning to small-time receivers—mainly Jews, he claimed. It was not only more difficult for his men to get to know who the receivers were, it was also now more likely that the crucial evidence in any burglary case—the stolen goods—would be altered and incapable of being identified in court because instead of selling off valuable items like silver or jewellery into the established circuits of stolen goods, receivers were now choosing to melt down plate and remove jewels from their settings. All of this required more developed policing, both detection and investigation on the part of his men, a more intense pretrial construction of evidence, and more careful preparation of cases to be sent to trial. It was these requirements and ambitions that lay behind a complex set of plans that Fielding put in motion in the late 1760s and the early years of the following decade.[3]

One element in Fielding's ideas about making policing of property offences more effective in these years involved an extension of the gathering and circulating of information about crime, offenders, and stolen goods. Bow Street had become a clearing house for information about crime across the metropolis, and to some extent for information about provincial crime too. From his first years in the office, Fielding had been in touch with provincial magistrates about problems in their jurisdictions or about offenders they wanted to track down who may have fled to London. In the policing plan he put before the government at the end of the Seven Years War, he had hoped to enlarge his budget to enable him to establish a newspaper that would be distributed across the country carrying information about offenders being sought for offences in London and elsewhere—a form of police gazette.[4] He returned to these ideas in 1772, with a much expanded scheme—a 'General Preventive Plan'—designed to create a national network of criminal information to be coordinated from Bow Street. The plan, outlined in five circular letters that Fielding sent to magistrates in towns and counties in England

---

[3] The commons committee duly reported a number of resolutions, incorporating the suggestions laid out by Fielding and the other witnesses—the high constable and deputy high steward of Westminster. But apart from the introduction and passage of legislation that made it possible for receivers of jewels and plate taken in the course of burglary or highway robbery to be convicted as principal offenders, whether or not those they dealt with were also convicted (10 Geo 3, c. 48 (1770), little else followed immediately. Fielding's recommendations about improving the night watch did give rise to further discussion both in parliament and in the parishes of Westminster, with the result that a major piece of legislation was passed in 1774, on which see Elaine Reynolds, 'Sir John Fielding, Sir Charles Whitworth, and the Westminster Night Watch Act, 1770–1775', *Criminal Justice History*, XVI (2002), 1–22; and *idem, Before the Bobbies*, 50–7.

[4] See ch. 3, text at n. 98.

and Wales between September 1772 and September 1773,[5] depended on the willingness of magistrates throughout the country to send him the names and descriptions of suspects who had fled from justice. Fielding undertook to include the names of such suspects in a printed list to be circulated to every bench of magistrates in the country four times a year in the hope that they would print copies and send one to the constables in their jurisdictions to be displayed on the doors of parish churches in the countryside and on boards in public places in towns.

This was 'the first stone' of his national policing plan, Fielding said in his initial circular letter of 22 September 1772. The second, described more fully in another letter a few weeks later, was a scheme to publish a weekly list of such offenders in a newspaper that he intended to send without charge to the chief magistrates in towns and to the active magistrates in counties, again in the hope that the information would be widely distributed. In its first year, from October 1772, Fielding arranged to have this information included on the front page of the Monday edition of the thrice-weekly London newspaper, *The London Packet* or *New Lloyd's Evening Post*. Thereafter, having received an addition of £400 to his budget for the purpose, he published it in his own paper, *The Hue and Cry*. Fielding's fundamental intention in establishing his General Preventive Plan, as he said in his third circular letter—repeating a theme he had emphasized from the beginning—was to save lives by reducing crime.[6]

A national system of criminal information, circulating throughout the country, would make it certain, so he believed, that offenders would be caught and brought to justice and that anyone contemplating an offence would be deterred from doing so. Like his brother before him, Fielding believed that serious crime would only be reduced if the criminal law was vigorously enforced. And, to this end, he also took steps in the early 1770s, as he developed his national plan, to intensify the prosecution of crime in London. He introduced innovations at Bow Street that were to have a profound effect on the nature of pretrial procedures and on the settings in which justices managed the crucial first stage of criminal prosecution. Fielding found ways to make the services at Bow Street available to the public for long and regular hours. In addition, he created a court-like setting that attracted and accommodated a large audience for his examinations of suspected offenders. Bow Street was transformed in this way from being merely the house of a busy London magistrate into a magistrates' court in which several justices served in

---

[5] Copies of the first three circular letters are at TNA: SP 37/9/275–7. Two of these and two others are printed by Radzinowicz, *History of English Criminal Law*, 3, Appendix I, 479–81, 482–4. Radzinowicz discusses Fielding's 'General Preventive Plan' at 47–54. The best account of the Plan, its context and implications, is John Styles, 'Sir John Fielding and the problem of criminal investigation in Eighteenth-Century England', *Transactions of the Royal Historical Society*, 5th series, 33 (1983), esp. 135–49, which goes beyond the circular letters to local newspapers and to the records of provincial benches to uncover their responses to Fielding's plan in 1772 and to its further development in subsequent years. And see John Styles, 'Print and Policing: Crime Advertising in Eighteenth-Century Provincial England' in Douglas Hay and Francis Snyder (eds.), *Policing and Prosecution in Britain, 1750–1850* (Oxford, 1989), 55–111, which illuminates the broad subject of advertising and criminal detection in the eighty years after 1750.

[6] Radzinowicz, *History of English Criminal Law*, vol. 3, 479–81.

rotation to keep the office open at stated hours every day. Fielding's determination to enlarge the magistrates' role in the prosecution of serious crime in the capital and to send stronger cases to trial at the Old Bailey also led him to create what was essentially a new stage in pretrial procedure—a stage in which some accused felons, already committed to trial, would be brought back to Bow Street to a special session held once a week through the 1770s at which they were 're-examined' before an audience in the hope that further evidence of their guilt would be produced. The impact of these special re-examination sessions was further magnified by Fielding's success in encouraging the London press to attend and to provide their readers with a weekly report on his efforts as a 'public servant' (as he thought of himself) to combat crime in the metropolis.

To strengthen prosecution cases being sent to trial at the Old Bailey, Fielding concentrated on the effective gathering and presentation of evidence. He was not content as a magistrate simply to accept and process whatever evidence the prosecutor/victim and his or her witnesses brought to him, which was inevitably the situation of virtually all justices of the peace in England since they had no investigatory or evidence-gathering machinery at their command. In Fielding's case, the runners provided independent evidence in at least some of the cases that came before the magistrates at Bow Street and, as William Mainwaring, the chairman of the Middlesex quarter sessions, said in 1792, they made it possible for Fielding and his successors to be prosecuting magistrates.[7] The runners also supported prosecutions by testifying at the Bow Street committal sessions and in cases sent to trial at the Old Bailey.

2. JOHN FIELDING AND THE BOW STREET MAGISTRATES' COURT

John Fielding and other magistrates who acted at Bow Street dealt with the full range of issues that came the way of the several dozen justices of the peace who served for Westminster and the Middlesex parishes within the metropolis. Apart from felony allegations, London magistrates took up a wide range of charges involving assault or other misdemeanours, and they acted in their own parlours or in association with others in petty sessions to adjudicate conflicts between employers and their workers over wages or mistreatment, and, among many other things, disputes between parishes over Poor Law issues or other administrative matters.[8] The work undertaken by the Bow Street magistrates was not in

---

[7] In the debate on the 1792 bill: *Parl. Debates*, 29 (1792),1179.

[8] For the work of justices of the peace, see Norma Landau, *The Justices of the Peace, 1679–1760* (Berkeley, 1984); and for magistrates' powers of summary justice in the late eighteenth and early nineteenth centuries, Peter King, *Crime, Justice and Discretion in England 1740–1820* (Oxford, 2000), ch. 4; *idem, Crime and Law in England, 1750–1840: Remaking Justice from the Margins* (Cambridge, 2006), ch. 1; *idem*, 'The Summary Courts and Social Relations in Eighteenth-Century England,' *Past and Present*, 183 (2004), 125–72; Bruce P. Smith, 'The Presumption of Guilt and the English Law of Theft, 1750–1850,' *Law and History Review*, 23 (1, 2005), 133–72; *idem*, 'Did the Presumption of

principle any different in this respect from their Westminster and Middlesex colleagues. As we have seen, the Bow Street magistrates were not among the leaders when it came to the prosecution of minor offences.[9] The balance of their work—certainly in John Fielding's day—was more on the side of felony allegations than that of other metropolitan justices.

Fielding made an effort to make the services of Bow Street available as widely as possible, and encouraged other magistrates in the metropolis to follow his lead. He had urged the government of George Grenville to increase the number of stipendiary magistrates who would be free to devote themselves full-time to the work of criminal prosecution in a system coordinated by Bow Street.[10] That having failed, he encouraged justices in Westminster and other parts of the metropolis to work together voluntarily to create offices in which, by attending in turn, they could provide magisterial service to the public at fixed times during the week.[11] Such so-called 'rotation offices' did indeed emerge over the next 30 years. Some were short-lived; others became more settled, though even those were stronger at some periods than others, dependent as they were on the personalities of the magistrates and their willingness to serve. But over the next three decades the public was able to find magistrates at regular hours at a number of busy locations—in Westminster, Clerkenwell, Shoreditch, Whitechapel, and Shadwell, and at St Margaret's Hill in Southwark, across the river.[12]

These offices were established in public places—in the Guildhall in Westminster, in the vestry rooms of parish churches—not in the private houses in which most magistrates had previously worked. From the beginning they were known as 'public offices'. They also attracted numbers of thief-takers who became 'attached', or who attached themselves, to the offices and performed some of the tasks that Fielding's runners carried out. Even the most stable of these rotation offices remained in Bow Street's shadow, however, in large part because they lacked its great advantage: resources. The government's subvention (increased for the purpose) enabled Fielding to create a fully-functioning and effective rotation system that was not matched by the other public offices until parliament provided them with financial support in 1792.[13]

From his earliest days in the office, Fielding had had the help of associate magistrates. When Saunders Welch moved to his own magistrates' office in Litchfield Street, Fielding found other Westminster magistrates to share the work of the office. John Spinnage acted occasionally in the 1750s and by 1765 he was sitting

Innocence Exist in Summary Proceedings?' *Law and History Review*, 23 (1, 2005), 191–9; Norma Landau, 'Summary Conviction and the Development of the Penal Law,' *Law and History Review*, 23 (1, 2005), 173–89; Drew D. Gray, *Crime, Prosecution, and social relations: the summary courts of the City of London in the late eighteenth century* (London, 2009).

[9] Ch. 4, text at n. 11.
[10] Ch. 3, text at n. 8.
[11] LMA: MC/SJ (Rotation Committee Papers, 1763–4).
[12] The complex history of the emergence of these rotation offices and of the magistrates who attended them has been masterfully unravelled by Ruth Paley, 'The Middlesex Justices Act of 1792: its origins and effects,' Ph.D. thesis (University of Reading, 1983), chs. 3–7.
[13] See ch. 6, section 4.

regularly one day a week, occasionally more frequently. Soon thereafter he was in receipt of a stipend from the government.[14] Two other justices, William Kelynge and Thomas Kynaston, were acting at Bow Street by 1763–64, and they too were given stipends to ensure their regular attendance when in 1768 Fielding persuaded the Grafton administration to increase its financial support for his work. All of this served Fielding's ambition to establish what he on one occasion called a 'Felony Rotation,'[15] that is, an office served by a sufficient number of magistrates that he could guarantee it would be open to the public on stated hours every day of the week. When Kelynge and Kynaston were given stipends in 1768, Fielding was able to announce that the Bow Street office would be open 'every day from Ten to Two, and from Five to Nine.'[16]

In an advertisement in the *Gazetteer* in 1771 setting out these regular hours, Fielding emphasized the public nature of the office. 'The freest access [is] allowed to every body,' he wrote, 'whether brought there by business or curiosity, so that any person may constantly have an opportunity of being present at the transactions of the Magistrates who sit there.'[17] To encourage that attendance and to support a new system of examination emerging in the early 1770s, Fielding also found the resources to create a new courtroom in 1772 which decisively confirmed Bow Street's difference from other public offices outside the City of London. Up to that point, the Fieldings and Sir Thomas De Veil before them had conducted magisterial business in what was essentially the parlour at Bow Street. This is the room illustrated in a print of 1743 showing De Veil smoking a pipe, examining a suspect in a relaxed and informal way. He is sitting back in an armchair, behind a table which has room at one end for Brogden, his clerk, who is shown apparently taking a deposition. In the background, a dozen or so figures wait their turn to appear before the justice, and the open door shows a crowd outside (Plate 1).[18] The room is also illustrated in a drawing by Marcellus Laroon, which may exaggerate the apparent disorder in the room in the interest of heightening the drama, but confirms an essential point that in the middle years of the century, pretrial hearings at Bow Street were conducted in an informal way.[19]

---

[14] Spinnage received £100 from the office funds in 1765 (TNA: T 1/449, f. 45).

[15] TNA: SP 44/138, 182 (I am grateful to Norma Landau for that reference).

[16] Sir John Fielding, *Extracts from such of the Penal Laws as Particularly relate to the Peace and Good Order of this Metropolis* (London, 1768; first edn. 1761), 7. Edward Sayer, the deputy high steward of Westminster, later recalled that a system of stipendiary magistrates was being discussed in 1768 for the City of Westminster. It may have been the failure of that more general plan that enabled Fielding to persuade the Grafton administration to increase their support for his office. Edward Sayer, *Observations on the Police or Civil Government of Westminster with a Proposal for a Reform* (London, 1784), 32–3.

[17] *Gazetteer and New Daily Advertiser*, 5 January 1771.

[18] Also reproduced in Clare Graham, *Ordering Law: The Architectural and Social History of the English Law Court to 1914* (Aldershot, Hampshire, 2003), 168.

[19] Reproduced by Martin C. Battestin with Ruthe R. Battestin, *Henry Fielding: A Life* (1989), Plate 52. It is entitled, 'Night Walkers before a Justice'. Laroon dated it 1740 towards the end of his life when, Martin Battestin suggests, his memory was seriously faulty. Battestin argues that the drawing dates from a decade later and that the magistrate pictured is Henry Fielding (at ix–x). What is mainly significant about this image for my purpose is the setting. It is simply a room. The only furniture is a table and chair, and there is no barrier between the magistrate and women accused of being prostitutes (and some of their male clients) who have been brought in by watchmen for questioning.

Plate 1. Sir Thomas De Veil conducting magisterial business at Bow Street, 1742 [City of Westminster Archives Centre].

On occasion committal hearings attracted an audience. Crowds in his 'office-room', as De Veil called it, were common enough that he complained about the opportunities they provided for men he called 'Newgate Solicitors, and other very crafty Persons' to attend the magistrates' pretrial proceedings to give advice to suspects under examination.[20] Such crowds of onlookers may explain why the settings in which those hearings were carried on were beginning to change by the second quarter of the century, why Bow Street magistrates were beginning to add features that in time created a space reserved for the justices and the clerical staff, a place where defendants would stand to be examined, and seats for the audience. Though neither artist chose to show it, De Veil's room included a 'bar' of some kind by 1747, behind which presumably the accused stood or that perhaps held back the crowd. In time, the magistrates' office-room came more closely to resemble the courtrooms in which trials themselves were conducted.

The idea for such a court-like setting in which magistrates would manage their criminal business may have arisen from developments in the City of London where, instead of acting individually in their own houses, the aldermen began in 1737 to act in rotation in a space marked off in a gallery in Guildhall, each taking a day's duty in turn. Provision was made in this new room for a bar that separated the magistrate and his clerk from prosecutors, constables, witnesses, and the accused.[21] An even more direct model was provided by the purpose-built courtroom included in the Mansion House, the official residence built for the lord mayor and opened in 1752. In this courtroom, the mayor presided daily during his year in office, in parallel with the daily session in Guildhall, carrying out all the duties expected of a magistrate in a setting that clearly separated him from the prostitutes, vagrants, accused felons, and other suspects brought in to be examined.[22]

These developments in the City may have encouraged John Fielding to go beyond the simple 'bar' that De Veil had introduced at Bow Street to create a more formal setting for this first stage of criminal prosecutions. There was still a good deal of informality in the early 1760s, with attendees standing and perhaps milling about. On one occasion in 1763, a suspect offered to write a confession, and when given pen, ink, and paper, began to write but soon asked Marsden how to spell 'Murder'. He refused to tell him, on the grounds that it would have been 'an improper Thing' for him to 'Dictate.' But, Marsden recalled, 'Several Noblemen were there, and I think it was the Earl of Sandwich told him how to spell it.'[23] Fielding's new courtroom provided a more formal setting. It was constructed in 1772 in the yard behind the house, and was approached by way of an anteroom in

---

[20] Sir Thomas De Veil, *Observations on the Practice of a Justice of the Peace* (London, 1747), 2, 4.

[21] This is the space illustrated by William Hogarth in Plate 10 of Industry and Idleness. See J. M. Beattie, *Policing and Punishment in London, 1660–1750: Urban Crime and the Limits of Terror* (Oxford, 2001), 109.

[22] Sally Jeffrey, *The Mansion House* (Chichester, 1993), 205, 214–17.

[23] *Select trials for murder, robbery, burglary . . . and other offences. . . .* (4 vols., London, 1764) IV, 246; quoted by Andrea McKenzie, *Tyburn's Martyrs. Execution in England, 1675–1775* (London, 2007), 44.

Engraved for The Malefactor's Register.

Dodd delin. Taylor sculp.

View of the **PUBLIC OFFICE** Bow Street, with Sir John Fielding presiding, & a Prisoner under examination.

Plate 2. Public Office, Bow Street, with Sir John Fielding presiding, 1779 [City of Westminster Archives Centre].

which defendants could be held while waiting to go before the magistrate.[24] Fielding retained a more private office in which he occasionally took depositions and examined accused offenders. James Hackman, who murdered Martha Ray, Lord Sandwich's mistress, was, for example, examined in Fielding's private room.[25] But virtually all magisterial business at Bow Street was conducted in this new public courtroom. It is illustrated in *The Malefactor's Register* (1779), where it is portrayed as very much Fielding's court. He is shown seated in an armchair on a dais, the familiar black band across his eyes, dominating the proceedings at what was undoubtedly a session held on Wednesday mornings in which accused offenders were re-examined. Other magistrates are present, but they had to be content with distinctly secondary places on benches on either side of him. A clerk sits at a table in front of the dais to record the proceedings, and a prisoner stands to be examined some distance in front of him behind a bar. In the room itself there are seats for prosecutors, witnesses, the public, and the press (Plate 2).[26]

The construction of the Bow Street court confirmed Fielding's leading role in the prosecution of serious crime in the capital. As a magistrate who encouraged the public to report offences to his office and who sent men to investigate crimes and apprehend and bring in suspected offenders, he was inevitably more concerned than most justices of the peace to collect and organize the evidence that would support the prosecution when he sent a case to trial at the Old Bailey. That certainly was his reputation. Victims of property offences looking to get back their stolen belongings, or at least to bring their assailants to justice, clearly thought that Bow Street offered the most effective help in the metropolis. The keeper of Newgate prison was exaggerating when he said in 1757 that he received 'commitments from [Fielding] almost every day'—that is, prisoners committed to his gaol

---

[24] It was described in a newspaper in 1778 as 'the large office at the back of [Sir John Fielding's] house, which was exceedingly crowded' and in which several suspects 'were put to the bar' (*London Evening Post*, 2–4 April 1778). For other glimpses of the room see, e.g., OBP, April 1775 (Daniel Gregory and Richard Barrett) t17750426–8; OBP, September 1783 (Thomas Booker) t17830910–38; OBP, May 1780 (William Edwards) t17800510–2. Contemporaries called it a room or large office. Although it is anachronistic to call it a courtroom, I do so to make the point that it represented something very different from a mere parlour in a justices's residence and that Fielding introduced a significant change in the way magistrates met the public.

[25] John Brewer, *A Sentimental Murder: love and madness in the eighteenth century* (New York, 2004), 24.

[26] *The Malefactor's Register: or, the Newgate and Tyburn Calendar* (5 vols., 1779) vol. 3, frontispiece. This engraving is reproduced in John H. Langbein, 'Shaping the Eighteenth-Century Criminal Trial', *The University of Chicago Law Review* 50 (Winter, 1983), 74, in Ronald Leslie-Melville, *The Life and Work of Sir John Fielding* (London, 1934), frontispiece, and in Graham, *Ordering Law*, 170. The gallery may be fanciful, possibly also the seats, at least the large number of seats shown. An attorney who attended Bow Street in 1780, just after Fielding's death, said that he had entered the room and 'sat on the bench,' making it sound like something provided for the audience not the justices (James Oldham, *The Mansfield Manuscripts and the growth of English law in the eighteenth century* (2 vols., Chapel Hill, 1992) 2, 1024). This man fell into conflict with justice Addington over his right to be there and to ask questions. See below text at n.145.

Plate 3. Sir John Fielding by Nathaniel Hone, 1762 [© National Portrait Gallery]

to await trial.[27] But (with respect to felonies) Fielding was certainly the most active magistrate in Middlesex. In his first decade in office, more than a third of the accused felons sent for trial at the Old Bailey from Middlesex were committed as a result of proceedings at Bow Street, the vast majority conducted by Fielding himself (Table 5.1). That predominance became even more striking when the three-magistrate rotation system was fully in place by the late 1760s, for in the years 1767 to 1773 almost half of all Middlesex felony commitments originated in the Bow Street office. By the last years of the 1770s increasing numbers of commitments were being made by the magistrates in the other emerging public offices—particularly Litchfield Street, Shoreditch, and Whitechapel—a pattern that was to continue and indeed to become more pronounced in the 1780s. But in Fielding's day prosecutors were most likely to go to Bow Street with their complaints, and there can be no doubt about his leading role in organizing the evidence in many of the felony cases tried at the Old Bailey.[28] After his death, the

---

[27] He had been asked in court if he could identify Fielding's signature and replied that he could do so because he saw his distinctive scrawl on the documents accompanying the commitment of accused felons very frequently (OBP, January 1757 (Charles Butler) t17570114–30.

[28] In a sample of eight sessions in the years 1782–92 (following Fielding's death), commitments from Bow Street were to fall to a level of just over 20%. For Bow Street commitments after 1780, see ch. 7, text at n. 35.

Table 5.1. Commitments by magistrates to trial at the Old Bailey, 1756–80[1]

Period	Sessions	Total Commitments	Bow Street Commitments	%
1756–66	6	303	109	36.0
1767–73	8	626	304	48.6
1774–80	6	564	213	37.8
N	20	1493	626	41.9

[1] Source: LMA: OB/SR, gaol calendars. Based on a sample of 20 of 192 sessions.

long-serving deputy high steward of Westminster, Edward Sayer, confirmed that he had been the most active Westminster magistrate.[29] That would also have been clear to those familiar with the printed *Proceedings* of the court, in which his name was commonly invoked and the work of the Bow Street office frequently mentioned.[30]

Frequent notices of his work in the *Proceedings* help to explain why Fielding acquired a wide reputation as an active and knowledgeable magistrate and why numerous private prosecutors giving their opening evidence at Bow Street said they had been advised to go to him, even if it meant a long journey across the metropolis. Magistrates at the rotation offices may to some extent have been in competition with Bow Street: unlike Fielding and the other stipendiary magistrates who worked there, their incomes depended on the fees that arose from the paperwork required by the prosecution process.[31] But his abilities were also recognized by other metropolitan magistrates who on occasion sent him cases that required knowledge and skill beyond their capacities; as a Shadwell justice said in advising a constable to take a suspect to Bow Street, 'Sir John knew better what to do [in the matter] than he did'.[32] The support available to the victim-prosecutor at Bow Street also helps to explain why the office became so dominant in the third quarter of the eighteenth century. No other magistrate in the metropolis could command the services of as experienced a group of men as the runners, whose help in finding and apprehending offenders might be provided gratis to private prosecutors if the Bow Street justices chose to send them. Bow Street could also

[29] Sayer, *Observations on the Police or Civil Government of Westminster*, iv.

[30] John Langbein detected Fielding's hand in the printed reports of half the cases tried in the October 1754 session in which the pretrial work of magistrates is disclosed, a figure that reflects both the level of his activity and the fact that he dealt more frequently than other magistrates with the kinds of serious cases that the printer of the Proceedings was likely to feature. Langbein, 'Shaping the Eighteenth-Century Criminal Trial', 69.

[31] Norma Landau has shown that Fielding was criticized by the Middlesex bench on at least one occasion for interfering in the prosecution of a case that had originated with another magistrate: 'The trading justice's trade' in Norma Landau (ed.), *Law, Crime and English Society, 1660–1830* (Cambridge, 2002), 58.

[32] OBP, December 1765, Stephen Wheat and Robert Tull (t17651211–48).

help by getting stolen goods advertised and getting handbills distributed immediately to the major pawnbrokers and other likely receivers, the cost of which might also be paid for by the office. But the principal attraction that drew prosecutors to Bow Street in the 1760s and 1770s was almost certainly John Fielding's reputation as an examiner, his ability to draw out prosecution evidence and uncover weaknesses in the responses of the accused, his capacity to frame and organize a strong and effective prosecution case.

John Fielding's growing reputation made Bow Street the leading centre of criminal prosecution in the metropolis and, indeed, in the country, for his advice and the help of the runners were frequently sought by provincial magistrates. The runners gave evidence from time to time at provincial assizes, particularly on the Home Circuit—in the counties surrounding the metropolis.[33] But what particularly distinguished Bow Street under Fielding was the way he expanded the pretrial process into a more extensive search for evidence than the law required. In doing so, he helped to accelerate a process that had been underway for several decades before he came to Bow Street, a process that was fundamentally changing the nature of magistrates' pretrial work.

In examining accused felons in the early years of the eighteenth century, magistrates appear to have continued to adhere to the requirements of legislation dating from the mid-sixteenth century under which they were given very little leeway in decision-making. They were instructed by the bail and commitment statutes of the reign of Mary I to take depositions of the victim and prosecution witnesses, and to examine the accused, summarizing any response they offered. They were required to ensure that a trial would take place by binding victims over in recognizances to carry on the prosecution and by committing defendants to a place of confinement, bail being only rarely allowed in felony cases.[34] Justices' handbooks through the eighteenth century—including the multiple editions of Richard Burn's authoritative guide—continued to advise magistrates not to interpose their own judgement, but simply to complete the paperwork and send every case on to trial.[35] Justices of the peace seem largely to have heeded that advice for 150 years. But by the third decade of the eighteenth century, London magistrates had assumed a discretionary power to dismiss cases that they thought should not go to trial—almost certainly because new elements on the prosecution side had begun to change the balance in criminal justice administration to the disadvantage

---

[33] The runners gave evidence, e.g., in felony cases tried at the assizes on the Home Circuit—the counties surrounding London. In four assize sessions in Surrey, surveyed between 1770 and 1790, a total of 18 Bow Street officers gave evidence in 26 cases; in Essex in four sessions in the same years, 12 runners appeared in seven cases; and in Kent, eight testified in five trials (TNA: ASSI/94/1059–62, 1124–7, 1329–35, 1258–61). For the runners' involvement in cases in Essex in the 1780s, see King, *Crime, Justice, and Discretion*, 78.

[34] For the statute of Queen Mary's reign governing the magistrates' committal procedures (2 & 3 Ph. & Mary, *c.* 10 (1555)), see John H. Langbein, *The Origins of Adversary Criminal Trial* (Oxford, 2003), 40–2.

[35] Richard Burn, *The Justice of the Peace and Parish Officer* (3rd. edn., 1756), 207.

of the defendant.[36] John Fielding was also prepared to dismiss the charges against an accused felon when he judged the evidence unlikely to lead to a conviction. But in his case such an exercise of discretionary power was only one aspect of a larger set of practices that he developed in the pretrial process that changed the character of committal procedures at Bow Street. Fielding's activism took him well beyond the passive role the Tudor legislation prescribed. For him, the pretrial hearing was not simply a bureaucratic step in the process by which the charges against accused felons came to be tried by a judge and jury, but rather a continuation and integral part of his policing activities. He expanded the role of the magistrate in the pretrial phase of criminal prosecution beyond any previous practice by developing what came to be known as re-examinations.[37]

Henry Fielding seems to have been the first magistrate to bring suspected felons whom he had already committed to trial back to Bow Street to answer further charges or to be further questioned.[38] He may have thought he was empowered to do so by a clause of the Disorderly Houses Act of 1752 which authorized magistrates to hold vagrants or suspected felons for a period no longer than six days 'for further examination' to give local authorities time to publish an advertisement (if they chose to do so) describing the man or woman being held and what they had been carrying when apprehended—an addition to magisterial authority Fielding had advocated.[39] That may have provided authority for a 'further examination' before a suspect was either committed or discharged. But John Fielding's practice went beyond that by bringing offenders already committed back to Bow Street to be examined again. Fielding used such 're-examinations' extensively, and advertised them ahead of time, in hopes that additional evidence would come to

---

[36] The principal changes were introduced by rewards offered in statutes in the 1690s and by the central government after 1720 to encourage the prosecution and conviction of violent offenders. They mainly seem to have encouraged thief-takers who sought to profit from the large sums being offered by arranging prosecutions and ensuring convictions by any means available. The dangers of corrupt prosecutions and of perjured evidence unsettled what had hitherto been perceived in felony trials as a balanced confrontation between two equally unprepared amateurs and brought responses from both judges and magistrates. London magistrates began to assume a discretionary power to dismiss some suspected felons brought before them on the grounds that the evidence was not persuasive and that the charges had not been made by prosecutors prepared to swear on oath that they believed the accused to be the perpetrator of the offence in question, but rather had made that assertion simply as a matter of suspicion. Langbein, *The Origins of Adversary Criminal Trial*, ch. 3; Beattie, *Policing and Punishment in London*, ch. 2.

[37] For a fuller account of Fielding's re-examination procedure at Bow Street in the 1770s, see J. M. Beattie, 'Sir John Fielding and Public Justice: the Bow Street Magistrates' Court, 1754–1780,' *Law and History Review*, 25 (1, 2007), 61–100.

[38] In January 1753 a defendant was said to have been 'brought from New Prison [to Bow Street] a second time.' OBP, January 1753 (Joseph Hall) t17530111-27.

[39] 25 Geo II, c. 36, s. 12 (1752). According to Henry Fielding's account of a Bow Street session at which he examined 30 'idle, dissolute, and suspicious persons,' several members of parliament who were present 'declared themselves sensible of the Necessity of a Law to detain all such suspicious Vagabonds, till they can be advertized, and seen by Persons lately robb'd.' *The Covent-Garden Journal and a Plan of the Universal Register Office*, ed. Bertrand A. Goldgar (Middletown, CT, 1988), 403. For Fielding's interest in this addition to magisterial authority, see King, *Crime, Justice, and Discretion*, 94–5.

light (if victims of similar offences were in attendance, for example) and thus bring further support to the prosecution when the charges were heard at the Old Bailey.[40]

In his effort to convict the highwayman, William Page, in 1757, for example, John Fielding announced his arrest in *The Public Advertiser*, along with accounts of his offences and a list of the watches Page had pawned (information supplied by his accomplice, who had turned king's evidence).[41] A later advertisement announced that 'Page will be re-examined before Justice Fielding, on Tuesday next at One o'Clock.'[42] The point of such re-examinations was made explicit in the case of a gang of five footpads apprehended at the same time and accused of committing robberies in and around London. An accomplice had provided Fielding with the details of 17 of their robberies—information about victims, locations, and property taken—and the re-examination was advertised as taking place on the same day as Page's, 'when all Persons that have lately been robbed are desired to attend.' The outcome, as another notice in the press a week later revealed, was that sufficient evidence had appeared at the Bow Street hearing to put these accused footpads to their trials.[43]

By the late 1760s re-examinations became weekly events and brought the Bow Street magistrates' court increasingly into the public eye. What had been an ad hoc system—a re-examination being announced whenever an appropriate suspect was to be returned to Bow Street on a particular day—became an established part of the Bow Street routine, with a session being held every Wednesday from 10 a.m. to 3 p.m. and occasionally continuing on the following Friday. The regularity with which these sessions came to be staged was made possible by the stipends given to Joseph Kelynge and Thomas Kynaston, and to their successors—Sampson Wright (by June 1772) and William Addington (in 1774). The addition of two salaried magistrates enabled Fielding not only to keep the Bow Street office open to the public every day at fixed times, but also to stage what was in effect a weekly petty session. By 1768, a bench of magistrates were to be in attendance at Bow Street on Wednesday mornings, Fielding announced, 'to hear complaints relating to public nuisances . . . and to transact such other public business as requires the presence of more than one Magistrate.' But in addition, the Wednesday session formed a key element in his effort to strengthen and support the charges being developed against accused felons whose cases would be going to trial at the Old Bailey. Fielding announced at the same time that he intended to bring back to Bow Street all 'Prisoners as have been committed in the preceding Week' in order to re-examine

---

[40] For the importance of the re-examination session at Bow Street under the Fieldings, see Langbein, 'Shaping the Eighteenth-Century Criminal Trial', 64, n. 243. I assume that the practice of re-examination explains why in the Old Bailey gaol calendars of the 1750s, some defendants are said to have been 'committed' for trial by a named magistrate on a given date and then 'detained' by the same or another magistrate on a later date (LMA: OB/SR). By the middle of the 1760s such entries are common in many sessions.

[41] *The Public Advertiser*, 10 August 1757 (repeated in the next five issues).

[42] Ibid, 1 September 1757.

[43] Ibid, 8 September 1757; on 26 September 1757, Fielding announced in the same paper that 'the supposed Highwayman Henry Clarke' had been arrested, and he encouraged victims of robberies near London over the previous three months to come to Bow Street the following day at 2 p.m. when Clarke was to be re-examined.

them.[44] In fact, not all prisoners were re-examined, and some of those coming before the magistrates on Wednesday mornings were there for the first time. But re-examining selected suspects was the main purpose of that weekly session.

Publicity was crucial to this enterprise and Fielding went out of his way to attract an audience to these weekly sessions—those who were simply interested in hearing the details of criminal charges as well as victims of recent offences. To attract the press, Fielding provided 'the printer of a morning paper . . . with a desk and pen, ink and paper,' according to a critic who disapproved of such publicity.[45] For their part the publishers of London newspapers found the re-examination sessions an attractive source of copy.

From 1772 to the end of the decade (when, as we will see, powerful objections were raised against the practice) London newspapers, daily and tri-weekly, provided accounts in their Thursday editions of the previous day's session.[46] They varied in length, depending on what other news there was to report and on the interest of the cases that had come before the justices. If there had been little business of interest, they might be brief. But more often the accounts of the Wednesday re-examination sessions at Bow Street occupied a good part of a column or more in papers that typically devoted only a page or two (each with four columns) to domestic news. Four of the eight reports in the January and February editions of the *Morning Chronicle* in 1775, for example, occupied more than a column each, and none was less than a half column. The number of cases dealt with in the weekly reports also varied. In a sample of two months every year between 1772 and 1780 the number of cases reported in the Thursday papers ranged between one and 17,with an average of about seven. Three-quarters of the cases included in these accounts of the magistrates' proceedings at Bow Street were felonies (five per session, on average)— overwhelmingly robbery, burglary and varieties of larceny (Table 5.2). They created pretrial publicity in ordinary felony cases on an unprecedented scale.

The examination of Thomas Broadhead in April 1773 provides a good example of the way in which Fielding used these Wednesday sessions to collect further evidence against an offender already committed to trial. Broadhead, accused of highway robbery, was examined on a Monday and brought back two days later at the re-examination session at which the magistrates worked hard to build a case

---

[44] Fielding, *Extracts from such of the Penal Laws* (London, 1768), 7.

[45] William Augustus Miles, *Letter to Sir John Fielding, Knt. Occasioned by his extraordinary request to Mr Garrick for the suppression of The Beggars Opera* (London, 1773), 22.

[46] Some newspapers headed these reports 'Intelligence from the Public-office in Bow-street' or 'Proceedings at the Public-office in Bow-street'; others simply began a paragraph 'Yesterday at the Public Office, Bow-street. . . .' I have depended on the following papers for the account of the Bow Street re-examination sessions in the 1770s: *Morning Chronicle, Morning Post, Public Advertiser, Gazetteer, British Mercury, London Evening Post, General Evening Post, St James's Chronicle*. The first five were dailies, the last three tri-weeklies. A comparison of the reports in all of these papers of the four Wednesday meetings of the Bow Street magistrates in January 1775 suggests that there were at least four reporters in court. Two of the papers regularly printed the same report as two others; the reports in the *Morning Chronicle* and the *Morning Post* were unique. The London press also reported re-examination sessions at some of the Rotation Offices, but not as regularly as those at Bow Street. See, for example, *General Evening Post*, 13 February 1772 (Litchfield Street) and 28–31 May 1774 (St Margaret's Hill).

Table 5.2. Reports in the press of Wednesday commitment sessions at Bow Street, 1772–1780[1]

	Total Cases	Felonies	% Felonies
Number	326	240	73.6
Range	1–17	0–12	
Average per session	6.9	5.1	

[1] Source: reports of the proceedings at the Public Office, Bow Street, in the Thursday editions of the *Public Advertiser* and *Morning Chronicle*, every January and July, 1772–1780 (47 reports altogether).

against him—clearly because Fielding believed him to be responsible for several unsolved robberies, including an attack on the Hampstead stagecoach in the previous January for which someone else had recently been convicted at the Old Bailey.[47] The runners brought in victims of other as yet unsolved offences, several of whom swore that Broadhead had robbed them. Other victims were less sure, but the outcome of this drive to pile up evidence against Broadhurst was his certain conviction at the Old Bailey and his execution for highway robbery.[48]

Fielding went beyond all previous practice in conducting these re-examinations every week as part of the established routine of the office and well beyond the requirements of the statutes governing the committal process. This was particularly true with respect to his encouragement of suspected felons to bring defensive evidence at the pretrial stage, including evidence that might give them an alibi. When he first announced that the Wednesday sessions would be held regularly, he said that they would provide accused felons with 'Time to send for Friends and Witnesses to shew their Innocence, and prevent their being unwarrantably precipitated into Trials for Fraud or Felony'.[49] And indeed more than one in 10 of those accused of committing a felony had their cases dismissed at Bow Street in the 1770s, either because their prosecutors failed to appear or because they successfully brought alibi evidence.[50] Other magistrates dismissed cases because of weak evidence and had done so for at least 40 years by then.[51] But, as far as I am aware, no magistrate before Fielding had positively invited defendants to submit counter evidence or to encourage them, as was said, to 'set up a defence'.[52]

---

[47] Presumably either Samuel Male, alias May, or James Wilson, who were convicted of stopping the Hampstead coach at the January 1773 sessions (OBP, January 1773, t17730113-19. Two other groups of offenders were also tried at that session for attacking the same stagecoach at other times in January, but were acquitted.

[48] *General Evening Post*, 3–6, 6–8 April 1773; OBP, April 1773 (Thomas Broadhead) t17730421-29.

[49] Fielding, *Extracts from such of the Penal Laws* (1768), 7.

[50] In a seven-month sample of reports of the proceedings before the Bow Street magistrates in the *Public Advertiser* and the *Morning Chronicle* between July 1777 and July 1780 in which 82 dispositions by the magistrates were recorded, 74% of those accused of felony were committed to trial, 15% were remanded for further examination, and the charges against the remainder were dismissed.

[51] Above, n. 36.

[52] *Morning Chronicle*, 13 January 1780. A woman charged with theft of bank notes testified at the Old Bailey that, having asked John Clarke, a runner, if she should tell Fielding that she had found

The pretrial publicity that Fielding's practice at Bow Street had encouraged was criticized soon after he established his new courtroom. William Augustus Miles voiced serious reservations about the innovations at Bow Street in 1773 in the course of criticizing Fielding for trying to suppress a revival of Gay's *Beggar's Opera* on the grounds that it encouraged young men to turn highwaymen. In a scathing analysis of Fielding's practice as a magistrate, Miles was particularly concerned with what he described as his wholly improper departures from the requirement of the Marian system of pretrial. He thought it particularly egregious that Fielding asked prisoners 'what they have to urge in their defence', a matter, he said, that was 'due only in a court of justice.'[53] More serious criticism and decisive opposition, arose in 1780 out of an incident in the Gordon Riots in June of that year.

Soon after the riots began, a number of men were arrested on suspicion of having taken part in the destruction of the Catholic chapels attached to the houses of the Sardinian and other foreign ministers.[54] They had been examined at Bow Street as the violence was still in progress. The names of the prosecution witnesses were disclosed in the course of this examination and the crowd took revenge on two of them, Sampson Rainsforth and Stephen Mabberley, by attacking and burning down their houses. The reporting of such evidence in the press was attacked in the report of a committee of the privy council set up to look into the causes and consequences of the riots. Obviously struck by the foolishness of conducting such a procedure in public and allowing the names of witnesses to be published in the press while the disturbances were in progress, the privy councillors called in Justice Addington and interrogated him about it:

> ... asked by whom the Evidence at Bow Street is taken down and published, answered by people employed to make paragraphs for the News papers; asked how he could think of taking the Evidence of Mr Rainsforth and Mabberly against the Rioters in public, answered that it was the general Custom of the Office; asked if it was always so, say'd that some times the first Examination was taken in private in the little Room, that when Committments were to be made out it was public, that it had certainly been wrong to make it public in this Case.[55]

When he was examined on this subject, Sampson Wright put the responsibility for Bow Street examinations being extensively reported in the press not on 'the general Custom of the Office,' but where it belonged: on Sir John Fielding. He claimed always to have differed from Fielding in this matter, and thought 'public Examinations a public inconvenience.'[56] At least one newspaper deprecated the reporting of

---

them, he replied that 'that was as good a defence as she could set up.' OBP, September 1776 (Ann Seabright, alias Forbes) t17760911–50. Newspaper accounts occasionally noted that accused felons had 'set up a defence' at Bow Street, or had been asked what defence they had to make, that they had said little in defence, or had made a poor defence (*General Evening Post*, 20–2 April 1773, 8–10 February 1774; *Gazetteer*, 15 January 1778; *Morning Chronicle*, 29 January 1778, 20 July 1780, 14 September 1780; *British Mercury*, 1 December 1780).

[53] *Letter to Sir John Fielding*, 7–18. For a fuller account of Miles's objections to Fielding's pretrial innovations, see Beattie, 'Sir John Fielding and Public Justice', 92–3.

[54] For the Gordon Riots, see below, ch. 6, text at nn. 42–9.

[55] TNA: PC 1/3097 [n.p.]   [56] Ibid.

evidence given at the pretrial procedure at Bow Street 'because of the effect it has on the minds of men, who from thence form prejudices, which they carry with them into court, and which pervade their judgment as jurymen.'[57]

Neither Wright nor Addington did anything to alter the practice in the aftermath of the riots, even after Fielding's death in September. But the attorney general, James Wallace, and chief justice Mansfield got a second opportunity to pronounce on the more general implications of these Bow Street procedures when Addington appeared as the defendant in a lawsuit for assault and unlawful imprisonment brought in King's Bench in December 1780 by Thomas Ayrton.[58] In the course of the trial before Lord Mansfield—in which the King's Bench special jury found in Ayrton's favour with full costs—it was reported in the press that the 'practices of [the] Bow Street office were publickly exposed and severely censured by the whole court.'[59] The censure was delivered in the first place by the attorney general, followed by Mansfield, both of whom criticized Bow Street on the grounds that vigorous examinations and re-examinations uncovered a great deal of evidence—including on occasion defensive evidence—which was then published at length in the press. They both pronounced this prejudicial and contrary to law and, as a consequence, the attorney general announced his intention 'to file informations, ex officio, against the printer of every news-paper who dared in future to publish the examinations of prisoners.'[60] It had an immediate effect. *The Morning Chronicle* announced a week after the trial that the attorney-general and the lord chief justice having pronounced as they had, 'the Printer thinks it becoming him to shew a proper deference to such high authority.'[61] All the papers followed suit, though reluctantly. Having reported Bow Street examinations on 7 December 1780, *The Morning Post*, *Gazetteer*, and *Public Advertiser* declined to do so a week later. *The British Mercury* offered a spirited defence in a few issues, but then conformed.[62]

Re-examinations of defendants who had been committed for trial were not abolished in December 1780. Nor were Bow Street and the other magistrates' offices closed to the public, as some of the papers initially thought would happen.[63] But the regular Wednesday sessions at Bow Street were abandoned—at least they were no longer reported at length and with the detail that had characterized newspaper coverage in the 1770s. Indeed, pretrial publicity in general became much more restrained. *The Gazetteer* announced in August 1782 that 'several persons now in custody are strongly suspected of having lately committed many footpad robberies near London [and that] they will be re-examined at [Bow Street]

---

[57] *London Courant*, 13 June 1780.

[58] See below, text at nn. 145–6; and Beattie, 'Sir John Fielding and Public Justice,' 94–6.

[59] *British Mercury*, 9 December 1780. Addington was no ordinary magistrate. Though he was by all accounts a difficult man, he was well versed in the criminal law, having published *An Abridgement of Penal Statutes* in 1775.

[60] *British Mercury*, 11 December 1780.

[61] *Morning Chronicle*, 14 December 1780.

[62] *British Mercury*, 11, 12, 13 December 1780.

[63] *London Courant*, 14 December 1780.

on Friday next, at eleven o'clock, when all persons lately robbed are desired to attend.' What passed at that session was not subsequently reported.[64] By the end of the decade an occasional case re-examined at Bow Street was briefly reported in *The Times*, but one case at a time, never a full session, and rarely more than a handful in a year. In 1794 the publisher of the *Morning Chronicle* confirmed that 'no detail of examinations at Bow Street has been given in any of the respectable papers' since the attorney general threatened them with prosecution in 1780.[65]

3. THE BROWN BEAR

Newspaper reports of re-examinations in the 1770s make it clear how important the runners were to the prosecutions conducted at Bow Street. They brought in some of the suspected offenders; they collected evidence to be produced in court; they sought out witnesses and ensured that they came to the magistrates' hearings as well as to the subsequent trial if the defendants were committed—and not just in the cases in which they had been directly involved; they alerted victims of as yet unsolved offences that a hearing was to be held at Bow Street at which they might recognize their attackers or the goods they had lost. The runners were on hand in the Bow Street court to manage the prisoners and to search them if required to do so by the magistrates. The runners also appeared as witnesses for the prosecution at Bow Street and the Old Bailey—and indeed before other magistrates and other trial courts.

Having made an arrest, the runners might take the suspect immediately to be examined by a magistrate, or, if none was available, to the neighbouring public house that served as a form of police station, where they could be searched and interrogated. The Bow Street house itself was not large enough to offer more than minimal facilities in which accused offenders could be held for long periods. There was a small room in the basement where a few prisoners could be kept. But not until the nineteenth century was there space for a more extensive lock-up, or for a room in which the runners could gather until work came their way or in which they could question the suspects they had apprehended. This was why the runners used a nearby public house for the purpose—at first and briefly the Barley Mow, but by 1756 the Brown Bear, directly across Bow Street from Fielding's house.[66]

The Brown Bear remained a public house. It took in lodgers and was obviously a favourite drinking spot in the Covent Garden area: its two parlours, bar, and tap were often reported to be crowded with locals when policing business was being

---

[64] *Gazetteer*, 15 August 1782.

[65] *Morning Chronicle*, 17 May 1794. This reminder of the attorney general's prohibition was prompted by complaints that the same rules were not being applied with respect to the trials of radicals currently underway, and that comments in the press 'have a most evident tendency to prejudice such persons on their trial.'

[66] For the Barley Mow, see OBP, February 1754 (Peter Sampson) t17540227–38; OBP, April 1754 (Silas Dowling) t17540424–31. The first mention of the Brown Bear is at OBP, May 1756 (Charles Cane and Thomas Williams) t17560528–22.

conducted there. But it also acted in effect as the runners' headquarters and played an indispensable role in Bow Street policing for decades. Prosecutors often reported in Old Bailey trials that, having discovered a theft, their first thought was to go to Bow Street to enlist the help of the runners—as in the case, for example, of a shopkeeper who sent his servant to follow two women he suspected of stealing from him while he himself 'went to the *Brown Bear* in Bow-street [and] got Atkins and Moses Morant', or the case of an 'old-clothes-man' who, thinking that the clothes he was being offered for sale 'were not honestly come by,' went 'to the *Brown Bear*, in Bow-street, opposite Sir John Fielding's, and told his people I had some men at my apartment that I suspected'.[67] The runners often reported that they had been sought out at the Brown Bear by victims of offences.[68] Parish constables and victims of offences also knew that they could take suspects they had apprehended to the public house across the street when the 'public office' was not open for business.[69]

The Brown Bear had a secure room in which stolen goods could be stored and one in which suspects ordered into temporary confinement by the magistrates could be held, overnight if necessary. We learn from Old Bailey trials of men being 'locked up at the *Brown Bear*' or being 'in custody' there,[70] a function the pub continued to serve into the nineteenth century as it became ever more fully integrated into the work of policing and prosecution. The chief magistrate told a parliamentary committee in 1816 that until 'a place of confinement' had been made available within the Office itself two years earlier, all prisoners committed to trial had routinely been taken to the Brown Bear for security until they could be transferred to gaol.[71] It was in fact still in use. Samuel Bamford, a radical accused of treason in 1820 and brought to London from Manchester to be interviewed by the privy council, was held overnight at the Brown Bear, along with seven other accused. They were 'secured by chains to the bed posts, and to each other,' he wrote, though they were otherwise well treated by the Bow Street officers, whose 'demeanor . . . was, without exception, such as might be expected from men who knew their duty, and had the full power to perform it'—treatment very different from that they had experienced in Manchester 'by men of the same station.'[72]

Perhaps the most important contribution that this public-house/ police-station made to the prosecution effort mounted by the Bow Street magistrates was its provision of a place where the runners could interrogate and search suspects, uncovering evidence that might well prove to be decisive at both the committal

[67] OBP, January 1784 (Sarah Partridge and Mary Stokes) t17840114–44; OBP, January 1774 (William Sheene et al) t17740112–3.

[68] OBP, September 1774 (Joseph Doggett) t17740951–50.

[69] OBP, February 1784 (Thomas Turner) t17840225–29.

[70] OBP, May 1779 (Richard Hutton) t17790519–15; OBP, April 1781 (Richard Sheering) t17810425–9; OBP, January 1790 (David Greville) t17900113–19; OBP, December 1792 (John Carney) t17921215–37.

[71] *Parliamentary Papers*, 1816, vol 5 (510): *Report from the Committee on the State of the Police of the Metropolis*, 23. There was also a secure 'cage' at the Brown Bear where stolen goods could be stored.

[72] Samuel Bamford, *Passages in the Life of a Radical* (6th. edn., 2 vols, London 1967, ed.. W. H. Chaloner; first published 1839–41), vol. 1, 103–4.

stage of the criminal process in the magistrates' court and at the Old Bailey in cases that were sent to trial. It provided a place where they could stage a form of identity parade that would enable them to claim at the preliminary hearing and at the Old Bailey that the victim had identified his or her attacker—though as we will see, this was more often done during the pretrial process itself. The runners also added corroborating evidence in numbers of cases heard at the Old Bailey as a result of having searched suspects at the Brown Bear—sometimes before they had taken them to be examined by the magistrates, sometimes in the course of that pretrial hearing. John Lacuse, an apprentice to a smith, who had a bag taken from him in a public house in Covent Garden that contained more than £40 of his master's money and some of his own belongings, was advised by the publican to go to Bow Street to get a runner and a search warrant and to seek out the man he suspected, Thomas Donnelly, a chairman, who he thought could still be found in a nearby pub. Lacuse did so, and Joseph Stephenson, an active Bow Street officer who was also a Westminster constable, arrested Donnelly, took him to the Brown Bear, searched him, and found the money, along with the apprentice's missing knee buckles and sleeve buttons. 'I took him over to Sir John Fielding,' Stephenson said at Donnelly's Old Bailey trial, 'and he committed him to Bridewell.'[73] That search was presumably authorized by the magistrate's search warrant. But in many other cases, searches were conducted at the Brown Bear as a matter of course—an area in which the runner's authority seems cloudy to say the least. In a typical case, Richard Bond described at the Old Bailey how he arrested the defendant, Joseph Guy, a black highwayman accused of stopping Nicholas Kemp and his wife, Anne, in a chariot near the Marylebone turnpike and of taking their money and a green purse. Bond said that he followed Guy's trail for two days until he came upon a man who answered his description. He took him to the Brown Bear, where he searched him and found the green silk purse and money that he produced in court.[74]

These searches appear to have been carried out in public in one of rooms in the Brown Bear, without any effort at concealment, even when, as in one case, the search involved 'pulling [a suspect's] breeches off' to find the five guineas he had hidden.[75] Searching suspects in the public rooms applied even to women, one of whom was said to have been 'stripped' in the course of the search, though what that meant is unclear. At some point, the runners appear to have acquired a screen that at least made more private searching possible. Two women accused of stealing gold rings from the shop of Ann Whitman objected to being searched by a man at the Brown Bear: 'they [the women] desired them to be decent', a witness told the court.

---

[73] OBP, April 1767 (Thomas Donnelly) t17670429–10.

[74] OBP, February 1767 (Joseph Guy) t17670218–38. As another example of a very large number, Richard Bond and two other officers, acting on a tip from a pawnbroker, arrested three men accused of burglary and stealing ten guineas, six half-guineas and other valuable goods, they testified at the trial that they had taken them to the Brown Bear and searched them 'in the back parlour.' They found several guineas and half guineas on each of them and a ring and handkerchief which the prosecutor immediately identified. Only then were they 'taken before Sir John', examined, and committed for trial (OBP, April 1773 (William Collins, Thomas Oats, and Thomas Spooner) t17730421–10).

[75] OBP, January 1779 (Susannah Watson and Anne Russel) t17790113–2.

Ann Whitman said 'I had better search them myself,' and perhaps because the officers 'bid me search them close as gold rings lay in a small compass' she took them behind 'a screen'. She found the rings.[76]

Not all prisoners were taken first to the Brown Bear. Many, perhaps most, were taken directly by prosecutors and the runners to the public office across the street, especially when the rotation system was established in the 1760s and the magistrates were available there at fixed hours every day. In that case, they would be searched there if the magistrates thought it necessary: one man said at his trial that he was 'not only searched, but stripped in a back room at Sir John Fielding's.'[77] But most complaints about rough treatment in the course of searches arose from the interrogations in the more freelance atmosphere of the public house. Prisoners claimed from time to time that in carrying out searches and interrogations at the Brown Bear the runners had used violence and intimidation, or that they had made threats or hinted at promises of favour to get them to confess.[78] One man said that they had taken him 'to a public-house, and wanted to get something out of me. They are some of Sir John Fielding's people, and live by what they can make that way.'[79] Certainly, if suspects resisted being searched the runners were not unwilling to use force, tying them up if necessary.[80] Occasionally they were accused of stealing prisoners' property and otherwise abusing them. Robert Morris was not the only defendant at the Old Bailey who complained about his experience at Bow Street. But he was wealthy enough to voice his outrage by means of a long advertisement in the press when he was taken to the Brown Bear after being arrested by the runners for acting as a second in a duel. His main complaint was against the magistrate, William Addington, who had published a handbill and issued a warrant for his arrest, but he was also offended by being manhandled by the runners, taken to a public house, and treated as a criminal. He had been, he said, 'not only insulted by the Bow-street runners, in the language in the true style of their wretched employer [Addington], but inhumanly treated in a hackney coach, when there was no witness; and instead of being carried before a magistrate, was, contrary to my remonstrance, forced into the justice's own ale-house, called the *Brown-Bear*, in order to be further bruised and insulted, before a parcel of witnesses ready at all times to swear the contrary'.[81]

---

[76] OBP, January 1780 (Mary Jones and Mary Smith) t17800112–22.

[77] OBP, February 1780 (Robert Anders and Richard Palmer) t17800223–34.

[78] For allegations of violence, see OBP, January 1759 (Edward Cleaver and Elizabeth Sharp) t17590117–30. Elizabeth Sharp, charged with receiving the banknote that Edward Cleaver had confessed to taking from a mail bag, claimed to have been harshly treated by the runners. She wanted to be taken before the lord mayor because the runners 'tore and dragg'd me about,' presumably at the Brown Bear. 'Mr Fielding's fellows us'd me cruelly', she said. For suggestions of favour being offered, OBP, May 1756 (Charles Cane and Thomas Williams) t17560528–22; OBP, December 1787 (Charles Berkley and John Claw) t17561212–9; OBP, October 1790 (Michael Sheridan) t17901027–60.

[79] OPB April 1767 (William Mallett et al) t17670429–71.

[80] OBP, December 1766 (Michael Cassody and Christopher Broaders) t17661217–36.

[81] *Morning Post and Daily Advertiser*, 23 January 1782.

Not many of the prisoners at the Old Bailey had an opportunity to complain in these ways about their treatment at Bow Street: Morris was clearly moved as much as anything by the insult to his social position. What he perceived as rough treatment in the hackney coach and at the Brown Bear was almost certainly the common experience of many of the suspected felons who found themselves in the hands of the runners. Many of them must have been relieved to be taken—as Morris requested—across the street to the magistrates' court where the real business of the pretrial process took place in a room that by 1772 was set up as a courtroom and in a procedure that John Fielding elaborated over the years of his tenure there in ways that were designed to produce as much evidence as possible for the trial that for most of them would soon take place before the jury and judges at the Old Bailey.

4. THE RUNNERS IN COURT

Sending strong cases to trial concerning the robbery, burglary, and larceny charges that preoccupied the Bow Street magistrates day in and day out, meant establishing (where this was appropriate) the victim's ability to identify the suspect as his or her assailant, or, in cases in which no confrontation had taken place between victim and assailant, uncovering evidence that linked defendants to the property alleged to have been stolen. A victim's willingness to swear to the identity of their assailant carried a great deal of weight with juries. When the opportunity arose, the runners might try to get such an identification established at the Brown Bear before taking the accused before the magistrates. One victim said at the Old Bailey that the runners had taken him into a back room at the Brown Bear, where 'there was a good many people. I immediately went to the prisoner', he continued, 'laid my hand on his shoulder, and said he was the man.'[82] Another was called to Bow Street some days after he had been robbed, where he was told 'there were sixty or seventy men in a room over the way at the Brown-bear, and bid me go and see if I could pick the men out.' Looking into the room, he told the runners that he saw one of the men. 'They bid me bring him out; I went in and brought [the prisoner] out.' No other evidence linked Lewis to this robbery, and the judge was clearly sceptical about the prosecutor's ability to recognize someone he had seen for only a few minutes on a dark night on an unlit road. Nonetheless, the jury convicted him simply on the basis of the prosecutor's identification of him as his attacker.[83]

Such tests were carried more often before the magistrates, sometimes, though not always, a little more formally. Thomas Carpmeal described one such identity 'parade' as follows:

---

[82] OBP, October 1757 (Abraham Bareive) t17571026–20.
[83] OBP, January 1772 (John Lewis) 17720109–13. He was pardoned before the following session and sentenced to 14 years' transportation to America.

[W]e brought them [the defendant and three other suspects] to Bow-street and sent to the people that had been robbed, this woman came; she had lodged an information about a week before. I was present, there were a great number of prisoners there, and the magistrates put them all together in a room with other people that are not prisoners; this woman came and fixed upon the prisoner immediately; there were about twelve prisoners and twenty others.[84]

William Randall, a servant who was attacked by two robbers on the Islington road and tried to fend them off with his stick against their cutlasses—losing not only his money but two fingers in the encounter—was brought to Bow Street to identify a man Charles Jealous and other runners had picked up as a suspect. Jealous told the Old Bailey judge and jury that

the prisoner was put amongst some of us and some strangers . . . we were all together to the number of fourteen. Mr. Bond sent a little boy for the prosecutor to come out of the [court]room into the yard where we were; when he came into the yard Mr. Bond desired him to go round and see if there was any body there whom he knew. He immediately pitched upon the prisoner.[85]

Jealous also said that 'None of us at Sir John Fielding's ever saw Randall from the time he came to give information' until the day on which he made this identification. He did so, no doubt, to remove suspicion that Randall's choice had been determined by hints from the runners—a suspicion that was always likely to arise, and that the runners were always at pains to deny. From time to time, defendants alleged that an identity test at Bow Street had been fixed, that the victim had been persuaded to identify the defendant because the magistrates or the runners were out to get him. 'Was he shown you by any body at Sir John Fielding's?' a post boy who had been attacked by a mail-robber and who had identified his assailant at Bow Street was asked by prosecuting counsel anxious to rule out any such suggestions.[86] Similarly, a servant who had identified a defendant as the burglar who had broken into his master's house, was asked in cross-examination if 'Sir John Fielding's people . . . [gave] you a hint?'[87] Both denied it, but both also revealed that the circumstances under which victims and their witnesses were asked to identify someone they had seen briefly, days or even weeks before, very often in the dusk or the dark, and under frightening circumstances were almost certain to have led to mistakes that could well have a crucial influence on the outcome of trials. Having denied that he was prompted by the runners, the post boy said: 'I went into the room where he [the defendant] and some more gentlemen were; I stood in the room some time; I heard his voice, and walked up to him.' It turned out, however, he had not been brought into some neutral space, but into the courtroom when the defendant was at the bar of the court and in chains. The accused's counsel asked pertinently, in cross-examination: 'Did you find him out by his voice, or the

---

84 OBP, September 1782 (William Mayhew) t17820911–57.
85 OBP, May 1780 (William Edwards) t17800510–2.
86 OBP, July 1770 (John Stretton) t17700711–26.
87 OBP, December 1778 (John Hartley and James Beane) t17781209–32.

situation he stood in while under examination?'[88] The servant, helping to prosecute an accused burglar, denied that the runners had pointed the defendant out to him, but he added that he had seen the accused entering the court in irons.[89]

It seems certain, given the conditions in which these crucial determinations were carried out and the fallibility of eyewitness evidence even when taken in the best of circumstances, that identifications made under oath in very brief eighteenth-century trials led to wrongful convictions.[90] There was clearly not a great deal of sensitivity, however, to the untrustworthiness of eyewitness memory. Even when a judge pointed out that the prosecutor in a highway robbery case had seen the defendant only briefly during the robbery three weeks or a month earlier, that 'he did not see him among a group of other people, or pick him out as the man that robbed him, but was led to the man as the man that had robbed him,' the jury failed to take the hint. When a juryman asked the prosecutor: 'Was he the first person that was brought to you, did you see more than this one?' and he insisted that he 'knew him to be the man as soon as I saw him,' he was convicted. Perhaps the fact that the prosecutor was a Middlesex justice of the peace explains the jury's willingness in this case to defer to his certainty that the defendant was the highwayman who had stopped his carriage and threatened to 'blow his brains out' if he did not hand over his purse.[91]

One might presume that the preferred outcome of procedures set up to encourage and support the efforts of private prosecutors was that the guilty would confess. A critic said in 1773 that Fielding strove too mightily for confessions.[92] But in fact there is little evidence of this, or at least of his doing so overtly. He would have known better than most magistrates that by mid-century the judges were increasingly unwilling to accept confessions obtained by force or favour.[93] Magistrates may have continued to induce some of those accused at Bow Street to confess by close questioning or by confronting them with incriminating evidence.[94] And prisoners continued to assert at the Old Bailey that they had been bullied into confessing at Bow Street or had been promised more lenient punishment if they

---

[88] OBP, July 1770 (John Stretton) t17700711–26.

[89] OBP, December1778 (John Hartley and James Beane) t17781209–32.

[90] For modern evidence on this point see, Elizabeth F. Loftus, *Eyewitness Testimony* (Cambridge MA, 1979; 2nd. edn., Charlottesville VA, 1992).

[91] OBP, September 1783 (William Sharman) t178730910–3. Defence counsel, who, as we will see, were engaged by prisoners more frequently in the 1780s than ever before, found it difficult to make headway against prosecutors who insisted on oath that they were certain in their identification of their assailants. One lawyer asked the victim of a robbery for which three soldiers were indicted a series of questions about the circumstances in which he had identified them at Bow Street, getting him to agree that he had gone to the magistrates' court in the expectation of seeing the men who had attacked and wounded him, that they were shown to him in chains as men presumed guilty, that after seeing them only briefly at 9 p.m. in December he was prepared to identify all three of them, that he was aware their lives were at stake. His identification was the strongest evidence against the three men—though they did not help their cause by engaging in a pitched battle with the runners who arrested them some hours after the robbery. They were convicted. OBP, January 1790 (Thomas Newton et al) t17900113–4.

[92] Miles, *A Letter to Sir John Fielding*, 21.

[93] Langbein has traced the emergence of the 'confession rule' in *Origins of Adversarial Trial*, 218–23.

[94] OBP, January 1780, John McCormick (t17800112–3).

did so.[95] But confessions were being too carefully scrutinized in the last decades of the eighteenth century for there to have been frequent intimidation or persuasion by promises of favour. By the 1780s, some judges would not accept confessions reported in oral evidence. When it was asserted in a case in February 1784 that the prisoner had confessed, Mr Justice Gould said that he would not admit it: the law required, he said, that 'it should be reduced into writing.'[96] It was presumably to ensure that confessions would be above suspicion that by the 1780s the Bow Street magistrates were using a printed form to record what suspects said at their examinations—not simply those who confessed, but the statements of all examinees.[97]

One form of confession that was obtained on the understanding that a very considerable favour would follow was regularly accepted at the Old Bailey: that is, the confession of an accomplice who admitted his guilt on the understanding that he would not be prosecuted (and might well also be given part of a reward) in return for the evidence that convicted his erstwhile associates. Allowing a defendant to turn 'king's evidence', as it was called, was left to the committing magistrate. It was a powerful instrument in the struggle to control serious crime, and it was frequently employed at Bow Street in the eighteenth century, having emerged in conjunction with the statutes that established the parliamentary rewards for the conviction of robbers, burglars, and coiners in the generation after the Revolution of 1689. But, like other confessions of guilt, it too had become subject to judicial control in the middle decades of the eighteenth century after the perception spread that the practice encouraged corrupt prosecutions and perjured testimony.[98] The adoption of a rule by the Old Bailey bench in the 1740s that the evidence of a crown witness, uncorroborated by independent testimony, would not be sufficient for conviction, was an effort to remove an obvious source of unsafe verdicts. It was firmly in place by 1751 when Henry Fielding complained

---

[95] A judge refused to allow a written confession to be read in court in 1774 when John Leigh, the chief clerk at Bow Street, acknowledged under questioning from the bench that Fielding had told the prisoner that if he confessed 'he would endeavour to save his life.' (OBP, September 1774, Amos Merritt (t17740907–62). Henry Morgan, on trial for murder in 1784 claimed that the Bow Street magistrate, William Addington, had pressured and persuaded him into signing a confession. He had taken him into a room by himself, Morgan said, and told him that 'if I did not make some confession or other I should be sent to prison, and locked up, and loaded with irons, and nobody should see me; and if I would make any confession I should have every thing done that could be, and should be pardoned.' Addington was not in court to be questioned, but Nicholas Bond, the clerk who had recorded the confession, was able to persuade a sceptical court that Morgan had given it freely and voluntarily and it was admitted. OBP, September 1784, Henry Morgan (t17840915–1).

[96] OBP, February 1784, John Jacobs, Samuel Selshire, and Richard M'Donald (t17840225–11).

[97] The printed form was headed: 'Middlesex. The Examination of [blank] charged with [blank] by [blank] of the Parish of [blank] in the County of Middlesex and taken before me one of his Majesty's Justices of the Peace for the County of Middlesex' with the date. The suspect's statement then followed (and might go on to the back side), beginning with the printed words 'who saith' occasionally struck through to become 'who confesseth' when he or she chose to admit their guilt and give an account of the crime. The statement was signed by the justice, and witnessed either by the prosecutor or one of the runners. The first surviving example is dated 28 October 1783 (LMA: SP/OB/Oct.1783/52).

[98] For a full account of the cases at the Old Bailey that reveal the adoption, functioning, and eventual modification of the corroboration rule, see Langbein, *Origins of Adversarial Criminal Trial*, 203–17.

that the need to bring corroboration to the evidence of a confessed offender was making it difficult to convict robbers.[99] But the magistrates' ability to name one of a group of offenders as king's evidence—provided he or she confessed before they were committed for trial—remained a potent weapon in dealing with crime in the metropolis.

The runners investigated offences, apprehended, questioned, and searched suspects, brought them before the magistrates for examination and re-examination, and in many of the cases in which they had had a role, gave evidence at both Bow Street and the Old Bailey. Their names appeared often enough in newspaper accounts of the pretrial examinations at Bow Street and in the printed reports of the trials at the Old Bailey that they must have become familiar to the public, especially since by the 1770s they tended to remain attached to the office for years on end. We learn about the evidence they gave before Fielding and the other Bow Street magistrates not only from newspapers, but also from their signed depositions or 'informations' as they were called. These statements, taken before a magistrate, were supposed to be forwarded to the trial court, along with similar statements given by the victim and his or her witnesses. They served as the basis of the indictment and were occasionally read in court when there was a dispute about what had actually been said before the justice. Depositions 'froze' the evidence, as Langbein has said.[100] Where they have survived—and since they were not part of the formal record of the courts their survival has been haphazard—depositions given by the runners report the results of their investigations. In the nine years 1781–89, in which these documents are particularly numerous among the Old Bailey manuscript records, close to 200 depositions given by 15 runners and men otherwise associated with Bow Street as assistants or patrolmen have survived.[101] As one would expect, the vast majority—indeed more than 90 per cent—were given by the men we have earlier identified as the most active of the runners: Charles Jealous led the way with 46 depositions; John Carpmeal and Patrick Macmanus (32 each); John Clarke (18); Moses Morant (14); John Atkins (13); and John Townsend (12).[102]

How often the runners followed up their having given evidence before the magistrate by appearing in the witness box at the Old Bailey to confirm that

---

[99] Henry Fielding, *An Enquiry into the Causes of the late Increase of Robbers (1751)* in Malvin R. Zirker (ed.), *Henry Fielding. An Enquiry into the Causes of the Late Increase of Robbers and Related Writings* (Oxford, 1988), 158–63.

[100] Langbein, *Origins of Adversary Criminal Trial*, 40–7, 273–7.

[101] The manuscript records of the Old Bailey, including gaol calendars, depositions, jury lists, and other documents, are in the London Metropolitan Archive, designated OB/SP for Old Bailey Sessions Papers. The collection is the result of the merging of several deposits: an original group that remained with the Sessions Papers; a second group, transferred from the Central Criminal Court, and a third collection that came to the LMA from the Corporation of London Record Office, the archive of the City of London. Depositions survive erratically among these papers from 1755 to about 1789. There are only a handful for some years—indeed none at all for several—and several hundred for others. For the purposes of an initial foray I concentrated on the years 1781–89. The papers were not entirely catalogued when I worked through them some years ago, and many were too damaged to be consulted. My data understate the number of depositions given by the runners.

[102] Based on LMA: OB/SP 1781–89.

evidence is impossible to answer with certainty. The best estimate is provided by the manuscript indictments among the sessions rolls (the formal charges brought against defendants), which record the names of witnesses sworn before the grand jury. A sample of the indictments in 22 sessions across the 1770s and 1780s suggests that eight or nine runners on average were included among the witnesses at each session in those years, ranging between three at the July 1771 session and 17 in July 1774. If all these men had actually been called to give evidence, the court would have heard from two Bow Street men every day—assuming that the average of five court days per session in the early 1770s remained the case through the whole period.[103] The number actually reported as giving evidence in the heavily edited and abridged Old Bailey *Proceedings* was inevitably much smaller than that—indeed not more than one a day.[104] There is no reason to think that the editor favoured one runner over another in reporting Bow Street evidence, so the *Proceedings* provide a reasonably reliable confirmation of the evidence obtained from the depositions with respect to the appearances of the runners in the witness box at the Old Bailey. I have counted their appearances using the online version of the *Proceedings*. Jealous and Heley led the way in the 1770s, and in the following decade the most active runners reported as giving evidence at the Old Bailey were Jealous, again, followed by Carpmeal, Macmanus, and Morant (Table 5.3). Despite the under-reporting in the Old Bailey *Proceedings* and the haphazard survival of depositions, the accumulated evidence suggests at the very least that the Bow Street men were frequently enough in court to have become familiar to the important decision-makers—the high court judges and the recorder of London, who presided over the trials, and to the jurors, who not only heard dozens of cases in a session, but in many cases served in several sessions and had as a result lots of opportunities to become familiar with the officers from Bow Street.[105]

How often the runners' evidence was decisive in the jury's deliberations and the sentences pronounced by the court is impossible to know. But having been involved in the investigation of offences and the interrogation of the accused, they frequently had important evidence to give. In property cases, in which they were most often called to give evidence, their testimony commonly involved how they had come to arrest the prisoner—whether through the disclosure of an informer, the victim's description, their own investigations or suspicions, the

---

[103] The indictments are included in the Sessions Rolls of the court: LMA: OB/SR. My estimate that the Old Bailey heard cases on five days on average at each session is based on the dates in the forematter of the printed *Proceedings* between 1771 and 1775—counting one of the days of the session as a non-trial day, that is, a day taken up with preliminaries and sentencing. After 1775, it is not possible to learn how long the sessions lasted, since the *Proceedings* give the dates as that of the opening day 'and the following days'.

[104] For the character, publishing history, and reliability of the printed Old Bailey *Proceedings*, see Langbein, *The Origins of Adversary Criminal Trial*, 180–90; Simon Devereaux, 'The City and the Sessions Paper: Public Justice' in London, 1770–1800,' *Journal of British Studies*, 35 (1996), 466–503; idem, 'The Fall of the Sessions Paper: The Criminal Trial and the Popular Press in Late Eighteenth-Century London,' *Criminal Justice History*, 18 (2003), 57–88; Robert B. Shoemaker, 'The Old Bailey Proceedings and the Representation of Crime and Criminal Justice in Eighteenth-century London,' *Journal of British Studies*, 47 (3, 2008), 559–80.

[105] For jurors' repeated service, see ch. 4, n. 83.

Table 5.3. Attendance of the runners as witnesses at the Old Bailey, 1760–1800.[1]

	1760s	1770s	1780s	1790s	Total	Period
John Noakes	30	23			53	1761–1774
W. Haliburton	18	32	19		69	1765–1785
John Heley	17	61	3		81	1766–1780
Charles Jealous		42	102	18	162	1775–1794
Thomas Carpmeal		2	78	42	122	1778–1800
Moses Morant		11	52	10	73	1776–1792
David Prothero		19	30		49	1776–1782
P. Macmanus			76	17	93	1780–1800
John Townsend			23	23	46	1785–1800

[1] Source: <http://www.oldbaileyonline.org>. John Clarke's name was too common to make recovery of his cases feasible. Had they been included, his appearances at the Old Bailey would have rivalled those of the leaders.

cooperation of a pawnbroker, or any of the other ways in which they had become involved in such cases. They could also disclose what they had found on the prisoner or in his or her lodgings, and other evidence that associated defendants with stolen goods.

The evidence given by Bow Street men at a burglary trial in 1776 was typical of the support the runners were able to bring to a prosecution. The break-in was at the house of Solomon Fell in Lincolns Inn Fields in which clothes, silver plate, and other goods worth close to £100 were taken. Fell reported the burglary to Bow Street. Nothing was learned about it until a week later when the runners were investigating another and even larger burglary in which a great deal of silver plate had been stolen. On this occasion, John Clarke said at the trial of William Wood, a publican, all the officers and some assistants went 'to all the noted houses,' that is, to the houses of known receivers thought capable of dealing with significant quantities of silver plate, including Wood's house. In his evidence, Clarke described the search they conducted, the goods they found, and where they found them: shoes and shirts bearing Fell's name in Wood's bedroom, along with other clothes that corresponded to those listed in a handbill sent around after the burglary. Clarke also found four ingots of silver, which led to an extensive search through the house for a furnace capable of melting silver. It was found in a garret with a charcoal fire still burning. Heley testified that he had discovered a false floor, beneath which he found two pistols, a crow-bar, and 'a large parcel of picklock keys.' He also found another pair of shoes which the shoemaker (having been brought to court by the runners) identified as having been made for Fell. The runners took charge of other items of stolen property found in Wood's house, keeping them in custody until they produced them for the jury.[106]

[106] OBP, September 1776 (William Wood) t17760911–1. Wood was convicted.

The runners' production of physical evidence and their accounts of how it had been found commonly worked in this way to support circumstantial evidence, or the testimony of an accomplice turned king's evidence, or the victim's identification of the offender. Haliburton's and Heley's evidence in a trial of two highwaymen in 1770 that helped to convict one of the robbers could be many times duplicated. Having received word from an informer about the robbery, they were sent by Fielding's chief clerk to investigate, searched the suspects' lodgings and found the goods reported missing which the victim identified in court. Their evidence supported the victim's willingness to swear to the identity of one of his attackers.[107]

In some cases the information from a pawnbroker provided the lead that enabled a runner not only to find the accused but also to create the chain of evidence that tied him or her to the stolen goods. When Thomas Shipley, for example, tried to pawn four pairs of silk stockings marked 'R.W.' and numbered 21–24 with John Heather, a pawnbroker in Long-acre, and refused to reveal how he came by them, Heather ordered two of his servants to seize and hold him while he sent another the short distance to Bow Street to summon a runner. Atkins came. He testified at the trial that he had searched Shipley and found that he was carrying a reading glass, an ink stand, two keys, three duplicates issued by other pawnbrokers, and a letter addressed to Dr Richard Warren, his former employer in Sackville Street. The runners brought Warren to identify the reading glass and ink stand as his property, as were the goods that Atkins had recovered from the other pawnbrokers. In court, Shipley confessed that, out of work and out of considerable necessity, he had taken advantage of his friendship with his former colleagues in service in Sackville Street and his knowledge of the house to return there from time to time when he knew the doctor was away to take a few things he thought he could pawn.[108] As in this case, the runners were often able to establish an accused's possession of stolen property by finding a pawn ticket and bringing the pawnbroker to Bow Street to identify the prisoner as the person who had brought the goods to his or her shop.[109]

The most effective support the runners could give to the efforts of private prosecutors in property cases at the Old Bailey was evidence that associated defendants in this way with the stolen goods listed in the indictments. Making a connection that 'traced [the property] home to the prisoner' was a 'medium of proof', a judge said in 1784, just as much as a victim's identification of his or her attacker on oath.[110] Other witnesses could provide evidence that helped to link a defendant to stolen property, but no body of men had ever before been in a position

---

[107] OBP, September 1770 (Edward Millson and Charles Macdonald) t17700912-39.

[108] OBP, December 1785 (Thomas Shipley) t17851214-6.

[109] OBP February 1767, Joseph Guy (t17670218-38); OBP, May 1767 (Thomas Donnelly) t17670429-10; OBP, April 1773 (William Collins *et al*) t17730421-10. In a deposition given before the Bow Street magistrates, Moses Morant, a runner, testified that he had found a pawn ticket on Alexander Duff which led him to the pawnbroker who had taken a stolen cloak in pawn and eventually to the shopkeeper who had lost it and the woman who had made it for him (LMA: OB/SP/ April 1783/49).

[110] OBP, July 1784 (Robert Moore) t17840707-2.

to testify as regularly to such matters, or with the authority that the runners could bring to the court after years and decades of describing how investigations had been conducted, what had been found and where, what suspects had said when they were apprehended or when they were examined before the magistrates. The runners preserved the evidence that linked defendants to the offence by taking stolen property into their custody and bringing it into court to be shown to the jury.[111] They occasionally made inventories of evidence found on searches, or marked particular items that enabled them or the prosecutor to identify them in court; when large bills of exchange were involved, they registered them before a magistrate and sealed them with his and their own seals.[112]

The Bow Street officers were frequently enough in court that they must have become not only used to being there and testifying in public, but more to the point, conscious of the most effective way to present evidence. They could also from time to time draw on the store of information that John Fielding had compiled at Bow Street about crimes reported and offenders suspected, information that aided their investigations and their testimony in court. The so-called 'watch book' was particularly useful in this respect. Watches, unlike money and many other things that were commonly stolen by robbers, pickpockets, and other thieves, were readily identifiable. From the beginning Fielding had understood the usefulness of having his clerks keep a separate record of stolen watches—of the makers' names and the numbers they had engraved on them—along with the addresses of all known London watchmakers and the names and addresses of the reporting victims. He also persuaded some of the largest pawnbrokers in the metropolis to cooperate in his policing efforts by holding and reporting to Bow Street people they suspected of having stolen the watches and other goods they offered in pawn. Robbers may have had some sense of the dangers that the evidence collected at Bow Street posed for them: some obviously did, since active and experienced highwaymen like William Page attempted to alter or eliminate the numbers on the watches they stole, or to disguise them completely by changing their cases. But disguise was difficult to manage successfully since alterations were easily recognized and the makers had ways of recording numbers not simply on watch cases, but hidden on the movements too.[113] Still, watches were among the robbers' favourite booty. They were valuable (or could be) and they were carried by a significant number of men by the second half of the eighteenth century—and not just very wealthy men—and by some women. Along with money and jewellery, gold or silver watches, with their chains and the seals that decorated so many, were the prizes that highwaymen looked for when they stopped passengers wealthy enough to travel by coach outside the metropolis and by footpads accosting victims in town.

---

[111] OBP, April 1772 (James Lucas and Luke West) t17720429–81. In court, John Heley 'produced a pair of shoe buckles set with stone, a cross, 69 oz. of silver melted down and a piece of silver skillet, I have had them ever since,' he said in evidence, 'in my custody.' The prosecutor swore that it was all his property except the silver which he assumed was his plate melted down.

[112] OBP, January 1775 (Edward Batsford) t17750111–65; OBP, April 1780 (William Bagnall and Elizabeth Rose, *alias* Bagnall); t17800405–19; OBP, October 1780 (George Bishop) t17801018–31.

[113] See ch. 3, text at n. 17.

A trial in 1775 illustrates the usefulness of the Bow Street watch book in the prosecution of highwaymen and street robbers. At the February session of the Old Bailey, John Armer was tried for robbing Hugh Boyd, Esq. near St Marylebone in the previous August, taking three guineas from him and a gold watch that had cost £20. Boyd had reported the offence to Bow Street, and given the name of the maker and number of the watch. Nothing followed immediately, and indeed, as was likely in most such cases, nothing might have ever have followed if Armer had not been taken up for another offence some months later. As a result of the charges brought against him then, his lodgings were searched by John Heley, the runner, a search that turned up the 'duplicate'—the pawn ticket—that Armer had received when he pawned Boyd's watch. This led Heley to the pawnbroker who had taken in the watch and who was still holding it, and from there to the maker who had sold the watch to Boyd and who was able to identify it even though it was no longer in its original case and attempts had been made to change its number. Armer could not provide a convincing story about how he had obtained the watch, and that—along with other more direct evidence—helped to convict him.[114] In a similar case a month earlier Edward Batsford was charged with attacking Thomas Roberts in the street along with two accomplices. Roberts, a coachman, was strong enough to get the better of two of them in a scuffle, but the third knocked him down, kicked him in the side and head and took a watch and four guineas from his pockets. Roberts reported the offence to Bow Street where the name and number of the watch were entered into the records. They provided evidence to bring Batsford to trial five months later when he was taken up for another offence and the runners found the watch in his lodgings.[115] In each case, Fielding's records enabled the runners to contact victims several months after a robbery and get them to come to Bow Street to undertake a prosecution. Watches were valuable. But, as Boyd told Armer as he was being robbed (not perhaps entirely self-servingly), they were also 'dangerous things' for thieves to take.[116]

In these cases the investigative work of the runners and the 'criminal information' kept at Bow Street led to convictions. Whether the interventions of the runners and their giving evidence at the Old Bailey made in general for a higher level of convictions in property cases—compared to those in which victims managed on their own in the old way, or sought help from parish constables or other thief-takers (including the men attached to the magistrates' rotation offices)—is impossible to know with any degree of certainty. Juries did not explain their verdicts and one could never be certain what had tipped their decisions one way or the other, even if we had complete records of the trials and not just the heavily-edited accounts that make up the printed *Proceedings* of the Old Bailey. Still, there is some reason to think that prosecutions in which the runners contributed evidence about their investigations and searches and their dealings with prisoners

---

[114] OPB, February 1775 (John Armer) t17750218–19.
[115] OBP, January 1775 (Edward Batsford) t17750111–65; for similar cases see OBP, February 1775 (Daniel Angus) t17750218–29; OPB, April 1780 (John Sparrow) t17800405–3.
[116] OPB, February 1775 (John Armer) t17750218–19.

Table 5.4. Verdicts in property cases at the Old Bailey, 1770–1790[1]

Verdict	Cases in which the Bow Street runners gave evidence		Cases in which the Bow Street runners did not give evidence	
	No.	%	No.	%
Guilty	105	61.1	1598	46.0
Guilty of a reduced (non-capital) charge	30	17.4	445	12.8
Not Guilty	37	21.5	1430	41.2
N	172	100.0	3473	100.0

[1] Old Bailey *Proceedings* (<http://www.oldbaileyonline.org>). Based on the trials held in 1770, 1775, 1780, 1785, 1790, including robbery and burglary.

strengthened the case against the defendants. A five-year sample of property cases tried at the Old Bailey between 1770 and 1790, reveals that in those in which the runners gave evidence the juries found 79 per cent of the defendants guilty, whereas the equivalent figure when runners were not in court to contribute their testimony to the prosecution case was 59 per cent (Table 5.4). There is no way to know that it was the runners' evidence that made the difference, but the figures do at least suggest that as a possibility.

More decisive evidence of the influence of the runners as witnesses at the Old Bailey can be found in the trial of offences in which expertise and a coherent assemblage of evidence were particularly important if the jury was to be convinced of the validity of the prosecution. This can be seen most clearly in cases concerning the counterfeiting of the coinage—making simulated silver half-crowns, shillings and sixpences, or copper halfpennies and farthings—and the putting off, or uttering, of false money. Making guineas and silver coins was treason, the coinage being the king's, and a conviction in such cases could lead to the horrors of the traitor's death—to be hanged, drawn, and quartered for a man, burned alive for a woman.[117] Most often by the late eighteenth century these offences were punished by hanging. Making false halfpennies and farthings was a misdemeanour that had been made punishable by two years in prison in 1742, but that was to be made a felony in 1771.[118] It was a

[117] For the law relating to counterfeiting, see Radzinowicz, *History*, I, 652–4, and John Styles, 'Our traitorous money makers': the Yorkshire coiners and the law, 1760–83' in John Brewer and John Styles (eds.), *An Ungovernable People. The English and their law in the seventeenth and eighteenth centuries* (London, 1980), 172–249. On the punishment of women, see Simon Devereaux, 'The Abolition of the Burning of Women in England Reconsidered,' *Crime, Histoire & Sociétés/Crime, History & Societies*, 9 (2, 2005), 73–98.

[118] 15 Geo 2, c. 28, s. 6 (1742); 11 Geo 3, c. 40 (1771). This latter act was almost certainly passed at the suggestion of the Mint. William Chamberlayne, the solicitor to the Mint and the man broadly in charge of coining prosecutions, set out for the master of the Mint in an undated letter of this period the difficulties of convicting counterfeiters of copper halfpennies and farthings so long as the offence remained a misdemeanour. The main problem was that the authorities were not allowed to search suspect houses for the kinds of evidence required to win a conviction in court. Nor was the evidence of an accomplice sufficient in itself to convict an accused counterfeiter of copper coins. Corroborating evidence was required in the form of tools and counterfeit coins, and such evidence could normally

felony that allowed benefit of clergy, and thus a non-capital offence that was usually punished by imprisonment or transportation.[119]

Coining was conducted in the metropolis in houses, cellars, and garrets, in hired lodgings, disused warehouses, and outbuildings of all kinds, by men and women, sometimes in twos and threes, more often in larger groups of up to seven or eight. A large group working in concert could produce a considerable number of coins in a day that must have gone to an established distribution network, rather than being hawked around the neighbourhood in the way coiners involved in smaller operations must have been content with. Silver coins could be cast in moulds from a mixture of silver and a base metal melted in a crucible, or they could be stamped out as round blanks from sheets of a similar mixture of metals that had been flattened in a mill, and then stamped with a die that had been prepared from a legitimate sixpence, shilling, or half-crown. In each case, the coin would be finished by being dipped in aqua fortis to draw silver to the surface, and then edged and polished. Both methods required files and scourers and other finishing materials. Copper halfpennies and farthings were stamped out from sheets of the metal. Stamping out blanks required machines and may have needed a minimum number of hands to run them. Casting may not have been so demanding, though several hands obviously made it easier to manage the furnace and the crucibles in which metal was melted, and the moulds and dies with which the coins would be produced.[120]

The runners were successful in apprehending and prosecuting at least some coiners. In part this was because several officers could go out together, along with assistants and Westminster constables if necessary, forming a large enough group to surround a target house, immobilize everyone inside, and search thoroughly for evidence, including looking for secret rooms dug out in cellars or other hiding places. A large group could also confront the potential danger involved in arresting men who might well resist. The runners went armed with pistols and cutlasses, and were ready to use force when it was necessary. Having been informed that seven

---

only be obtained by searching the work site. In addition, so long as the offence remained a misdemeanour, the uttering of copper coins was no offence. So counterfeiting copper coins should be made a felony, he concluded, in order to give the magistrates and the police the authority they needed to collect effective evidence and to bring uttering charges against those who 'put off' copper counterfeits (TNA: Mint 1/12, 123–5). The Act of 1771 did so.

[119] As with all offences in which benefit of clergy or, in the case of women, benefit of the statute, applied, it was strictly speaking available only for the first offence; the courts could refuse the plea for a second conviction and pass a death sentence—though always with the possibility that a conditional pardon would result in transportation or some other substitute. Occasionally in the late eighteenth century, the Mint solicitor instructed the prosecuting barrister to oppose clergy, and convictions in a number of cases of uttering of silver coins and the making of copper halfpennies resulted in a death sentence. See, e.g., OBP, September 1783 (William Rothwell) t17830910–35; OBP, April 1786 (William Smith and James Robinson) t17860426–13; OBP, September 1787 (Thomas Dean) t17870912–22.

[120] I have drawn this description of coining processes from the Old Bailey trial accounts, some of which were long and detailed. For an illuminating account of the context in which coining flourished in the eighteenth century and the distinctive form of coining in Yorkshire in the 1760s and 1770s, see Styles' brilliant essay noted above (n. 117), "'Our traitorous money makers'".

men were at work in a house producing false half-pennies, four runners and two Westminster constables forced their way in, separated the inhabitants, and tied them up. John Clarke, who was leading the runners, threatened to shoot one man who refused to come out of a hiding place and the Bow Street men dealt roughly with others who resisted efforts to bind their hands. (A man who was innocently repairing the doorway when they arrived scuttled off immediately, saying later in court that he left when he 'heard a cry of Fielding's men; I did not care to be in their mess; I should not like to meet them any where, much less in a house').[121]

Evidence-gathering was crucial to a successful prosecution. A large group of knowledgeable officers could conduct a systematic search, and carry away presses and crucibles and other machinery, tools, and materials to be taken to court as evidence at a subsequent trial. All the coins in various states of production (as well as the good ones that served as 'patterns' for dies) had to be collected and their location in the house noted. Evidence that the defendants had actually been at work making false coins was also important, and notes had to be taken of their clothing and general appearance when they were arrested—whether they were dressed for hard and dirty work, with their coats off, their sleeves 'tucked up', their stockings down, and whether their hands were discoloured from having used aqua fortis and from rubbing and polishing counterfeits. This was all strong circumstantial evidence. But what came to be the crucial issues in coining trials in the 1770s and 1780s were technical matters concerning the tools, machinery, and materials that had been found at the scene. The implements and machinery had to be carted away to be produced in court—or at least to be available to be seen.

The ability of a large group of officers to investigate coining operations, collect evidence on the spot, bring it to court and explain its significance to the judge and jury—which is, as we will see, what the Bow Street men became skilled at doing—transformed the detection and prosecution of coining offences. In the 1730s and 1740s, trials at the Old Bailey for the high treason of counterfeiting the king's coinage were invariably conducted by lawyers acting for the crown, and evidence was frequently given by an officer from the Mint or the Mint solicitor. But successful prosecutions depended fundamentally on the testimony of informers and accomplices who had worked with the defendants or who had distributed counterfeit coins on their behalf. Evidence about the tools and machines used in the production of false coins might be given in the course of such trials, and publicans or shopkeepers who had taken counterfeits in trade testified in some cases. But, to judge from the accounts of coining trials in the printed *Proceedings*, material evidence was most often haphazardly presented and rarely seems to have provoked much interest from judges or jurors.[122] Dependence on the evidence of an informer or an accomplice made for uncertain outcomes, especially when it emerged in the course of a trial that the main prosecution witness was in fact the principal offender, and the defendant such a marginal player that a judge might feel

---

[121] OBP, April 1774 (Thomas Hayward *et al*) t17740413–90.
[122] See, e.g., OBP, December 1731 (John Taylor) t17311208–42; OBP, April 1737 (John Irons) t17370420–45; OBP, July 1746 (Johannah Wood) t17460702–27.

obliged to order an acquittal or drop the charges.[123] It is hardly surprising in these circumstances that in the 50 years before 1770 only one coining offence a year on average came before the Old Bailey court.

That was to change in the 1770s and 1780s. After dealing with 51 coining cases in the half century before 1770, juries at the Old Bailey heard more than 200 over the next two decades, a tenfold increase. About a third of that number were the direct result of the statute of 1771 that made the counterfeiting of copper coins a felony.[124] The other two-thirds, some 133 cases, were for activities that had been prosecuted in previous decades—the counterfeiting of silver half-crowns, shillings, or sixpences, the uttering of such money, or the possession of equipment that would have made it possible to engage in its production.

Why prosecutions of those offences increased after 1770 is unclear. It is possible that more coiners were at work in London in the last quarter of the century, or that the public became more hostile to counterfeiters. I do not know if either of those conditions obtained, and it should be said that those who made and circulated fake silver had never had a great deal of public support. But some part of an explanation of the significant increase in prosecutions after 1770 may lie in the way the offence came to be prosecuted when men like the Bow Street officers and those who became attached to the emerging rotation offices in this period enabled informers, inclined to act on their suspicions that counterfeiting was underway, to pass on information without having to appear in court to carry on a prosecution. Where earlier, informers would most often have been obliged to testify at a trial, putting themselves at risk of retaliation from relatives or friends of the accused, the emergence of prosecuting policemen provided informers a means by which they could report their suspicions about coining operations (in return for some form of pay-off from the officers or the Mint) without exposing themselves. By the 1770s, virtually every coining case prosecuted by the runners was set in train by suspicions passed on to them by someone who did not subsequently appear in court or whose identity was not divulged.[125]

For more than two decades from the late 1760s, the Bow Street officers also had the very considerable advantage in dealing with coining operations that one of the runners, John Clarke, had knowledge of the metal trades and had been involved in the prosecution of coining offences on behalf of the Mint for two or three years before becoming attached to the Bow Street office.[126] He was not simply a specialist in counterfeiting cases, but became one of the leading runners, involved in the whole range of investigations undertaken by Fielding's men. But he was particularly prominent in the prosecution of coining, and may have been recruited for that purpose. The Mint solicitors continued to call on him to give evidence in

[123] OBP, September 1743 (William Cotes) 17430907–53; OBP, April 1746 (Jane Wilson) t17460409–48.

[124] 11 Geo 3, c. 40 (1771).

[125] For the willingness of the judges at the Old Bailey to shield the identity of informers who passed useful information to the runners, see the Roberts case, above, ch. 4, text at nn. 59–62.

[126] Clarke said at the Old Bailey in 1782 that he had been 'employed for the Mint thirteen years' (OBP, January 1782 (John Morgan *et al*), that is since about 1769.

such cases and to pay him a fee for doing so.[127] Over the 1770s and 1780s he emerged as an expert witness in coining trials—acknowledged as such, as we will see, by judges and lawyers at the Old Bailey, in the assize courts of the Home Circuit and indeed around the country. Under Clarke's leadership and example, Bow Street cases were presented with a high level of skill and, from the prosecution point of view, with a good deal of success.

Clarke had been apprenticed to a button maker and had practised that and related metal trades before coming to Bow Street.[128] At various points over the next two decades he called himself (with what justification is unclear) a silversmith, a silver-canehead maker, a chaser, a jeweller, and a coin dealer, as well as a button maker, but it seems likely that the latter was his real metier.[129] In any event, whether or not he exaggerated the scope of his experience, no one seems ever to have challenged his knowledge of metal working and of the implements and materials used in the making of counterfeit coins. Informers clearly thought he was the right man to go to, as did the Mint solicitor and metropolitan magistrates faced with difficult coining cases. He organized Bow Street's raids and was clearly deferred to by the other runners once they were in a house. Coming unexpectedly upon what seemed to be a coining operation, having searched a house for other reasons, Charles Jealous said at the Old Bailey trial that 'finding something that made us suspect that coining was going forward, we sent for Mr Clarke...; we made no search till Mr Clarke came.'[130] It was assumed by the runners that Clarke would direct the way evidence was gathered, since, as one of them said, 'he understands these things better than myself.'[131]

---

[127] Clarke's ongoing connection with the Mint was confirmed in a case of uttering in 1786 when a Clerkenwell magistrate to whom it was reported sent the informer to the Mint Solicitor, Vernon, who in turn sent him to Bow Street to ask Clarke to investigate and encourage the suspect into committing the offence again, then to arrest him and manage his prosecution (OBP, April 1786 (Thomas Bassett) t17860426–106.

[128] Clarke's first case as a runner was at the October sessions, 1770 (OBP, October 1770 (Joseph Knight *et al*) t17701024–60). He said several times in Old Bailey trials when asked why he could speak with authority about coining that he had worked as a button maker, a trade that involved fine metal work (e.g. OBP, May 1771 (Samuel Byerman) t17710515–21). Early in his career at Bow Street, a barrister asked him at the Old Bailey after he had given evidence if he was 'a moneyer [i.e. a maker of coins] in the Mint?' 'No,' he replied, 'I have made buttons.' (OBP, May 1771 (Edward Vaughan) t177010515–19. He claimed on one occasion to know more about button making than anyone (OBP, September 1783 (William Moore and Sarah Moore) t17830910–56); when asked in court why he seemed to know something of chemistry, he replied that 'We are obliged to use it in the business I was brought up in.' (OBP, February 1774 (Thomas Ives *et al*) t17740216–58).

[129] These additions are given in recognizances he entered into to appear to give evidence in trials at the sessions of the peace as well as the Old Bailey: LMA: MJ/SP/1772/09/28; MJ/SP/1778/07/39i; MJ/SP/1778/06/17; OB/SP/1774/09/19; OB/SP/1775/02/19; OB/SR/150 (September 1774).

[130] OBP, September 1776 (Robert Walker) t17760911–56. Because he was lame, Clarke was never in the vanguard if he was a member of a raiding party. The runners generally touched nothing until he arrived.

[131] OBP, April 1774 (Thomas Hayward *et al*) t17740413–90. For the runners deferring to Clarke, see also OBP, October 1790 (James Royer *et al*) t17901027–30. The judges came to share the runners' appreciation of Clarke's knowledge and experience. Asked from the bench at a trial in 1782 whether the coins before the court were counterfeit and he confirmed that they were, the judge said that 'Nobody knows better than you do.' OBP, September 1782 (Richard Harper *et al*) t17820911–104.

It was in court that Clarke's preeminence was most visible and his knowledge most valued. For the most part, Bow Street officers giving evidence in coining cases at the Old Bailey described what had been found at the scene. Clarke gave the detailed technical evidence. The precision and authority with which he gave such evidence seems to have been influential in changing the way the courts dealt with such charges. As I have suggested, technical issues had rarely been of major concern in coining cases in London before the runners became involved in their prosecution. By the 1770s, the nature of the machinery and the tools found at the scene (along with the coins they had produced) were becoming the central matter of the trial, the issues around which verdicts were based.

Clarke gave evidence in 108 coining trials between 1769 and 1793, sometimes in the form of a narrative in response to a request from the bench to 'explain to the Court and Jury, the several uses of these things,' when the runners had brought into the courtroom the presses and dies and other tools found at an alleged coining operation. At others he responded to a series of questions from a judge or prosecuting counsel. In both cases the point was to explain how the evidence the runners had assembled had produced the coins laid before the jury. In a typical statement in a case in 1775, in which two men and a woman were accused of casting counterfeit shillings, Clarke told the court that

> I received an information on the 7th of May, of coiners in that house. I sent Phillips [a runner] on the 9th to look at the house.... The next day we went to the house, and Morris and Broomwich being taken into custody, I searched Morris, and found upon him two counterfeit shillings and a sixpence. In the right-hand room I found a crucible on the fire, and hot metal in it; there was a pair of flasks in that room, on the window, and a bench, with counterfeit shillings upon it. Somebody must have been at work there, there is no doubt of it. On the same board there was some file-dust, (producing it) it appears to be a composition of silver and copper. On the table, in the middle of the room I found some good shillings (produces a good shilling, and two counterfeits). The counterfeit shilling appears to be cast from that good one. He produced several other good shillings and counterfeits, that were cast from them, particularly one good crooked shilling, and two counterfeits cast from it, with a little defect on one side of the good one, and likewise of the counterfeit, and observed, there was a crooked mould in the flask, answering to it. The inside of the moulds are made of sand, and there is a facing that closes the pores, that what is cast might not come out full of spots. The instruments produced, are applicable to coining; they [the coiners] can't work without them: there was some aqua-fortis and water, the uses of which, is to force the silver on the outside of the shillings, and by rubbing it comes off again. Morris said, he had been at work in the garden; but on looking at the hands of Morris and Broomwich, they were all over with the dust and filings of the coining business: and on the trowsers of Broomwich was the mark of the lathe, which was in the left-hand room, and is turned with the foot, and may be used in the coining business for edging of silver. The dust upon the lathe appeared to be the same as that on the working board. In the right-hand room I found this piece of box wood, to which a shilling had been fixed, in order to take the edge off: there was no coin, but only filings where the lathe was.[132]

[132] OBP, May 1775 (George Morris *et al*) t17750531–54.

Clarke was particularly knowledgeable about processes that involved the use of cutting engines, the making of dies, the machines used for striking of blanks and the tools for finishing the edges and polishing the resulting coins. In a trial of men accused of making copper halfpence, he described how the suspects had been secured, and continued:

> I found in the room a press and two dies for coining halfpence; and there was a great quantity of warm halfpence, and copper ready for scowering, and several other dies; in another cellar I found a cutting out press and several slips of copper (produces a gauge) this is a thing they use to mark the copper so as to cut it out the size of a halfpenny; that I found in the garrett; in the one pair of stair' s room I found some counterfeit halfpence (producing them); when there are a great quantity to coin it will take at least seven men; the other presses I found are too big to be brought into court; they are at the door; (he produces the copper cut in slips, and also that which was ready for scowering; and also a great quantity of counterfeit halfpence); in one of the dies there is a stroke just under the Britannia's head; some of the halfpence have the same stroke on the impression, and therefore I am sure they were struck with that die.[133]

Some judges preferred to ask Clarke a series of questions, a strategy that had the advantage of isolating each piece of evidence brought into court, better enabling the jury to understand its function and importance. In the trial of Joseph Lewis for counterfeiting shillings in October 1783, Mr Justice Nares asked Clarke to confirm that 'You have been employed for many years for the Mint, and therefore you can describe to us the several implements that are here?' and followed with two dozen questions that took Clarke through the casting process. 'What is the use of these crucibles?' 'What is that little pipkin?' 'Is the whole apparatus for coining compleat?' 'Look at these shillings, are they cast or struck?' 'What are these filings?' When he got to the process by which the metal was poured into the moulds, Nares asked Clarke to go to the jury and show them precisely how it was done. Then came a series of questions about the coins that had been found: which were the good ones that were used as patterns, which were the counterfeits. As in all coining cases, an artisan from the Mint was sworn as a witness to confirm Clarke's judgements about good and bad coins.[134]

Clarke's explanations of the various techniques by which false coins could be produced instructed judges, jurors, and lawyers in the kinds of materials and tools required for the job and in doing so shifted the evidentiary requirements for convictions in coining cases. The authoritative way in which he explained the uses of particular pieces of equipment focussed attention over time on the question of whether the machinery brought into court in support of a prosecution was in fact capable of making the coins that were the principal evidence against an alleged offender. Evidence about the appearance of the defendants at the time of their

---

[133] OBP, April 1774 (Thomas Hayward *et al*) t17740413–90.
[134] OBP, October 1783 (Joseph Lewis, alias Harris) t17831029–68. For other trials in which Clarke was asked a series of questions about the evidence, see OBP, February 1774 (Thomas Ives *et al*) t17740216–58, OBP, January 1780 (Benfield and Turley), OBP, April 1783 (William Harcourt *et al*) t17830430–108.

arrest—whether they looked as though they had been working—remained important, but insufficient in itself. The evidence increasingly required to bring the
charge home to defendants in coining cases was that the equipment put in evidence
was sufficiently complete to do the job. 'We wish you to explain to the Court and
Jury, the several uses of these things,' a judge asked Clarke at a trial in 1788,
referring to the tools and machines the runners had brought into court. And then,
when he had done so at some length: 'Is there a complete apparatus for coining
there?'[135] That emphasis on the completeness of the equipment could work
potentially to the advantage of a defendant. In another case in the following year,
when Clarke was asked the same question and replied in the affirmative, the
defendants' lawyer, William Garrow, showed how expert testimony could be
turned against the prosecution by taking Clarke through his evidence again and
getting him to admit that in fact not everything required for the production of the
coins in question was present in court. Garrow's own knowledge of the processes of
coining, acquired in the course of years of dealing with Clarke and other prosecution witnesses, enabled him to cast sufficient doubt in the minds of some jurors that
the jury retired for an hour and a half—an unusually long time in this period for a
jury to consider its verdict—before they returned to convict George Dawson and
acquit his wife.[136]

In most of the cases in which he was involved, John Clarke was able to satisfy
juries not only because of his obvious expertise and long experience, but also
because of the way he testified in court. It is clear from his dozens of appearances
at the Old Bailey that he did not strain the evidence, push it beyond its limits, or
appear to strive mightily for convictions. He did not bring weak or frivolous cases.
Judges recognized and commented on his restraint; Mr Justice Gould said in a
coining trial in 1783 that he had 'never heard him too forward,' by which, I take it,
he meant too assertive in the witness box.[137] That reticence, along with his careful
assembly of evidence and the skill he displayed in presenting it to the jury, explains
his success in court. Over the 24 years in which John Clarke was attached to Bow
Street (1770–93) he gave evidence in almost half of the 216 coining trials heard at
the Old Bailey. The conviction rate in the 106 cases in which he appeared was over
90 per cent; in the remaining 110, it was 44 per cent (Table 5.5).

It is difficult to know how many of the latter he might have been involved in as
an investigator without giving evidence because not only were the *Proceedings*
heavily edited, a large number of the trial accounts in coining cases are what
John Langbein has called 'squib' reports, simply brief statements of the substance
of the indictments—the offences charged and the names of the defendants—
mainly in minor cases of uttering or cases that ended in acquittals. The conviction
rate in those in which he did give evidence can only be a rough and ready indication
of his importance to the prosecution of coining in this period since in most of his
cases he was not the only police witness. But it may be significant that the 24 cases

[135] OBP, April 1788 (William James, alias Levi *et al*) t17880402–48.
[136] OBP, September 1789 (George Dawson and Deborah Dawson) t17890909–46.
[137] OBP, February 1783 (Abraham Butler) t17830226–77.

Table 5.5. Verdicts in trials for counterfeiting and uttering at the Old Bailey, 1770–1793[1]

	Cases in which John Clarke gave evidence			Cases in which John Clarke did not give evidence		
	Guilty	Not Guilty	Total	Guilty	Not Guilty	Total
Number	96	10	106	48	62	110
%	90.6	9.4	100.0	43.6	56.4	100.0

[1] Source: <http://www.oldbaileyonline.org>

the Bow Street and rotation office men prosecuted without Clarke resulted in a distinctly lower conviction rate (58 per cent). These varying conviction rates are noteworthy mainly because they support the conclusion that emerges from a reading of the trial accounts—that in coining trials in this period, Clarke's was most often the decisive and persuasive evidence.

5. THE RUNNERS AND DEFENCE COUNSEL

The involvement of the runners in the prosecution of coining at the Old Bailey provides a useful insight into the ways in which they helped to strengthen prosecutions of other offences. Although they were never involved in a large proportion of the cases tried in London, they added a new element to the trials in which they took part by bringing evidence gathered in the course of investigations and interrogations of suspected offenders. They could describe crime scenes, how they discovered and apprehended defendants, what suspects said and did, what they were carrying, and what was in their lodgings. They brought forensic evidence into court to be shown to the jury. They could occasionally bring documentary evidence from the Bow Street records to support prosecution cases. Along with the changes introduced by John Fielding into the magistrates' committal hearing at Bow Street, the detective work of the Bow Street men contributed in a variety of ways to support prosecution cases. It seems likely to me that this addition to the prosecution side at the Old Bailey helps to explain one of the fundamental changes in trials in this period, that is the involvement of solicitors in the pretrial process at Bow Street and the striking increase in the number of defendants who opted to engage a lawyer to assist them in court.

In the early decades of the century, efforts to encourage prosecutions by the provision of massive rewards had resulted in such unfairness, perjury, and corruption in trials at the Old Bailey that the judges had broken a fundamental rule of court and allowed defendants in felony trials to engage counsel to help ensure that prosecution evidence would be more effectively tested. What these lawyers were able to do for their clients was closely controlled by the bench. In effect, defence counsel were allowed to do only what the judges themselves had always done for prisoners on trial: that is, to examine defence witnesses and to cross-examine the victim and his or her witnesses as they presented the evidence for the prosecution.[138] Despite these restrictions, a number of defendants in the 1730s clearly thought it worth their while to engage barristers to help them in court. Over the next 40 years, lawyers can be found acting on both sides in felony trials at virtually every session of the court, though never in more than a few cases. It would have been rare over the middle decades of the century for more than five per cent of defendants, for example, to have counsel at a session of the Old Bailey.

The number of defence counsel acting at the Old Bailey was to increase strongly, however, beginning in the late 1770s, but particularly as the American war came to an end in 1782.[139] In the years that followed, as many as a quarter to a third of accused felons sought the help of defence counsel. Some of the sudden increase in the number of barristers being engaged by defendants at the Old Bailey may have resulted simply from the large increase in prosecutions for property offences, and especially robbery and other violent offences, that followed the end of the American war and the demobilization of the forces.[140] It may have been encouraged too by the government's announced determination to fight the rising crime levels by making it known that pardons would be difficult to obtain if the judges did not reprieve convicted capital offenders.[141] But more fundamentally, the increased willingness of defendants to engage counsel and the apparently changing attitudes of lawyers towards their role in court may have resulted from the strengthening of prosecution cases at the Old Bailey as a consequence of John Fielding's innovations at Bow Street.

It is an important issue whether Fielding's efforts to bolster prosecution cases by more extensive pretrial examining, along with his willingness to allow defendants to bring counter evidence, encouraged accused felons to bring lawyers to their aid at pretrial proceedings, and whether his re-examinations over several days made it easier for them to do so. It remains unclear how commonly lawyers had attended magistrates' committal hearings over the first half of the century. So long as the Marian dispensation was strictly enforced, under which virtually every accused person was to be sent to trial, there was presumably little scope for a lawyer's engagement in these proceedings. There were complaints at the end of the seventeenth century, however, about some of the better-organized thieves in London getting the help of 'Newgate solicitors,' and both De Veil and Fielding himself warned against such men as troublemakers.[142] These were presumably men in the

---

[138] Langbein, *Origins of Adversary Criminal Trial*, 106–77.

[139] For the following account of defence counsel at the Old Bailey in the eighteenth century, particularly in the 1780s, see Langbein, *Origins of Adversary Criminal Trial*, 167–70, 291–310; Allyson N. May, *The Bar and the Old Bailey, 1750–1850* (Chapel Hill, 2003), ch. 2; J. M. Beattie, 'Scales of Justice: defense counsel and the English criminal trial in the eighteenth and nineteenth centuries', *Law and History Review* 9 (1991), 221–67; Stephan Landsman, 'The Rise of the Contentious Spirit: Adversary Procedure in Eighteenth-Century England,' *Cornell Law Review* 75 (1990), 497–609.

[140] J. M. Beattie, *Crime and the Courts in England, 1660–1800* (Princeton and Oxford, 1986), 582–7.

[141] Ibid, 583.

[142] Langbein, *Origins of Adversarial Criminal Trial*, 136–47; Beattie, *Policing and Punishment*, 395–9.

lower reaches of the legal profession. When better-established lawyers began to attend magistrates' hearings in large numbers remains unknown. There is some evidence of attorneys being present on behalf of accused felons not long after Fielding created the new courtroom in 1772 when the scope for defensive efforts in the re-examination process may have broadened. A man accused of stealing from the mail was reported as having had the help of 'an eminent attorney' in 1773; a suspect was advised by a 'Gentleman of the Law' in the following year, who argued to no avail that the charge against his client was no felony; a man whose social standing was sufficiently respectable that the publisher of the *General Evening Post* referred to him as 'Mr W—', but who was nonetheless charged in 1776 with stealing a lady's gold watch, engaged John Silvester, a barrister of 10 years' standing who was to become increasingly well known at the Old Bailey and ended his career as Recorder of London.[143] It was clearly a well-established practice by 1792, when, in an advice book written for students at the Inns of Court, Thomas Ruggles expressed his disapproval of what he called the 'modern practice' of attendance at Bow Street examinations.[144]

Whether Fielding allowed such 'respectable' lawyers to ask questions or cross-examine prosecution witnesses, I do not know. But there is a suggestion in the conflict at Bow Street between an attorney Thomas Ayrton, and the presiding magistrate William Addington a few months after Fielding's death that lawyers had become accustomed in the 1770s to intervening in the pretrial process on behalf of their clients.[145] Ayrton had attended a committal hearing in support of a man accused of robbery. He became embroiled in a dispute with Addington when he took notes and attempted to cross-examine the prosecutor, interrupting the magistrate's questions to do so and insisting 'that he had the right to ask the Prosecutor any questions.' Addington was aggressive and a bully, so perhaps not too much should be read into his conflict with Ayrton. But in asserting in his defence against the suit for assault and false imprisonment at King's Bench that changes in the pretrial process at Bow Street were 'contrary to his own sentiments of judicial enquiries,' he seems to suggest that attorneys had been allowed to ask questions and in other ways to become involved on behalf of defendants at Bow Street in the previous decade in a procedure entirely shaped, as he said, by Sir John Fielding.[146]

If attorneys were attending at the pretrial stage at Bow Street by the late 1770s, taking notes and writing briefs, that would certainly help to explain the increase in the number of barristers appearing in trials for felony at the Old Bailey when prosecutions rose sharply in the 1780s. And it is possible, too, that a changing climate of prosecution explains why at least some counsel appear to have been more

---

[143] *General Evening Post*, 2–4 March 1773; *Morning Chronicle*, 7 July 1774; *General Evening Post*, 7–9 May 1776. For other evidence, see May, *The Bar and the Old Bailey*, 89–90. For Silvester's career, see ibid, 36–40.

[144] Thomas Ruggles, *The Barrister; or, Strictures on the Education Proper for the Bar* (London, 1792), 209.

[145] For the wider implications of this case, see above, text at nn. 58–63.

[146] *British Mercury*, 9, 11 December 1780; Mansfield's notes, in Oldham, *The Mansfield Manuscripts*, 2, 1023–6. *British Mercury*, 11 December 1780.

committed then than ever before to defending their clients by the only means open to them—a searching cross-examination of the evidence supporting the charges. William Augustus Miles had objected to what he thought was Fielding's bombastic and aggressive examinations of suspects before the Bow Street magistrates. He particularly disliked his encouraging printers to publish the evidence so obtained which he thought would be bound to influence the jury in cases that went to trial. Such pretrial publicity was wrong because 'the mild laws of this country suppose every man innocent till he is convicted by the unanimous determination of his peers'.[147] That too was an emerging sentiment that would soon become a commonplace and that may have played some part in a conviction that the balance in the trial of criminal offences had swung too far to the side of the prosecution.

The leading proponent of vigorous defence in the 1780s was a young man who took up practice at the Old Bailey in 1783, William Garrow. He was only 23, but Garrow had trained himself for criminal practice while he was a student by regular attendance at the Old Bailey—an indication in itself of a changing climate around the prosecution of felonies.[148] He acquired a deep knowledge of the criminal law, and when he was called to the bar plunged in immediately, volunteering in his very first session to act *pro bono* on behalf of two women who were without counsel. Within months he was being noticed in the press. The sharpness of his mind and power of his speech, his ability to seize on weaknesses in prosecution evidence, his knowledge of the law and skill in elucidating the details and relevant points of leading cases, were to take him to the leadership of Old Bailey barristers in the 1780s. During the decade in which he was active in that court, he was engaged overwhelmingly for the defence.[149]

Garrow was a domineering and intimidating presence in the courtroom, in large part because of his determined and insistent probing of witnesses who struggled to avoid answering his questions. He was a formidable opponent. It is thus revealing of the standing and reputation of the officers attached to Bow Street to consider how Garrow dealt with them in court. Having undertaken investigations and made arrests, searched and questioned suspects, the runners were frequently in a position to add weight to the prosecution in felony trials at the Old Bailey. But the runners were also vulnerable to the charge that their evidence was tainted by financial interest when there was a parliamentary reward in the offing that depended on the conviction of the defendant. All prosecutors and their witnesses in such cases were open to such charges, and it was a natural defence tactic in trials of robbers and burglars to remind jurors that the case may have been motivated by the prospect of 'blood money'. It was a tactic that William Garrow was always willing to employ. It was no doubt more effective against some witnesses than others, and Garrow seems to have shaped his cross-examinations of witnesses in accordance with his sense of jurors' own attitudes and biasses.

---

[147] Miles, *A Letter to Sir John Fielding*, 19.
[148] Beattie, 'Scales of Justice,' 237.
[149] The following account of Garrow's career at the Old Bailey is based on May, *The Bar and the Old Bailey*, 40–2, Beattie, 'Scales of Justice', 237–47, as well as the Old Bailey *Proceedings*.

Garrow was particularly hard on thief-takers not attached to Bow Street or one of the rotation offices. He made a distinction between public officers of the law and men he called 'private traps', those who sought out and prosecuted offenders without being in any way connected to a magistrate. Such men had been common in the first half of the century and there were still thief-takers in the 1780s not employed by the magistrates at Bow Street or not working from one of the rotation offices.[150] Garrow treated such men with open contempt, presumably feeling that the jurors would have little regard for those who were simply in the business for money and who worked without the implicit authority that the runners derived from operating under the auspices of magistrates. Garrow took a hard line with private thief-takers when they refused to acknowledge that they stood to gain financially from a conviction. 'How long have you been engaged in this honourable business of thief-taking?' he asked Joseph Levy, and then, when Levy denied that he had helped prosecute cases in the previous session, 'What, there was no blood money last Sessions?'[151] He asked another thief-taker, Christopher Sanders, giving evidence in a robbery case in 1792, how often he had been in court, how many rewards he had collected, and whether he had other cases 'of the same sort' pending in other courts (he had). Garrow concluded his cross-examination by observing in the form of a question, and for the benefit of the jury, that 'you are neither a police officer nor a parish officer, but a gentleman having time to do this business', to which Sanders replied lamely 'it is for the good of the public.'[152] That was precisely the point that Garrow intended to deny by his insistent cross-examinations of both private thief-takers and the prosecutors who hired them—cross-examinations aimed at forcing them to admit that they were well aware of the rewards they were looking forward to earning while putting defendants' lives at risk.

When the opportunity arose, Garrow occasionally subjected the Bow Street officers and the men who had attached themselves to the rotation offices to vigorous cross-examinations—and particularly the latter who occupied a more tenuous position in the policing world than the Bow Street men. The magistrates in those offices were not themselves highly regarded; indeed, they were looked down upon as men of indifferent character, men who made a trade of the justice business, and who were not concerned or able to exercise the same kind of control over the runners attached to their offices as the Bow Street magistrates.[153] The Bow Street runners had the great advantage of attachment to a public office better established and more highly regarded in the 1780s than those emerging public offices. They were also much better rewarded and had more stable employment. These differences in

---

[150] Giving evidence for the prosecution in a coining case in 1790, Edward Ryland said 'I am a cordwainer by trade; sometimes I act as a constable when I see a thief.' He had been dismissed as a parish patrolman for theft of beer, and, foregoing the shoemaking business, had became, as he called himself, 'a common thief-taker.' He had not had much success at that either. OBP, October 1790 (James Royer *et al*) t17901027–30.

[151] OBP, January 1785 (George Norris, et al) t17850112–20.

[152] OBP, December 1792 (Edward Egerton) t17921215–3.

[153] Landau, 'The trading justice's trade', 46–70; Ruth Paley, ' "An Imperfect, Inadequate and Wretched System"?: Policing London before Peel', *Criminal Justice History*, 10 (1989), 98–102.

standing and reputation registered in the Old Bailey courtroom. Garrow treated the men attached to the magistrates' offices around the metropolis notably more roughly than the runners who worked under the direction of the justices at Bow Street. He was not unwilling to cast doubt on their motives and integrity by calling them thief-takers, and asking them in court how much money they expected to earn from the conviction (and possible execution) of the defendants in the dock. He accused them of encouraging victims to charge more serious offences than the facts warranted in the hope of earning rewards, and of extracting confessions by threats or the promise of favours.[154] In cross-examining two such officers—including one he called 'a trap belonging to Mr Staples's office'—Garrow asked them repeatedly about the blood money they had earned in recent years, before getting other witnesses to reveal that an officer had planted evidence on one of the accused. The jury acquitted the four defendants.[155]

The Bow Street officers were also vulnerable to such charges, but lawyers rarely made much of the fact that they stood to gain from rewards in some of the cases they helped to prosecute. 'Do you not expect a share of the reward on the conviction of this man?' a defence lawyer asked Thomas Carpmeal in a robbery case in 1783 that was not going well for the accused. 'Yes, you know this as well as you get your own fee,' was the reply, and the matter seems to have rested there, presumably because the lawyer recognized that many of the jurors knew the Bow Street men and were not likely to be swayed by being reminded of their interest in the outcome of the case.[156] The Bow Street runners were also open to the suspicion of encouraging victims to lay more serious charges than the facts warranted—as when, for example, a thief and his accomplices took someone's watch in a crowd by shoving or hustling or otherwise distracting the victim. If pushing could be turned into the appearance of violence that put the victim 'in fear', the offence might be successfully indicted as robbery and bring all concerned in its prosecution some share of a parliamentary reward. Defence counsel frequently wanted to know in such cases on whose advice the more serious charge had been laid. A prosecution witness, asked by Garrow how the indictment had been drawn, revealed that John Townsend, a Bow Street officer, had had a hand in it. 'He is a better lawyer than you,' said Garrow; 'he knows how to make out a highway robbery.'[157] Another prosecutor was asked if he had any conversation with anyone about the indictment and how it was best to charge it, and in particular whether he had spoken with the Bow Street men about sharing the reward. And, he went on, was it at the Brown Bear? Well, yes, it turned out that he 'used' the Brown Bear, that he was a regular there. Garrow then got to the point:

[154] OBP, September 1784 (John Lawrence) t17840915-37; October 1786 (John Lightfoot and John Tyrrell) t17861025-16; December 1787 (John M'Carty and Thomas Hartman) t17871212-24; April 1790 (John King) t17900424-16; December 1783 (Sarah Slade) t17831210-44.
[155] OBP, January 1785 (George Norris *et al*) t17850112-20.
[156] OBP, December 1783 (James Roberts, alias Yark, and Ruth Mercer) t17831210-2.
[157] OBP, April 1787 (John Wheeler) t17870418-96.

Q: So you have heard a great deal about the reward?

A: It was spoke of to be sure.

Q: Who have you had words with about it?

A: Why Mr Atkins, who is here in Court; he is one of the Bow Street officers.

Q: Have you had conversation with Atkins about it?

A: I have had some little conversation with him, I begged him not to speak of it.

Q: Have you never had any conversation with Townsend?

A: No, Sir, nor nobody else.

Garrow clearly thought that Townsend was particularly active in coaching victims and witnesses to exaggerate the violence in these street confrontations.[158]

As we have seen, Bow Street officers were also accused from time to time of managing informal 'identity parades' at the magistrates' office or the Brown Bear public house in a way that encouraged victims to identify as their attackers the suspects the Bow Street men had arrested.[159] And they were occasionally suspected of pressing suspects to confess, either by offering favours if they did, or threatening dire consequences if they refused—both of which forms of persuasion were sufficient by the middle decades of the eighteenth century to have the confession ruled inadmissible.[160]

The Bow Street men were thus not immune from a variety of charges that could undermine the cases they helped to prosecute. Garrow certainly did not regard them as beyond criticism. But he seems rarely to have treated the Bow Street officers to the kinds of damaging cross-examinations to which he subjected some of the private thief-takers and occasionally the runners from the rotation offices, or indeed any witness who attempted to evade his questions. One finds few examples of his attempting to undermine their credibility by sarcasm or scorn or to shake their testimony by the powerful and insistent cross-examinations that made some witnesses tremble at the thought of having to face him. Indeed, one might characterize his attitude towards them as familiar, occasionally verging on friendly, and at worst neutral. Questioning Charles Jealous about an exchange between a defendant and the magistrate at Bow Street during a pretrial hearing some weeks earlier, Garrow asked if he was sure he remembered that conversation accurately. 'If it was for seven years,' Jealous replied irrelevantly, 'and I saw your face, or any man's face, I could remember him.' To which Garrow said that he had 'seen so many instances of your recollecting faces, that I can believe that; but I say as to the conversation?' And when Jealous said that he remembered it well, Garrow left it, not asking him to swear that on oath to unsettle him, as he might have done with another witness.[161] Garrow engaged in similar exchanges with other runners, on

---

[158] OBP, July 1787 (Benjamin M'Cowl and George Brace) t17870711-7.

[159] OBP, December 1784 (Thomas Wood and George Brown) t17841208-2; February 1785 (William Channing) t17850223-122; May 1787 (William Stone) t17870523-7; January 1790 (Thomas Newton et al) t17900113-4; April 1790 (George Wakeman) t17900424-8). See above, text at nn. 82–9.

[160] OBP, October 1785 (John Adamson and Burgell Tranter) t17851019-40; December 1787 (Charles Berkley and John Claw) t17871212-9; October 1790 (Michael Sheridan) t17901027-60. On the emerging rules re confessions, see Langbein, *Origins of Adversary Criminal Trial*, 218–23.

[161] OBP, February 1784 (Thomas Turner) t17840225-97.

one occasion emphasizing Townsend's long experience when he got him to confirm from his own knowledge that his client might have been previously indicted under two aliases, but had never been in custody at Bow Street.[162]

Perhaps the most revealing exchanges between Garrow and the Bow Street men came in cases involving counterfeiting of the coinage and in particular in his dealings with John Clarke. Clarke was an effective witness, not only because of his expertise, but because, as we have seen, of the way he testified in court—by not straining the evidence, not pushing it beyond its limits, or appearing to strive mightily for convictions at any cost. His reputation at the Old Bailey can be seen in the way Garrow (as well as the judges and other lawyers) dealt with him. Garrow questioned him carefully, and often with a certain respect. In a trial in October 1785, he interrupted Clarke's evidence to raise an objection, saying when he did so that 'you are the last man I should stop; but I should object the same if my Lord Mayor was a witness.'[163] Perhaps the clearest testimony to Clarke's reputation came in a trial in 1789 when, being questioned by Garrow, he said that he wished to go out of court, no doubt to visit the necessary house, and promised that 'I will not speak to anybody I assure you.' The printer of the *Proceedings* thought it worth reporting the following exchange:

Mr Garrow. I can trust you; but for the satisfaction of the prisoners, whose lives are at stake; you say you will not speak to anybody.

Mr Clark, to the Prisoners. Gentlemen, will you trust me, I will not say anything to any person.

Prisoner John Jones. You have too much honour to do anything of the kind Mr Clark, we are sensible.[164]

6. CONCLUSION

Garrow frequently referred to the Bow Street men as officers of justice or officers of the law. In so doing, he recognized the quasi-official position they had come to occupy since the middle of the eighteenth century. Despite their reliance on rewards for a good part of their income, the runners had successfully established a public and professional character which owed a great deal to Sir John Fielding's efforts over the quarter century before his death in 1780. It had been Fielding's ambition to create a centre of policing and prosecution in Bow Street that would encourage the public across the metropolis to report offences and help to diminish crime by ensuring that offenders were apprehended, charged, convicted, and punished. He had persuaded the government to grant stipends to two associate justices who helped him to keep his house in Bow Street open for long and regular hours. He created the first courtroom outside the City of London which attracted

---

[162] OBP, February 1786 (John Kitsall, alias Wilmot, alias Smith) t17860222–55.
[163] OBP, October 1785 (James Scott *et al*) t17851019–45. And see OBP, April 1786 (Joseph Yelland *et al*) t17860426–9; September 1789 (George Dawson and Deborah Dawson) t17890909–46.
[164] OBP, June 1789 (Thomas Denton and John Jones) t17890603–50.

and accommodated an audience for his examinations of suspected offenders. And he ensured that Bow Street and the work of his runners would become widely known by inviting the press to report on his pretrial examinations. In these ways, Fielding opened the early stages of criminal prosecution to the public much more than they had ever been before and made Bow Street not only the best known and the busiest magistrates' office in the metropolis, but what was more important, a public institution—an institution that continued after his death to be a permanent part of the administration of the criminal law in the capital.

The runners were a crucial element in Fielding's practice of public justice. Under his control and direction—and with the financial support they drew from the government's subvention—they became a stable group of experienced investigators who made detection an acceptable element in policing, and acquired reputations that distinguished them from the shadowy thief-takers who had so corruptly manipulated the opportunities provided by massive state rewards in the first half of the century. The runners were no doubt motivated by the prospect of rewards, and they almost certainly helped to convict men innocent of the charges they faced by rigging identity parades and encouraging hesitant prosecutors. But there seems to have been little perception in the public in the late eighteenth century that the Bow Street men were corrupt or untrustworthy, at least among those in and out of parliament whose opinions were crucial to the shaping of the police, including members of the juries who sat on the felony cases tried at the Old Bailey. This, I presume, is why Garrow made little effort to undermine the runners' credibility as witnesses, whatever his own view of them might have been.

6

Fielding's Legacy: Police Reform in the 1780s

1. THE GOVERNMENT AND POLICING IN THE 1780s

John Fielding died in September 1780 on the eve of a renewed crisis in the administration of the criminal law that drew the central government more directly than ever before into the management of policing and prosecution in London and into the construction and support of new penal arrangements. The immediate crisis arose from three intersecting issues. One was the familiar and now seriously amplified post-war crime problem, as reports of violent offences and property crime of all kinds escalated over the first half of the1780s, not only in London, but now also in the expanding industrial areas in the Midlands and the North. The second problem troubling the government as crime began to increase was a serious penal issue that was a consequence of the break with America—the closing of the former colonies to English convicts. Transportation to the American colonies had been established in 1718 as the principal sanction imposed on convicted felons, and it had provided six decades of stability in penal administration. When the possibility of transportation was removed in 1776, convicts piled up in inadequate gaols all over England, and they did so in increasing numbers as prosecutions mounted in the post-war years and convicted offenders continued to be sentenced to terms of transportation, with the destination left to be decided.[1] Such problems in the penal realm were not easily solved, and certainly not rapidly. Prison ships moored in the Thames (the dreaded hulks) had provided some small relief during the war, but after 1782 the government was faced with the difficult matter of finding either an alternative destination for offenders sentenced to transportation or an alternative sanction.

The third issue that revealed problems in the administration of the criminal law as the American war came to an end arose from the week-long period of protest and violence that had taken place in London in June 1780, known as the Gordon riots, in which the civil authorities lost control of the streets and mobs attacked and burned down public and private buildings. These alarming events underlined the weakness of London policing, and most especially the inadequacy of the magistrates

---

[1] For transportation and its termination, see A. Roger Ekirch, *Bound for America: The Transportation of British Convicts to the Colonies, 1718–1775* (Oxford, 1987); Gwenda Morgan and Peter Rushton, *Eighteenth-century Criminal Transportation: the formation of the criminal Atlantic* (Basingstoke, 2004); J. M. Beattie, *Crime and the Courts in England, 1660–1800* (Princeton and Oxford, 1986), ch. 9.

in Westminster and the parishes of Middlesex and Surrey within the ambit of the larger metropolis.

These were problems only the government could solve. They fell to what was in effect a new department formed in 1782 as a result of the reorganization of the work of the two secretaries of state.[2] Hitherto, both secretaries had shared the work, dividing foreign affairs along geographical lines and sharing, though unevenly, the small amount of domestic business that came their way.[3] The new arrangement in 1782 assigned domestic and colonial business to one secretary, foreign affairs to the other. It was a division that had been agreed for political rather than administrative reasons—in particular George III's anxiety to have as little as possible to do with Charles James Fox when he came into office with Lord Rockingham after the fall of the North government in 1782.[4] But it had important administrative consequences, most especially for domestic issues, which became for the first time the sole concern of one of the leading ministers of the crown. The establishment of the Home Department made it likely that the administration of the criminal law would receive more focussed attention from the government than ever before. In time, the office would provide a setting, a centre, where knowledge and expertise with respect to penal policy, prisons, policing and other aspects of criminal administration could accumulate, where issues could be discussed, suggestions received, outside help sought, policy formulated, and when necessary, legislation debated and drafted. This did not happen immediately, but some of the early fruits of the emerging focus on criminal issues can be seen in efforts undertaken in the 1780s to improve the policing of London.

Apart from the transportation question and penal policy in general, the most immediate issue the government faced as the American war came to an end was the extent of reported crime and violence in the published *Proceedings* of the Old Bailey, in the London newspapers, and in the monthly magazines. The crime reported in this way amounted to a fraction of the offences that might have been prosecuted if more victims had gone to the trouble of finding a magistrate and to the bother and expense of undertaking an investigation and laying charges. But even the fraction that came to the attention of the courts was sufficient to create another period of anxiety about the criminal justice system, another post-war crime wave. As had been common in previous conflicts, prosecutions had fallen away during the American war, not as sharply as in the past perhaps, but nonetheless from an annual average of 658 felony trials involving the taking of property in the first half of the 1770s to an average during the war of just over 500, reaching a low point of 346 in 1779 (Table 6.1). As in the past, prosecution levels rose as the war drew to a close, and then spiked sharply in the early years of peace. In 1784, the judges heard a thousand cases involving property offences at the Old Bailey, and

---

[2] Simon Devereaux, 'Convicts and the State: the administration of criminal justice in Great Britain during the reign of George III', Ph.D. dissertation (University of Toronto, 1997), ch. 2; *idem*, 'The Criminal Branch of the Home Office, 1782–1830' in Greg T. Smith, Allyson N. May, and Simon Devereaux (eds.), *Criminal Justice in the Old World and the New* (Toronto, 1998), 270–308.

[3] M. A. Thomson, *The Secretaries of State, 1681–1782* (Oxford, 1932).

[4] Boyd Hilton, *A Mad, Bad, and Dangerous People. England 1783–1846* (Oxford, 2006), 39–40.

Table 6.1. Property offences at the Old Bailey, 1770–1789[1]

Years	Robbery	Burglary[2]	Other capital[3]	Larceny[4]	Receiving	Total
1770–74	279	319	492	1928	188	3206
Annual Average	56	64	98	386	38	641
1775–82	406	360	776	2545	150	4217
Annual Average	51	45	97	318	19	527
1783–89	546	570	1145	3369	205	5857
Annual Average	78	81	164	481	29	837

[1] Source: <http://www.oldbaileyonline.org>
[2] Burglary (85%) and housebreaking (15%)
[3] Shoplifting, theft from dwelling house, from other specified place, picking pockets, horsetheft.
[4] Grand larceny (96%) and petty larceny.

well over 800 in subsequent years. Where the annual average had been 527 during the war years, in the seven years from 1783 to the end of the decade it had risen to 837, an increase of almost 60 per cent. Robbery and burglary, widely regarded as the most serious offences and the most likely (after murder) to be reported in the press and given the most space in trial accounts, led the way in the immediate post-war years, almost doubling in 1784 over their levels in the two previous years.

As had been the case after every war in the eighteenth century, alarm about the dangers on the roads, about violent attacks on houses, and the mounting levels of offences of all kinds was a constant theme in the press in the early 1780s. The seriousness of the violence was brought home to members of parliament and the cabinet by the number of prominent victims of robberies and other serious offences. Thomas Fellows, a Middlesex magistrate, was one such victim: making his way home to Uxbridge, having attended the county quarter sessions in Clerkenwell in September 1783, his coach was stopped by three highwaymen one of whom presented a pistol and took his watch and five guineas in gold.[5] Sir Thomas Davenport and his wife were similarly held up in the post-war years on the outskirts of London by two mounted and armed men (to whom they handed over their gold watches and their money), as was Sir William Jarvis Twissden and an Irish peer, the earl of Clermont.[6] Other men of more than middling rank were mugged on the

[5] OBP, September 1783 (John Burke) t17830910–3; OBP, October 1783 (John Burke) t17831029–1.

[6] OBP, December, 1783 (Robert Cross) t17831210–6; OBP, September 1784 (George Drummond) t17840915–21; OBP, December 1784 (Thomas Wood) t17841208–2. Simon Devereaux has noted the large number of upper-class victims in the early 1780s ('Convicts and the State,' 1–3). For other examples in the eighteenth century, see Nicholas Rogers, 'Confronting the Crime Wave: the Debate over Social Reform and Regulation, 1749–1753' in Lee Davison *et al* (eds.), *Stilling the Grumbling Hive: the response to social and economic problems in England, 1689–1750* (Stroud, 1992) 79–81; and Norma Landau, 'Gauging crime in late eighteenth-century London,' *Social History*, 35 (4, 2010), 396–417.

streets of London in these years, including William Wickham, (who was studying law, having left Oxford two years earlier and who was to be appointed a police magistrate in 1792 and to work in the Home Office, organizing spies against what were thought to be insurrectionary threats). He was hustled and beaten by a group of men near the Theatre Royal in Drury Lane ('where the robberies generally are done,' John Townsend observed at the trial).[7] As a writer in the *Gentleman's Magazine* complained in 1784, the amount of violence on the roads 'must make every man tremble for his safety, who is under the necessity of frequently visiting the metropolis.'[8]

Reports of violence against the wealthy and well-connected may well have added to the sense of urgency felt in the Home Office as the number of offences mounted in the post-war years. But almost certainly as compelling were the difficulties experienced by magistrates, gaolers and indeed everyone involved in the administration of the law. An increase in commitments to trial on the order of well over 50 per cent in a matter of months put pressure on institutions that could quickly fill to capacity. The numbers of offenders involved were tiny by modern standards, but so were the institutions called upon to deal with the prosecution of felonies. Magistrates' offices, courtrooms (including the Old Bailey), gaols and houses of correction, could all easily become overcrowded. In the case of the gaols in which defendants were kept while awaiting trial and to which the guilty were returned, the pressures of accommodation were much more severe in the 1780s' crime wave than they had been for decades because of the failure of the government to find an alternative destination for the hundreds of convicts sentenced to transportation and those pardoned from execution on condition that they too be sent out of the country.

The alternative punishment of imprisonment at hard labour was being advocated in several quarters even before the American war closed the door to transportation. But there were huge impediments to its implementation. There were few institutions capable of housing men and women so convicted. County houses of correction had been established in the sixteenth and seventeenth centuries to impose discipline upon vagrants, prostitutes, disobedient servants, and similar minor but troublesome offenders. But they were in no state to take up the management of the hundreds of felons convicted of noncapital offences after 1782. Nor, despite a

---

[7] OBP, February 1785 (James Coyle) t17850223–13. The theatres notoriously attracted pickpockets, particularly when the king and queen were in attendance, as they were in this case, because they drew a large crowd of spectators around the doors. John Fielding was said to have devised a plan in 1773 to keep the streets around the Drury Lane and Covent Garden theatres clear *(London Evening Post,* 9 November 1773). If so, it had little effect.

[8] *Gentleman's Magazine,* 54 (1784), 712. The proprietors who staged public concerts in Ranelegh House in Chelsea were conscious of the bad effects that the danger on the road from Westminster could have on their attendance. They announced at the beginning of their 1773 season that a horse patrol would guard the road. Two years later they promised an 'armed horse patrol'. During the war that began soon thereafter (when robberies declined) they withdrew the arms and then the patrol itself. When the roads were again thought to be dangerous, in 1783, a patrol that guarded the Chelsea road had been established at Bow Street. For their advertisements, see the *Public Advertiser,* 10 May 1773, 9 March 1775, 27 June 1777, 20 April 1778; and for the Bow Street patrol, below, section 2.

statute of 1779 that authorized the creation of two new prisons in London—penitentiaries, as they were called—did the government take on the burden of building such institutions. Those who were in charge of planning the London penitentiaries failed to agree on where they might be sited, and the government was in any case unwilling to find the considerable sums of money required when, as always after wars, the management of the bloated national debt was an overriding priority.[9]

Unwilling, perhaps unable, to do a great deal to solve the serious penal difficulties experienced in many parts of the country, the government that replaced Lord North's disgraced administration in the Spring of 1782 sought for ways to reduce the number of offenders crowding into the courts and gaols. Their initial moves were familiar responses to increasing prosecutions. On the one hand, as a way of discouraging the most serious offenders, the government tried to enlarge the terror surrounding capital punishment by limiting the granting of pardons. The possibility of obtaining a pardon, many believed, not only gave offenders some hope that they might not be hanged, but also delayed the carrying out of the penalty and thus weakened the connection in the minds of offenders between crime and its consequences. In a crime wave in the middle of the century, the Pelham government had sought to discourage violent offences by making the punishment of murder as gruesome as possible by the so-called Murder Act.[10] After the American war the government made a similar effort to frighten men contemplating robbery by announcing that the king would refuse to pardon violent offenders—a threat that was sufficiently carried out that the middle years of the 1780s were the bloodiest of the century.[11] In addition, as a further effort to impress potential offenders and spectators with the solemnity of execution, the government accepted the long-standing criticism of the harmful effects of the ancient three-mile procession of the condemned from Newgate to the hanging place at Tyburn by ordering in 1783 that London executions henceforth would take place outside the gaol, where a scaffold was to be erected for the hanging days several times a year.[12]

Lord Shelburne, the first principal secretary of the new Home Office (to give it the name it later acquired) in March 1782, and Thomas Townshend, who

---

[9] For penal ideas and the extent of incarceration in the late eighteenth century, see Michael Ignatieff, *A Just Measure of Pain: the Penitentiary in the Industrial Revolution, 1750–1850* (New York, 1978); Randall McGowen, 'A Powerful Sympathy: Terror, the Prison, and Humanitarian Reform in Early Nineteenth-Century Britain,' *Journal of British Studies*, 25 (3, 1986), 312–34; idem, 'The Body and Punishment in Eighteenth-Century England,' *Journal of Modern History*, 59 (4, 1987), 651–79; Devereaux, 'Convicts and the State', ch. 4; idem, 'The Making of the Penitentiary Act, 1775–1779,' *The Historical Journal*, 42 (2, 1999), 405–33; Beattie, *Crime and the Courts*, ch. 9.

[10] 25 Geo II, c. 37 (1752).

[11] Simon Devereaux, 'Recasting the Theatre of Execution: the Abolition of the Tyburn Ritual,' *Past and Present*, 202 (2009), Fig. 1, 135 (annual convictions at the Old Bailey across the eighteenth century) and Fig. 3, 149 (executions); Beattie, *Crime and the Courts*, 582–92.

[12] Devereaux, 'Recasting the Theatre of Execution'; Andrea McKenzie, *Tyburn's Martyrs: Execution in England 1675–1775* (London, 2007), ch. 1; V. A. C. Gatrell, *The Hanging Tree: Execution and the English People 1770–1868* (Oxford, 1994), 602–3.

followed him in July when Shelburne moved to the Treasury,[13] also made an effort to reduce serious crime by attacking what were widely regarded as its fundamental causes—the high levels of vice and immorality in the metropolis and the large number of petty offences left unpunished by the failure of the magistrates to put the law into effect. As Simon Devereaux has shown, Shelburne defended this approach to crime prevention as an effective alternative to the more expensive and no doubt more contentious programme of penitentiary building contained in the 1779 Act. He was to say later that he had been assured that 'if the number of ale-houses could be lessened, the Vagrant act enforced, and the general administration of justice as it stood invigorated,' there would be no need for new penal institutions.[14] This may have been a useful excuse. But the attack on minor crime as a way of limiting more serious offences was a strategy that any government was likely to have followed in the circumstances of 1782 and after. Certainly the Pelham government had made a serious effort to introduce such measures in the mid-century crime wave—an effort that was well known in the secretary of state's office since copies of several documents dating from the early 1750s are among the 1781 office papers.[15]

The difference in the post-American war years was that, whereas the Pelham administration had relied on a parliamentary committee to propose legislation, the new Home Office took the lead in 1782 and after. In October 1782, Townshend wrote to urge the leading magistrates of the cities of London and Westminster and the chairmen of the Middlesex and Surrey benches, to persuade the justices in their jurisdictions to pay more attention to the licensing of public houses, to enforce the vagrancy laws, to do more to control gambling, and to meet more often in petty sessions if that was necessary—in general to strive to halt the corruption of public morals that everyone agreed was the fundamental cause of crime. The magistrates in petty sessions were required to send in an account from time to time of their proceedings in putting these orders into effect.[16] Beyond that, Townsend introduced two pieces of legislation in 1783 designed, in one case, to increase the punishment of those convicted of receiving stolen goods, and, in the other, to

---

[13] For the politics of the two years following the fall of the disgraced administration of Lord North at the conclusion of the American war in March 1782—a period that saw a succession of administrations headed by Lord Rockingham (March–July 1782), Shelburne (July 1782–April 1783), Fox and North in coalition (April–December 1783), and William Pitt (from December 1783)—see John Cannon, *The Fox-North Coalition: Crisis of the Constitution, 1782–4* (Cambridge, 1969).

[14] *Memoirs of the life of Sir Samuel Romilly* (2nd. edn., 1840), I, 328–9, quoted by Simon Devereaux, 'Strategies of Prevention: London Police Reform in Context, 1782–1792,' a paper delivered at the meeting of the North American Conference on British Studies, San Francisco, 2007.

[15] TNA: SP 37/15, 474–84, 491–8 ('Propositions relating to the Causes and Prevention of Robberies etc.'; 'Matters proposed to be given in charge to the Judges now going the Circuits'; 'Precedents in the Reigns of King William the 3rd, Queen Anne, and his late and present Majesty [George I and George II] of Proclamations and Orders issued for punishing Prophaneness and Immorality, and for apprehending Street Robbers and Rioters etc.'

[16] TNA: HO 43/1, 43–8; Devereaux, 'Convicts and the State,' 202–3. The requirement to report appears to have been largely ignored: only two such reports are to be found in the department records (TNA: HO 42/2, 112–16, 117–18).

broaden the Vagrancy Act (1744) to bring within its purview persons found carrying housebreaking implements or arms at night. The first bill failed to pass, the second was adopted.[17]

These gestures did little to improve matters, as was made clear by the continuing increase in reported and prosecuted crime in 1783 and after. With that problem becoming ever worse, and no doubt with the continuing penal issues and the anxieties caused by the Gordon riots in mind, Townshend (Lord Sydney after April 1783) encouraged an effort in the department to do something more fundamental to improve the policing of the metropolis beyond attempting to persuade the magistracy to intensify the policing of minor crime and tinkering with the criminal law. He had said when introducing his two legislative measures in February 1783 that it was his intention to 'make some regulations for the improvement of the police of the metropolis'.[18] He took that up on his return to the department, or at least supported an examination by others of what police reform might mean and how it might be accomplished. The result was to be a dramatically innovative (though politically insensitive) bill in 1785 that failed to gather support and disappeared virtually immediately, though it left traces that were to be important in the future. The question was taken up again, some years later in different circumstances, and resulted in a statute that was less ambitious than the previous bill, but that nonetheless introduced significant changes in the way the criminal law was administered in the metropolis.

These two pieces of legislation, the second in particular, owed a good deal to the ideas and practices that John Fielding had developed at Bow Street. They form the main subject of this chapter. But I will begin with another development at Bow Street that also derived from Fielding's ideas and that was successful because of the commitment of the Home Office to strengthening the policing of London. This was the introduction of an armed and salaried foot patrol (or 'patrole,' as it was called) in the winter of 1782–83, established as a means of countering the highwaymen who were so common in the post-war years on the main roads on the outskirts of the city. It was initiated by Sampson Wright, the chief magistrate, but it was taken up, generously funded, and strongly supported by the Home Department. That it was to become accepted in the 1780s as an element in London policing is a measure both of the seriousness with which the crime problem was regarded and of the intentions of the government to do something to confront it. The bill that followed in 1785 and the statute in 1792, which we will then go on to study, were further expressions of those intentions.

---

[17] As 23 Geo 3, c. 88 (1783). See Sir Leon Radzinowicz, *A History of the English Criminal Law and its Administration from 1750*, 4 vols, (London 1948–68), vol. 3, 92–3; and Devereaux, 'Convicts and the State', 203.

[18] *Parliamentary History*, 1783, 23, 364–5.

2. THE BOW STREET PATROL

Patrolling the streets of the metropolis by the night watch as a way of preventing crime and catching perpetrators was a well-established policing activity by the 1780s. And both the make-up of the parochial night watch and the way it was organized had been steadily improved over the previous century. It had become a force of paid officers supported by local taxes, rather than being made up of reluctant citizens taking their turns to guard their neighbourhoods at night as a civic duty. By the early eighteenth century, watchmen were each assigned a beat in their parish or ward which they were supposed to traverse twice each hour through the night, and in the course of the century they became more effective guardians of the night streets than they once had been. They were certainly not all as old or feeble as their critics made out. Their policing efforts were also immensely aided by the remarkable transformation of the lighting of the streets of the capital that took place in the second quarter of the eighteenth century and after.[19] But even the most attentive watchmen could not do a great deal to prevent theft and violence, certainly not the most serious offences. In the best of circumstances, one man walking an established beat twice an hour, announcing his presence by calling the time, was not likely to discourage determined robbers and burglars, especially men working in gangs. In any case, watchmen were particularly thin on the ground in the large populous suburbs on the edges of the expanding metropolis, many traversed by busy roads that provided tempting targets for both mounted robbers and footpads.

This was one of the policing problems that John Fielding had taken up early in his years at Bow Street. As we have seen, he spent some of his small budget in his first years in the office sending officers to patrol parts of the metropolis in which robberies were common and especially along the major roads surrounding the capital. Some of this patrolling was undertaken in order to catch a persistent highwayman or a gang of burglars; once that had been achieved, or the offenders had moved out of the district, the patrolling was withdrawn. But some was a little more general than that, a group of men being sent into an area for a number of days or weeks as a way of diminishing crime more broadly, or to provide protection for coaches and travellers along a particular road. The first annual report Fielding submitted to the secretary of state in 1756 included payments for men patrolling Westminster squares and for two mounted officers 'patrolling the Great Roads to prevent Robberies.'[20] The accounts for the following three years include many such entries.[21]

---

[19] Elaine A. Reynolds, *Before the Bobbies: the Night Watch and Police Reform in Metropolitan London, 1720–1830* (London, 1998); J. M. Beattie, *Policing and Punishment in London, 1660–1750: Urban Crime and the Limits of Terror* (Oxford, 2001).

[20] TNA: T 38/671, f. 4.

[21] For numerous examples of Fielding's use of patrolling, see ch. 3, text at nn. 39–40, 54–5, 67–8, 98–104.

When his budget allowed it, Fielding invested a considerable portion of his annual allowance on patrolling as a deterrent to highway robbery. In the winter of 1761–62, for example, as the Seven Years War was coming to an end and London experienced a surge of robbery and other property offences, he sent out mounted patrols along some of the major roads on the outskirts of London. He was unable to sustain that effort once the peace was signed, however, because the increase in business coming into the office forced him to send his officers to investigate crimes and chase suspects. To maintain some form of patrolling on the roads around the city as part of the larger policing plan he put forward in 1761, he made the provocative suggestion that a regiment of light cavalry be stationed near the metropolis to take up the task of patrolling the highways (under his direction). That had drawn no response, but he did persuade the Grenville administration to pay for an eight-man horse patrol to guard some of the main roads every night. That was not an expenditure Grenville was anxious to sustain, given his anxiety as the head of the Treasury to reduce the national debt in the post-war years, and after a year he withdrew the government's subsidy. Policing, he said in justification—invoking the established wisdom—was a matter for local communities.[22]

For the most part, patrolling from Bow Street was carried out during the remaining two decades of John Fielding's magistracy whenever his ordinary budget made it possible. It was largely limited to forays by groups of officers when an active highwayman or footpad threatened a particular stretch of road or locality. In the description of the office written in 1777 referred to earlier, the author included among the officers 'A Conductor of Patroles and pursuits—to fix patroles in places particularly infected and pursuits after those against whom informations are made'. This was Nicholas Bond, who combined the chief clerkship of the office with leadership on the policing side. It is clear that the patrols he was expected to organize were still ad hoc, sent out to deter offences 'in places particularly infected' and for as short a time as possible.[23]

Fielding remained persuaded of the value of surveillance of all kinds, and not just on the major roads. The plan he put to the government in 1761 had included foot patrols within the city; and in the evidence he gave to the house of commons committee set up in 1770 to examine the state of crime in Westminster, he emphasized the importance of the night watch and ways in which it could be improved. His notion that the various parish watches should be put under the control of a committee of magistrates with himself in the chair was ignored, but his suggestions helped to promote the reform argument that, after a good deal of local consultation, led to a major reform of the watch in legislation in 1774 that improved the methods of recruitment of watchmen in Westminster, regulated their numbers, gave them better pay, imposed more control over their work, and

---

[22] Radzinowicz, *A History of English Criminal Law,* 3, 58–62; and see above, ch. 3, text at nn. 102–3.
[23] NLI 15929 (3)

sought to improve cooperation among the separate parish forces. Following the lead of one of the parishes, the Act also created armed parish patrols—essentially groups of watchmen who were not bound to fixed beats, but free to move around the whole parish at night.[24]

The impulse also remained strong at Bow Street to institute patrolling in a more permanent way to deal with violent street and highway offences. Fielding's successor as chief magistrate, Sampson Wright, took up the cause in the early 1780s, when the need for more effective policing of the roads became increasingly obvious as the American war drew to a close. 'The present deplorable state of the police of the metropolis and its environs', a London newspaper commented in August 1782, 'demands the consideration of government—not an hour passes now that the most daring depredations are not made upon the passenger even in the face of day; and to add to the calamity, we understand that near 200 more desperadoes are to be discharged from the hulks, in the course of next month, to reinforce the present powerful corps of housebreakers, highwaymen, and footpads.'[25] And, essentially for the first time, the policing problems of London did indeed receive the sustained consideration by the government, part of their effort to reduce the burden placed on the criminal justice system by the sharply increasing number of offenders.

The spur for the formation of the patrol was provided by Sampson Wright's initiative to use his office funds to hire what the *London Packet* said in August 1782 was a group 'of stout men, who are to go armed, and patrole in different parts, from the dusk of the evening till 12 o'clock at night' as a way of countering the 'numerous robberies that are committed almost every evening in the vicinity of London.'[26] Bow Street confirmed in the following month that 'a well-appointed patrole is now established to guard the principal avenues leading into the metropolis.'[27] At the same time, Wright sent a plan for a patrol to Townshend, the secretary of state for the Home Department, who, as we have seen, was developing a preventive strategy in the face of the continuing increase of property offences and the threat of more as winter approached. Wright's plan called for the metropolis to be divided into three districts in each of which a patrol of 10 men would be set up to guard the main roads. It would be difficult and dangerous work, he thought, so a smaller number would not 'think themselves safe or be equal to the Undertaking.' They would have to be paid five shillings a night each, the costs of which, he was confident, would be covered by reduced reward payments when potential robbers realized that 'Detection will henceforth follow the Commission of Crimes with greater Certainty than heretofore.'[28] Secretary Townshend seized on the idea. Wright recalled in the account of the office he drew up a few months later— probably in March 1783 for Lord North, who became secretary of the Home Office in the coalition government he formed then with Charles James Fox:

---

[24] Reynolds, *Before the Bobbies*, 51–4, 63–4, 78–9.
[25] *London Packet*, 28–30 August 1782.
[26] *London Packet*, 28–30 August 1782.
[27] *Gazetteer*, 25 September 1782.
[28] TNA: HO 42/1, ff. 290–3.

... at the beginning of [last] Winter I presented a Plan to Lord Sydney, one of the Secretaries of State, for protecting the Roads round London (which at that time were so much infested by Footpads and Highwaymen that scarce a Night passed without several Robberies being committed, and very often accompanied with great Cruelties) by establishing a Patrol of able Men properly armed for that Purpose. This Plan was immediately adopted and is still continued.... The Expence attending the execution of this Plan, from the great Number of Men necessary to be employed on so many different Roads is about fifty Pounds a Week, which bears no proportion to the Benefits that have arisen from it.[29]

Wright went on to say that the plan had been adopted by the government 'only on the Spur of the Occasion' and that it was unclear 'whether it will be continued or not.' And indeed, it had been accepted as a six-week experiment out of the usual concern in the Treasury about the costs involved.[30] At about £2,600 a year, those costs were not insignificant, considering that the Bow Street office had never received more than a quarter of that sum for its main policing activities. For some time, the Treasury queried the need for its continuance. As each six-week payment became due, and successive heads of the Home Office who had to bear the brunt of complaints about the state of crime—Sydney, who had instituted it, Lord North, in his short-lived coalition with Charles James Fox, and Sydney again, in the Pitt administration that came into office in December 1783—put political differences aside in their continued support for the new patrol against the Treasury's insistent opposition. The Home Department's attitude was summed up by North when in June 1783 the Treasury Board enquired whether in his view 'so very expensive an Establishment' should continue to be funded. The Board was informed that

Lord North has taken into his Consideration the utility of continuing the Patroles, employed under the Direction of Sir Sampson Wright for preventing Footpad and Highway Robberies, his Lordship has also consulted Sir Sampson and some of the other Justices upon this occasion, and has obtained from the former the inclosed Paper, containing a comparative State of the Robberies committed last Year and in the present, within the same Period, by which it appears that the number has considerably decreased, the cause of which, Sir Sampson attributes, principally to the Patroles, who, though they have apprehended but few, have been vigilant in preventing Robberies and Violences, which might otherwise have been committed on the public Roads leading to this Metropolis.

North's view, the letter went on, was that it would not be advisable to discontinue the patrol now 'particularly as so many Men have lately been discharged from the Sea and Land Services.'[31] In the following year, his successor, Sydney, was asked once more if the 'Patrol should be continued at the same Expence it has now long occasioned to the Public,' and gave the same answer. He agreed with the Treasury's concern that the costs should be controlled, while insisting on the patrol's

[29] NLI 15929 (3). For the dating of this document and Wright as the author, see ch. 4, n. 5.
[30] The six-weekly payments in early 1783 are recorded in the 'Special Service Book'—TNA: T 38/741, 11, 15, 16.
[31] TNA: HO 35/4, 23 June 1783; T 27/35, 259; HO35/4, 8 August 1783.

continuance. It had been, he said, 'of so much advantage to the Public ever since its Establishment in preventing many outrageous Offences against the Peace, which were daily increasing, that it is his opinion, that it would be productive of most serious and alarming consequences, if the Patrole was to be discontinued at this present time.'[32]

It remained in place, and indeed the patrol was to be expanded on several occasions over the next four decades. Sampson Wright had asked for 30 men, to be divided into three parties, but in the event the government provided funds to support 46 men who worked in eight groups of five or six, with one man in each named as the 'conductor', or 'captain'. Their principal duty was to guard the main roads around the metropolis. Each of the eight parties was assigned to one of the major routes: one worked on the main road to the east, along the Balls Pond and City Roads to Shoreditch and beyond; two patrolled roads to the north—one to Kentish Town and Hampstead, the other to Holloway and Islington; three parties went to the west—towards Acton and Kilburn, to Fulham and Chelsea, and along the Hammersmith Road respectively; and finally, two worked south of the river, one along the Clapham and Wandsworth roads, west from Southwark, the other to the east, along the Deptford and Greenwich roads.[33] They divided into smaller parties at several points along those roads.

Each ordinary patrolman was paid 17s.6d a week (£45.10.0d. a year) the captains double that—providing decent incomes which might occasionally have been improved by payments for extra work from office funds, a share of a parliamentary reward for helping to arrest and convict a highwayman, or part of a private reward.[34] It was an income sufficient to attract and retain recruits, especially the leadership post of conductor/captain, in which men tended to serve for many years.

The patrols went out every night, armed with cutlasses. They went on foot, though they occasionally hired coaches to bring in those they arrested. And they soon began to make arrests and to give depositions before the magistrates at Bow Street and evidence in trials at the Old Bailey and the Surrey assizes.[35] Being told about a robbery by two footpads in the fields near Chelsea, in November 1783, the men on patrol on the route that began at Hyde Park corner and ran west to Kew Bridge, gave chase. Having no success, John Shallard, James Macmanus (the brother of Patrick, the runner), and the rest of the patrol retraced their steps from Pimlico and found the two suspects in Hyde Park with the money they had stolen. Having committed them overnight at a nearby watchhouse, they resumed their patrol, but returned the next morning and took them to Bow Street where they were examined and committed.[36] In December, another group of patrolmen going along the City Road to begin the beat to the east, came upon a coach that had been

---

[32] TNA: HO 36/4, 149–50.
[33] TNA: T 1/598, 315–24.
[34] For the identity of the early patrolmen, their beats, and weekly pay see TNA: T 1/598, 315–24.
[35] For depositions taken at Bow Street, see LMA: OB/SP. In 1784, e.g., the depositions that have survived include nine given by members of the patrol.
[36] LMA: OB/SP/December1783/35.

stopped and robbed by two men who were running away with drawn cutlasses. Three of the patrolmen gave chase and apprehended one of the footpads.[37]

Patrolmen gave evidence in a sufficient number of Old Bailey cases over the 1780s and their engagements with suspected robbers and others were reported sufficiently often in the newspapers that they became familiar figures in the metropolis and their patrol routes became known to the public. When a man and his wife, going home in their chaise, were stopped and robbed at about 11 p.m. near Turnham Green by a single highwayman, the man went immediately in search of the patrol that he knew would be somewhere in the vicinity. He told the court that

> I came up the road to Hammersmith, and enquired for some of the Bow-street people; I stayed twenty minutes, and then proceeded to Hammersmith turnpike, and from thence to Kensington, where I found them; I believe this was about a quarter before twelve; and a quarter before one, the person took [the highwayman]; and brought word he was taken, the next morning. Having left my address at the turn-pike gate, they came down to acquaint me they had taken him; and the next day, between eleven and twelve, I saw him at Bow-street.[38]

This was only one of several reports of robberies that that particular patrol received during the evening. There were five men on duty and, as one explained in court, they agreed to divide into two parties:

> [T]hree went up the gravel pits, two staid at Kensington gate, and a quarter before one the prisoner came up to the gate; . . . I discovered his horse to be very warm, and from the description I had of the man, I thought he was like him; I dismounted him, and searched him; out of his right hand pocket I took one of these pistols [producing it in court]; the mean while the prisoner delivered one up himself; after that I took him into the turnpike house; Thomas Dyer afterwards searched him in my presence, and found the property [that had been reported stolen].

One of the patrolmen went the next day to search the defendant's lodgings and found a bullet-mould and powder.[39]

The patrol had been created to go after men like this and indeed in their first two years 70 per cent of the 32 cases in which they appeared to give evidence at the Old Bailey were street or highway robberies.[40] In time, in part because highway offences diminished, patrolmen came to play a more general role in the office and to be sent out on jobs by the magistrates or to be engaged by victims. They came to be regarded by the Bow Street magistrates as officers available to be employed on their own, or with one or more of the runners. For example, in January 1784, Archibald Ruthven, one of the first captains of the patrol, accompanied John Clarke in a sting operation to catch a counterfeiter.[41]

---

[37] LMA: OB/SP/December1783/70.
[38] OBP, July 1787 (Thomas Alger) t17870711-9.
[39] OBP, July 1787 (Thomas Alger) t17870711-9.
[40] Based on OBP, 1783-84.
[41] OBP, January 1784 (John Gilbert) t17840114-78.

While patrolmen were never to achieve the status of the runners in the eyes of the magistrates, or indeed of the public, the fact that they came to do the same kind of work carried significant implications for the runners themselves. We will take up these issues more fully in the following chapter. In the meantime, we need to return to the issue of police reform in the years after 1782.

3. THE LONDON AND WESTMINSTER POLICE BILL, 1785

The establishment of the patrol was an indication of the government's commitment to reducing crime in and around London. They had at the same time issued exhortations to the magistrates to play their part by removing the temptations and encouragements that were widely believed to lead men into committing criminal offences in the first place and to draw them down the slippery slope that led to disaster for themselves and danger for society. Beyond that, the Shelburne and Pitt governments had a further ambition in mind, another way in which the policing of London might be strengthened and the preventive programme given some backbone—that is, an intention to improve the magistracy itself.

Concern about the character of the men who sat on the Westminster and Middlesex commissions of the peace was of long standing. They were fundamentally suspect in the eyes of the propertied elite because as urban middle class men, most of whom depended on the fees their magisterial work generated, they lacked the natural authority that the gentry and aristocracy brought to the magistracy of the counties. Those were ancient concerns by 1780. What seems to have persuaded Shelburne and Sydney that something needed to be done of a more fundamental kind was not only the pressing post-war crime problem but also the obvious failure of the London magistracy (with a few exceptions) to respond effectively when, in June 1780, the protests of the Protestant Association against some minor concessions granted to Catholics led to the events known as the Gordon Riots—a week of violence and destruction that included attacks on the main institutions of criminal administration. Civil authority was simply non-existent for the best part of a week, and order was only restored by the brutal intervention of the military. The riots confirmed for many that the magistrates could not be relied on. A brief account of the riots and conclusions drawn from them by the governing class helps to explain why in 1785 the government introduced legislation that, had it been passed, would have transformed the magistracy and the policing of the metropolis.

The riots had begun on Friday 2 June, when Lord George Gordon, the son of a Scottish peer, an M.P, and the head of the recently-formed Protestant Association, led a large crowd of followers to present a petition to parliament urging repeal of recent legislation that had granted some partial relief from the restrictions long imposed on the Catholic population in Britain.[42] When parliament adjourned

[42] The following account of the riots is based very largely on: John Paul de Castro, *The Gordon Riots* (London, 1926); Christopher Hibbert, *King Mob: the Story of Lord George Gordon and the Riots of 1780* (London, 1958); George Rude, *Paris and London in the Eighteenth Century* (London, 1970), 268–92;

without acting on the petition, segments of the crowd expressed their discontent and their anxiety about Popery by attacking the chapels of foreign ambassadors in London, widely believed to be centres of Catholic missionary activity. Over the next few days, a number of houses and businesses of Catholics were also torn down or burned. The attacks broadened ominously on the following Tuesday when parliament reassembled and failed again to address the demands laid out in the petition. The rioters now took out their anger on a wider array of targets, most immediately, the houses and public offices of those few magistrates who had confronted the rioters at the chapels of the Catholic ambassadors and who had ordered the arrest of several rioters. Those accused men had been brought before the Bow Street magistrates on the Monday when a large crowd had been in attendance to hear the evidence given by prosecution witnesses. The names of those witnesses became known to those in attendance and they were further broadcast when the pretrial hearings at Bow Street were reported in the press on the following day. The result was that the houses of several of those witnesses, as well as of the magistrates responsible for the arrests, became immediate targets of the crowd's vengeance.[43]

As a further consequence of those arrests and the commitment of several rioters to await trial, the leading institutions of the criminal justice system were also besieged by different sections of the crowd: the sessions house at the Old Bailey; Newgate gaol, which was gutted and its prisoners released; and other penal institutions in the metropolis, including the Middlesex Bridewell, the New Prison in Clerkenwell, and two prisons in Southwark, King's Bench and the Fleet. The Bow Street office was among the targets demolished on the Tuesday. A crowd milled about in the street much of the day, supplied with beer by a publican hoping to protect his house, until in the early evening a small group broke down the door at Fielding's office, took out the furniture and the records—dozens of volumes (all required by future historians)—and made a bonfire of them all. Three officers had been present most of the day: Nicholas Bond, who went early to find help and never returned; and Macmanus and Prothero who tried to discourage the crowd from carrying out their threats to demolish the building, but then left by the back door when the attack began in the evening. Macmanus said at the subsequent trial of two of the rioters that he went home to get his pistols, cutlass, and great coat, but when he returned he could do little. He merely watched from 'the top of Bow

---

John Stevenson, *Popular Disturbances in England, 1700–1870* (London, 1979), 76–90; Tony Hayter, *The Army and the Crowd in mid-Georgian England* (London, 1978); and two illuminating essays on the character and consequences of the riots by Nicholas Rogers, 'Crowd and People in the Gordon Riots' in Eckhart Hellmuth (ed.), *The Transformation of Political Culture. England and Germany in the Late Eighteenth Century* (London, 1990), 39–55, and *Crowd, Culture, and Politics in Georgian Britain* (Oxford, 1998), ch 5.

[43] *London Courant*, 5 June 1780. A dark cloud was thrown over the public nature of the criminal justice practised at Bow Street—the proceedings open to the public and the press that Fielding had striven so hard to establish—by these acts of vengeance against those identified as enemies of the Protestant cause. The committee of the privy council set up to enquire into the riots criticized Sampson Wright and William Addington for allowing newspapers to publish this information (see below, text at nn. 51–2).

Street', with Prothero and Morant, who had also arrived.[44] Similar attacks were carried out on the houses of some of the rotation office magistrates who made efforts at various times to confront the crowd.[45]

Wednesday brought a further broadening of targets which now included Thomas Langdales's large distillery in Holborn. Perhaps most alarming to the government, Wednesday also saw two attempts to break into the Bank of England, both fended off not by the civil authorities, but by the military. It was indeed to be soldiers, aided by associations of armed property owners, who were to bring the riots to a halt over the next few days. The troops who were in London at the beginning of the riots had been engaged in crowd control to some extent from the beginning, but they had been, as always, hesitant to act without a magistrate being present to read the Riot Act.[46] And very few magistrates had been willing to become involved when crowds of rioters were threatening to pull down or burn houses. Their hesitancy to authorize the use of force in defence of private houses and public buildings meant that on some occasions soldiers stood by while houses were being demolished and their contents burned. Particularly egregious in the eyes of the privy councillors who subsequently examined the origins and nature of the riots was the behaviour of the lord mayor and aldermen of London, the magistrates of the City, who had done little themselves (either out of fear or out of sympathy with the rioters' cause) and had refused to call on troops to confront the rioters in their attacks on the chapels of foreign ambassadors and on the houses and businesses of the largely Catholic population in and around Moorfields.[47]

The legal position of troops confronting a rioting crowd was indeed not entirely clear, or at least not believed to be clear.[48] But all doubt was to be swept aside on Wednesday when the riots seemed to escalate out of control with the attacks on the Bank. On that day, acting on the advice of the chief justice, Lord Mansfield, and of the attorney general, and with the king's approval, the privy council announced that the troops who were by then pouring into London from around the country were authorized to use force in the defence of life or property without waiting for the Riot Act to be read or for a magistrate's explicit authority. The results were predictable. The troops, many of whom had been pelted, taunted, and mocked over the previous days, brought the riots to a swift and bloody end, killing and wounding many in the crowds in doing so. By the Friday, a week after the

---

[44] OPB, 28 June 1780 (William Laurence and Richard Roberts): t17800628–1. Both defendants were convicted. Roberts was hanged and Lawrence pardoned.

[45] Including the houses or offices of William Hyde (Bloomsbury), John Sherwood (Shadwell), John Staples (Whitechapel), and David Wilmot (Worship Street).

[46] Hayter, *The Army and the Crowd*, ch. 12.

[47] The lord mayor, Brackley Kennet, was particularly blamed for failing to call on troops to prevent the attack on the foreign ministers' houses and chapels when he might have done so and then—whether out of fear or out of sympathy with the Protestant Association's programme—for discharging some of the rioters who had been arrested in the early stages of the riots. There can be no doubt that the conduct of the City magistrates was one of the more alarming aspects of the riots to the king's ministers and to the committee of the privy council appointed subsequently to discover the 'authors and abettors' of the disturbances and who examined Kennet at length (see text at nn. 50–3).

[48] Hayter, *The Army and the Crowd*, ch. 1.

Protestant Association petition had been presented to parliament, about 300 people, mainly rioters, were dead. Of the 450 suspects arrested, 134 were tried for various offences, of whom 58 were convicted. Twenty-five rioters were eventually hanged.[49]

Within a few days the privy council created a committee to enquire into the causes of the riots, the state of the gaols, and the behaviour of the magistrates.[50] Several Westminster and Middlesex magistrates were called to give evidence, including the four from the rotation offices who were known to have been active during the riots and whose offices or houses had been destroyed. The most extensive evidence was given by the Bow Street magistrates, Wright and Addington, both of whom gave accounts of their movements in the early days of the riots and of their efforts to intervene in various riotous situations—in particular of their attempts on the first day to find a sufficient number of constables to disperse the crowds around parliament and the Westminster Guildhall. Both had initially been criticized by the house of lords for their failure to organize the defence of parliament since government ministers claimed they had been warned ahead of time by Lord North, the prime minister, that trouble was anticipated.[51] The notice had in fact gone to Fielding at his house in Brentford, where he was seriously ill, and took some time to reach the office. But Addington and Wright were more praised than blamed by the committee of privy councillors. They were supported in particular by the secretaries of state, Stormont and Hilsborough, who said about Addington that 'it was impossible for any Magistrate to be more Zealous and Active than [he] had been.' Wright was similarly defended in the house of lords by the duke of Northumberland, lord lieutenant of Middlesex.[52]

The privy council committee was, however, harsh in its conclusion about the failure of the main body of Middlesex and Westminster magistrates to disperse the rioters or to call on the military to do so. Their report and the reaction in parliament and the press to the week of protest make it clear that the Gordon riots brought to a head the long-standing criticism of so many of the men who acted as justices in the metropolis. The committee's conclusion was that significant changes needed to be made in the way justices were recruited and in the way the criminal law was administered in London. The riots had revealed, they wrote, 'a general remissness in the Officers to whom the preservation of the peace is entrusted.' The way the civil authority was administered, they concluded, 'was inadequate to the purposes of suppressing the Riots, and that some Method is necessary to be taken for the better securing and preserving the peace within the

---

[49] These are Radzinowicz's figures (*History of English Criminal Law*, vol. 3, 89).

[50] The committee report and related papers are at TNA: PC 1/3097 (n.p.).

[51] *Parl. Debates*, 31 (1780–81), 671, 687–8; *Gazetteer*, 3 June 1780; *London Chronicle*, 1–3 June 1780.

[52] *Parl. Debates*, 31 (1780–81), 671, 687–8; TNA: PC 1/3097 (n.p.); *Gazetteer*, 5 June 1780; *London Chronicle*, 3–6 June 1780. Wright and Addington were also commended in the press. See, e.g., *London Chronicle*, 10–13 June 1780.

said Districts'.[53] Lord Shelburne had expressed the same view when parliament was besieged on the first day. It was plain, he told the house of lords, that the policing of Westminster was in every way inadequate, that the commission of the peace, 'was filled by men, base to the last degree.' Recent events, he went on, made it plain that the Westminster police 'ought to be new modelled and that immediately.'[54]

Shelburne's views were important since—as the first head of the new Home Office for a few months in 1782 and then briefly prime minister—he was in a position to act on them. He ensured that the policing of London became for the first time a matter that the central government needed to take up directly, and he passed on his concerns to his successor in the Home Department, Thomas Townshend. Policing issues were being actively canvassed there in 1782–83.[55] David Wilmot, an experienced magistrate at the Worship Street rotation office, submitted a plan that called for the creation of six public offices, besides Bow Street, each staffed by two stipendiary magistrates, four salaried constables, and a clerk.[56] Another magistrate resubmitted a plan he had drawn up at the time of the Gordon riots, similarly recommending that the rotation offices be closed in favour of five or six public offices with three 'sitting magistrates with proper allowances for their attendance.'[57] These ideas were taken up by what turned out to be the most stable government since Lord North's resignation—the administration formed in December 1783 by the young William Pitt who had been brought in by George III to form a government to which the king could give his fullest support. It was to remain in office for more than 20 years. Among the ministers who came back into office with Pitt was Thomas Townshend, now Lord Sydney. He would have preferred a less arduous post, no doubt because he knew the difficulties ahead.[58] Two matters in particular were high on the agenda: the need to establish a destination for felons sentenced to terms of transportation; and the need to do something about the police of the metropolis in the face of the weaknesses widely recognized in the magistracy of Middlesex and Westminster and the continuing, indeed mounting, problem of crime.

Reluctantly or not, Sydney became engaged in the discussions underway in the Home Department to find ways of improving the metropolitan police. Joseph

[53] TNA: PC 1/3097 (n.p.).

[54] *Parl.* Debates, 31 (1780–81), 680; *London Courant*, 5 June 1780, 2. For the influence of the riots on ideas about the reform of the magistracy, see Radzinowicz, *History*, 3, 90–3; Reynolds, *Before the Bobbies*, 60, and her unpublished thesis, 'The Night Watch and Police Reform in Metropolitan London, 1720–1830', Ph.D. thesis (Cornell University, 1991), 237–42.

[55] For discussions of police reform ideas after 1782, see Ruth Paley, 'The Middlesex Justices Act of 1792: its origins and effects', Ph.D. thesis (University of Reading, 1983), chs. 6–7; Devereaux, 'Convicts and the State', 119–217, 343–50; Radzinowicz, *History of English Criminal Law*, vol. 3, 106–7.

[56] TNA: HO 42/1, f. 474: 'A Plan for establishing a certain Number of Offices in Westminster and Middlesex under the Auspices of Government for the Administration of Justice. . . .' A copy, dated 22 November 1784, is enclosed is at TNA: HO 42/5, ff. 390–3.

[57] TNA: HO 42/1, ff. 481–5.

[58] Lord Fitzmaurice, *Life of William, Earl of Shelburne*, 2 vols. (London, 1912), 2, 280–1.

Cawthorne, a writer on magisterial and police issues, recalled in the early 1790s that these matters were 'much attended to by Lord Sydney when Secretary of State.'[59] At any event, it is unlikely that the concentrated activity over 18 months that led to introduction of a major bill in the house of commons could have been carried on without at least his tacit approval. Discussions were in progress when he returned to the department in late December 1783. Earlier in the month, Sampson Wright had been asked if Sir John Fielding had left a plan of police for Westminster. None could be found, Wright replied; if he had left such a plan, he continued, it was probably 'destroyed at the Time of the Riots when all his Books and Papers in Bow Street were burnt by the Rioters.'[60] Suggestions were solicited or sent in to the Home Department by interested parties—mainly versions of ideas that Fielding had advocated and put into practice at Bow Street over the previous 20 years, centering on the need for more public offices and more salaried magistrates.[61] There was broad agreement that the metropolitan magistrates were the problem, and that nothing would be done to reduce crime until there were active and honest magistrates to engage in efforts not only to apprehend and punish serious offenders but to deal with the causes of offending by doing something about the proliferation of public houses, the large number of receivers, and the spread of vice and petty offences. More such suggestions along those lines were sent in as it became known that the Home Department was preparing reform legislation. It was eagerly anticipated in some quarters by the early months of 1785. The *Morning Chronicle* bemoaned in May that nothing yet had been done 'in amendment of our Police'; another paper regretted to report two weeks later that 'the much talked of, and surely much wanted bill for the amendment of the Westminster police' was to be deferred to the next session of parliament.[62] Proposals involving an increase in the number of stipendiary magistrates beyond the three at Bow Street were common enough knowledge that at least one objection was raised on the grounds that appointing 'hirelings' would cause the few remaining 'respectable justices who continue to act' to withdraw from the commission.[63]

Legislation had indeed been prepared. It was laid before the house of commons at the end of June as 'A Bill for the further Prevention of Crimes, and for the more speedy Detection and Punishment of Offenders against the Peace, in the Cities of London and Westminster, the Borough of Southwark, and certain Parts adjacent to them.'[64] It had been drafted by John Reeves, a young barrister and legal writer,

---

[59] A handwritten note inscribed on a copy of Cawthorne's pamphlet, *Considerations on the Authority of the magistrates, commonly called the Police* (London, 1788) which he sent to Henry Dundas during the latter's tenure as secretary of the Home Office (1791–4): NA: HO 42/20, 90.

[60] BL: Add Mss 35621, f. 229.

[61] TNA: HO 42/6, ff. 182–3, 224, no. 398.

[62] *Morning Chronicle*, 12 May 1785; *Public Advertiser*, 25 May 1785.

[63] TNA: HO 42/6, f. 182.

[64] Copies are rare. An early draft is in Sheila Lambert, *House of Commons Sessional Papers of the Eighteenth Century*, vol. 46, 503–32. For other copies, see Radzinowicz, *History of English Criminal Law*, 3, 108, n. 2. For discussion of the bill, see ibid, 110–21; Paley, 'Middlesex Justices Act', 220–6; Reynolds, *Before the Bobbies,* 73–6, David Philips, '"A New Engine of Power and Authority": The

hired by Sydney for the purpose. Reeves had no obvious specialized knowledge, but he was a lawyer, and he had written a two-volume work on the early history of English law.[65] Having some interest in public issues, he was hunting around for a job in 1784 and wrote to Sydney after trying the lord chancellor.[66] No one could have anticipated the legislation that emerged from a process that appears to have been far from smooth and straightforward. One of the problems with its subsequent discussion in the house was that there were several versions in circulation and to some extent that muddied the debate. But its central points were very clear and it was remarkable in its geographical reach and in its ambition to achieve a radical and extensive reform.

The 'principle of the bill,' Reeves said, 'was for a strong executive,' by which he meant that it was intended to provide a measure of central control over the disparate policing forces across the metropolitan area.[67] He claimed to have found an outline of such a proposal in papers given to him by William Mainwaring—'I mean,' he said, 'the idea of a head office.'[68] Those papers do not appear to have survived. There is little other evidence that the need to provide some form of central direction over the policing forces in London was discussed in the planning of the bill, though this may well have been raised, given the conclusions about the magistracy that the privy council committee had reached after the Gordon Riots, and given John Fielding's frequent advocacy of some form of coordination among the magistrates. Reeves' proposals went well beyond that. To 'strengthen the executive,' he proposed that the metropolis be considered a unified police district and be placed under the supervision of three commissioners—'commissioners of police', he called them in correspondence[69]—to be appointed by the government. These men would be salaried and have a clerical staff in a central office. They would also have the authority of justices of the peace—to issue warrants and the like—but without having to carry on day-to-day magistrates' work. The unified district of the metropolis was to be divided into nine policing divisions under these commissioners, each with a public office staffed by stipendiary magistrates who together would monopolize the administration of the criminal law. The policing divisions included the City of London, the Borough of Southwark, and seven areas in Westminster and Middlesex parishes within the metropolis, areas that had an emerging identity because they were places in which rotation offices had been established over the previous two decades. Within that framework, the bill envisaged a new range of police officers. A high constable directly under the

---

Institutionalization of Law-Enforcement in England, 1780–1830' in V. A. C. Gatrell, Bruce Lenman, and Geoffrey Parker (eds.), *Crime and the Law. The Social History of Crime in Western Europe since 1500* (London, 1980), 162–8, Devereaux, 'Convicts and the State', 210–17.

[65] *A History of the English Law from the Saxons to the End of the Reign of Edward the First*, 2 vols, (London, 1783–84).

[66] Devereaux, 'Convicts and the State', 212–13.

[67] Ibid, f. 258.

[68] Ibid, f. 258.

[69] TNA: HO 42/7, f. 197.

commissioners would be in constant communication with a chief constable in each of the nine divisions to pass on orders from the commissioners. Within each division, a force of 25 petty constables would be required to patrol their territory, during the day as well as at night, some on foot, others on horseback, all armed, and all to be devoted to seeking out and apprehending offenders. These new officers would be under the command of the commissioners, who paid their stipends and had the right of appointment and dismissal.

The bill thus proposed to establish a new police force: centralized, hierarchical, and, with more than 200 paid constables. Some elements clearly derived from existing institutions—the rotation offices, and particularly Bow Street, with its paid magistrates and its large force of patrolmen who not only went out to guard the roads, but also joined the runners in investigating offences and apprehending suspects. But the heart of the suggested structure was entirely new—the metropolis as a unified district, a central command overseeing several policing divisions, forces of policemen on guard night and day. And the new police constables were to receive their orders from their chief constable and through him from the high constable and the commissioners, not from magistrates. The stipendiary magistrates in the nine divisions would no longer be the active leaders of policing forces—a separation of magistrates' judicial and administrative/ministerial powers that had never previously been contemplated and that was not to be realized in law until 1839.[70]

Reeves intended these structural changes to have major consequences, and to go on transforming the policing of London. Day-to-day, centralized leadership was fundamental to his plan. Without the active engagement that the commissioners would supply, continuing improvements would not be possible, since the secretary of state, 'as you know,' he wrote to Nepean, was 'always too much engaged in politics to enter minutely into them.'[71] One of the improvements, Reeves envisaged, was that the commissioners would gradually establish effective control over the local bodies of watchmen and constables by dint of the authority granted to them by the bill to replace current holders of these offices as they died or retired. In time, the whole policing force of the metropolis would come under the central office.

Beyond these structural changes in the policing of the metropolis, the bill included several other far-reaching proposals. Several clauses sought to enhance the preventive powers of the police to search and arrest on suspicion. They provided constables, for example, with powers well beyond anything ever previously suggested, and authorized the commissioners to grant search warrants that would allow constables to enter any house in search of stolen goods or receivers. Resistance would bring punishments that could rise to imprisonment or even transportation. Constables with appropriate warrants were also to be authorized to enter any place licenced to sell beer or liquors and to arrest journeymen, apprentices, servants, and labourers drinking there. Other clauses extended the provisions of the Vagrancy Act of 1744 to include a wider range of persons who could be considered rogues and vagabonds and to enable the police to control by a system of licensing certain kinds

[70] See ch. 8, text at nn. 201–3.
[71] TNA: HO 42/7, f. 197.

of tradesmen—silversmiths, watchmakers, old clothes dealers, and the like—who were suspected of acting as receivers. Indeed, the prevention of crime that had been sought by Shelburne and Sydney in 1782–83 would be a hallmark of the new force. As the solicitor general said in introducing the bill in the house of commons—in phrases that anticipated the ambitions of the metropolitan police established by Robert Peel in 1829—the commissioners' leadership and control would ensure that this new police would patrol the dangerous parts of the town with a 'constant and unremitted duty . . . to keep upon the look-out, to maintain an active search after offenders.' The magistrates of Westminster and Middlesex had signally failed to ensure such surveillance.[72] In Reeves' view, even the most engaged magistrate had neither time nor authority to do so effectively.[73]

The bill proposed several other major alterations in the administration of the criminal law in London, two of which are particularly notable. On the one hand, it declared that parliamentary rewards would no longer be paid. In their place, the commissioners would be able to reward at their discretion anyone who assisted in the apprehension of offenders. The solicitor general said in debate that this had been included on the advice of the Bow Street magistrates, who thought that rewards 'rather tended to promote perjury and perpetrate murder, under pretence, and under colour of law, than to prevent crimes, and punish the guilty,' an interesting indication of the limited importance of state rewards in the incomes of Bow Street officers by the 1780s.[74] A second intervention was even more notable. Because Reeves took the view that the current pattern of eight sessions a year at the Old Bailey did not deliver sufficiently swift justice, the bill proposed that the court should meet weekly—that is, virtually continuously. To meet the objection that the civil work of the 12 high court judges, who principally conducted the Old Bailey trials, would prevent this, Reeves further proposed that a number of barristers of 10 years' standing be added to the commission to hear the less complex felony cases when the judges were not available.

In short, the intention of the London and Westminster police bill, the solicitor general said in the house of commons, was to achieve 'a total reformation . . . in the regulation of the police' and to bring such vigour into the administration of justice as to make it unnecessary (thinking about the experience of the Gordon Riots) for constables to call on the aid of the military. 'To keep the bayonet out of employ,' he added, 'the power of a civil officer must be rendered efficacious.'[75] In his effort to persuade the house of commons to allow the bill to go to committee, where it might be changed and improved if necessary, the solicitor general also said that the bill had been seen by many people in the administration and by numerous lawyers, including 'persons . . . of the first rank' in the profession. The result had been that

---

[72] *Parl. Debates*, 25 (1785–86), 911–12.

[73] TNA: HO 42/7, ff. 257–9.

[74] *Parl. Debates*, 25 (1785–86), 893. For the runners' incomes, see below ch. 7, section 4.

[75] *Parl. Debates*, 25 (1785–86), 890, 911. There were two brief debates on the bill, one on 23 June when the solicitor general sought leave to bring in the bill, the other on 29 June in response to a petition from the City of London. Both are reported in *Parl. Debates*, 25 (1785–86), 888–913. The second is slightly more fully reported in the *Morning Chronicle* of 30 June.

a great deal had been 'chopped' from Reeves' original offering.[76] Despite the foot-dragging and the chopping, the bill as presented to the commons introduced a remarkable range of new ideas about the police of London.

It is difficult to be certain whose ideas they were—how much of the bill arose from discussions in the Home Office among Sydney, Nepean, Reeves and perhaps others, and how much came from Reeves' own notions of how the problems of crime and policing might best be met. George Reid, a London magistrate who had knowledge of the bill and who claimed to have been involved in discussions with the Home Office over several years about police reform, thought the honour of the bill's success would go to Sydney.[77] But the strikingly original and radical ideas at the centre of the bill seem to have been Reeves' own. The solicitor general said so in introducing the bill in the house of commons.[78] In correspondence with Evan Nepean, the under-secretary of state, Reeves referred to the bill as 'our scheme'. He may have been closer to the truth when at a later date he called it 'my scheme'.[79]

If that was the case, it seems likely that Reeves believed that he had created a structure that embodied proposals submitted in recent years to the Home Office, the elements of which owed a great deal to John Fielding's practice at Bow Street over a quarter century, especially the idea of public offices staffed by stipendiary magistrates and paid constables, some form of central coordination, and the value of preventive patrolling, to which Reeves could add the frequently declared necessity of diminishing minor offences in order to prevent serious crimes, and the appetite for reform expressed by the privy council committee and others after the Gordon riots. He may have been influenced to some extent by the organization of the police in Paris, where a Lieutenant of Police presided in his administrative functions over a complex system of police and civil administration.[80] It was a charge that would be made by the bill's opponents.[81] But Reeves must have thought that he had material enough and warrant enough in emerging practices in the metropolis and the plans suggested to the Home Office in recent years. What he added was a clear mind, political naivety, and perhaps above all, an authoritarian temperament.

Reeves made it clear that he wanted to 'strengthen the executive'—better leadership of the police in London, but also leadership under the ultimate authority of the king's ministers. His views about the importance of the central government to the maintenance of public order were not perhaps revealed in 1785, but they were to be fully on display a few years later when the country became sharply divided about political and constitutional questions in the years after the French Revolution. Reeves was not merely hostile to the ideas of the Revolution and

---

[76] *Parl. Debates*, 25 (1785–86), 896.

[77] TNA: HO 42/6, no. 383.

[78] *Parl. Debates*, 25 (1785–86), 894.

[79] TNA: HO 42/7, f. 197; HO 42/7, f. 218. For Reeves and his authorship of the bill, see Paley, 'Middlesex Justices Act', 220–1.

[80] It is possible that Reeves acquired knowledge of the police of Paris (if not from personal experience) from the English diplomat William Mildmay's account of the French police, originally written for the government in the early 1750s and subsequently published as *The Police of France* (London, 1763).

[81] *Parl. Debates*, 25 (1785–86), 896.

opposed to the popular radical societies that arose to advocate a reform of parliament, but actively engaged in opposing them as the founder and leader of an anti-radical society—the Association for Preserving Liberty and Property against Republicans and Levellers.[82] Perhaps more expressive of his ideas about authority was the pamphlet he published in 1795 in which he asserted the superiority of the monarch over parliament in the constitution—a heresy against the principles of England's own revolution of a century earlier that led to his prosecution by the house of commons for seditious libel. He was brought to trial, but acquitted by the jury.[83] Given an outlook that favoured order and obedience and strong leadership from the centre, it is perhaps understandable that in re-thinking the police problem in London in 1785 he developed present practices and the ideas that had been sent into the Home Office to what he thought their logical conclusions—seeing as he did so no objection to what others found provocative. When the bill was rejected, he said in some bemusement that the subject had long been discussed and had been 'more agitated and was better understood, than most subjects of executive government, particularly since 1780.'[84]

Reeves seems to have been genuinely surprised when the bill met with immediate hostility. There were strong objections to some of its central proposals, especially the extension of the authority of the police to arrest and to break into houses on suspicion and to threaten respectable tradesmen with a system of licensing. The threat the bill posed to the liberty of the subject was among several objections raised by the Foxite whigs in parliament, by the magistrates of Middlesex, led by their chairman, William Mainwaring, in a meeting called for the purpose, and by several newspapers.[85] Others objected to the prospect of barristers being added to the Old Bailey commission.[86] Criticism of the substance of the bill did not, however, get much of an airing, because it was immediately engulfed by vociferous objections from the City of London. Reeves was unprepared for the anger expressed by the mayor and aldermen of the City to this frontal attack on the way they managed the administration of the criminal law and particularly on their ancient and chartered privileges of self-government. It was at the least politically inept to propose the

---

[82] Eugene C. Black, *The Association. British Extraparliamentary Political Organization* (Cambridge, MA, 1963), ch. 7.

[83] Philip Schofield, 'Reeves, John (1752–1829)', *Oxford Dictionary of National Biography*.

[84] TNA: HO 42/7, f. 258.

[85] The magistrates resolved that the bill was 'a dangerous innovation and encroachment on the rights and security of the people' (LMA: MJ/OC/11, f. 147, quoted by Paley, 'Middlesex Justices Act', 223), and see, *Parl. Debates*, 25 (1785–86), 905 and *Public Advertiser*, 8 July 1785. The press was divided on the merits of the bill. *The Gazetteer* (1 July), *General Evening Post* (30 June), and the *Daily Universal Register* (subsequently *The Times*, 29 June) were opposed; the *Public Advertiser*, *Morning Chronicle* (1 July), and *Morning Post*, (7, 11, 18, 23 July) supported the bill, the latter, Paley suggests ('Middlesex Justices Act', 224), at Reeves' instigation. 'It will be a public misfortune,' the *Public Advertiser* commented on 8 July, when it seemed possible that a revised bill might be reintroduced, 'if the Solicitor General's Bill, for the prevention of robberies, should not pass into a law during the present Session of Parliament.'

[86] *Parl. Debates*, 25 (1785–86), 897, 909–10. Even alderman Newnham, anxious to get in as many blows as he could against the bill, objected to barristers sitting as judges at the Old Bailey when he knew very well that he and other aldermen—none of them qualified in any way—did so.

appointment of stipendiary magistrates in place of the lord mayor and aldermen without any attempt to smooth the way and to fail—as the Home Office did—to give the mayor and aldermen adequate opportunity to comment on the bill before it was introduced. The City's anger was expressed in no uncertain terms in a petition against the bill, vigorously supported by the four aldermen who represented the City in parliament. Reeves continued to think that the aldermen were wrong to hold out against changes that would benefit the whole metropolis. If the City was excluded from the bill, he argued, some notoriously criminal areas on its borders, like Chick Lane and Petticoat Lane, would continue to be poorly policed and everyone would suffer.[87] This was possibly true, but seriously wrongheaded. Before debate could be engaged on this or any other matter, the overwhelming hostility of the City forced the government to abandon the bill. It had been introduced on 23 June 1785, and given its first reading on 27 June. It was withdrawn two days later for technical reasons.[88] The solicitor general said he would bring it back when a minor adjustment was made. He never did.[89]

Why the bill failed is clear enough. Why Sydney and the members of the cabinet who had read it and the lawyers who had chopped it about had not seen the error—fatal in retrospect—of including the City is less clear. It was one thing to think, as Sydney was later to say, that the policing of the City was in need of improvement;[90] it was quite another to seek to amalgamate the City into the larger metropolis for policing purposes. It seems to me that the conclusion to be drawn from this is that the problems they were attempting to solve appeared to the government, at that moment, so large and so threatening that whatever the City might say was unimportant compared to the need to do something to reduce the number of offences. It is important to remember the conditions under which these decisions were made: levels of violent crime that showed no signs of abating; record levels of capital punishment; fundamental penal problems that seemed insoluble; the memory of the failure of the magistrates during the riots of 1780. In moving for leave to introduce the bill, Archibald MacDonald rehearsed the familiar arguments about the increasing dangers on the streets of the metropolis—the ways that perpetrators of crime were being drawn into increasingly serious offences by deepening immorality. Although magistrates had been instructed and encouraged to act to reduce levels of vice and minor crime, nothing had been achieved to stem this enlarging

---

[87] TNA: HO 42/7, f. 259.

[88] JHC, 40 (1784–5), 1100, 1105, 1109, 1123.

[89] It was withdrawn on the technicality that because it carried financial implications it would have to be dealt with in two separate pieces of legislation. Reeves expressed his disappointment in a letter to Sydney hours after the bill was withdrawn, blaming the coolness of the solicitor general, the attorney general, and prime minister Pitt (TNA: HO 42/7, ff. 257–9). He remained optimistic that it would be brought back in a future session and be passed. That was contemplated but dropped, in part perhaps because of Pitt's concern about the cost (Devereaux, 'Convicts and the State', 214–15).

[90] In a later debate, when the City of London was proposed as a model of how policing might be organized in the metropolis, Sydney said that he 'doubted whether altogether the Police of the city of London deserved to be considered as a system to be imitated,' on the grounds that there were infamous drinking establishments in the City as well as in Middlesex (*Parliamentary Register* (1790–2), vol. 33, 534).

criminal world. Indeed, the level of violent offences seemed to be higher than ever. Nor had capital punishment had any effect. As Macdonald pointed out in introducing the bill, more convicted offenders—mainly young men—were being executed than ever before. A further level of anxiety was added by the incarceration of men in the hulks moored in the Thames. Most of them would have been transported before the war; the independence of the American colonies had made that impossible. Now they were kept in harsh and brutalizing conditions and then released when their sentences were completed. It must have seemed in 1785 that there was no way forward, no way to stem the violence that threatened everyone in society, including the middle class and the wealthy. The bill that Reeves constructed, as radical and in some ways extreme as it was, presented a solution that he and perhaps Sydney and others in the Home Office may have thought simply developed the structures and practices that John Fielding had created. After years of fumbling, it must have seemed not only to Reeves, but to the bill's supporters in the government, that, despite its problems, this bill promised a way forward.

Reeves expressed his unhappiness to Sydney with the failure of prime minister Pitt to bring political weight to bear when the bill got into immediate trouble in the house of commons.[91] His disappointment was also more personal, since he appears to have expected to hold some office under the new arrangement, perhaps as a stipendiary magistrate, possibly one of the commissioners of police. In acknowledging a payment of £300 for his work on the bill in July 1786, he spoke about 'expectations that were disappointed' by the bill's failure.[92] Such a generous payment may have been to some extent compensation for that disappointment— and perhaps also the appointment he was to receive in 1792 as receiver of the police, a post created by legislation we will discuss in the following section. Reeves may also have felt some satisfaction when his failed bill formed the basis of an act of the Irish parliament in 1786 that created a police establishment for Dublin.[93]

4. THE MIDDLESEX JUSTICES ACT, 1792

Seven years after that disastrous attempt by the government to establish London policing on a new foundation, parliament did pass legislation that introduced a measure of reform. The Middlesex Justices act of 1792 included two elements of the 1785 bill that almost certainly would have been enacted into law had they been proposed then on their own. One was the establishment of public offices in which stipendiary magistrates monopolized the administration of the criminal law in Westminster, in parishes in Middlesex that were within the larger metropolis of London, and in the borough of Southwark, across the river. Difficulties were

---

[91] TNA: HO 42/7, ff. 257–9.
[92] TNA: HO 42/9, f. 537.
[93] 26 George III, c. 24 (1786); Stanley H. Palmer, *Police and Protest in England and Ireland 1780–1850* (Cambridge, 1988), 97–100.

avoided by the City of London being excluded from the Act. The second element consisted of measures to increase the powers of the police.

The main aspect of the Act, the creation of public offices, had been at the heart of the police reform plans discussed in the Home Office before Reeves was invited to bring his imagination and his authoritarian temperament to bear on the issue. There had been virtually universal agreement in the years following the American war that a reform of the magistracies of Westminster and Middlesex was essential if the policing of London was going to be improved. That sentiment was not diminished by the failure of the 1785 bill; indeed, it was if anything strengthened in the last years of the decade.[94] The problems that had earlier driven reform ideas became even more obvious towards 1790.

For one thing, though the numbers of offences being prosecuted at the Old Bailey diminished to some extent, there were increasing concerns about the levels of violent crime on the streets of the metropolis. This was becoming a problem in the middle years of the decade. In his introduction of the 1785 bill, the solicitor general had noted that while the Bow Street patrol, established two years earlier, had been successful in reducing the number of attacks by highwaymen in the suburbs and on the outskirts of the metropolis, one of the side effects of their work was to cause offenders to move to the inner streets of the city, where the number of robberies and other offences had increased notably.[95] Sampson Wright had not predicted this displacement effect when he persuaded the government to set up the patrol in 1783; he merely promised that even if the patrols did not make a lot of arrests and failed to bring large numbers of charges, their presence would discourage robberies on the main roads. That had happened, and the patrols got the credit. They 'had been the means,' the minister who followed Sydney at the head of the Home Department, W. W. Grenville, agreed in 1790, 'not only of preventing numerous Robberies, but of detecting and bringing to punishment a number of Persons who had committed such Offences.'[96] Grenville also came to accept, however, that the consequence had been an increase in violent attacks on the inner streets of the capital.

The questionable security of the London streets had also been revealed in the Spring of 1790 by the slashing attacks on fashionable young women carried out by Rhynwick Williams, the man who came to be known as the 'Monster'. His bizarre behaviour—stalking his victims, muttering obscenities while engaging them in conversation, and finally slashing at their clothes with a knife—was followed in intense press reporting over several months.[97] As Greg Smith has said, the case underlined the ineffective policing of the streets and the broader dangers of life in

---

[94] Paley, 'Middlesex Justices Act,' chs. 6–7.

[95] *Parl. Debates*, 25 (1785–86), 891.

[96] TNA: HO 43/3, 190–1.

[97] Greg T. Smith, 'The State and the Culture of Violence in London, 1760–1840', Ph.D. thesis (University of Toronto, 1999), ch. 5; *idem*, 'Policing and Punishing a Monster: Law, Violence, and Renwick Williams, London's other "Ripper"' (forthcoming); Jan Bondeson, *The London Monster* (London, 2000); Robert Shoemaker, *The London Mob: Violence and Disorder in Eighteenth-Century England* (London, 2004), ch. 10.

the city.[98] The Bow Street office was involved in the search for Williams only to the extent of issuing an advertisement offering a reward of £100 for his conviction. But the sense of panic the case generated may well have been the spur, along with continuing concern about the level of robberies, that encouraged Sampson Wright to seek an enlargement and reorganization of the patrol. In April 1790, when publicity about the 'Monster' was at its height, Grenville agreed to bolster the policing forces at Bow Street to enable Wright to add patrols to guard the inner streets of the metropolis while retaining those on the main roads.[99] Instead of 46 men working in eight parties, the nightly foot patrol would henceforth consist of 13 parties of four or five, each led by a conductor, or captain—a total of 68 men.[100]

Evidence of increasing street violence is perhaps sufficient in itself to explain the renewal of interest in the Home Office in the last years of the 1780s in the prevention of crime in the metropolis. But Devereaux has shown that those sentiments were also again encouraged, as they had been before 1785, by the difficulties the government continued to face in matters of penal policy, particularly the pressures to build gaols. Opposition in the house of commons to the reliance on the hulks and transportation (especially as news was received of fearful mortality on the early fleets sent to establish the penal colony at Botany Bay) increased the ambition of penal reformers to persuade the government to support the construction of penitentiaries in which inmates could be subjected to labour discipline and instructed in religious principles. Seeking ways of reducing the number of serious offenders to be managed was one way of deflecting those ambitions. And that meant attacking the sources of serious crime by controlling the vice and immorality and petty crime that were universally believed to be the source of the more damaging offences.[101]

Government support for a campaign against vice and immorality—the behaviours and attitudes that were the foundation of all criminality—was also encouraged by an initiative undertaken in 1787 by William Wilberforce, a well-connected and respected member of parliament.[102] Recently converted to evangelical Christianity, Wilberforce took up two principal reforming causes. He joined other evangelicals and Quakers in a vigorous campaign against the slave trade, a campaign that brought the cruelty of the trade before the public and laid the groundwork for its abolition in 1807 and of slavery itself in British colonies in 1833. Wilberforce's second project was to stimulate another campaign against gambling and drinking and other socially harmful and immoral habits and behaviour—sins, in his eyes, of

---

[98] Smith, 'The State and the Culture of Violence,' 231–2. In his 'Sketch of a Plan to Prevent Crimes', which he sent to Dundas at the Home Office in 1791 (TNA: HO 42/20, 124 ff), John Donaldson pointed to the case of the 'Monster' as evidence of the need for improved policing in the metropolis. His 'Sketch' was subsequently published (London, 1792).

[99] TNA: HO 43/3, 190–1.

[100] For the expanded patrol, see below, ch. 7, text at nn. 36–40.

[101] Devereaux, 'Convicts and the State', 336–50.

[102] The following account of the Proclamation Society, is based on Joanna Innes, *Inferior Politics. Social Problems and Social Policies in Eighteenth-Century Britain* (Oxford, 2009), ch. 5.

which the rich were as guilty as the poor. He proceeded by persuading George III, with the help of the Archbishop of Canterbury, to issue a proclamation encouraging constables to enforce the numerous laws on the books that authorized the punishment of drunkenness, gambling, and vice. Magistrates were also ordered to oversee their work more effectively and to be fully engaged in carrying out their duty to govern their neighbourhoods, being careful, for example, in awarding alehouse licences. Sydney gave his support by circulating the proclamation to all local authorities with his encouragement that they strive to put it into effect. Wilberforce followed this initiative by recruiting a group of men to promote the intentions of the Proclamation, a society that would direct and encourage without becoming engaged in mounting prosecutions, as Societies for the Reformation of Manners had done in the past. The Proclamation Society remained small, but it was well placed to do this work of encouragement because its members were men of influence—members of the higher clergy, peers, members of parliament, and a number of prominent magistrates, including William Mainwaring, the chairman of both the Middlesex and Westminster benches.

The convergence of concerns about crime and immorality encouraged a renewal of interest by the early 1790s in measures to promote preventive policing.[103] Inevitably this refocussed attention on the character and capacities of the magistrates of Westminster and Middlesex. It did so at a time, Ruth Paley has shown, when the Westminster and Middlesex benches were particularly weak, and when it was becoming difficult to find good candidates to sit regularly at the rotation offices that had emerged in the metropolis since the 1760s.[104] This was one reason why Middlesex magistrates had been so prominent in the discussions leading up to the 1785 bill. It also explains why Mainwaring, a figure of considerable importance to the government, and Nathaniel Conant, who was to be one of the first stipendiaries and later chief magistrate at Bow Street, remained persuaded after the failure of Reeves' bill that the paucity of good candidates for the rotation offices needed urgent attention.[105] The solution, Mainwaring and Conant believed, had been included in the 1785 bill (though obscured by its more extreme elements): the

---

[103] It is possible, too, that some further impetus towards establishing a more effective magistracy in the capital was provided by the Revolution in France. After some initial euphoria among the governing class in the early months of the Revolution when it seemed that the French were in the process of establishing a constitutional monarchy, the growing radicalism and violence across the channel came to be seen as posing a decided threat to the British constitution, as radical groups at home organized to demand political reform. There is not a great deal of evidence that the threat of sedition provoked the search for strong magistracy and police, but it may have helped to confirm the value of such a project. On that point, see Devereaux, 'Convicts and the State', 345–6; Paley, 'Middlesex Justices Act', ch. 9.

[104] Paley, 'Middlesex Justices Act', 213–18.

[105] As an example of the problem of recruitment, Paley cites the appointment of Nicholas Bond, the chief clerk of the office, as a magistrate at Bow Street in 1785 ('Middlesex Justices Act', 213). Certainly, it was unusual for a clerk and active officer to be raised to the bench, but it seems to me likely that this appointment was made with a purpose. Bond was greatly valued by Sampson Wright and by the Home Department (as he had been by Fielding). He had long been the leader of the runners, as register clerk, and had just recently been given an addition to his salary of £100 a year for his 'activity in apprehending the most desperate offenders' (*General Evening Post*, 4 October 1785). My sense is his appointment was a sign that difficult times required a strong figure on the bench.

appointment of stipendiary magistrates at the rotation offices, magistrates like those at Bow Street, with a group of constables at their command, and with salaries sufficiently large to eliminate their dependence on fees taken at the office and to enable them to be present for magisterial business at regular hours during the week.

Conant sent such a plan to the Home Office that may have sparked interest in reviving the ideas proposed by magistrates between 1782 and 1785 for a more preventive policing system.[106] The first move did not, however, come from the department directly. Perhaps, with the drama of 1785 in mind, the Home Office did not draw up a bill or overtly take a lead. But Henry Dundas, the secretary of state in 1792, was clearly ready to step in when in March 1792 Francis Burton, a backbencher with ties to the administration, introduced a bill into the house of commons for 'the more effectual Administration of the Office of a Justice of the Peace, in such Parts of the county of Middlesex as lie in and near the Metropolis.' The need for such legislation, Burton said, was well understood on both sides of the house and consisted mainly in 'a deficiency of [magistrates] in the metropolis, and an abuse of the office itself.'[107] The initial bill concerned simply the magistrates of Middlesex—Burton had no intention of raising a storm by including the City of London—and made the relatively modest proposal that five public offices be established in Westminster and those parts of Middlesex that lay on the northern and eastern edges of the metropolis, each to be staffed by three salaried magistrates. The new stipendiaries would be given exclusive control of the administration of the criminal law in their districts. All other justices would be forbidden to collect fees for such work. The salaries of the new justices and their clerks would be paid out of the fees collected in the offices, which fees would be remitted to a treasurer or paymaster who would send in regular accounts to the Home Department.[108]

The bill had not come directly from the Home Department, but it was taken forward and managed in the house of commons by the Home secretary, Henry Dundas. He too was obviously content with the limited nature of the bill: its principle, he said in moving second reading, was simply 'to correct abuse in the conduct of trading justices.'[109] It was opposed by the Foxite whigs on the grounds that the creation of stipendiary magistrates appointed by the crown meant an increase in patronage and an expansion of the influence of the crown in the metropolis.[110] Despite that, it was not likely to have been a deeply contentious bill, and would almost certainly have gone through as written had it not been for the presence in the house of William Mainwaring, one of the members for Middlesex and chairman of

---

[106] Paley, 'Middlesex Justices Act,' 227–8.

[107] *Parl. Debates*, 29 (1791–92), 1034.

[108] Copies of the original bill and of two subsequent bills as amended in committee are in Sheila Lambert, *House of Commons Sessional Papers of the Eighteenth Century*, vol. 79, 409–39. The Act as passed was 32 Geo III, c. 53. For accounts of the Act and the debate surrounding it, see Paley, 'Middlesex Justices Act', ch. 7; Radzinowicz, *History of English Criminal Law*, 3, 123–34; Philips, 'A New Engine of Power and Authority', 165–71.

[109] *Parl. Debates*, 29 (1791–92), 1181. As Jerome Hall noted, the bill was designed 'to improve the magistracy, not to create any changes in police.' 'Legal and Social Aspects of Arrest Without a Warrant', *Harvard Law Review* 49 (1936), 588.

[110] *Parl. Debates*, 29 (1791–92), 1164, 1182–3.

the county bench. As a member for the county and as its leading justice of the peace, he spoke with a good deal of authority and, as he said, with 'local knowledge.'[111] Mainwaring said at its first reading that the proposal was inadequate on several grounds, and at the committee stage he got his additions accepted, additions that made the bill more complex and more controversial.

There were three changes of note. In the first place, the number of offices was increased to seven, including one in Southwark, when Mainwaring and others pointed out that the proposed five offices left several of the most populous parts of the metropolis without adequate magisterial services.[112] The second addition was a clause, proposed by Mainwaring, similar to that in the 1785 bill giving constables and watchmen the right to apprehend people they merely suspected of being in public places with the intention of committing felonies. The intention was to increase the power of the police to govern the streets and, as Mainwaring said, 'to strengthen the arm of the magistrate to suppress vice.'[113] A suspect taken before a magistrate could be declared 'a person of evil fame and a reputed thief' simply on the oath of one witness and be deemed a rogue and vagabond subject to the harsh provisions of the Vagrancy Act of 1744.[114] Though an appeal to the sessions was allowed, in practice it would have been difficult for most of those so arrested to enter into the recognizance and find the sureties required to launch an appeal. For the most part, it meant that men and women merely suspected of intending to commit a felony—picking pockets was almost certainly the felony that the proponents of the legislation had in mind, and constables who came into contact with them day in and day out, their likely accusers—faced the possibility of a sentence of six months' imprisonment at hard labour. This clause raised bitter opposition in parliament, as it had in the 1785 bill, largely on the grounds that the constitution, and the liberties and freedoms it upheld, protected citizens against mere suspicion and from a procedure that imposed punishment without a finding of guilt. Again, the Foxite whigs led the opposition to these enhanced policing powers and gathered some support before losing on the crucial vote in committee.[115]

Mainwaring's most general complaint about the initial bill concerned the conception of the magistracy it presented and the weak position in which it left the justices in the face of the most serious violent offences. He was articulating the established view of magistrates as both judicial officers and the leaders of policing and prosecution activities when he asked whether magistrates were to be active or passive. Were they 'to wait for persons to come and exhibit their complaints?' If so, he said, the bill would do little to curb the violence that so plagued the city that 'no man at this

---

[111] *Parl. Register*, 32 (1792), 296; General *Evening Post*, 18 April 1792.

[112] To allay anxieties in the City that their accustomed jurisdiction in justice matters in Southwark was being invaded by the addition of a public office at St Margaret's Hill in the Borough, s. 18 of the Act explicitly confirmed the right of the mayor and aldermen and the recorder of London to continue to act as justices of the peace there.

[113] *Parl. Debates*, 29 (1791–92), 1179.

[114] Section 17 of the Act, referred to as Clause D in the debates.

[115] *Parl. Debates*, 29 (1791–92), cols. 1464–5 For the debate on this clause in the house of lords, see Philips, 'A New Engine of Power and Authority,' 169–70.

moment could hardly be secure at noon day.'[116] If the new magistrates were not to have the ability to investigate offences, to identify and apprehend offenders, robbery could not be suppressed. And if it was intended that they lead the fight against crime, Mainwaring argued, they would need the help of active constables.[117]

Mainwaring was thus drawing a contrast between what had long been the expectation that magistrates would simply wait to receive complaints from victims of crime, and the altogether new engagement in investigation and apprehension of suspects introduced in recent years by the Fieldings. His concern was that, other than the general supervision of the home department, there was no provision in the bill for the management of policing efforts against robbers and burglars and other serious and violent offenders. His view was clear, that in the absence of other leadership, John Fielding's ideas and practices had to be preserved and strengthened. 'He wished to know,' he said, 'on what foundation the offices were to proceed. Were they to be something similar to that at Bow-street? He owned he should in that respect like them.'[118] At the committee stage, he pressed further. As matters stood, the magistrates would have 'no means . . . of enforcing the execution of the laws, which was surely a terrible deficiency in a metropolis, where shocking outrages were committed day and night.'[119] In response, Dundas invited Mainwaring to provide clauses to be inserted in the bill, with the result that the statute subsequently passed included provision for seven, not five, offices, and provided each office with a staff of six constables who would be paid 12 shillings a week, with additions for their expences in conducting investigations and making arrests.[120] What came to be known as the Police Act was passed for three years only and came up thereafter for periodic renewal. In effect, it created the police force that, along with Bow Street, remained the subject and target of reform ideas and discussions about how the police might be strengthened for a generation—indeed, until 1829, when Robert Peel's Metropolitan Police changed the conversation and established a police force as a substitute for the parochial night watches.[121]

It is worth noting that no objections were raised to the addition of 42 paid constables when the bill was reported back to the house, nor in the house of lords. If there were anxieties among members of parliament or in the public at large about legislation that added a significant number of police officers who were at least indirectly at the service of the government in the person of the home secretary, they were not expressed. No alarms were raised about government agents or concerns that what was being created was a police force on the Parisian model. Mainwaring's argument was accepted without complaint that paid officers dedicated to the apprehension of felons were needed if dangerous offenders were going to be caught and punished, since private thief-takers, he reminded the house, had proved to be

---

[116] *The Times*, 18 April 1792.
[117] *Parl. Debates*, 29 (1791–92), 1179.
[118] Ibid.
[119] *Gazetteer*, 4 May 1792.
[120] 32 Geo III, c. 53, ss.15, 16. The seven public offices were to be in Westminster (two), Clerkenwell, Shoreditch, Whitechapel, Shadwell, and Southwark, each with three stipendiaries and other justices of the peace who chose to attend.
[121] See ch. 8, section 5.

mainly corrupt and 'never touched a thief till he was worth their taking.'[122] It is an interesting reflection on the question of why Sydney had allowed Reeves to present such a flawed piece of legislation in 1785, that in speaking strongly in favour of the 1792 bill in the house of lords debate, he reflected on his own experience and perhaps revealed the reason he had been in favour of the earlier effort to strengthen the police. In reply to an argument that it was unnecessary legislation and that consideration of the bill should be postponed, Sydney said that 'the bill should be passed as soon as possible; the daily assaults and robberies in the streets, which their Lordships were no strangers to, pointed out the necessity of it. It had been his lot to have many schemes of the same kind proposed to him, and they had generally been put off upon the idea of waiting another year. . . . The sooner the bill passed the better.'[123]

The 1792 Act was in many ways evidence of the success of John Fielding's innovations at Bow Street. He had long sought the replication of the Bow Street structure throughout the metropolis. And its passage, I suggest, is further evidence of the good reputation the Bow Street officers had acquired under the direction of Fielding and his successors. Dundas called on that reputation in defending the clause in the Act that increased police powers to arrest on suspicion. He told the house of commons that he had that morning spoken to Macmanus—a man to whom he 'did not like to apply the word thief-catcher' since he was 'so respectable a character'— and in 'a long conversation' sought his opinion as to the necessity of such a clause. Lord North, following, was more sarcastic about the parliament 'entrusting dictatorial power into the hands of Mssrs. Townsend and Macmanus', but his referring to them by name at least reveals how familiar they were to members of parliament.[124]

The 1792 Middlesex Justices Act was thus in the end based on the model of Bow Street, on Fielding's conception of the magistrate, and his view of how to deal with the threats posed by serious crime. The Act needs to be understood not as a failed attempt to create a police force for the metropolis as a whole along the lines of Peel's Metropolitan Police Act of 1829, but as the culmination of John Fielding's work, and, more broadly as the culmination of changes in the prosecution of violent crime that had begun exactly a century earlier with the first reward statute (1692) that had offered £40 for the conviction of a highwayman. The failure of efforts in the first half of the eighteenth century to encourage private detection and prosecution by offering large parliamentary and government rewards had drawn the central government in the middle of the eighteenth century into limited and guarded support of the Fieldings' efforts to build a more public group of thief-catchers. That financial support had been crucial to the Bow Street project. But it was John Fielding's ideas and vision that had transformed his house into the principal centre of policing and prosecution in the metropolis. And it was Bow Street that provided the model when, after 1780, the government took another step into direct engagement with the problems of policing the metropolis when it committed public resources to establish a new force of patrolmen and to reform the magistracy—providing, in doing so, eighteenth-century solutions for an eighteenth-century problem.

---

[122] *The Times*, 4 May 1792.
[123] *The Parliamentary Register*, 33 (1790–92), 532.
[124] *Parl. Debates*, 29 (1791–92), 1473–4; *Gazetteer*, 24 May 1792.

7

The Runners in a New Age of Policing, 1792–1815

1. BOW STREET AND THE POLICE ACT

The Middlesex Justices Act (1792)—or the Police Act, as it came to be called—established public offices at seven locations across the metropolis: two in Westminster, one in Clerkenwell, three in the East End, and one across the river in Southwark. They were intended to provide magisterial services across the metropolis, outside the City of London. Each was staffed by three stipendiary magistrates, two clerks, and six constables. When in 1800 the Thames Police was established with a central office in Wapping to deal with offences on the river and the neighbouring docks and warehouses, the original office in Shoreditch became redundant and was eventually moved to Queen's Square.[1] Thereafter, the public offices were to remain largely unchanged in their locations, size, and structure.

The Act also established a receiver of police who was to collect the fees generated at each office that were expected to meet the bulk of their expenses and to distribute necessary additional funds provided by the Treasury. The first occupant of the post was the same John Reeves who had written the ill-fated 1785 police bill. He was a busy man in 1792–93. He had served most recently as chief justice of Newfoundland (1791–92), and was still involved in establishing the judiciary there when he took up the receivership of police.[2] At the same time, he was deeply involved in anti-radical politics, as the founder of the 'Association for Preserving Liberty and Property against Republicans and Levellers', also known as the 'Crown and Anchor Society'.[3] One consequence of these engagements was that he left his first principal task as receiver—setting up the seven new offices, finding them suitable buildings, arranging the furnishings, and so on—to the man appointed as surveyor of the

---

[1] Sir Leon Radzinowicz, *A History of the English Criminal Law and its Administration from 1750*, 4 vols, (London 1948–68), vol. 2, ch. 13; Ruth Paley, 'The Middlesex Justices Act of 1792: its origins and effects,' Ph.D. thesis (University of Reading, 1983), ch. 10.

[2] Jerry Bannister, *The Rule of the Admirals: law, custom, and naval government in Newfoundland, 1699–1832* (Toronto, 2003), 177–8, 197.

[3] E. C. Black, *The Association: British extra-parliamentary political organization* (Cambridge, MA, 1963), ch. 7. Reeves seems to have organized this association when he learned from his friend, Evan Nepean, that William Grenville, the foreign secretary, had such a group in mind as support for the government's prosecution of radicals (Robert R. Dozier, *For King, Constitution, and Country: the English loyalists and the French Revolution* (Lexington, KY, 1983), 57–9).

police offices, Benjamin Latrobe.[4] Reeves was not interested in such details anyway. He seems to have thought that he might make the post into something like the commissionership of police that he had failed to create for himself earlier. He was clearly seeking more superintending authority than the Act provided him, when early in his tenure he observed to Dundas that 'it is very desirable that a concurrence, and uniformity should be effected between them all [the new police offices], and that is very likely to be best brought about and preserved by a person in my situation.'[5] The post remained much less grand, however—more book-keeper than leader—and he seems largely to have neglected it.

The new police offices had been modelled on Bow Street, but the institution that John Fielding had created remained essentially separate and very different from them. Perhaps the most obvious difference was that, unlike the police offices, its work was not confined to a particular district within the metropolis. The new stipendiary magistrates were expected mainly to serve the populations in their immediate areas, areas that were not at first precisely defined, but that took shape in practice.[6] Bow Street too was assumed by the Home Office to be responsible for policing the area around Covent Garden, and thus to have a 'district' in that sense for purposes of local policing. But its jurisdiction had never been defined or limited. From the beginning its officers had conducted investigations across the metropolis, the Home Counties, and further afield. That continued to be the case after 1792. Indeed, the runners were if anything more active outside London than before, even more likely, as John Wade said in 1828, to be 'despatched into the country, to Scotland and Ireland, and even to the Continent, for the apprehension of offenders.'[7]

Bow Street was also different from the police offices in that its magistrates had a closer relationship with their masters in the Home Office than the other stipendiaries. The police magistrates were appointed by the secretary of state and one from each office was required to attend the department once a month to report on the state of crime in their districts. But Ruth Paley has shown that the Home Office was not deeply concerned with the day to day working of the offices and did little to discipline the stipendiaries for absenteeism or even gross misbehaviour. On the other hand, the Bow Street office was increasingly important to the government as a centre of policing, in some senses as a national police, and was even more closely tied to the Home Office after 1792 than it had been earlier.[8] The chief magistrate

---

[4] TNA: HO 42/21, ff. 162–5, 263–4. Talbot Hamlin, *Benjamin Henry Latrobe* (New York, 1955), 46–7, 125. Latrobe was to become an important architect, particularly in America, where he went in 1796. Among other buildings, he designed the restored Capitol in Washington.

[5] TNA: HO 42/21, f. 278.

[6] For the parishes they served, see Patrick Colquhoun, *A Treatise on the Police of the Metropolis*, 7th edn. (London, 1806; reprinted Montclair, NJ, 1969), 505–6; John Wade, *A Treatise on the Police and Crimes of the Metropolis*, (London 1829; reprinted Montclair, NJ, 1972), 37–9. They acquired powers to act as constables in Middlesex and Surrey in 1801 (by 42 Geo III, c. 76) and additionally in Essex and Kent in 1821 (2 Geo IV, c. 118).

[7] Wade, *Treatise on the Police*, 39. For the runners' provincial work, see below, text at nn. 46–59; ch. 8, text at nn. 60–3.

[8] Paley, 'Middlesex Justices Act,' 272–8, 286.

was in daily contact with the secretary or under-secretary, and received more frequent communications from the Home Office than other stipendiaries. As we will see, Richard Ford (magistrate 1793–1806, chief magistrate for the last six years) kept an office at the Home Office, so busy was he in examining men suspected of plotting insurrection. But even in less heated times, the chief magistrate at Bow Street was in constant contact with the government and acted as the secretary of state's principal advisor on policing issues.[9]

Bow Street's distinctive character was further enhanced by the financial arrangements that followed the 1792 Act. The statute laid out the salaries of the magistrates, clerks, and constables of the seven new offices, and required that they be paid out of fees collected in the offices, supplemented when necessary by funds from the Treasury. It also set a maximum of £2,000 that each office was allowed to spend for salaries and all extras, including police work, a sum that was never to change and that clearly placed constraints on the policing activities they would be able to carry out. Bow Street was not mentioned in the Police Act. It continued to be financed as it had from the beginning, simply by an annual grant of £600 from the Treasury that had to be accounted for and renewed every year. The salaries of the magistrates and the costs of the patrol were paid separately. These arrangements changed in a fundamentally important way in 1793 when Henry Dundas, as the head of the Home Department, ordered Reeves to prepare a budget for Bow Street and to take its finances under his management along with the police offices. Dundas's first thought seems to have been to formalize this in legislation. Patrick Colquhoun, one of the new stipendiaries, certainly thought that a bill for that purpose was being prepared in May 1793.[10] But if so, Dundas changed his mind, and in July he simply wrote to Reeves to order him to prepare a budget for the Bow Street office that would include the salaries of the magistrates and clerks, the costs of the patrol, office expenses, and for the first time a stipend for the runners that was essentially a retainer in the form of a weekly wage.[11] This decision had important consequences. The informality of the new arrangement increased the policing resources available to the Bow Street magistrates (and the Home Office), and did so in a way that avoided the financial straight-jacket imposed on the other police offices by the 1792 Act. Legislation would almost certainly have established a limit on Bow Street spending. Under the informal arrangement, no such constraints were established— a consideration that Dundas may well have had in mind, since the government was coming increasingly in 1793 to call on the policing services of Bow Street in the face of growing internal security issues.[12]

---

[9] When Samuel Bamford, the radical, was examined before the privy council in 1820 on suspicion of treasonable activity, he was first interviewed by Sir Nathaniel Conant, the chief magistrate, in his room in the Home Office and then taken by him before the council (Samuel Bamford, *Passages in the Life of a Radical* (6th edn., 2 vols, London 1967, ed. W. H. Chaloner; first published 1839–41), I, 105.

[10] TNA: PRO 30/8/124, 197.

[11] TNA: HO 35/13, 23 October 1793.

[12] See below, section 3.

Henceforth, Reeves submitted an account of the office's charges every quarter, dividing the expenditures into three categories.[13] First were charges on the 'establishment', that is, the salaries of the magistrates, the clerks, the six officers (or eight, as of 1802), the patrol, and those who kept the office going—the office keeper, housekeeper, and messenger. In time, this list would also include pensions paid to officers' widows and superannuated patrolmen. Established payments also included the cost of publishing and distributing the *Hue and Cry*. By the early nineteenth century all those charges together came to a total of a little more than £8,000 a year. Beyond that, there were two other categories of payment in the quarterly accounts: one for 'incidental' charges, as they were called; the other for 'extraordinary' charges.[14] Incidentals were the variable costs of running the office—rent, lighting, heating, cleaning, stationery supplies, and the like. 'Extraordinary' payments were for policing. They were payments 'allowed by the magistrates for expences and trouble incurred by the different officers and patroles in the exercise of their public duty'—that is, for the work on which they were dispatched on behalf of the office: investigating offences, searching for witnesses, gathering evidence, making arrests, testifying at the Middlesex sessions and the Old Bailey—all the activities that the Fieldings had wanted funds to reward.

Nothing changed in principle as a result of this new system, but a great deal changed in practice. The annual grant of £600 received by Bow Street before 1793 had supported both the costs of running the office and the expenses and rewards paid to the runners for their policing activities. By the mid-1780s the office costs had been taking up so much of the budget that much less money was available for direct payments for detection and prosecution than had been the case in the 1760s. The account drawn up for the year 1784–85, the only one that has survived from the quarter century after 1767, shows direct payments to the officers for their policing work making up only about 7 per cent of a budget that went overwhelmingly for the salaries of the clerks and office keepers, other office expenses, printing costs, and so on.[15] Indeed, it is clear that the runners had been suffering financially for some time, having to rely entirely on payments from private clients at a time when the large number of patrolmen were also available to take on such investigations. This almost certainly explains why, as Reeves complained when he first examined the Bow Street accounts, for some time Sampson Wright had not filled patrol vacancies in order to give the runners some financial support.[16] Dundas's placing the financing of Bow Street in the hands of the receiver of police created a budget for the office that not only provided salaries on the establishment for both the patrol and the runners, but also made it possible for them to claim payments for every aspect of the policing work they did on behalf of the office.

---

[13] TNA: T 38/673–4.

[14] These terms seemed to be interchangeable in first year or two, but thereafter the policing charges were labelled as 'extraordinaries'.

[15] TNA: T 1/626, ff. 247–51.

[16] TNA: HO 35/13, 23 October 1793.

Before 1793, the chief magistrate at Bow Street had received money *in advance*, roughly at Michaelmas, for the forthcoming year's requirements. This in effect placed a cap of £600 on expenditures. Under the new financial regime, payments were made *retrospectively*, following the submission of an account at the end of each quarter. The officers and patrolmen were allowed to put in vouchers, or bills, for the work they had been sent to perform, bills that were supposed to be validated by the signatures of at least two magistrates and sent in with the quarterly accounts.[17] This provided a form of control over the expenditures of the office, though that control was in practice loose at best. But the main point is that, even with tight controls, the budget for 'extraordinary' payments was open-ended in a way it had never been before. As we will see, these payments were to be substantially larger in total than they had been before the new financial system was put in place following the passage of the 1792 Police Act.

This was clearly one of the reasons why the Bow Street officers were always better-off than their equivalents in the police offices. The magistrates at those offices complained to the house of commons committee set up by prime minister Pitt in 1797 to investigate financial issues across the administration that with their budgets fixed at £2,000 and virtually all of that sum required for salaries and other necessary charges, they lacked 'the Means of rewarding [their constables] for special Services in the Discharge of their Duty.'[18] That was not entirely true. They too were allowed to include 'extraordinary' payments for police work in their accounts.[19] But they were clearly more constrained than the magistrates at Bow Street, and, as a result, the constables at the new offices were never to be as fully engaged as the Bow Street men in the investigation of crime. They may not have been as frequently called upon by the public, but it was equally, perhaps more important that the magistrates in the policing offices were held on a tighter financial rein. The Bow Street magistrates, on the other hand, sent their runners and patrolmen out on jobs as they saw fit. As John Reeves told the commons committee in 1798, 'there is no other Limit to the Expenditures [at Bow Street] than the Discretion of the Justices.'[20] This was confirmed in a description of the police of

---

[17] The duke of Portland, Home Secretary, ordered the Bow Street magistrates in May 1795 to certify the fitness of each voucher or bill in response to the concerns of the Treasury about how these expenditures for policing were going to be controlled (NA: HO 65/1, 1 May 1795). As we will see, not every claim in the future was accompanied by a bill, certified or not.

[18] The committee issued its report on the financing of the police offices as *The Twenty-eighth Report of the Select Committee of the House of Commons on Finance: Police and Convict Establishments* (1798). It is included in Sheila Lambert (ed.), *House of Commons Sessional Papers of the Eighteenth Century*, vol. 112. Although John Reeves was one of three witnesses before the committee (the others were Patrick Colquhoun and Jeremy Bentham) not all of his evidence was included in the report. The quoted passage about the limited ability of the stipendiary magistrates to reward their constables is in a statement of 'Observations' that Reeves prepared for the committee. It is included in a version of the report published in the following year to highlight Patrick Colquhoun's proposals for a reform of the police, which was the burden of his evidence before the committee. This was published as *The Report of the Select Committee of the House of Commons relative to the Establishment of a New Police in the Metropolis* (1799). The quote from Reeves's 'Observations' is at 114.

[19] TNA: HO 65/1, 10 December 1795.

[20] *Report of the Select Committee* (1799),115; HO 61/1, 148–9.

London among the Home Office papers in 1812. 'The money allowed for the Establishment of the 7 Police Offices,' it observed, 'is fixed by Act of Parliament, but the Establishment at Bow Street is paid out of the Civil List and may be extended upon its present foundation so as to meet the peculiar exigencies of the times.'[21]

The result was that the costs of Bow Street policing rose strongly after 1792 over earlier levels. Under John Fielding, Bow Street had drawn a total of roughly £1,600 a year from government sources for the salaries of the magistrates (£600), the publication and distribution of the *Hue and Cry* (£400), and the running costs of the office, including payments to the officers (£600). With the addition of a permanent patrol in 1783 and its expansion in 1790, those costs had risen to over £4,000. Under the new arrangements by which Bow Streets's finances came to be managed by the receiver of police, the costs of the office increased further. The precise amount varied from quarter to quarter, depending on the level of discretionary payments, but even in modestly busy periods the resources made available to Bow Street went far beyond anything John Fielding had dreamed of receiving. And with the further expansion of the patrol—the addition of a mounted patrol in 1805, a dismounted patrol (1818), a day patrol (1822), and the engagement of so-called 'supernumerary' patrolmen when they were required for extra duty on the streets[22]—the costs went up even more sharply. An informal and rough account drawn up in 1822 put the cost of the Bow Street office itself at £7,400 a year. The foot patrols required an equal amount, and the hugely expensive mounted patrol more than double that. Fielding would have been astonished to learn that the office he had run for so long on £1,600 a year was by then costing the government about £31,000.[23]

This massive increase was mainly the result, as we will see, of successive extensions of the patrol, along with the stipends for the officers (since 1802 eight rather than six), and increases in the magistrates' and clerks' salaries. It also reflected a broadening of the policing carried out by the office, new tasks taken on in the 1790s largely as a result of the domestic consequences of the Revolution in France and of the war that began in 1793 and (with a brief respite) only concluded with the defeat of Napoleon in 1815. The stimulation that the Revolution encouraged of a movement for political reform in London and in many provincial centres raised concerns in the government and in the governing class more broadly about threats to the constitution in church and state, about domestic security and the safety of the king and the royal family. Bow Street was drawn into a concern with some aspects of these matters in part because the new financial arrangements after 1792

---

[21] TNA: HO 42/119, f. 162. This undated description of 'Police of the Metropolis of London and its environs', may have been prepared for Henry Addington, later viscount Sidmouth, who became home secretary in 1812.

[22] In 1795 and 1798, e.g. OBP, April 1795 (James Jamison) t17950416–45; TNA: T 38/673, January–April 1798 (payment for pistols for the extra patrol).

[23] TNA: HO 61/1, 148–9. The cost of the eight police offices, including the Thames police, was estimated in that same account as £36,740. Including Bow Street, the total cost of London policing in 1822 was thus £67,740.

placed the office more than ever under the control and supervision of the secretary of state and the under-secretary in charge of criminal matters at the Home Office. The flexibility of Bow Street's finances made it possible for the government to use the runners and the patrolmen as they thought necessary. The consequence was a shift in the balance of policing carried out by the runners. The years after 1792 saw them taking on a wider range of investigations that included more work outside London and more engagement with threats to national security and social disorder, tasks that were not entirely new, but that came to occupy much more of their time than they had before 1792.

2. CRIME, THE RUNNERS, AND THE PATROL, 1792–1815

This shift in the balance of their work did not mean that the runners withdrew from dealing with violent offenders or with the ordinary run of property offences. They continued to be engaged by private prosecutors to catch and prosecute thieves and robbers, and the Bow Street magistrates continued to send the runners out to investigate offences when the public interest was sufficiently engaged. In November 1798, when a rash of robberies was reported on Hounslow Heath, two officers— Henry Edwards and Thomas Dowsett—were sent in a post-chaise 'to scour that neighbourhood.' They were greeted by being themselves attacked by two highwaymen. Shots were exchanged. One of the robbers escaped, the other (John Haines) was found because he had been seriously wounded, and the runners got information about him from the stable-keeper who had rented him a horse. He had lost a great deal of blood and had to be attended to at the Brown Bear until he could be examined and sent to trial. He was charged at the January 1799 sessions at the Old Bailey under the harsh and rarely-enforced Black Act of 1723 with the capital offence of shooting at someone, convicted, sentenced to death, and hanged.[24]

The runners continued to carry out investigations into property offences—as when, for example, Townsend was able to show that an apparent burglary in a coffee shop was the work of an insider, the head waiter.[25] They still responded to tips from informers. John Sayer and Henry Edwards, learning where they would find a trunk that had been cut from behind a post-chaise, went with others to a house in a dangerous part of town and arrested two men after a violent encounter in which some of the Bow Street men were injured.[26] The runners also continued to work when necessary in large groups. Charles Jealous—in his last months in the office before he took up duties at Windsor Castle—described at the Old Bailey how

---

[24] OBP, January 1799 (John Haines) t17990109–11; *The Times*, 17 November 1798; 14 January 1799. Haines's accomplice was caught some months later and he was also convicted and sentenced to death under the same statute since he too had shot into the chaise in which the Bow Street men were riding (OBP, September 1799, Thomas Clark (t17990911–2)). The offences are mistakenly categorized as assaults in the Old Bailey website.

[25] *Morning Chronicle*, 13 July 1791.

[26] OBP, February 1799, John Groves and George Bamber (t17990220–35); *The Times*, 25 January 1799.

he, Macmanus, Townsend, and five other Bow Street men had apprehended seven footpads when they got 'information' that they were drinking at a pub in Islington.[27] In other cases, the runners mounted long stake-outs,[28] and carried out the same kind of dogged searches as they had in John Fielding's day, as when William Atkins traced a hackney coachman when a woman inadvertently left luggage in his coach and the only thing she could remember about the vehicle was that one of its doors was fastened by a peg.[29]

The runners also continued to be called upon by departments of the government like the Post Office to investigate offences on their behalf—responsibilities that were noted in an account of the office's work presented to a new secretary of state in 1812.[30] Examples of Bow Street men working for the Post Office—investigating thefts from the mail, typically thefts of bank notes by sorters or letter carriers—are not difficult to find.[31] The Bank of England also employed Bow Street officers to detect and assist in the prosecution of forgers. To take just one example, in the last three months of 1794 the Bank's solicitor engaged virtually all of the runners to run down a number of forgers in London. Over a period of 85 days all six runners were involved at one time or another, sometimes singly, more often in groups of two, three, or four, in conducting searches in all parts of the metropolis, including the City of London, and in apprehending and interrogating suspects and informers. Christopher Kennedy, whose short career as a runner had begun in 1792 and who was to die in 1795, was the most active, being in receipt of expenses and payments for his time and trouble on 56 occasions. Townsend was involved on 22 days, Jealous on 19, the other three runners between 10 and 19. Altogether the Bank paid just over £70.[32]

The Bank later engaged in a major national campaign against forgers when, as a consequence of a run on specie brought on by the demands of the war, the government suspended cash payments in 1797 and the Bank was allowed for the first time to issue small-denomination notes of £1 and £2. These became an immediate target of forgers, and an extraordinarily large number of forged notes were released through a dense network of distributors over the next quarter century before cash payments were restored in 1822. The runners were drawn into this campaign, as were constables from the other police offices in the metropolis as well as a number of provincial constables, all of whom responded to the Bank's offer of generous rewards for the detection and prosecution of the forgers and those who

---

[27] OBP, April 1794, Thomas Stunnell (t17940430–8).

[28] *The Times*, 18 January 1805.

[29] *The Times*, 7 April 1804.

[30] TNA: HO 42/119, f. 162.

[31] See, e.g., OBP, September 1792 (Isaac Moore) t17920912–85; January 1795 (James Pepperday) t17950114–36; October 1807 (George Palmer) t18051028–39; September 1809 (Thomas Roles) t18090920–81; for cases noted in the press, *The Times*, 27 October 1804; 9 November 1812; 31 December 1812; 27 October 1813.

[32] Bank of England Mss, Roehampton, F48. I am grateful to Randall McGowen for providing me with copies of his notes on this material.

uttered the notes. The campaign stretched to every part of the country, supervised by a Bank committee and managed by a firm of London solicitors.[33]

Much of the runners' work continued after 1792 along the lines established under John Fielding. But the balance of that work had begun in the 1780s to shift away from the dominant position that detection and prosecution of crime in London had held for so long, and it continued to do so in the last decade of the century and after. The runners came to be much less frequently concerned with property crime and run-of-the-mill felonies and made fewer appearances in the witness box at the Old Bailey than they had 10 years earlier. This shift in the runners' work was a consequence in part, as we shall see, of new policing demands that engaged their attention. But it was also a consequence of the expansion of other policing forces, notably the patrolmen attached to the Bow Street office, and the constables in the new police offices established by the Middlesex Justices Act of 1792.

The effect that the new police offices had on the level of criminal business carried on at Bow Street can be seen in the commitments of suspects recorded in the Old Bailey gaol calendars. Under John Fielding, Bow Street committed over 40 per cent of all accused felons from Middlesex who went to trial at the Old Bailey; the remainder were committed by Westminster and Middlesex magistrates acting on their own or, beginning in the 1760s, by magistrates in the so-called rotation offices that were taking shape then and in the following decades, offices in which magistrates in several parts of the metropolis began to cooperate in carrying out their duties in order to establish sites at which the public would be able to find a justice at regular hours.[34] Such offices made little initial impact on criminal prosecutions, but emerged to take a much stronger and more active role in the years following the American war. The effect on the Bow Street magistrates' share of criminal commitments was being felt in John Fielding's last years in the office and became particularly clear in the 1780s when they were responsible for committing about a fifth of the men and women sent for trial at the Old Bailey. After 1792, the balance moved even more towards the new police offices that were staffed by salaried magistrates and more conveniently located than Bow Street for the vast majority of victims of felonies. By the early years of the nineteenth century, the

---

[33] Randall McGowen, 'The Bank of England and the Policing of Forgery 1797–1821', *Past and Present*, 186 (February, 2005), 81–116. (Bow Street involvement is at 89–90.) Along with an illuminating discussion of the nature and extent of the forgery problem, McGowen's essay provides interesting evidence of the emergence in some of the larger provincial towns of active constables taking up detection and prosecution along the lines of Bow Street and the metropolitan police offices. McGowen has published other articles in his continuing study of forgery in eighteenth and early nineteenth century England. Two in particular relate to the Bank of England campaign against forgers in this period: 'From Pillory to Gallows: the Punishment of Forgery in the Age of the Financial Revolution', *Past and Present*, 165 (November 1999), 107–40; and 'Managing the Gallows: The Bank of England and the Death Penalty, 1797–1821', *Law and History Review*, 25/2 (2007), 241–82.

[34] See ch. 5, text at nn.11–12.

contribution of the Bow Street magistrates to the calendars of suspected felons awaiting trial had fallen to just over 15 per cent.[35]

Another fundamental change was even more important in ensuring that the runners' work did not remain after John Fielding's death entirely as it had been in his lifetime. That was the creation of the Bow Street patrol in 1783 and its enlargement at the end of that decade to enable patrolmen to guard the inner streets of the capital as well as the suburbs. The new financial arrangements after 1792 confirmed support for a patrol of 68 men, working in 13 parties of four or five patrolmen, each led by a conductor, or captain. There were to be further expansions of the patrol in the early decades of the nineteenth century to enlarge its capacity to guard the roads on the outskirts of the metropolis, beyond the zone in which the foot patrols worked. Early in 1798, the home secretary, the duke of Portland, obtained extra sums from the Treasury to extend the patrolling beyond its current range because of some 'very daring Robberies on the Kentish and Windsor Roads.'[36] But there was an inevitable limit to what foot patrols based at the centre of the city could do, and the difficulties of dealing with offences being committed further and further out beyond the expanding suburbs were not solved until a new form of patrolling (one that John Fielding had advocated 40 years earlier) was established in the early years of the nineteenth century. Faced with an increase of highway robberies beyond the reach of Bow Street forces, Richard Ford, then chief magistrate at Bow Street and, as we will see, a man with very close contacts with the Home Office, persuaded the government in 1805 to create a mounted patrol to guard the roads outside the metropolis. After a six-month experiment on three roads, the Home Office deployed a full complement of 54 horsemen to guard 'all the great roads leading from London to such distances as the particular local nature of each may consider necessary'—a range that came in time to be up to 20 miles from the centre of the city. For the most part, mounted patrolmen were recruited from among men who had served in the Light Dragoons, men who would be fully capable of using the sabres and pistols they were to carry.[37] They were part of the Bow Street establishment, but since the horse patrol required stabling and other accommodation, its men, horses, and equipment were stationed in the areas they were to guard—along the highways outside the metropolis. It was virtually

---

[35] For commitments recorded in the gaol calendars before 1780, see ch. 5, Table 5.1. A sample of eight sessions between 1782 and 1792 shows Bow Street responsible for 21.8% of the 1,150 accused felons committed to trial; in a sample of 10 sessions, 1794–1812, the Bow Street share had fallen to 15.3% of 947 commitments (source: LMA: MJ/SR (gaol calendars). A very large number of calendars are missing after 1812).

[36] TNA: HO 36/10, 387.

[37] TNA: HO 36/14, 55–6; HO 42/80 ff.33–4, 35–6, 38; HO 36/14, 158–9. In a description of the office written in 1813 by John Read, the chief magistrate, the horse patrol was then said to consist of two inspectors and 41 men. They were armed with pistols and sabres. Their patrols began between three and seven miles from London 'according to the Security of the Road [information] arising from the Bow Street Foot Patrole and local Watchmen in the Suburbs, and patrole a distance of about 8 miles of Road to an extent of from 12 to 15 Miles from London. A Man and Horse are stationed at each end of the Ground patroled and they patrole to the opposite points and back again meeting each other on their outward and inward Journeys. In the open Commons and Heaths the Patrole is Doubled.' (Devon R.O., Sidmouth Mss, 152 M/OH 38.

impossible in those circumstances for the Bow Street magistrates to exercise any real control over their work, supposing they had wanted to, and within a few years its actual management was put in the hands of its own 'conductor', based in the Home Office.[38]

The foot patrol of 68 men remained very much an integral part of the Bow Street policing establishment. Their principal duty remained to guard the main inner streets of the metropolis and the major roads bringing traffic into the capital. They worked at those tasks from dusk until midnight, for which they received a weekly stipend that provided them with what in the 1790s would have been (at about £45 a year) the foundation of a reasonable income. They were at liberty to add to that—or perhaps they were expected to add to that—by engaging in policing duties during the day at the behest of the magistrates. And from their first days in the office in 1783 they had done just that. Indeed, they came to share many of the tasks hitherto carried out by the runners. In the 1780s and after, the patrolmen can be found investigating offences, making arrests, and giving evidence for the prosecution at Bow Street, the Middlesex Sessions of the Peace, and the Old Bailey.

By the 1790s, the patrolmen were engaging fully in the more general policing work of the office. They were sent by the magistrates and hired by private prosecutors to investigate not only the offences they might come upon in their patrolling of the inner streets of the city and the highways leading out through the suburbs—robberies by footpads and mounted highwaymen, pocket picking, burglary—but offences that required their attendance and engagement during the daylight hours when they were not officially on duty. On Christmas Day in 1798, for example, *The Times* reported that '[i]n consequence of the number of highway and footpad robberies which have lately been committed in the day time, as well as in the night, on Epping Forest, the Magistrates ordered a party of the patrole there,' where they made two arrests and brought the suspects to Bow Street for examinations.[39] Other press and trial reports reveal patrolmen investigating and making arrests in cases of housebreaking, coining, and larcenies of every kind. They can be found working on their own, with some of their fellow patrolmen, and with one or more of the runners (one of whom may have had some loose superintendence over them).[40] They were also sent by the magistrates to keep watch at fairs and, as in the case of the Epping Forest investigation, to carry out other duties outside the metropolis.

---

[38]   TNA: HO 65/2, 7 October 1813.

[39]   *The Times*, 25 December 1798.

[40]   In 1798, it was reported in the press that Rivett had been recommended 'as a chief Officer to superintend and inspect the patrol' in Dublin. 'In that situation,' the report went on, 'he will be like Townsend in London' (*Morning Chronicle*, 10 January 1798). Within three weeks Rivett had gone and returned, the Irish government having taken it amiss that an English outsider had been brought in to do that job. The report of his return in the *Morning Chronicle* (30 January 1798) assumed, however, that he had gone as the 'Inspector of the Press' and that he had been sent away because Ireland was in no need of 'practised treason-finders'—an interesting confusion considering the extent to which the runners had become involved by the late 1790s in anti-sedition work on behalf of the secretary of state, with Rivett prominently among them, for which see below, text at nn. 77–91.

Table 7.1. Bow Street witnesses at the Old Bailey, 1795–1817[1]

	Robbery	Burglary/ Housebreaking	Picking Pockets	Other Capital Felonies	Larceny	Forgery/ Fraud/ Coining	Total
Runners	4	8	-	11	20	14	58
Patrolmen	20	21	8	28	62	12	156
Total	24	29	8	39	82	26	214
Runners %	16.7	27.6	-	28.2	24.4	53.8	27.1

[1]Source: <http://www.oldbaileyonline.org>. Based on the years 1795, 1800, 1804, 1810, 1817

The work of the patrol and the runners came to overlap to such an extent that patrolmen came to outnumber runners in the witness box at the Old Bailey in the last years of the eighteenth century and the first decades of the nineteenth. Between 1795 and 1817, the runners gave evidence in court much less frequently than they had in John Fielding's day. Where several runners might have been present every day the Old Bailey sat in the 1770s, barely one runner made an appearance at each *session* by the early nineteenth century. Their place had been taken by patrolmen, even in cases that it is reasonable to think were regarded as the most serious— robbery and burglary (Table 7.1).

The runners' withdrawal from the investigation and prosecution of crime in London is further confirmed by two bodies of Bow Street evidence that have survived fortuitously in this period: a small group of bills submitted by officers in claiming payments for work done on behalf of the office; and the chief clerk's distribution of small cash payments known as 'disbursements'. Most of the bills sent into the Treasury have not survived. But a group of just over 50 from 1811 and a few from the following year remain among the quarterly accounts, and provide some further evidence of the division of work between the runners and patrolmen in those years. They confirm the changing division of work at Bow Street suggested by the Old Bailey evidence: three quarters of the bills had been submitted by patrolmen, the other quarter by runners.[41] The 'disbursements' tell the same story. These small cash payments were made by the chief clerk to cover some of the out-of-pocket expenses officers had incurred in carrying out an investigation—coach fares, for example. They were obviously useful, especially to the poorer paid patrolmen.[42] The clerks' accounts of their disbursements have largely disappeared, but three survive for nine months in 1800–01 showing payments of less than £40 a month on average. They too confirm the changing balance of duties in the office. In the account for the second quarter of 1800 (April–July), for example, 40 of the entries were for payments to single patrolmen and another eight name two

[41] TNA: T 38/673.
[42] Up to 1807 the patrolmen were paid once a quarter. They were henceforth given a weekly wage on John Reeves' suggestion (HO 36/14, 362).

patrolmen working together. Only 14 payments went to runners, either working alone, with other officers, or with patrolmen.[43]

The surviving office accounts in the quarter century after the 1792 Act confirm the growing importance of the patrolmen as the men most likely to respond to appeals for help from victims of property crime in London. Addington attempted to emphasize the distinction between the two groups of Bow Street men in the public mind by ordering in the summer of 1799 that they all wear badges announcing their status as officer or patrolman.[44] Whether that happened or not, it had little effect on the tendency by then of the press to call them all Bow Street 'officers', which no doubt explains why the runners were insisting within a few years on being known as 'principal officers' or even 'senior principal officers'. And it had even less effect on their sharing the work of investigation and prosecution of property crime and other felonies, or on the patrolmen increasingly taking the lead in such work. The author of a memorandum on the police of London written for a new Home Secretary, Earl Spencer, observed in 1806–07 that while each of the police offices included 10 constables, the equivalent force at Bow Street was near a hundred—that is, he recognized the runners and the patrolmen as being equivalent with respect to criminal work.[45]

By the 1820s, virtually the only Bow Street officers giving evidence in the trials at the Old Bailey—across the whole range of serious criminal offences, including robbery, burglary, housebreaking, pocket picking, coining, and the array of larcenies—were members of the day and night patrols. By then, the captains of the patrol had become as knowledgeable about the London underworld as the runners, and, like the runners, many of them remained in office over many years. Their experience also made the captains natural recruits for vacancies in the ranks of the runners. Edward Fugion was an early recruit from the patrol to be a runner in 1796. By the second decade of the nineteenth century it was a common pattern: John Vickery (1811), Samuel Taunton (1811), Daniel Bishop (1816), William Salmon (1820), and James John Smith (1821) had each captained a patrol party for several years before being named as 'principal officers'.

One consequence of the increasing prominence of the patrolmen in the policing of London was that the runners were free to take up new tasks. In one area, they did not so much take up new tasks as respond to a growing demand for their services—that is with respect to criminal investigations outside the capital, which became more numerous and more diverse in the late years of the eighteenth century and the early decades of the nineteenth.

---

[43] TNA: T 38/673. The money for the 'disbursements' came from fines and fees collected in the office, which Bow Street was allowed to keep, unlike the police offices, in which this income went in support of the established costs—another way in which Dundas's decision to allow the policing activities at Bow Street to be financed in a looser and more generous way favoured the office. The additional income amounted only to a few hundred pounds a year, depending on the level of office business, but it clearly helped to facilitate the office's policing work.

[44] *The Times*, 13 July 1799.

[45] BL: Add Mss 75900 ('Police arrangements').

Bow Street had never been restricted to a particular local jurisdiction. From the earliest days of the office, the Bow Street officers had chased offenders across the country, and on occasion across the Irish Sea and the Channel; they had sought out provincial suspects who had taken refuge in London and escorted them back to face justice; and they had been sent to fetch suspects back to Bow Street who had fled the capital and had been picked up by constables in other jurisdictions. Such work continued after 1792. In a typical case in 1805, two of the runners, Rivett and Miller, were dispatched by the chief magistrate, Sir Richard Ford, to find a land-tax collector who had absconded from Edinburgh with several thousand pounds and was thought to be in London. They got a line on him from the boat that had brought him to the Thames and traced him through a succession of lodging houses and pubs. When he was caught and examined before the Bow Street magistrates, they took him back to Scotland.[46] Bishop traced a similar absconder to Paris and brought him back to be tried at the Winchester assizes.[47] John Sayer was sent to Gloucester gaol in 1799 to identify three men being held there who were suspected of committing offences in London. He knew two of them, and brought them back: a robber who went by the name of Galloping Dick; and the accomplice of a man who had been executed in the previous week for shooting at two Bow Street officers.[48] In another case, Carpmeal and Jealous, no doubt acting on a tip, went to Birmingham to apprehend two accused robbers who had slipped away from the Kingston assizes two years earlier and had since been at large.[49]

Policing of this kind had been part of John Fielding's vison of a national network constructed by magisterial correspondence and cooperation. He had regularly sent his officers to help with investigations across the country when that support was requested. After 1792, that aspect of the runners' work not only continued but increased sharply. *The Times* regularly reported their journeys around the country. They can be found going to Hull to combat a gang of robbers, to Bury St Edmunds to guard against thieves at a fair, to the Isle of Sheppey in Kent to discover the identity of a man washed ashore with his throat cut and to trace his murderer to Walmer, near Dover, to investigate the murder of four revenue officers by a smuggling gang, to the village of Exening in Suffolk to look into a suspected case of arson involving a wool-barn, a parsonage, and several houses.[50]

The runners' work in the provinces expanded after 1792, no doubt in part because of an increase in requests for their help in investigating serious offences and apprehending dangerous offenders. But demand for their services is only part of the explanation. As important had been the increase in resources available to them, resources that allowed the Bow Street magistrates and the Home Office to pay for the runners' investigations in the provinces in cases in which the victim or the local authorities were not able to meet the costs. The increased resources that the

---

[46] *The Times*, 11 October 1805.
[47] *The Times*, 7 March 1818.
[48] *The Times*, 4 March 1799. For Haines, see above, text at n. 24.
[49] *The Times*, 17 January 1794.
[50] *The Times*, 13 November 1798, 21 October 1802, 10 May 1814, 15 November 1815, 21 August 1818.

government made available after 1792, along with the runners' reputation for skill and courage and the increase in requests from provincial prosecutors, all help to explain the emergence after 1792 of an expanded line of work that—along with other new tasks we will take up presently—helped to make Bow Street the centre of a national police even more than it had been under the Fieldings.

Little had been known about the runners' work outside London in the early nineteenth century before the publication of David J. Cox's recent study of the provincial activities of the men he prefers to call by their more official name of 'Principal Officers'.[51] Cox has recovered evidence of their work from two provincial papers, *The Times,* the Old Bailey website and Home Office records. He has compiled a sample record of 601 cases in which Bow Street officers conducted investigations into criminal offences outside London between 1792 and 1839, the year in which the police forces at Bow Street were disbanded. He has, in addition, gathered the evidence from the Old Bailey court records of their metropolitan investigations over the same period, a total of 292 trials. Cox is thus able to compare the runners' provincial and metropolitan work—the offences they were called to investigate, where they mainly worked in the provinces, the identity of the 'employers' who had called on Bow Street for help, and other matters. In the case of the runners' London investigations, Cox's findings confirm that in the late eighteenth and early nineteenth centuries the runners were not as deeply engaged in the prosecution of felonies in the capital as they had been under John Fielding and that they had left that work very largely to the patrolmen.[52]

Inevitably, it cost more to employ Bow Street help outside London than in the metropolis itself. For the most part those who called for help were expected to pay the runner's expenses and fees for service, though when that was not possible and the public interest was involved the Home Office might allow the charges to be carried in the Bow Street accounts—mainly coach fares, lodging, and subsistence at a set rate; the officers normally charged a guinea a day for their work. Cases that involved long journeys from London, or a good deal of moving about to conduct investigations, or that simply stretched over many days and weeks, could be expensive. Cox has found bills of £50 and more.[53] Nonetheless, the runners were called to investigate cases in every county of England, and a few in Scotland and Wales, though 70 per cent of their work was conducted in the south, particularly in the Home Counties around the metropolis.[54] Given the costs involved, it is no

---

[51] David J. Cox, *A Certain Share of Low Cunning. A History of the Bow Street Runners, 1792–1839* (Cullompton, Devon, 2010). The following brief account of the runners' work outside London largely depends on Cox's research. It is worth noting that his thesis, on which the book is based, includes data on each case in Cox's sample, details which are summarized in tabular form in the book. Dr Cox's thesis is: '"A Certain Share of Low Cunning": an analysis of the work of the Bow Street principal officers, 1792–1839, with particular emphasis on their provincial duties', Ph.D. thesis (Lancaster University, 2006).

[52] Cox, *A Certain Share of Low Cunning,* 76.

[53] Ibid, 149–50.

[54] Ibid, 148–56.

Table 7.2. Types of cases investigated by Bow Street runners, 1792–1839[1]

Provincial Cases				Old Bailey Cases			
Rank	Offence	No.	%	Rank	Offence	No.	%
1	Murder/attempt	99	16.5	1	Larceny	160	54.8
2	Arson/damage	93	15.5	2	Forger/fraud	63	21.6
3	Larceny	86	14.3	3	Burglary	25	8.6
4	Forgery/Fraud	71	11.8	4	Robbery	14	4.8
5	Burglary	66	11.0	5	Recapture of escapees	12	4.1
6	Robbery	61	10.1	6	Pocket picking	7	2.4
7	Sedition/rioting	42	7.0	7	Murder/attempt	6	2.1
8	Recapture of escapees	14	2.3	8	Arson/damage	3	1.0
9	Pocket picking	14	2.3	9	Sedition	2	0.7
10	Other or not recorded	55	9.2				
	Total	601	100.0		Total	292	100.0

[1]Source: Cox, *A Certain Share of Low Cunning*, 105, 126.

surprise that in the 40 per cent of provincial cases in which the costs were paid by private citizens, the 'employers' of the runners were mainly large landowners or mill-owners or men similarly in a position to afford outside help to prosecute someone who had committed a major theft or done serious damage to their property. A quarter of the cases had been initiated by public or private institutions, including the Bank of England, a further quarter by the Home Department or the Bow Street magistrates, and 10 per cent by provincial magistrates.[55]

Few of these cases were trivial. Most were regarded as serious by their victims or the authorities, either because they had involved violence, or the theft of or damage to property of considerable value. The three leading offences the runners were called to investigate outside London—each accounting for about 15 per cent of the 601 cases—were murder, arson or damage to property, and larceny, followed by forgery, burglary and robbery, each about 11 per cent of the total (Table 7.2).

The prevalence of murder is striking, given how infrequently—as Table 7.2 confirms—the runners were involved in homicide cases in the metropolis. As we have seen, the investigation of homicide remained the province of the coroner in London. Only rarely did such cases enter the criminal justice system in the way other felonies came to court—via the magistrates' examination and committal procedures. From time to time, John Fielding had sent the runners (perhaps at the request of the family of victims) to investigate a suspicious death, but it had never been a major aspect of their work. And as Cox has discovered from his examination of the Old Bailey *Proceedings*, that remained the case after 1792. He has found a mere six cases of murder or attempted murder in which runners gave evidence at the Old Bailey in the following four decades. Their investigation of 78 murder cases in the provinces over the period 1792 to 1839 is thus at first sight

[55] Cox, *A Certain Share of Low Cunning*, 74.

surprising. But the explanation lies in the close connection of these homicides with the cases that make up the second largest group of provincial offences investigated by the runners—arson and damage to property—or with the activities of smuggling or poaching. Most of the provincial homicide charges arose not from narrowly interpersonal encounters, but rather involved the killing of officials arising out of confrontations between the authorities and protestors, or from attempts by gamekeepers to arrest poachers, or customs officers to prevent smuggling. In some of these cases the runners had been sent by the Home Office; others were initiated by landowners and by magistrates troubled by the complexity of the problems they faced in dealing with large numbers of violent offences and the dangers involved in discovering and prosecuting the perpetrators—as well as the threats of retribution that would hang over any local constable brave enough to take up the challenge of bringing such offenders before the courts.[56]

On average (in Cox's sample of their work), the Bow Street officers were called to investigate an offence outside London on just over 12 occasions every year between the Police Act of 1792 and the disbandment of the force in 1839. What proportion of the runners' time these provincial cases occupied would be impossible to calculate even if we knew the full extent of their work outside London. Some took a good deal of time, others very little, and the demands for their services rose and fell with changing local circumstances: serious deprivation, shortages of food, the reduction of wages, or changes in labour practices and in the availability of work following the introduction of new machinery in textile production or of steam-driven threshing machines in agricultural areas were met with protests and 'disturbances' that were likely to lead to the kinds of offences that caused local authorities or landowners to seek the runners' help. Much higher involvement of Bow Street men can be seen in 1812, at the time of the Luddite protests, and in general in the difficult years towards the end of the war in 1815 and the several years of peace thereafter.[57] Cox shows that the demands for Bow Street help also rose sharply in the 1830s.[58]

As important as provincial cases were by the early nineteenth century, they by no means monopolized the runners' time. The broadening scope of their work no doubt made Bow Street even more a national police force after 1792 than they had been under John Fielding: as the chief magistrate, Sir Richard Birnie, was to tell a house of commons committee in 1822, they were 'police officers for the country at large.'[59] But there was another sense in which they had become more of a national force by the early nineteenth century, that is in the work they increasingly took up under the immediate direction of the Home Department. The runners never ceased

---

[56] Ibid, 104–10. And see ch. 6, in which Cox discusses these issues in the course of providing detailed case studies of the Bow Street officers' investigations into six types of offence, including murder, arson, and poaching.

[57] Based on annual data included in Cox's thesis: '"A Certain Share of Low Cunning,"' App. 4, 333–9.

[58] Cox, *A Certain Share of Low Cunning*, ch. 7.

[59] *Parliamentary Papers*, 1822, vol. 4 (440) *Report from the Committee on the State of the Police of the Metropolis*, 14.

to deal with ordinary crime, but a new range of issues claimed their attention after 1792. These came directly from the government's demand for policing services.

3. NEW POLICING DEMANDS

Although the policing of felonies in the metropolis had largely fallen to the patrol by the early nineteenth century, the runners continued to receive the largest proportion of 'extraordinary' payments for work done on behalf of the office. What that work was is revealed in a number of the quarterly accounts from the early years of the century. For the most part, the sums paid to individual officers for their work on behalf of the office are not categorized or distinguished in the accounts. But in five quarterly accounts between 1800 and 1803 Reeves arranged the entries in three groups.[60] One set of payments were for the work the runners had always done at the behest of the magistrates—investigating offences, making arrests, finding witnesses, and the like. This was always going to be a variable amount, but in these five quarterly accounts it averaged about 44 per cent of the total money distributed by Reeves to the runners and patrolmen. The two other batches of payments were for what were essentially new policing tasks: on the one hand, work undertaken on behalf of the secretary of state, which accounted for 20 per cent of Reeves's outlays; and a further group, amounting to 35 per cent of the whole, for the work shared by several runners and patrolmen of guarding the king and other members of the royal family (Table 7.3).

There is no indication in the accounts of the precise nature of any of this work. But the fact that more than half of the payments to the runners and the patrol in the early years of the nineteenth century was for work on behalf of the government and the royal family confirms that the runners had been drawn into forms of policing that were essentially new after 1792, or at least that constituted a much larger part

Table 7.3. Payments showing the division of Bow Street work, 1800–1803 (to nearest £)[1]

Work on behalf of:	Expenditure	
	£	%
Royal Family	813	35.2
Secretary of State	469	20.3
Bow Street Magistrates	1025	44.4
Total	2307	99.9

[1] Source: TNA: T 38/673: accounts for April–July 1800, July–October 1800, July–October 1801, April–July 1802, April–July 1803.

---

[60] TNA: T 38/673: April–July 1800, July–October 1800, July–October 1801, April–July 1802, April–July 1803.

of their work than they had under John Fielding. It is not a surprise to learn that the bulk of this new work arose from the government's concern about the domestic consequences of the Revolution in France—the rise of militant radicalism and a perceived threat of sedition and insurrection supported by a French invasion.

(a) National security

Ruth Paley has observed that it is tempting to see the 1792 Police Act not simply as a means of correcting the inadequacies of the Middlesex magistracy, but as an effort to put in place a political police to control emerging radicalism and to counter seditious activity in Britain.[61] The early stages of the revolution in France had provided encouragement to a renewed political reform movement that aimed at making the house of commons more representative of the English population and more responsive to the needs and opinions of a wider section of society than could be the case in a chamber filled with the landed gentlemen, placemen, and the nominees of aristocratic patrons. Proposals for parliamentary reform had first arisen in the 1760s as a consequence of the government's treatment of John Wilkes, and had been pursued again seriously in the late 1770s and the following decade as a result of the failed war in America. Reformers within the political class, especially those allied with the whig opposition, tended to favour minor adjustments that would increase the number of independent members of parliament and reduce the influence of the crown in the house of commons. But during and after the American war, ideas were also canvassed that would have introduced much more significant changes—proposals largely from middle class political and religious leaders aimed at eliminating the overweening power of the aristocracy and making parliament more responsible to the people by introducing universal male suffrage and secret ballots, creating single member and equal electoral districts, eliminating placemen, and paying members. Efforts to win some measure of reform—including one put forward by the prime minister William Pitt—failed on three occasions in the early 1780s, and the movement subsided until events in France in 1789 as well as the centenary celebration of England's own Glorious Revolution, brought the issue of the inequalities in the system of representation once more onto the public agenda.[62]

The difference in the 1790s was that the leadership of the reform effort passed largely into the hands of men outside the political class, many of them skilled working men, who drew inspiration from the radical proposals of Tom Paine and the possibility of political renewal that the French Revolution seemed to promise. The London Corresponding Society and similar societies in urban centres across the country staged mass public meetings to endorse proposals for thorough-going political reform, developments that came to seem increasingly dangerous as opinion

---

[61] Paley, 'Middlesex Justices Act', 294.

[62] John Brewer, *Party Ideology and popular politics at the accession of George III* (Cambridge, 1976); Ian Christie, *Wilkes, Wyvill, and reform: the parliamentary reform movement in British politics, 1760–1785* (London, 1962).

in the government and more generally in the governing class became concerned about the growing violence in France in the fall of 1792. Opinion hardened further with the execution of Louis XVI in January of the following year, as well as with the aggressive determination of the revolutionary government to expand French power into the Low Countries and beyond, and its announced willingness to help democratic movements everywhere achieve their own remaking of the political order. Despite their assurances that they had no intention of turning to violent measures to achieve their political ambitions, the London Corresponding Society and other radical groups were regarded with increasing suspicion, particularly when France declared war on Britain in February of 1793. By continuing to hold public meetings to discuss the need for fundamental alterations to the constitution, the radical movement came to be viewed by broad sections of the middle and upper classes as posing a threat to political and social stability at a dangerous time for the country. Whether or not prime minister Pitt and those closest to him were persuaded that English security was under threat, the government moved aggressively to counter threats of insurrection and to promote loyalty to the monarch and the constitution. Thomas Hardy and the other leaders of the London Corresponding Society were arrested early in 1794 and charged with treason, *habeas corpus* was suspended, making it possible for the authorities to arrest on suspicion without charge or trial, and increasingly stringent powers were obtained from parliament that defined seditious practices more narrowly and prohibited large-scale public meetings of the kind they disapproved.[63] Over the next seven years, there were to be more than 200 prosecutions for sedition in England.[64]

It is not implausible to see the creation of the seven police offices in 1792 as an element in that programme of opposition to radicalism and sedition. On the other hand, the fact that constables were added to the bill only because the chairman of the Middlesex bench pointed out that the new stipendiaries would be impotent without them, suggests that the government had mainly set out to improve the quality of the Middlesex magistracy.[65] And, in the event, even with a body of constables who might have carried out investigations, the police offices did not turn out to be particularly useful in the government's campaign. Ruth Paley's detailed investigation of their work reveals that the stipendiaries did not do a great deal themselves to uncover credible evidence of the kinds of activities the government was anxious to prosecute. They were occasionally called upon by the Home Office to send men to report on meetings of the London Corresponding Society. But for

---

[63] Albert Goodwin, *The Friends of Liberty: the English Democratic Movement in the age of the French Revolution* (London, 1979), chs. 7–9; E. P. Thompson, *The Making of the English Working Class* (1963, rev. edn. 1968), ch. 5; H. T. Dickinson (ed.), *Britain and the French Revolution, 1789–1815* (New York, 1989); Eugene C. Black, *The Association. British Extraparliamentary Political Organization*, (Cambridge, MA, 1963); John Ehrman, *William Pitt* (3 vols, 1969–96), II, ch. 11; John Barrell, *Imagining the King's Death: Figurative Treason, Fantasies of Regicide, 1793–1796* (Oxford, 2000); Clive Emsley, 'The London "Insurrection" of December 1792: Fact, Fiction, or Fantasy?' *Journal of British Studies*, 17 (2, 1978), 66–86.

[64] Clive Emsley, 'An Aspect of Pitt's "Terror": Prosecutions for Sedition during the 1790s', *Social History*, 6 (2, 1981), 155–84.

[65] Above, ch. 6, text at n.118.

the most part they simply passed on information that came their way about seditious talk and the like, much of which was mere gossip and rumour.[66]

Bow Street seems to have been rather more actively engaged than that in the government's programme to suppress the radical societies and counter threats of sedition. One of its three salaried magistrates, Richard Ford, played a leading role in the government's campaign, and he, and the Home Office, could call upon a group of officers at Bow Street who were experienced in tracking offenders and collecting evidence. Bow Street's flexible budget was also of fundamental importance since it could be increased at will to meet the costs of policing carried out by the runners and patrolmen.[67] This may well have been Dundas's intention when he ordered Reeves to take charge of Bow Street's finances. He seems to have deliberately turned away from bringing the office under the legal structure created by the 1792 Act, opting instead for an informal arrangement that placed no cap on Bow Street's expenditure of the kind that controlled the costs of the public offices. The consequence was that the Home Office could make full use of Bow Street's resources. Richard Ford explained to a new Home Secretary in 1802 that the 1792 Police Act had enlarged 'that part of the police of the metropolis which is under the control of Government.' And, he added, because Bow Street's functions were undefined and its expenditures unlimited by legislation, the office could be 'extended upon its present foundation so as to meet the peculiar needs of the times.'[68] In the 1790s and the first years of the new century, the needs of the times had meant that, under Ford's direction, Bow Street was drawn into the anti-democratic effort waged by the government and its loyalist allies throughout the country.

Richard Ford was unusual among London magistrates not only in that he had been called to the bar and had practised on the Western Circuit, but he had also briefly been an M.P. He was also well connected. His father had been personal physician to George III and *accoucheur* to the queen. He was, in addition, a principal shareholder with Richard Brinsley Sheridan in the Drury Lane theatre, a circumstance that brought his son into contact with the theatrical world and the famous actress Dorothy Jordan—Mrs Jordan—who became his mistress.[69] It also brought him into contact with the Foxite whigs and led to his close friendship with the duke of Portland. Financial problems in the theatre had encouraged Richard to abandon the house of commons in favour of paid work just as the police offices were being opened, and it seems likely that it was through his political connections (and his obvious talent) that Ford became a magistrate at Shadwell and then at the Bow Street office, following the death of Sampson Wright in 1793. Ford did not

[66] Paley, 'Middlesex Justices Act', 300–24.

[67] Above, text at nn.13–21.

[68] BL: Add Mss 33122, f. 79.

[69] Elizabeth Sparrow, 'Ford, Sir Richard'', *Oxford Dictionary of National Biography*, 2004. Ford had promised marriage when they set up together, but by 1791 (and after the birth of three children) she tired of waiting and shifted her affections to the third son of the George III, William, Duke of Clarence, the future Willam IV, with whom she had a further 10 children (Claire Tomalin, *Mrs Jordan's Profession* (London, 1994)).

immediately succeed Wright as chief magistrate at Bow Street only because William Addington insisted that the right of succession was his, having been passed over in favour of Wright at John Fielding's death.[70] But, chief magistrate or not, Ford's legal training and his abilities made him an important asset to the government, faced as they were with a host of domestic problems in the months following the declaration of war. Addington was allowed to assume the title of chief magistrate, but Ford was treated by Dundas and his successor at the Home Office, the duke of Portland, as the real leader of Bow Street, indeed as the leading London magistrate. Dundas and Portland essentially took Ford into the Home Department and provided him with an office so that he could attend daily to be on hand to deal immediately with suspects brought in for examination—including printers and publishers of material regarded as seditious or blasphemous and anyone whose actions or utterances gave rise to suspicions about their loyalty to the king and constitution. He was to say in 1802 that his daily attendance at the Home Office had been one of his most important duties over the previous eight years [71]

Ford's magisterial work at the Home Office, as at Bow Street, blended with his actions as a policeman. He was in effect put in charge of London policing over that period, acting as a third under-secretary in all but name. In January 1795, he set up a separate Entry Book to segregate policing matters from the more general correspondence of the Home Office, and he seems to have composed many of the circular letters that were sent out to the police offices under the signature of the under-secretary in charge of criminal matters, John King.[72] He also organized and coordinated the government's campaign against foreign spies and domestic radicals, sending Dundas's and Portland's instructions to the police offices to conduct surveillance over public meetings and the radical societies, occasionally to send someone to infiltrate their meetings. Ford received and evaluated the reports of the government's own spies and managed the work of at least one himself. At one point he briefly took over the superintendence of the Alien Office, the agency set up by statute in 1793 to keep track of refugees coming into the country from the Continent. In short, from 1795 until his death in 1806, Richard Ford was at the centre of the government's campaign to repress the radical movement in England.[73] He was not a 'fanatical counter-revolutionary', according to Ann Hone, who has studied the large body of evidence concerning his work at the Home Office and Bow Street.[74] But Dundas valued him highly, showing his regard by arranging an addition

---

[70] *St James's Chronicle*, 1 March 1781.

[71] BL: Add Mss 33122, ff. 80–1.

[72] R. R. Nelson, *The Home Office, 1782–1801* (Durham, NC, 1969), 116.

[73] For Ford's work at the Home Office, see Paley, 'The Middlesex Justices Act', 288–93; Hone, *For the Cause of Truth*, chs. 2–3; Sparrow, *Secret Service*, 17; *idem*, 'The Alien Office, 1792–1806', *Historical Journal*, 33/2 (1990), 361–84; Clive Emsley, 'The Home Office and its sources of information and investigation, 1791–1801', *English Historical Review*, 94 (July, 1979), 532–61.

[74] Hone goes on to say that Ford knew members of the London Corresponding Society and retained their respect, even though he was responsible for the arrest of many of their colleagues (*For the Cause of Truth*, 81). Certainly, Francis Place thought it possible to ask him to persuade the government to provide support for the families of members of the general committee of the LCS who were arrested

of £500 to his £400 salary as a magistrate.[75] He was named chief magistrate at Bow Street (and knighted, as was the custom), when Addington retired in 1800, even though Nicholas Bond was the more senior man in line.[76]

Ford's activism ensured that the Bow Street runners and patrolmen would be drawn into the campaign against the popular societies in the middle years of the 1790s and against the more serious threats of insurrection that emerged after 1796. They were involved in some of the most important investigations, and arrests of suspected traitors. Macmanus and Townsend, for example, were prominent among those who arrested Thomas Hardy, the founder and leader of the London Corresponding Society, at 6 a.m. one day in May 1794. They were in charge of collecting evidence of Hardy's supposed treason, a task they went about in a way that caused him to object to their ransacking 'trunks, boxes, drawers, and desk,' seizing and carrying away 'hundreds of letters and manuscript papers belonging to the London Corresponding Society' and his own private correspondence and pamphlets.[77] All went to the Home Office where Ford categorized and analysed them for the prosecution at Hardy's subsequent trial at the Old Bailey, a trial at which, despite the government's massive effort to persuade the jury of his traitorous intentions, he was acquitted.[78]

In his account of his arrest, Hardy revealed the low esteem in which the runners had come to be held by men like him. He called them 'constables of Bow St Office, more generally known by the name of thief takers.'[79] This became a common denigration among the radicals, a reflection of the runners' part in the government's campaign to control and silence them. When a man was denounced as a suspected spy at a London Corresponding Society meeting in September 1794, he denied the charge, saying that he was 'no Runner or Thieftaker at Bow Street, but a man respected in my Neighbourhood and of a far different profession from that of Thief-catching.' One of his supporters agreed that he was 'too much of a Gentleman and too well respected to accept of such a disgraceful employment.'[80] Townsend may have been particularly disliked because of his zealous pursuit of radicals and his violent behaviour in making arrests. Some of this was revealed when the runners took part in a major operation in 1798 to arrest the leaders of the London Corresponding Society—arrests ordered in the belief that they were involved in

---

in 1798 and held for three years without trial. Ford did so. Mary Thale (ed.), *The Autobiography of Francis Place (1771–1854)* (Cambridge, 1972), 182–3; TNA: HO 36/11, 386–7, 412–13.

[75] TNA: HO 36/11, 378. Writing to the lords of the treasury, Portland said that this was in consideration of his work not only at Bow Street but in executing his (Portland's) orders respecting 'the police of the country in general.'

[76] Ruth Paley makes the point that while Addington had been able to muster significant support for his claim to succeed Sampson Wright in 1793, Bond, who was a man of humble social origins, had no such support ('Middlesex Justices Act', 290).

[77] Mary Thale (ed.), *Selections from the Papers of the London Corresponding Society 1792–1799* (Cambridge, 1983), 157–8.

[78] Thomas Jones Howell, *A Complete Collection of State Trials*, vol. 24 (London, 1818); for Hardy's arrest and trial, see Albert Goodwin, *The Friends of Liberty* (London, 1979), 332–53.

[79] Thale, *Selections from the Papers of the London Corresponding Society*, 157.

[80] Ibid, 218–19.

plans to take part in an insurrection to coincide with a French invasion. A meeting at which the members of the general committee were debating how they should respond to the government's call for demonstrations of loyalty in the face of this threatened French invasion was interrupted by the arrival of four runners, led by Townsend. While the others were said to have behaved with 'great civility,' Townsend, 'on entering the committee room, uttered a volley of horrid imprecations, and in an instant, without any provocation whatever, struck one of the delegates a violent blow on the head with a large stick; and... continued the same brutal behaviour, repeatedly declaring he cared for none of them, and would not be dictated to'.[81]

The runners were involved in other major arrests in the late 1790s, years in which the possibility of a violent rising was more than mere rumour and was met by heightened government vigilance.[82] Much of the planning for an insurrection on both sides of the Irish Sea centered on members of the United Irish Society, particularly the Rev. James O'Coigley (or Coigley), who sought to recruit members of the Manchester and London Corresponding Societies to adopt a violent course of action in support of their political and social aims, and who also acted as the link between English and Irish radicals and the French government. O'Coigley's activities were regularly reported to the government in 1797 and 1798 by spies and informers. His movements were also closely tracked by two Bow Street runners, John Rivett and Edward Fugion, who followed him for months and arrested him with several companions in Margate in February 1798 as he was preparing to depart once more for France. A copy of an address from the 'Secret Committee of England' to the Directory, encouraging the French invasion and setting out the conditions under which British radicals would come forward in support, was found in his greatcoat pocket. It was sufficient to convict him of treason some months later.[83] Revitt and Fugion were given £100 each as a special reward on the recommendation of the duke of Portland because they had devoted 'most of their time' over a six-month period in tracking O'Coigley and his associates.[84]

Apart from such major investigations and arrests carried out on behalf of the secretary of state and under his warrant, scattered items in the press reported the Bow Street runners and patrolmen going after more minor suspects of all kinds, bringing in members of radical societies for questioning, arresting booksellers and printers for producing or selling material considered seditious, carrying out surveillance on French refugees, and travelling to various parts of the country—including Manchester, Portsmouth and Chelmsford, among other places—to investigate rumours or apprehend suspects. They were particularly active following the passage

---

[81] Thale, *Selections from the Papers of the London Corresponding Society*, 435; Goodwin, *Friends of Liberty*, 442–50; Hone, *For the Cause of Truth*, 57–9.

[82] Goodwin, *Friends of Liberty*, 432–49; Hone, *For the Cause of Truth*, 41–117; Thompson, *Making of the English Working Class*, 179–203; Roger Wells, *Insurrection: the British Experience, 1795–1803* (Gloucester, 1986).

[83] Goodwin, *Friends of Liberty*, 432–8; William Cobbett, T. B. and T. J. Howell (eds.), *A Complete Collection of State Trials*, 33 vols. (London, 1809–26), XXVI, cols. 1266–77.

[84] TNA: HO 36/10, 498.

of the so-called Two Acts of 1795 which broadened definitions of treasonable activity to include written or spoken words and placed strict controls on public meetings of more than 50 people.[85] A sarcastic item in the *Courier and Evening Gazette* reported that

> Jack Townsend and all the other Officers who can read, are at present busily engaged in conning over the late Act of Parliament against Seditious Meetings. Jacky tells them as how 'to interpret the Laws', and transact State business, is much grander and more genteeler than looking after pitiful petty-larceny rascals.[86]

In 1798 and 1799, groups of Bow Street men—almost entirely runners—were mentioned in the London press (particularly in papers in sympathy with the government's campaign to repress radicalism) in connection with about two dozen arrests of men accused of seditious words or of participating in suspected treasonable practices, arrests made very commonly on warrants from the secretary of state, the duke of Portland. Rivett led at least half of these raids, Fugion and Dowsett were each involved in several, and virtually all the remaining runners—Carpmeal, Townsend, Sayer, Macmanus—had a hand in one or two.[87] They were sufficiently active that the attorney general felt it necessary in December 1798 to defend 'the Bow-street Runners . . . who had been called Spies and Informers, from the calumny with which they had been loaded.'[88]

Confirmation of the engagement of Bow Street men after 1792 for work on behalf of the government can also be found in the five quarterly accounts in which Reeves divided the 'extraordinary' payments he had made into three broad categories: for tasks undertaken on behalf of the secretary of state; for the royal family; and for the Bow Street magistrates.[89] The work for the Home Department in those five quarters between 1800 and 1803 amounted to 20 per cent of the total sum of £469 paid for the work of the Bow Street officers (Table 7.3, above). The accounts do not disclose the nature of the work undertaken; nor, in these early years is it possible to learn how much each officer earned, since before 1803, payments were made not to individuals, but to groups that had carried out particular tasks.[90] But, we do know how much was paid for work for the Home Office in these years, and

---

[85] Wells, *Insurrection*, ch. 3.

[86] *Courier and Evening Gazette*, 4 August 1797.

[87] Many of these arrests of men suspected of treasonable activities were reported in the *Sun*, a paper closely allied with the government, and, to quote Boyd Hilton, one of the 'most alarmist newspapers' in these years (*A Mad, Bad, & Dangerous People? England 1783–1846* (Oxford, 2006), 65. See 14 April, 1 June, 21 June, 13 July, 19 October 1798, 7 August, 9 August, 5 September, 11 September 1799. Reports of the runners' arrests of suspects also appeared the *Oracle and Public Advertiser*, 19 April, 4 May, 8 August, 18 August, 10 September 1798, 26 March, 16 April, 17 April, 25 April, 29 May, 15 August 1799. *The True Briton*, another 'alarmist' paper, carried reports on 30 June and 8 August 1798, and 9 April 1799.

[88] *Courier and Evening Gazette*, 22 December 1798.

[89] See above, 184, Table 7.3.

[90] There is a suggestion in the account for July–October 1795 that payments made to groups of officers who had worked together on one task were delivered as a lump sum to one of the runners and (in the case of a group of patrolmen) to one of the patrol captains, who then distributed it to those with some claim to payment. After 1803, the police receiver calculated the total owed to each runner and patrolman for all the work they had done in the quarter and submitted that as a single sum.

that information confirms newspaper reports and other scraps of evidence that suggest that from time to time—and especially when the government was particularly concerned about sedition and the threat of insurrection—the runners were drawn into policing operations directed at suppressing radicalism and, as those who supported the effort would have said, defending the constitution. In 1800, for example, the most frequent recipients of the money paid to officers working on behalf of the secretary of state were Rivett and Dowsett, who, in the six months covered by the accounts were each paid for taking up nine investigations, for the most part investigations they had carried out together.[91]

(b) Royal security

Closely connected with their concern about threats to the national security the government also became alarmed in the 1790s about the safety of the king and royal family, with the result that Bow Street was called upon to take up another set of new tasks—providing security for the court. The protection of the royal palaces in the eighteenth century was largely assigned to soldiers of the guards regiments, whose presence, as has been said, was 'more ceremonial than practical.'[92] What little protection afforded the royal family by the 1780s was provided by Bow Street, but until the later years of that decade protection was occasional, not ongoing. The need for more permanent control of access to the court and to the royal family became evident in 1786 when George III was stabbed outside St James's palace by Margaret Nicholson, who had clearly been driven mad by her wrongful dismissal from an aristocratic household and by numerous failed attempts to get royal help. Several other intruders, suffering from delusions of various kinds, gained access to St James's palace in the next few years, some threatening to harm the king, all of them raising questions about the security of the palace and the king's safety.[93]

Those threats became more serious in the following decade, when it was widely rumoured after the execution of Louis XVI that the new French regime intended to send agents to England to assassinate George III. By the middle years of the 1790s, conflicts on the home front over the war and over the high price of bread increased domestic hostility to the government and exposed the king to public abuse and physical harm. In October 1795 his carriage was assaulted and damaged by a mob on his journey to the house of lords to open parliament. And on several other occasions over the next months—when the king went to parliament to approve legislation broadening the meaning of treason and placing restrictions on the size of crowds at public meetings without a magistrate's permission, or when the royal family went to the theatre—angry crowds beset the king's coach, despite the protection of cavalry, foot soldiers, and large numbers of constables (including

---

[91] TNA: T 38/673: April–July 1800 and July–October 1800.

[92] Steve Poole, *The politics of regicide in England, 1760–1850: troublesome subjects* (Manchester, 2000), 52.

[93] Poole, *Politics of regicide*, 1–3, ch. 4.

special constables) brought together from the police offices and from parishes around the metropolis.[94]

It was in these circumstances that the royal family was for the first time provided with some measure of permanent police protection by Bow Street officers—protection that was designed to shield them in public and to provide more control over access to the court. This had already begun in a small way in 1788 when Patrick Macmanus was sent to deal with a mad clergyman, Henry Norman, who had made threats against the king.[95] Macmanus continued to attend at St James's palace and the queen's house for several months thereafter, attendance that became more permanent later in that year when the king had his first serious attack of porphyria, a disease that resulted in such mental derangement that for a few months he was rendered incapable of carrying out his duties. Some form of protection had obviously come to be regarded as essential even after the king recovered early in 1789.[96]

Macmanus remained at St James's and accompanied the king when in the summer he made the first of many annual visits to Weymouth on the south coast—an ideal place for the sea bathing that was recommended by the king's doctors and that was widely believed to be highly beneficial to health. Thereafter, he was invariably accompanied to Weymouth by a Bow Street officer and occasionally a magistrate. By 1790, Macmanus was drawing £25 a quarter plus expenses for his attendance at St James's palace and Weymouth, costs that were paid directly from contingency funds at the Home Office, not from the Bow Street budget.[97]

From this beginning, the police presence at the several palaces gradually expanded as the perceived threats to the king and the royal family increased. By 1792, Macmanus had been joined by two other experienced officers, Jealous and Townsend, when the king was in residence at St James's or Windsor or at the White House at Kew.[98] Their service fell into a regular pattern thereafter, with Macmanus attending at Windsor and the other two at St James's and Kew. The attack on the king's carriage in 1795 and fears about future assaults no doubt explain the further increase in security at court. It also owed a great deal to Richard Ford, who was by then well placed at the Home Office to shape decisions about security matters and who, as Steve Poole has said, 'took his responsibilities towards the Royal Family extremely seriously.'[99] In 1796, Jealous moved permanently to Windsor, where he was soon joined by another runner, William Anthony, while Macmanus and Townsend were joined by John Sayer in their service at St James's and Kew. Jealous received his moving expenses and rent for a house in Windsor (at £30 a year) and he

---

[94] TNA: HO 36/9, 521; HO 36/10, 376–7; HO 36/11, 7 December 1798; Poole, *Politics of regicide*, 108–11.

[95] TNA: HO 36/6, 161.

[96] Ida Macalpine and Richard Hunter, *George III and the Mad Business* (London, 1969), parts 1–2.

[97] TNA: HO 36/7, 50; HO 82/3.

[98] For the royal palaces favoured by George III and his pattern of residence, see Jeremy Black, *George III: America's Last King* (New Haven, 2006), 174–8.

[99] Poole, *Politics of regicide*, 54.

and the other runners also enjoyed an increase in their salaries to £42 a quarter. At the end of 1801, that was further increased to £50.[100]

That pattern of five of the most senior officers acting at the three main palaces—and with one or more of them accompanying the king to Weymouth for the summer visits that he undertook between 1789 and 1805—continued unchanged until at least 1810 when there is a decade-long gap in the Home Office account in which these payments are recorded. When the accounts are again available, in January 1822, four men—Townsend, Sayer, Thomas Dowsett, who had been acting at Windsor since 1800, and John Rivett—were sharing the work. They continued to do so until Townsend and Sayer died in 1832. Thereafter, two runners served at Windsor (with the new Metropolitan Police presumably guarding the other royal residences) until the Bow Street police were disbanded at the end of the decade.[101]

The runners assigned to Windsor Castle had entered into permanent duty there, which is no doubt why the number of runners was increased from six to eight in 1802.[102] Those in town were called on only when required. They were in the procession, carrying silver staffs, when the king went in state to parliament, or to the Abbey, or St Paul's.[103] A more frequent duty brought one or more of them to the palace several times a week when the king held a levee or a drawing room—the former for men only, the latter for men and women—each of which George III was in the habit of holding twice a week when he was in residence in London.[104] On such occasions, the runners managed access to the palace, controlling the traffic, preventing suspicious characters from getting in, and no doubt also being on the lookout for the pickpockets who were always drawn to crowds. Ford was to say in 1802 that the job of the runners at court was 'to prevent improper people from approaching His Majesty or committing depredations on the persons of those who go to court.'[105] Keeping order at the entrance to St James's was an especially difficult problem on the 'high' court days—the king's birthday, for example—when there was a large turnout of the social elite and large crowds of onlookers. But even that must have been easier to manage than the many occasions on which the king and the royal family went out in public—to the theatre and the concerts of 'ancient music,' to the Royal Academy, to open parliament, to visit the houses of peers or foreign ambassadors or, in George IV's time to Ascot or Egham races. After

---

[100] TNA: HO 82/3.

[101] In summary, the evidence in TNA: HO 82/3 is that Macmanus served on his own 1790–92, and was joined by Jealous and Townsend (1792–95). From 1796 to at least 1810, two runners were on duty at Windsor when the king was in residence, and three at St James's and Kew. Four were in service in 1822, when the record resumes, two at St James's and Kew, and two at Windsor. When Townsend and Sayer died in 1832, only the two runners at Windsor continued. They were disbanded in 1838. Between 1792 and 1801 they had received a salary of £43 a year, raised to £50 in 1802.

[102] Cox, '"A Certain Share of Low Cunning"', App. 1.

[103] *The Times*, 23 November 1803. They regularly accompanied the Prince Regent in 1811 and after when he reviewed troops on Wimbledon Common or Hounslow Heath (TNA: T 38/673 (bills dated 10, 14, 17 June 1811).

[104] Black, *George III*, 124.

[105] BL: Add Mss 33122, f. 79.

the assaults on the king's coach in 1795, the runners walked on either side of the coach on state occasions, when the king went in procession to parliament, to Westminster Abbey or St Paul's. The members of the foot patrol were likewise engaged at such times, along with soldiers, to stand guard at intervals along the route.[106]

How much close protection to the king the runners provided on those occasions is unclear. In 1804 the lord chamberlain, the marquis of Salisbury, may have been responding to an emerging practice when he ordered that 'none of the Bow-street Officers be permitted up stairs at St James's Palace in either the Guard or Presence Chambers'—in the latter of which the king would have met those attending a levee or drawing room.[107] Like many such orders, that may have been ignored. The runners' close attendance on the king was likely to have been common at Weymouth, where the royal family not only attended the Assembly Rooms from time to time and received the social elite, but where the king was also fond of sea bathing and walking on the esplanade.[108] The runners' protection of the royal family extended to similar duties when other crowned heads came to England. The Treasury paid close to £800 for their time and expenses (which no doubt included numerous assistants) when Townsend, Sayer, and Macmanus provided cover for the emperor of Russia and the king of Prussia on their celebratory visit to England in 1814, which included events in London and a tour to Oxford, Portsmouth, and other towns.[109]

Palace work provided some of the senior Bow Street men with a substantial addition to their incomes. Along with the £200 a year that Sayer and Townsend received from the Home Office contingency fund for their work for the royal family, they and other runners and a number of patrolmen also drew on the Bow Street office funds for some aspects of this work. We have seen that the five early nineteenth century quarterly Bow Street accounts that separated 'extraordinary' expenses into three groups included a total of £813 for duties performed on behalf of the royal family. If we assume, as we did with respect to payments made on behalf of work for the Secretaries of State, that the sums of money awarded to groups of men for particular pieces of work were divided equally among those named, about 60 per cent went to the runners—with Macmanus and Townsend leading the way at £133 and £93 respectively. The remainder went to members of the patrol who were called into service from time to time to line the routes of royal processions or to provide support around the entrance to St James's on high court days. Altogether, eight runners were in receipt of these funds, and 13 patrolmen, including most of the patrol captains, who almost certainly would have passed payments on to members of their patrol parties, listed as 'others' in the accounts.[110] The runners, too, may have had significant expenses connected with their work for

[106] TNA: HO 42/119, f. 160.
[107] *Morning Chronicle*, 14 March 1804.
[108] Black, *George III*, 125, 142.
[109] TNA: HO 36/17, 419.
[110] TNA: T 38/673, April–July 1800. See above, text at n. 60.

the royal family. But, as we will see, several of them—Townsend and Sayer in particular—enjoyed handsome rewards as a result of their duties protecting the royal family, not only from the Bow Street and Home Office funds, but also from private work that came their way as a result of contacts they made at the royal palaces with members of the aristocracy and with court society more generally.[111]

(c) Public order

Although the Bow Street magistrates dealt routinely with charges arising from the gaming, drunkenness, and prostitution that could be found in abundance around their office in the notorious Covent Garden area, John Fielding had not made the prosecution of such offences a prime target of his policing endeavours, a neglect for which he was criticized.[112] This may have changed soon after his death and as the American war came to an end, at least with respect to gaming, perhaps in response to the Shelburne government's call for magistrates to be more active in the prevention of crime by suppressing 'night houses and cellars in which drinking and gambling lead men of inferior rank into immoral habits and thus to crime.'[113] In 1782, the Middlesex bench petitioned the house of commons to outlaw the new and fashionable game of E.O. (Even and Odd), an early form of roulette, which, the magistrates claimed, was attracting gamblers from all walks of life and in many parts of London. A bill to outlaw the game was introduced in the house of commons in June 1782, to wide press coverage. Though it failed to pass, a campaign to close down gaming houses was joined vigorously by the Bow Street magistrates, with the runners' assistance. Addington and Sampson Wright led raids over several days in August 1782 that destroyed 17 E.O. tables, many of them in houses in the most fashionable parts of town.[114]

Bow Street raids on gaming houses continued to be reported sporadically in London newspapers thereafter, no doubt further encouraged by the reform drive that followed a royal proclamation in 1787 calling for a return to piety and religious observance, and the formation of a society to support those aims that had a strong upper-class base.[115] In the Spring of 1796, the Bow Street magistrates were applauded in King's Bench by lord chief justice Kenyon for their 'determination ... respecting the gambling houses.'[116] What he no doubt had in mind were raids like that led by Edward Lavender, the principal clerk of the office—acting here, as his predecessors often had, as a leader of the policing efforts of the office—on a gambling house in Leicester Square. The press reported that the

---

[111] See below, section 4.
[112] For his critics, see above, ch. 4, text at nn. 14–15.
[113] TNA: HO 43/1, 43–4.
[114] TNA: HO 42/1, ff. 246–7. For the campaign against E.O. in 1782 and the failed bill, see Donna Andrew, ' "How Frail are Lovers' Vows, and Dicers' Oaths": Gaming, Governing, and Moral Panic in Britain, 1781–1782' in David Lemmings and Claire Walker (eds.), *Moral Panics, Media and Law in early modern England* (New York, 2009), 176–94.
[115] Joanna Innes, *Inferior Politics. Social Problems and Social Policies in Eighteenth-Century Britain* (Oxford, 2009), ch. 5; see above, ch. 6, text at n. 103.
[116] *Oracle and Public Advertiser*, 25 May 1796.

officers were thwarted by 'a very strong door' from getting sufficiently quickly to the gaming room to catch the principals or most of the players, and they had to settle for two young men trying to hide themselves, one of whom, the report noted, proved to be French.[117] Three months later, Edward Fugion, a Bow Street officer, led a party of the patrol on a raid on another gambling house in Leicester Square in which on this occasion they caught two Englishmen and 17 Frenchmen at play. At their examination before the Bow Street magistrates, the Englishmen 'were admitted to bail, and the Frenchmen were committed to Tothill-fields Bridewell, till their cases were laid before the Duke of Portland', the Home Secretary.[118] Over the next two years, a dozen or more such raids were reported in the press, for the most part in Covent Garden, Charing Cross, and Leicester Square. One of the targets was described as 'a notorious gaming house frequented by foreigners,'[119] a point that was emphasized in the press in about half of these police raids. This concern about the presence of 'foreigners', especially French immigrants, among those arrested, as well as the involvement of Portland and the Home Office in the 1796 raid noted above, suggests that Bow Street's interest in gambling houses may have arisen as much from an anxiety about sedition as about vice. The raids were concentrated in years in which there was, as we have seen, a heightened alarm about the possibility of insurrection at home supported by an invading French army. They were also in years following the Two Acts that had prohibited meetings of more than 50 people. Any occasion on which large numbers of people met essentially in secret—as gamblers inevitably had to do—were likely targets of the government's interest. Bow Street was almost certainly drawn into a concern for gaming on orders from the Home Office, conveyed through Richard Ford.

That supposition is strengthened to some extent by other raids made by the runners in these years on public houses that provided centres of sociability for the Irish population in some of the most crowded parts of the city, including St Giles's and Drury Lane. Some pubs provided space for what were known as Cock and Hen clubs, assemblies that met regularly for drinking and dancing and perhaps for discussion, for at one the landlady of the house was said to 'take the chair.' These were no doubt viewed with some anxiety in the late 1790s in which fear of armed revolt, led by the United Irish, was particularly keen, and this may explain at least three raids reported in the press in 1797 and 1798 led by the Bow Street runners and involving large numbers of armed patrolmen.[120] The raids were authorized by a clause of the Vagrant Act of 1744 that gave magistrates power to send constables to conduct privy searches of premises in which they had reason to believe vagrants and the idle and disorderly were being sheltered. This provided wide scope for any kind of search. The Bow Street incursions were ostensibly to look for men and women who could be charged under the Vagrant Act, but the constables were also

---

[117] *True Briton*, 8 August 1796.
[118] *The Times*, 9 August 1796; *Lloyd's Evening Post*, 2 November 1796.
[119] *The Times*, 19 April 1798.
[120] *The Times*, 24 May 1797, 25 December 1798, 26 December 1798. There was another such raid in 1805, on the excuse that the Bow Street men were looking for deserters (*The Times*, 5 February 1805).

sent to look for deserters from the armed forces, and perhaps more generally to disrupt meetings of large numbers of men and women for the same reason they sent men to close down gaming houses.

Unlike the latter, however, while pubs were not defended by locked doors, some were well defended by their inmates. On at least two of these raids, the Bow Street men were met with strong resistance. In one, it was reported, a scuffle ensued in which the police were disarmed and beaten, and the inmates all made their escape.[121] Another was much more serious and ended in tragedy on both sides. On the day after Christmas 1798, 50 officers and patrolmen staged a provocative raid on a public house in St Giles's between 9 and 10 p.m. on a night on which it was well known the Irish would be celebrating St Stephen's day. The Bow Street force assembled at the Brown Bear, were armed with cutlasses, and moved in order to St Giles's with a warrant authorizing a privy search. They found a large crowd of men and women in the pub's tap-room and a meeting of a Cock and Hen club taking place one floor up, where 30 men and women were dancing to a fiddler. The officers went upstairs in force to serve the warrant, handcuffed many in pairs and were taking them away to be examined as rogues and vagabonds when the neighbourhood was raised against them. A battle ensued in which many on both sides were wounded and a captain of the patrol, Duncan Grant, was stabbed and killed. Several arrests were made and at a subsequent trial, eight men and two women were indicted for murder. The trial lasted from morning until nine at night, largely because the two prosecuting and two defence counsel conducted a lengthy argument about the legality of the warrant and other issues bearing on the crucial question of whether the charge should be murder or manslaughter. In the end the judge summed up in a way that encouraged the jury to find that the act had been conducted with malice: while the charges against four of the men and the women were dismissed, and one man was acquitted, three defendants were convicted and hanged outside Newgate three days later.[122]

Bow Street and the runners came to play another role that fits broadly into the area of public order by intervening to prevent duels being fought in the metropolis. Duels were not simple acts of public violence, but conflicts staged according to prescribed rules between two men (virtually always men) one of whom had issued a challenge that the other had accepted. They were not invariably fatal for the protagonists, though they were nonetheless deadly, and could easily end in death or serious injury. Duels were most often spurred by disputes, insults, or rude behaviour that might be entirely trivial, but that caused a man to think that his honour and reputation had been derogated or his courage or honesty called into question. The code of honour required in those circumstances that his self-esteem and his standing as a gentleman be restored by issuing a challenge to his antagonist to meet him in combat. Causes were multifarious. Some arose from simple matters

---

[121] *The Times*, 24 May 1797.

[122] OBP, May 1799 (Brian *et al*) t17990508–21. *The Times*, 11 May 1799. The Home Office anticipated that 'several of the lower orders of the Irish' would create a riot and attempt a rescue at the place of execution, but nothing developed. (TNA: HO 65/1, 12 May 1799).

of opinion that had nothing to do with honour, as for example whether 'Gabrielle or Sestini was the better singer, and the handsomest woman,' or whether Blackstone's *Commentaries* were 'a most superficial, empty performance,' as one lawyer insisted in a tavern dispute with another, who was 'violently extolling them.'[123] But for the most part challenges were issued by men who thought their honour and reputation had been sullied and that the duel provided the only satisfactory way to restore their standing in the world.[124]

Despite a growing opposition to the practice,[125] there seems to have been a renewed increase in duelling by the 1770s that came to a sharp climax in the last decade of the eighteenth century and the early years of the nineteenth, when numerous duels were reported in the press, some involving the most prominent men in the country, including William Pitt while he was prime minister. After 1815, the evidence of the newspapers is that the incidence of duelling fell away again, until the practice came to an end in the 1840s.[126]

In addition to the increase in the number of duels in the last third of the eighteenth century, a significant change in their character was also taking place by then, as swords gave way to pistols as the weapons of choice. So long as gentlemen wore swords as an item of fashion and practised the art of swordmanship, it was the natural weapon for settling disputes of honour. But the fashion and the habit both fell away in the first half of the eighteenth century, and, although swords continued to be used into the later eighteenth century, the majority of duels came to be fought with pistols. (From time to time, both weapons were employed, beginning with one and going on to the other if the first shot or thrust failed to have effect.)[127] Pistols introduced significant changes in the way duels were fought. They required rules to be agreed ahead of time about how many paces would separate the combatants, how many shots each would be allowed to take, who would shoot first. Negotiations about these matters may have encouraged the engagement of 'seconds', men who would typically deliver the challenge and receive the acceptance, and if opportunity arose, attempt to arrange reconciliation once the claims of honour had been satisfied. Seconds had been present earlier in sword fights, but they may have been even more common as pistols became the usual weapon. Pistols may also have made it possible for others besides gentlemen and military officers to challenge men to combat. Few outside the elite were trained in swordsmanship, but

---

[123] *Morning Post and Daily Advertiser*, 29 March 1776; *Gazetteer*, 25 September 1775.

[124] Donna T. Andrew, 'The code of honour and its critics: the opposition to duelling in England, 1700–1850', *Social History*, 5/3 (1980), 409–34; idem, *The Attack on Aristocratic Vice: Cultural Skirmishes in Eighteenth-Century Britain*, ch. 2 (forthcoming); Robert B. Shoemaker, 'The Taming of the Duel: Masculinity, Honour and Ritual Violence in London, 1660–1800', *The Historical Journal*, 45 (3, 2002), 525–45; Antony E. Simpson, 'Dandelions on the Field of Honor: Duelling, the Middle Classes, and the Law in Nineteenth-Century England', *Criminal Justice History*, IX, 1988, 99–155.

[125] Andrew, 'The code of honour and its critics'.

[126] Ibid, 410; Shoemaker, 'Taming of the Duel', 527; Simpson, 'Dandelions on the Field of Honor', 106–7, 110.

[127] *London Evening Post*, 5 April 1777; *General Evening Post*, 24 May 1777. A German nobleman who continued to wear a sword in England in the 1770s gave up the practice when, having become involved in a duel, he was advised by John Fielding to do so (*General Evening Post*, 23 July 1776).

anyone could shoot a pistol, and pistols could be hired for the occasion and loaded by an aide. Duellists remained overwhelmingly upper-class or military men, but pistols enabled men of the middle class, even the lower middle class, to issue challenges, and a number did.[128]

Historians have disagreed about the effect of pistols on the mortality rate in duels.[129] But the fact that skill or expertise in shooting came to be frowned on, and that practising beforehand or taking careful and deliberate aim were thought unfair, it would seem that whatever the reality, pistols were thought to be deadly. My supposition is that the prospect of staring down the barrel of a loaded pistol a few paces away (and there were no hard and fast rules about how far apart the duellists should be) must have concentrated the minds of some prospective participants, and encouraged second thoughts. And duellists did have time for second thoughts, and time to change their minds since combat was generally arranged for a day hence. There was time too for others to intervene and prevent the duel taking place at all. And here, the Bow Street magistrates and the runners proved to be very useful.

Bow Street provided a means by which one of the duellists, their friends or family, or some third party who knew of the arrangements, could bring proceedings to a halt. It became common for duels to be prevented by a timely visit to the site by the Bow Street police (and in a few cases by men from other police offices) armed with a magistrate's warrant to take all the parties involved into custody.[130] Such interventions were reported in the press, beginning with a few cases in the 1770s and 1780s, increasing strongly over the next two decades, before falling away again in the 1810s and after.[131] According to reports in the London press, Bow Street was

---

[128] Simpson, 'Dandelions on the Field of Honor', 115–25. Among the duellists, especially during the Revolutionary and Napoleonic wars when refugees were common in England, were members of the European nobility, who seem to have been particularly determined to defend their honour against any slight. Baron Hompesch, a Swiss nobleman and a general in the British army, provides a good example in that he challenged a man to a duel for jostling him in the Strand, and, when they met on Blackheath, insisted on firing a third round which seriously wounded his opponent, even though the seconds thought that honour had been served with the second round. A year later he challenged the barrister, William Garrow, to a duel for cross-examining him vigorously in a civil suit the baron had brought against a neighbour, making fun of him in court, and generally engaging in 'ungentlemanly conduct'. *The Times*, 23 and 24 September 1806; John Beattie, 'Garrow for the Defence', *History Today*, 41, (February 1991), 53.

[129] Shoemaker provides evidence that pistols made death less likely, whereas Simpson's perhaps less complete data suggested the opposite: Shoemaker, 'Taming of the Duel', 531–5; Simpson, 'Dandelions on the Field of Honor', 112–14.

[130] Shoemaker, 'Taming of the Duel', 538; for this and other ways men appealed to the courts and the authorities in the late eighteenth and early nineteenth centuries to prevent duels taking place, see Andrew, *The Attack on Aristocratic Vice*, ch. 2 (forthcoming).

[131] The following item is typical of the press reports:
'Information having been given on Sunday evening at the Police Office, in Bow-street, that a duel was intended to be fought on the following morning in the vicinity of Chalk Farm, Carpmeal and two of the patrole, went at an early hour to the spot, and soon discovered the parties with their seconds in a state of preparation to commence their warfare: they immediately interposed with great activity, got possession of the pistols, and secured both the combatants and their seconds, who were taken to the Office, and underwent an examination before James Read, Esq. Francis Jefferies, Esq. of Edinburgh, and Thomas Moore, Esq. of Bury-street St. James's, were the gentlemen who appeared on the ground. They were admitted to bail, and gave security for maintaining the peace, themselves in £400 each, and two sureties in £200 each' (*The Times*, 12 August 1806).

called in and prevented an impending duel on at least 87 occasions between the 1770s and the 1840s—fully three-quarters of which were concentrated in the 17 years between 1793 and 1809, as many as eight in a year (1803).[132] They were common enough that, in reporting one such event in 1806, *The Times* said that 'the *usual* communication having been given to the Bow-street Magistrates,' the officers were dispatched to take the parties into custody.[133]

If some of these disclosures, as I have speculated, were made with the knowledge of one of the protagonists, seeking an honourable and safe way out of a commitment that was not possible to be shirked without serious loss of face, it seems likely that Bow Street's standing in the metropolis made such a tactic acceptable. A duel being brought to an end by the principal magistrate of Middlesex ordering that a reconciliation take place, with or without forcing the combatants to enter into recognizances to keep the peace, offered what might have been seen as a palatable alternative to men who had second thoughts about what was ahead and what was at stake. And the fact that several of the senior runners, who commonly made the arrests, were known as men who provided security at the royal palaces, that some of them were in close attendance on the king, and who always accompanied the royal family on public occasions, offered some assurance that they were likely to be deferential in carrying out the magistrate's warrant.

4. THE VALUE OF OFFICE: 'EXTRAORDINARY' PAYMENTS

While the Bow Street officers received income from several public and private sources, their steadiest returns after 1792 came from office funds in the form of salary (essentially a retainer) and payments for the work they had been asked to undertake for the variety of occasional jobs carried out for the magistrates, including the investigation and prosecution of crime in the metropolis, and work on behalf of the royal household and the Home Department. As we have seen, the bills setting out the claim for payment most often included two elements. On the one hand, officers requested repayment of their expenses in conducting investigations, expenses that might include subsistence, and travelling costs if they had had to leave London, including coach fares (in London as elsewhere), and occasionally the costs of forwarding a prosecution (fees for subpoenas, and other documents, occasionally money they had laid out in support of prosecutors or witnesses). The second element was money for their 'time and trouble', based on a daily rate—most often a guinea in the case of the runners, though sometimes less—which would include time spent in carrying out the investigation and, where this was appropriate, in attending courts to give evidence for the prosecution, though any money

---

[132] Based upon a search of the *Times Digital Archive, 17th–18th Century Burney Newspapers*, and *Nineteenth Century Newspapers on Line*. In compiling these data, I have benefitted from the considerable help of Donna Andrew. I also owe thanks to Professor Andrew for information about the total number of duels in this period.

[133] *The Times*, 1 September 1806 (emphasis added).

they received from the courts for their participation as a witness for the prosecution (as authorized by statute) would be deducted from their claims.[134] A bill sent in by Samuel Taunton included three guineas for apprehending three men for burglary, conveying them to Bow Street and attending their examination, five shillings for attending at Clerkenwell sessions to prefer a bill of indictment, five shillings for giving evidence at the Old Bailey, and 14 shillings for an extra indictment charging one with returning from transportation. The total came to £4.7.0 from which he deducted 11 shillings allowed by the Old Bailey judges as a witness fee. Another, also submitted by Taunton for work out of town, included two guineas for two days carrying out enquiries at Windsor, 16 shillings for his coach fare there and back, two shillings for the coachman, another guinea and similar coach costs for returning to Windsor on another day for further enquiries, two guineas for two days expenses, all to a total of £7.1.6.[135]

The sums requested in individual bills naturally varied a great deal, as did the total amounts for these policing costs from one quarter to another. The bills have mainly disappeared. The accounts themselves have survived haphazardly from the early years. Over the 16 years, 1796–1812, in which the receiver would have sent in 64 requests for payment to the Treasury, only 22 are extant. Fortunately, the accounts of the following six years, 1812–17, are complete, almost certainly because they were requested by the house of commons committees looking into the state of the police in the metropolis in 1816 and the following two years.[136] We thus have a total of 46 accounts for the years 1796 to 1817 which reveal that the costs of policing ranged between £49 to £618 per quarter, with an average of £310 and a median of £299. One cannot make too much of the fluctuations in the early years when the data are scattered and when the nature of the policing that Bow Street was undertaking is largely unknown, but it is noteworthy that the costs of policing were at higher than average levels in the early years of the nineteenth century, particularly in 1801–02 and in the last quarter of 1804 and the first half of 1805 (at an average per quarter of £587 and £518 respectively). Without the evidence of the bills for the work behind these charges, one cannot be certain about the reason for these elevated levels. It seems reasonable to think, however, that there was some connection with the government's concern about national security issues in these years, and also with the increase in violent offences noticeable at the time of the Peace of Amiens (1802) that had been sufficient to encourage Sir John Ford,

---

[134] TNA: T 38/673: bills dated 16 January, 3 April, 24 April, 12, 29 June, 12 August, 26 September 1811. Compensatory payments from the courts to prosecutors for their time and expenses began in a small way in 1752 and were gradually broadened in several statutes thereafter to include witnesses as well as prosecutors. A clause in Bennet's Act of 1818 authorized the courts to grant all prosecutors and witness in felony cases an allowance for expenses, trouble, and loss of time (58 Geo. III, c. 70). See Beattie, *Crime and the Courts*, 42–8, and David Philips, *Crime and Authority in Victorian England: the Black Country 1835–1860* (London, 1977), 110–16.

[135] TNA: T 38/673: bills dated 7, 8, 11, 29 June 1811.

[136] TNA: T 38/673. For the work of the committee that sat in 1816, see ch. 8, section 3. The committee reprinted the Bow Street accounts for the years 1814–18 (and those of other police offices) as an appendix to its reports.

the chief magistrate, to push successfully for the establishment of the mounted horse patrol that came into service in 1805.[137]

The 'extraordinary' policing costs that the receivers of police applied for in these quarterly accounts were based on bills sent in by individual officers or groups of officers. For the first few years, Reeves reported the sums being claimed just as he received them, job by job, reflecting the way the Bow Street men worked— sometimes individually, more often in groups of two or more, and in groups that might include both runners and patrolmen. For example, the account of extraordinary charges in the third quarter (July–October) of 1796 consisted of 26 claims arising from the work the Bow Street men had been ordered to carry out by the Home Department or the magistrates. Three bills had been submitted by individual runners, 23 by groups of runners and patrolmen who had worked together on a particular assignment. The list begins as follows:

Townsend, Sayer, and Taylor £3.10.6
Townsend, Sayer, and others 10.17.6
Macmanus and Sayer 1.3.6
Sayer, Miller, and others 1.4.0
Carpmeal, Fugion, and Rivett 3.5.6
Macmanus, Sayer, and others 5.9.6
Townsend, Carpmeal, and others 8.12.6
Townsend, Sayer, and others 7.10.0

And so on. Such a list of charges suggests that the runners continued to work together, most often in pairs, sometimes in larger groups. Townsend appears twice more in this list with Sayer, three more times with Macmanus, as well as in a group with Carpmeal and in another with Carpmeal and Macmanus. The 'others' in the list were almost certainly patrolmen, two of whom (Thomas and Christopher Jones, both captains) are later named five times as working together. They claimed substantial sums that were likely meant to be distributed to members of their patrols. The list ends with single sums to be paid to three runners: Miller, Fugion, and Rivett.[138]

Sending in an account of this kind that in effect listed the bills he had received from the officers, totalled for the quarter, was clearly the easiest way for Reeves to request payment from the Treasury. On the other hand, it must have made for difficulties when the money arrived, for he (or his clerk) had to calculate how much to pay each runner and patrolman. There is evidence in the account for the third quarter of 1796, noted above, that Reeves got around this difficulty by giving the total sum due to the runners (£116) to John Townsend, and the £51 due to the patrolmen to one of the Jones brothers, to distribute on his behalf. The handwriting on the document makes it clear that this was done only when the money arrived from the Treasury.[139]

---

[137] For concern about sedition in this period, see above, text at nn. 82–8, and for elevated crime levels, ch. 8, section 1. For the mounted patrol, see above, text at n. 38.

[138] TNA: T 38/673, account for July–October 1796.

[139] TNA: T 38/673, account for July–October 1796.

Table 7.4. Top 10 recipients of 'extraordinary' payments at Bow Street, 1803–1817[1]

Officer	Status	Total received to nearest £	Number of quarters in which recipients submitted bills	Average amount received per quarter
		£		£
John Townsend	Runner	1,391	26	54
John Sayer	Runner	707	16	44
John Vickery	Runner	386	9	43
Patrick Macmanus	Runner	149	4	37
John Rivett	Runner	220	10	22
Christopher Jones	Patrol Captain	129	6	21
William Bacon	Patrol Captain	717	34	21
Samuel Taunton	Runner	505	28	18
John Pearks	Runner	401	22	18
George Ruthven	Runner	182	11	17

[1] Source: TNA: T 38/673: Accounts survive for a total of 34 quarters of the 60 submitted.

Such an arrangement may not have worked to everyone's satisfaction and there may have been complaints, for by 1803 Reeves had adopted another solution. He began then to send in an account to the Treasury that provided total amounts due to individuals for all their work that quarter. Each runner and patrolman making a claim is named once only to receive a sum for all work undertaken in the quarter. The Treasury seems to have accepted this new arrangement without complaint, even though it obviously made it difficult to match up the claims being made with the bills that supported them, a difficulty that might explain why no one seems to have made a fuss when bills were not sent in.

The new system of total quarterly payments to individuals makes it possible for us to know after 1802 how much individual runners and patrolmen received each quarter. I have listed the top 10 earners over the years 1803–1817 in Table 7.4, above. Not surprisingly, John Townsend came out well ahead of others, and the runners in general well ahead of most of the patrolmen, even the captains. Of course, these payments did not represent a simple addition to any of the Bow Street men's incomes. Most of the bills on which they were based included expenses as well as the payments for 'trouble' that were the real additions to their salaries. What proportion of the total each amounted to cannot be known, and thus the crucial question of how much into pocket the runners and patrolmen were cannot be answered. Nonetheless, the substantial sums going to Townsend, Sayer, Macmanus, and other runners suggest that the leading Bow Street men had prospered under the financial arrangements that followed the Police Act of 1792 and from the new lines of work the circumstances of the 1790s opened up for them. From a situation in the 1780s in which Sir Sampson Wright had found himself having to leave a number of patrol positions vacant in order to pay the runners for their work, there was now a virtually unlimited fund from which they were apparently being well rewarded. And of course, the office money was not their only source of funds. The runners continued to accept requests from private prosecutors for help in investigations, though by the 1820s, only with the permission of the magistrates. And, as we will see, some of the runners—Townsend and Sayer in particular—almost certainly benefitted significantly from private work and from rewards for favours that came their way as a result of the contacts they made at St James's and elsewhere with some of the wealthiest families of the country who were at the heart of court society.[140]

There is no doubt that the costs of policing in general increased substantially in the decades following the 1792 Act, especially the costs of the Bow Street office. Indeed, the costs of policing in London, including the incomes of the Bow Street men, were to become matters of public interest after 1815, when criminal prosecutions in the metropolis and in the country at large were to increase in a sharp and sustained way. In the difficult years that followed the conclusion of what had been a very long war, fundamental questions were to be raised again about the sort of police that would best serve the metropolis in the face of significant changes in the nature of the crime problem.

[140] See ch. 8, text at nn. 45–51.

8

Prevention: The Runners in Retreat, 1815–1839

1. LONDON CRIME IN THE EARLY NINETEENTH CENTURY

As the long wars against France finally came to an end in 1815, England experienced the expected rise in criminal prosecutions that had followed the conclusion of every war in the previous century. Prosecutions had been increasing for some years by then, but the coming of the peace and the demobilization of the quarter million soldiers and sailors who had made up the largest army and navy the country had ever raised brought a steeper acceleration in the number of accused felons sent to trial.[1] It was by then a commonplace that the reduction of war-related work and the re-integration of the forces in the transition from war to peace also brought a transition, as *The Times* remarked casually in 1821, 'from plenty to poverty or from full to incomplete employment of the people.'[2] Difficult labour markets had always led to increased prosecutions at the Old Bailey for robbery and theft.[3]

For the first time the public knew how many property offences were being prosecuted in the country since the government had agreed in 1810 to collect evidence of the annual number of indictable offences brought to trial in every county. The 'criminal statistics' that resulted were gathered at the insistence of men pressing for the reform of capital statutes and were at first focussed on the most serious offences. Over time, the collection of data was broadened to include the full range of felonies and misdemeanours brought before the courts, including those tried summarily by magistrates—figures that presented a much fuller account of the extent of prosecuted crime.[4] But the reports relating simply to indictable offences were striking in themselves, for they revealed a remarkable national increase across the first four decades of the

---

[1] Douglas Hay, 'War, Dearth, and Theft in the Eighteenth Century: The Record of the English Courts,' *Past and Present*, 95 (1982), 138–9; Charles M. Clode, *The Military Forces of the Crown*, 2 vols. (London, 1869), I, 272–4.

[2] *The Times*, 9 November 1821. The consequence, the editorial continued, was that 'a large portion of the lower class of inhabitants of London have acquired habits of determined profligacy and of idleness, which nothing can stimulate to action but that morbid zest which criminal enterprizes impart to the bosom of the incuriably wicked.'

[3] Hay, 'War, Dearth, and Theft'; John Beattie, 'Crime and Inequality in Eighteenth-Century London' in John Hagen and Ruth D. Peterson (eds.), *Crime and Inequality* (Stanford, 1995), ch. 6.

[4] V. A. C. Gatrell and T. B. Hadden, 'Criminal statistics and their interpretation' in E. A. Wrigley (ed.), *Nineteenth Century Society: Essays in the Use of Quantitative Method for the Study of Social Data* (Cambridge, 1972), 336–96.

nineteenth century in prosecutions for crime against property. The returns began with the offences charged in 1805, just over 4,000 nationwide, a level that remained roughly stable over several years. By 1812, the numbers had risen above 5,000, and by 1815, when the war ended, to 7,000. In 1817, more than 12,000 men and women were charged with an indictable offence involving the taking of property, a level that was sustained over the next two years. A slight falling back in the early 1820s was followed by another relentless rise, with only brief pauses, through the next two decades. By 1840, indictable offences against property charged in courts across the country stood at almost 23,000. The population of England had also risen in the first four decades of the century, from roughly nine million to close to 15 million, a strong increase indeed, but not sufficient in itself to explain the sixfold expansion in indictable offences since the early years of the century.[5]

Prosecutions for property offences in London followed a similar path (Figure 8.1).[6] In the first decade of the nineteenth century, the number of cases brought to trial at the Old Bailey fluctuated without much pattern between 600 and 800 a year, averaging 736. As in the country as a whole, those numbers were increasing by 1812–14, when the judges dealt with more than 900 property offences in each of those years. They increased sharply with the peace. Just over 1,500 trials involving crimes against property were heard at the Old Bailey in 1817, by far the largest number ever recorded, and although that rate of change was not immediately as sustained as it was in the rest of the country, the upward trend was renewed after six years of stable (and still historically high) numbers. Another sharp upward push began in 1824 and continued through the 1830s, with occasional pauses and one serious disruption in 1833–34 when the Middlesex magistrates decided to deal with more cases at their quarter sessions and send fewer for trial at the Old Bailey.[7] By the end of that decade what had become the Central Criminal Court was dealing annually with more than 2,500 cases involving property crime.[8]

The Old Bailey dealt almost entirely with felonies, so these figures by no means represent the full extent of prosecuted crime in the metropolis over those years. A number of property offences were also dealt with at the quarter sessions, and an

---

[5] Ibid, 372–4, 387–8 (Table I); V. A. C. Gatrell, 'The Decline of Theft and Violence in Victorian and Edwardian England' in V. A. C. Gatrell, Bruce Lenman, and Geoffrey Parker (eds.), *Crime and the Law: the Social History of Crime in Western Europe since 1500* (London, 1980), 239. V. A. C. Gatrell, 'Crime, authority and the policeman-state,' in F. M. L. Thompson (ed.), *The Cambridge Social History of Britain 1750–1950*, 3 vols (Cambridge, 1990), vol. 3, 251; Clive Emsley, *Crime and Society in England 1750–1900* (3rd edn., Harlow, 2005), ch. 2. David Taylor, *Crime, Policing and Punishment in England, 1750–1914* (1998), ch. 1. For the population, see E. A. Wrigley and R. S. Schofield, *The Population History of England 1541–1871. A Reconstruction* (Cambridge, 1989; first published, 1981), 534.

[6] The data on prosecutions at the Old Bailey in the following five paragraphs are derived from the website, <http://www.oldbaileyonline.org>.

[7] A copy of the decision at the meeting on 1 May 1833 at which the Middlesex bench agreed to that suggestion (as 'a saving of expense to the County') is among the Home Office papers at TNA: HO 59/3.

[8] The jurisdiction of the Old Bailey was expanded by statute in 1834 to include those areas in Essex, Kent, and Surrey that came within the new Metropolitan Police District and was henceforth known as the Central Criminal Court (4 & 5 Wm. IV, c. 36). See Allyson N. May, *The Bar and the Old Bailey, 1750–1850* (Chapel Hill, 2003), 146–50.

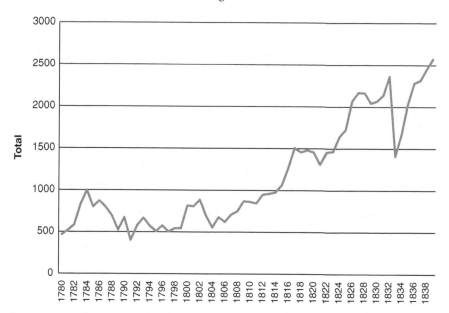

Figure 8.1. Defendants charged with property offences at the Old Bailey, 1780–1839[1]

[1] Source: <http://oldbaileyonline.org>

increasingly large number of petty offences were being dealt with summarily by magistrates in the police offices, and by the lord mayor and aldermen of the City of London, at the Mansion House and the Guildhall.[9] But the reports of the Old Bailey sessions in the printed *Proceedings* and in the press provided an accessible and regular source of information about crime in this period, and particularly about the kinds of offences that were most likely to shape opinion in the government, in parliament, and among the public about the problems to be tackled and the way the policing institutions of the metropolis needed to be changed.

A common perception emerged about crime in the early nineteenth century that although offences increased sharply, there was much less violence than there had been in the past.[10] The evidence taken by a house of commons committee enquiring into the state of the police in the metropolis in 1816 supported that

[9] Faramerz Dabhoiwala, 'Summary Justice in Early Modern London,' *English Historical Review*, CXXI (492, 2006), 796–822; Drew D. Gray, *Crime, Prosecution and Social Relations. The Summary Courts of the City of London in the Late Eighteenth Century* (Basingstoke, 2009); Peter King, 'The Summary Courts and Social Relations in Eighteenth Century England,' *Past and Present*, 183 (May, 2004),125–72; *idem, Crime and Law in England, 1750–1840* (Cambridge, 2006), ch. 1; Bruce P. Smith, 'The Presumption of Guilt and the English Law of Theft, 1750–1850,' *Law and History Review*, 23 (1, 2005), 133–72; *idem*, 'Did the Presumption of Innocence Exist in Summary Proceedings?' *Law and History Review*, 23 (1, 2005), 191–9; Norma Landau, 'Summary Conviction and the Development of the Penal Law,' *Law and History Review*, 23 (1, 2005), 173–89.

[10] For changing perceptions of robbery in the late eighteenth century, see Robert B. Shoemaker, 'The Street Robber and the Gentleman Highwayman: Changing Representations and Perceptions of Robbery in London, 1690–1800,' *Cultural and Social History*, 3 (2006), 381–405.

view,[11] as did the pattern of indictments at the Old Bailey with respect to crime in the metropolis. Mounted highway robberies, for example, were rare by the first decade of the new century; Sir Richard Birnie, the Bow Street chief magistrate, told a house of commons committee in 1828 that 'there has not been a mounted highwayman these thirty years.'[12] Many of the cases indicted as highway robberies at the Old Bailey in the eighteenth century had been muggings by footpads on the streets of the capital, charged as offences on the highway because the streets of London had been purposely designated as 'king's highways' in 1720 to make victims eligible for the £40 reward established by parliament in 1692 and thus to encourage prosecutions.[13] Even when the £40 parliamentary reward was abolished in 1818,[14] street offences continued briefly to be charged as highway robberies, perhaps out of clerical inertia or because prosecutors wanted to impress juries with the seriousness of the charge. But that too came to an end in 1830 when the last trials for highway robbery were held at the Old Bailey.

There were also many fewer indictments for all other forms of robbery at the Old Bailey in the quarter century after 1815 than there had been in the last quarter of the eighteenth century—both in simple numbers and as a percentage of the total property offences charged. There was some increase after 1815 in robbery cases from the very low levels that had prevailed during the war years, but the numbers of violent offences did not match those of the post-war peaks of 1783–84 (Figure 8.2). As a proportion of the total number of offences, robbery fell steadily after 1816, and very sharply over time. Whereas in the 1780s, almost 11 per cent of trials for property offences had been for some form of robbery, in the 40 years after 1800, the proportion was overall no more than two per cent, and barely half that by the late 1830s. Even the raw number of violent offences had been slightly higher on average in the 35 years before 1815 than over the subsequent quarter century, despite the increase in the population of the metropolis and the even stronger increase in the number of property crimes in general.[15]

The decline in robbery prosecutions suggests that there was indeed a decline in serious violence over the early decades of the nineteenth century. And it does seem to have been the case that not as many pistols and knives were in evidence—the violence in robberies coming now from fists, from victims being thrown to the ground or being hustled by a group of offenders, not being hit with a bludgeon or threatened with a weapon. 'Three men laid hold of me,' William Sweetman told the court in a typical case in 1815. One of them threw him down and 'put his hand into my breeches pocket and took two three-shilling pieces and some halfpence.' 'A person rushed violently against me,' another man said at the Old Bailey. 'I felt my watch instantaneously taken from me.' And in another case, the prosecutor

[11] For the committee, see below, section 3.

[12] *Parliamentary Papers*, 1828, vol. 6 (533): *Report from the Committee on the State of the Police of the Metropolis*, 35.

[13] J. M. Beattie, *Policing and Punishment in London, 1660–1750: Urban Crime and the Limits of Terror* (Oxford, 2001), 430–1.

[14] Below, text at n.78.

[15] Above, text at n. 4.

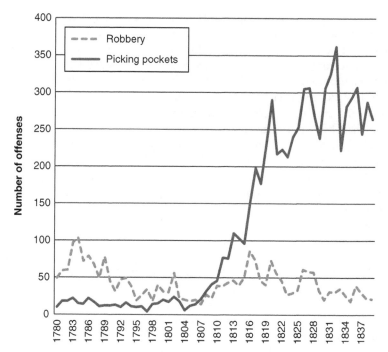

Figure 8.2. Defendants charged with robbery and picking pockets at the Old Bailey, 1780–1839[1]

[1]Source: <http://oldbaileyonline.org>

reported that 'there were nine men standing round me . . . all pushing me about . . . one tore my money out of my pocket.'[16] Almost half the cases tried at the Old Bailey between 1810 and 1830 were robberies in which victims were surrounded by a group of offenders and hustled while their pockets were rifled or their watches snatched.[17] These were clearly intimidating experiences and sometimes worse: some victims were treated very roughly, punched and badly beaten. Nonetheless, street robbers seem by the early nineteenth century to have been less cruel and vicious and to have inflicted fewer and less serious maimings on their victims than they often had in the previous century.

This decline of violence in robbery was one manifestation of a much broader falling away of violence in England in the late eighteenth and early nineteenth centuries.[18] But the number of offences charged as robbery (and perhaps to some

[16] OBP, April 1815 (William Sweetman) t18150405-17; OBP, May 1815 (Thomas Jones) t18150510-34; OBP, October 1815 (William Price) t18151025-6.
[17] Based on a 20% sample of the 973 trials for robbery and highway robbery at the Old Bailey, 1810–29 (<http://www.oldbaileyonline.org>).
[18] Greg T. Smith, 'The State and the Culture of Violence in London, 1760–1840', Ph.D. thesis (University of Toronto, 1999); *idem*, 'People don't want to see that sort of thing'; Robert Shoemaker, 'Male honour and the decline of public violence in eighteenth-century London,' *Social History*, 26 (2,

extent the behaviour of street robbers) were also clearly related to changes in the criminal law, particularly the way street offences came to be categorized as a result of a statute of 1808 concerning pocket picking. Picking pockets, a capital crime since the sixteenth century, was defined as the taking of something 'privately' from the person of another, that is, without the victim being aware of the theft. It had been a capital offence since Elizabeth's reign, but the harshness of that penalty for what was usually a trivial loss of property had long ensured that it would be seriously under-reported. It was known to be common in London wherever crowds gathered—at hangings, in and around the theatres, when the king went in state to parliament, at the royal palaces on the king's birthday and other similar celebrations, and so on—but it was rare in the eighteenth century for there to be more than two or three pocket-picking cases before the judges at each session of the Old Bailey. That some of these cases involved charges against prostitutes for stealing from their clients—men who had been asleep or too drunk to know their money, watches, or pocket books were being taken—suggests that the shame involved in confessing to being a victim in such a case was another reason why the crime was seriously under-reported. But the decisive issue was almost certainly the death penalty. That became clear when the threat of execution was removed in a statute of 1808, introduced by Samuel Romilly as one element of the broader programme of criminal law reform he had long promoted. With the death penalty removed, prosecutions increased substantially.[19]

Romilly's repeal of the capital punishment provision in pocket picking had been opposed by the high court judges on the grounds that removing the death penalty would lead to a massive increase in the offence. The movement in prosecutions seemed to justify their anxiety. From the 15 or 20 cases a year that had been the eighteenth century norm at the Old Bailey, prosecutions shot up after 1808—to over 100 by 1813, more than 200 six years later and over 300 by 1826 (Figure 8.2). The initial increase caused such concern at the Home Office that the police magistrates were asked in February 1811 to report on the effect of the abolition of capital punishment on pocket picking. Had there been a reluctance to prosecute before the Act was passed? Are there now more or fewer offences? Are more pockets being picked, the officials at the Home Office wanted to know, or are there simply more prosecutions?[20]

The magistrates' answers to these questions are unknown. There is no way of knowing whether the rapidity and extent of the increase in Old Bailey cases (226 per cent in the five years, 1810–14) were due to victims being encouraged to prosecute by the removal of capital punishment or pickpockets being more active. But one reason was almost certainly related to an element of the 1808 statute that

2001), 190–208; *idem*, *The London Mob: Violence and Disorder in Eighteenth-Century England* (London, 2004), ch. 6; John Beattie, 'Violence and Society in early-modern England' in Anthony N. Doob and Edward L. Greenspan (eds.), *Perspectives in Criminal Law* (Aurora, ON, 1985), 36–60.

[19] 48 Geo. III, c. 129 (1808). Sir Leon Radzinowicz, *A History of the English Criminal Law and its Administration from 1750*, 4 vols, (London 1948–68), Vol 1, 497–525.

[20] TNA: HO 65/2, 23 February 1811.

may well have encouraged *both* victims and offenders—that is, a clause that fundamentally changed the nature of the offence. To convict a defendant of the capital crime of pocket picking it had always been necessary to show that the stolen goods had been taken without the knowledge of the victim, that the offence had been committed 'privately', as the law said.[21] Romilly's bill eliminated that requirement when he accepted the advice of the solicitor general, or perhaps acceded to his request, to change the definition of pocket picking simply to theft from the person, whether done 'privately' or not.[22] In addition, whereas previously an indictment for picking pockets could only be laid against the person who had actually taken the goods, not his or her accomplices, the statute now made such charges possible—in a clause that was clearly intended to encourage prosecutions not only of pickpockets who continued to steal surreptitiously, but also the gangs of offenders who had in recent years taken up the tactic of surrounding victims in order to steal from them. The new statute declared hustling and harassing a victim to be a species of pocket picking, and thus non-capital, so long as the violence involved was not such as to 'constitute the crime of robbery.' In effect, Romilly's Act made robbery non-capital if no weapons or serious physical violence had been involved, and in so doing perhaps affected the way robbers went about their business.

An average of more than 30 cases of picking pockets were prosecuted at every session of the Old Bailey in the third and fourth decades of the century, at least a tenth of them carried out by groups of men swarming their victims—offences that might earlier have been charged as robbery.[23] Some of the apparent reduction of robbery was clearly the result of changes in the law relating to pocket picking. But not all. There is a good deal of evidence that the streets of London were less violent by 1815 than they had been in the previous century. The house of commons committee examining the state of the police of the metropolis in 1816 took testimony from men who had good reason to know about the violence on the streets first hand, including several runners and magistrates. None, certainly not the runners, had anything to gain by denying the widespread perception that violence had diminished; indeed, the reverse. Virtually every witness agreed that the roads and streets in and around the capital were much less dangerous than they once had been. Townsend and Sayer were both in a position to compare their experience of London in the 1780s with the current post-war period and both agreed there had been a remarkable change. Sayer remembered gangs of more than a dozen men committing robberies in Westminister when he joined Bow Street just before the Gordon Riots of 1780. Several parts of the town were then very dangerous, Sayer told the committee: no officer could walk alone down Duck Lane or other lanes around Smithfield without being assaulted. There were, he said, no such gangs now and no such danger. Townsend told the committee that he had recently spoken to

---

[21] Radzinowicz, *History of English Criminal Law*, vol. 1, 660–6.

[22] 48 Geo. III, c. 129, s. 2 (1808).

[23] Based on a 15% sample of more than 1,000 pickpocketing cases reported in OBP. in the years 1800, 1805, 1810, 1815, 1820, 1825, and 1830. For typical cases, see OBP, September 1820 (Isaac Wolfe *et al*) t18200918-251; OBP, September 1820 (Charles Smith) t18200918-255; OBP, December 1820 (Samuel Davis) t18201206-108.

Lord Eldon, the lord chancellor—not missing a chance to drop a name, as usual—about the changes he had experienced. 'Where are the highway-robberies now?' he had asked rhetorically: 'there are no footpad robberies or road robberies now, but merely jostling you in the streets. They used to be ready to pop at a man as soon as he let down his [coach] glass, that was by the banditti.... People travel more safely now'. John Vickery, the runner, and Conant, chief magistrate at Bow Street, added their agreement about violence on the streets. John Silvester was perhaps the best witness of all because he had attended the Old Bailey as counsel in the 1780s, sat on the bench there as common sergeant of London (1790–1803), and since becoming recorder of London in 1803, had prepared an account for the cabinet of the trial of every convicted capital offender. He confirmed for the committee that 'we now have no cruel offenders, no extraordinary violence against the person, as we have had formerly'.[24]

In the absence of significant levels of serious violence, the central problem of post-war crime in London was the sheer volume of largely petty offences, along with one other consideration that made the policing issues all the more difficult—the evidence that very large numbers of offences were being committed by young offenders. Concern about the involvement of adolescents in thievery and petty crime or about the numbers of children loose on the streets of the city, detached from parents and family, was by no means new in the early nineteenth century. Critical views of the behaviour of young people had been voiced at least since the sixteenth century and were certainly common in the eighteenth.[25] But the scale of juvenile engagement in crime seemed in the early decades of the nineteenth century to be beyond anything experienced in the past. It raised sufficient anxiety by 1815 to lead a group of London philanthropists to organize a 'Committee for Investigating the Alarming Increase of Juvenile Delinquency in the Metropolis' that concluded after their investigations that 'some thousands of boys in the Metropolis were daily engaged in the commission of crime.'[26] This may have been exaggerated, indeed alarmist. But it was widely believed. As Peter King has said, 'Juvenile delinquency had arrived as a separately identified social problem and as a source of intense concern.'[27]

Whatever the reason might have been, whether juveniles were committing more offences or, as King has argued, fears about the social consequences of urbanization and industrialization encouraged a greater determination in these years to prosecute adolescents 'as powerful representatives of the shape of the future,' the numbers of young offenders before the courts certainly increased sharply over the early decades

---

[24] *Committee on the Police of the Metropolis* (1816), 144, 177, 212–13, 223. For Silvester, see Allyson N. May, *The Bar and the Old Bailey, 1750–1850* (Chapel Hill, 2003), 258 and *passim*.

[25] Paul Griffiths, *Youth and Authority: formative experience in England, 1560–1640* (Oxford, 1996); Ilana Krausman Ben-Amos, *Adolescence and Youth in Early Modern England* (London, 1994); Heather Shore, *Artful Dodgers. Youth and Crime in Early 19th-Century London* (Woodbridge, 1999).

[26] Peter King, *Crime and Law in England 1750–1840. Remaking Justice from the Margins* (Cambridge, 2006), 104.

[27] Ibid, 105.

of the nineteenth century.[28] It is difficult to form a comparison with eighteenth-century experience because information about the ages of defendants was not included in Old Bailey trial reports until the last years of the century. Even then, ages were recorded only in the case of those found guilty, their ages having been determined in court, presumably as an aid to the judges in sentencing—in the decision whether to order transportation or imprisonment, and if the latter, in which institution and for how long. That evidence confirms that there was a large number—and an increasing proportion—of juveniles among convicted felons in the early decades of the nineteenth century. In broad terms, over the quarter century after 1815 about 40,000 prisoners were convicted of crimes against property at the Old Bailey, roughly 15,000 of them (37 per cent) were under the age of 20, convicted overwhelmingly of simple larceny and pocket picking.[29]

I have tabulated in Table 8.1 total convictions for larceny and pocket picking in 10-year periods over the first decades of the century of young male and female offenders—those under 17 years of age and the larger group under 20. The growing number of adolescent males among convicted offenders began in pocket picking soon after the 1808 act that removed capital punishment, and increased after the war ended in 1815 in the case of offences involving simple theft. The strongest increases were recorded in the 1820s when the total number of boys 16 and younger convicted of larceny had multiplied sevenfold since the first decade of the century and by a factor of more than 50 in the case of the pickpockets: altogether, close to 2,000 boys under 17 were convicted of these two felonies in the third decade of the century compared to a tenth that number in the first. Convictions of girls and young women increased at a much less pronounced rate until the 1830s, when their numbers moved up a little more sharply.

The increase in numbers of convictions is even more striking when one adds the convictions of older teenage boys, 17–19, and measures the changing proportion they represented of the total body of thieves and pickpockets. By the last years of the 1820s males under the age of 20 made up fully 60 per cent of all convicted pickpockets, having been about 20 per cent at the beginning of the century; in the case of larceny, the proportion of young offenders more than doubled to 40 per cent over the same period.

In setting out these changes in the number of prosecutions for property crime and in the number of adolescent offenders over the first four decades of the nineteenth century, I am not as much concerned to examine the difficult issue of whether they represent real changes in crime or changes in attitudes towards crime among the middle and upper classes that might have affected their propensity to prosecute. My concern is the effect of the increase in relatively minor property offences being prosecuted at the Old Bailey in the early decades of the nineteenth century on the way criminal justice was

---

[28] Peter King, *Crime and Law in England 1750–1840. Remaking Justice from the Margins* (Cambridge, 2006), 106–8.

[29] For a much fuller study of the ages of property offenders and of the proportion of juveniles among them in the late eighteenth and early nineteenth centruies, see ibid, ch. 2.

Table 8.1. Ages and gender of defendants convicted of larceny and picking pockets at the Old Bailey, 1800–1839[1]

Years	Male				Female			
	>17 years %	17–19 years %	Total <20 %	N	>17 years %	17–19 years %	Total <20 %	N
A. Larceny:								
1800–9	7.5	9.0	16.5	2345	7.9	9.5	17.3	877
1810–9	10.2	14.4	24.6	4103	5.9	9.4	15.3	1039
1820–9	20.2	21.7	41.9	6736	9.7	12.1	21.9	1637
1830–9	18.4	22.8	41.2	7180	10.5	17.8	28.3	2243
B. Picking pockets:								
1800–9	9.6	15.0	24.4	94	–	9.5	9.5	42
1810–9	18.1	28.4	46.6	811	2.7	19.5	22.2	185
1820–9	32.2	34.9	67.1	1756	8.5	25.6	34.1	317
1830–9	25.9	37.3	63.2	2211	6.3	22.8	29.1	394

[1] Source: <http://oldbaileyonline.org>

administered. It can be seen, for example, in an expanded workload at the Old Bailey that required the opening of a second courtroom in 1824.[30] It can also be seen in a significant change in the composition of the bench, in that the 12 high court judges, who were facing increasing burdens on their assize circuits as well as in London, came to play a less prominent role in ordinary trials than they had earlier. By the early years of the nineteenth century the judges had turned over the trial of straightforward non-capital cases to other senior legal figures at the Old Bailey, notably to the common serjeant of London, a second serjeant, and the recorder. The high court judges remained on the commission, but by 1815 they sat only on capital cases, one of their number dealing normally with these cases in a day or two.[31]

The character of the offences that largely filled the docket by the early nineteenth century had also contributed to a change at Bow Street since John Fielding's day. The process under which Fielding had brought suspected offenders already committed to trial back to the Bow Street office to be re-examined was still practised,

[30] David Bentley, *English Criminal Justice in the Nineteenth Century* (London, 1998), 55.

[31] The judges presiding at each trial are named in the Old Bailey *Proceedings* (<http://www.oldbaileyonline.org>). Serjeants-at-law ranked between king's counsel and barrister in the three gradations of lawyers called to the bar (Bentley, *English Criminal Justice*, 99). And see J. H. Baker, *The Order of Serjeants at Law* (Seldon Society, London, 1984).

Plate 4. Bow Street in 1810, in Rudolph Ackermann, *Microcosm of London*, vol 1 [Fisher Library, University of Toronto].

but on a much reduced scale. His special Wednesday sessions and the extensive reporting of the proceedings in the newspapers had not survived the prohibitions pronounced by the attorney general soon after Fielding's death. Nor, apparently, had the courtroom he had constructed to support his effort to bolster prosecution cases. Fielding had wanted to create a space in which an audience would be able to follow proceedings and perhaps bring further evidence, especially in cases in which highwaymen and other serious offenders had committed a series of offences. To facilitate that, he had provided chairs for the middle- and upper-class audience he hoped to attract.[32] That seating had disappeared by the early nineteenth century and with it the notion that committal hearings were being held with an interested audience in mind.

The illustration of the Bow Street office in Rudolph Ackermann's *Microcosm of London* shows a very different scene from Fielding's court (Plate 4),[33] the result of a re-organization that had apparently taken place at some point before August 1796, when *The Times* refers to an examination taking place in 'the new Office' in Bow Street.[34] In the Ackerman image of 1808, the magistrates are no longer looking out past a prisoner at the bar and to a sizeable group of people who may have been paying attention to the proceedings. Instead, they are conducting their committal hearing at the end of the room, their backs to a wall, looking directly at the prisoner in a raised dock against the opposite wall. A witness is giving evidence in a stand in the well of the court between them. There is no suggestion in the way the rest of the room is depicted that there was anything resembling an 'audience'—that is, people interested in what was being said by the magistrates or by lawyers, witnesses, and the accused. Other prosecutors and witnesses are simply waiting their turn, chatting and gazing about, having filed in through an unseen door on the left. The intention of the illustrator, Thomas Rowlandson, is to focus our attention on the main actors, particularly the magistrates and the accused, by dispensing with the crowd that, as newspaper accounts report, was often present when an offender aroused the interest of the curious or because he or she had committed so many offences that large numbers of victims turned up to add their evidence. At such times, the office could easily become 'excessively crowded', or 'crowded almost to suffocation.'[35] At a robbery trial at the Old Bailey in 1796, a witness said that the room at the committal hearing at Bow Street was so full that the magistrate ordered that 'a lane be made' through the crowd so he could get to the box. The victim similarly said that the crowd had been asked to 'make a line' so he could see the men accused of robbing him.[36] There was also likely to have been a more orderly organization in

---

[32] Above, ch. 5, text at nn.20–6.

[33] Rudolph Ackermann, *The Microcosm of London; or, London in Miniature*, 3 vols. (1808–11), vol. 1, 82.

[34] *The Times*, 30 August 1796.

[35] For a few examples, *The Times*, 7 September 1799, 7 February 1800, 4 October 1819, 4 October 1819, 20 August 1822, 14 and 22 December 1822.

[36] OBP, February 1796 (George Wakeman and Alexander Dew) t17960217-9.

the well of the court than Rowlandson depicts—more room for clerks, for example, and for the shorthand reporters, whose accounts of the proceedings continued to appear regularly in the press.[37]

The house next door to the Bow Street office was acquired by the Home Office in 1813, and eventually the two houses were joined, enabling the courtroom to be much enlarged.[38] But the form of the courtroom as Ackermann represented it seems to have been retained.[39] Charles Dickens, who had attended hearings there as a reporter,[40] describes the courtroom in *Oliver Twist* (1838) essentially as it appears in Ackermann, except that it is much less attractive and the placement of the magistrates' bench and the dock are reversed. Noah Claypole, sent by Fagin to report how the Artful Dodger fared at his committal hearing at Bow Street after he was arrested for pocket picking, 'found himself jostled among a crowd of people, chiefly women, who were huddled together in a dirty, frowsy, room, at the upper end of which was a raised platform railed off from the rest, with a dock for the prisoners on the left hand against the wall, a box for the witnesses in the middle, and a desk for the magistrates on the right'.[41]

If the Bow Street committal hearings in the early nineteenth century no longer attracted the kind of upper-class audience that had regularly attended John Fielding's Wednesday re-examination sessions, it may have been in part because the docket no longer included significant numbers of cases—highway robberies in particular—that caught the attention of the propertied elite. The daily grind of petty offences that characterized committal hearings at Bow Street by the early nineteenth century made for an entirely different experience. It also helps to explain why the runners continued after 1815 to play a less and less prominent role in the policing of the metropolis.

2. THE RUNNERS AND POST-WAR CRIME

The perception that petty crime was increasing steadily, particularly among the young, raised questions in the early decades of the nineteenth century about the criminal law and all the institutions of criminal administration—about the effectiveness (as well as the fairness) of capital punishment, the usefulness of imprisonment as a penal weapon, and, to an extent never before publicly broached, the nature and condition of policing in London. There was an emerging sense that

---

[37] That space (and presumably a table) was made available for the press is suggested by a report in 1827 that the Bow Street magistrate, Halls, 'after reading an article in the *Morning Herald*, reflecting on one of his decisions, called for the person who reports for that journal' and told him to warn his editor against making unfair comments on the court's proceedings. *The Times*, 13 October 1837.

[38] Clare Graham, *Ordering Law: The Architectural and Social History of the English Law Court to 1914* (Aldershot, 2003), 172.

[39] For plans depicting the changing forms of the ground floor of Bow Street, see Anthony Babington, *A House in Bow Street: crime and the magistracy, 1740–1881* (London, 1969), Plates 9–12. They are rendered in a useful form in Graham, *Ordering Law*, 172.

[40] Babington, *A House in Bow Street*, 231–2.

[41] Charles Dickens, *Oliver Twist*, book 3, ch. 6.

what was required from the policing forces was not an effort to find and prosecute more offenders, but ways in which the numbers of offenders crowding the courts and filling the gaols could be reduced. Prevention of crime was not a new idea. It had long been the duty of the night watch, the parish constables, and the godly magistrate. But the notion of a preventive police took on new meanings and became a more urgent requirement in the early decades of the new century.

How such policing was to be achieved, how it needed to be organized and led, emerged as pressing issues of public policy—questions to which there were no obvious answers. In exploring how those ideas developed after 1815, I will be particularly concerned with their consequences for the runners, the men at Bow Street who had been at the centre of earlier struggles against gangs and violent offenders. Their policing role had been changing since the 1780s, as we have seen—by the emergence of the patrol, by changes in the dominant forms of crime in the capital, by increasing demands from the Home Office, by work for the royal household and for magistrates and victims of crime in the provinces. That pattern of work continued after 1815. I will note that briefly, before going on to examine the confusion of ideas about policing that emerged in the second and third decades of the century, the passing of the Metropolitan Police Act in 1829, and the consequences of the establishment of the new force for Bow Street and especially for the runners.

Eight runners remained on the Bow Street establishment in 1815. Three were veterans with more than 30 years' service each—Patrick Macmanus, John Townsend, and John Sayer. The latter two remained in place until they both died in 1832. Macmanus retired within a year and was replaced by Daniel Bishop, who had been a captain of the patrol, and who became one of the most active of the Bow Street men over the next 15 years. The other runners in place in 1815 were John Pearks, who had been appointed a runner in 1802, and was to be replaced by George Ruthven in 1818; Steven Lavender, appointed in 1807, who became deputy high constable of Manchester in 1821 and was replaced by James John Smith; Harry Adkins, a runner since 1810, who gave way to William Salmon in 1820; John Vickery, appointed in 1811 and replaced in 1822 by James Ellis; and Samuel Hercules Taunton, promoted from the patrol in 1812, who remained in place until 1835. Besides Bishop and Taunton, Vickery, Smith, and Salmon had been conductors of the patrol before their promotion to the more lucrative post and were thus deeply experienced in the criminal work of the office at their appointment.

The group of runners had been increased from six to eight in 1802 because of the extra work that the protection of the royal family required. After 1815, two of the men who had long been among the leading runners, Sayer and Townsend, more or less abandoned police work entirely—at least on the evidence of press reports and the printed *Proceedings* of the Old Bailey. Sayer's absence from the *Proceedings* and Townsend's appearance at the Old Bailey to give evidence on only four occasions in the immediate post-war years and never after 1819, reflects the extent of their withdrawal from the investigation of London crime. Cox records them taking on one or two investigations in the provinces on their own, and on three occasions as members of larger groups of officers, but essentially they also left that work to others.[42]

They had done so in order to take on, more or less full-time, the job of royal protection. Indeed, Sayer said in 1816 that they were normally not allowed to take work outside London so as to be available to attend at court or to follow the court to the country when required.[43] They were regarded by the 1820s as men who 'always follow in the train of royalty', and were 'constant attendants' of the king.[44] Townsend, in particular, was frequently at court and his closeness to the royal family and court society made him a well-known figure in the upper-class world—indeed more widely than that, since he was frequently to be seen on the streets of London, smartly dressed, cane in hand, and wearing what became a familiar large white hat. It also provided him opportunities for handsome rewards from the wealthier members of court society—ensuring that they could come and go with some dignity on busy court days when onlookers crowded around St James's Palace and Buckingham House and dozens of members of the *bon ton* struggled to make comfortable entrances and departures. Sayer confirmed in his evidence before the house of commons select committee on the police of the metropolis in 1816 that they did private work for the upper-class families who had come to know them at court and that they had profited from it handsomely. 'I believe that, taking Townsend and myself,' Sayer told the committee, 'we get more money than the other officers; we attend the nobility and gentry, and if any accident might happen to them, we might get five or six guineas... this is from our being publicly known.'[45] Townsend became particularly well known when the prince regent ascended the throne in 1820 as George IV because the new king was said to be fond of his company and it seems clear that despite a previous prohibition against the Bow Street detectives appearing in the drawing room, this did not apply to Townsend in the new reign, if it ever had. He regularly attended the king on his frequent visits to Brighton and on his other favourite activities—attending the horse races, for example, or reviewing the troops.[46]

---

[42] David J. Cox, '"A Certain Share of Low Cunning": an analysis of the work of the Bow Street principal officers, 1792–1839, with particular emphasis on their provincial duties', Ph.D. thesis (Lancaster University, 2006), App. 4.

[43] *Committee on the Police of the Metropolis* (1816), 216.

[44] *The Times*, 31 January 1827, 15 March 1827.

[45] *Committee on the Police of the Metropolis* (1816), 215.

[46] Townsend's access to the inner circles of the court clearly encouraged his sense of self-importance, his name-dropping, and garrulous pomposity. This was on full display in his appearance before the house of commons committee in 1816. No one was more prolix, no one's paragraphs were longer; a question that other witnesses answered in a line or two as often elicited a story of his exploits and experience, of the 'as-I was-saying-to-the-chancellor' variety, that the committee appeared to listen to patiently (ibid, 137–41). Townsend's snobbery and ego are encapsulated in an exchange with Sir Richard Birnie, the chief magistrate, in 1827, as reported in *The Times*. This may be a spoof; Townsend was often lampooned in the press. But its placement in the paper in the regular column headed 'Police: Bow Street,' and the long list of duels it records, make it seem genuine enough. In either case, the short-hand reporter who took the conversation verbatim (if it is genuine), and the editor who printed it in full, clearly wanted to expose Townsend's inflated view of his own standing in the world. The exchange arose when a baker came to the office to complain that he had been challenged

Townsend's court and aristocratic connections undoubtedly explain why, having started life as a coster-monger (a street seller) or possibly a coal-porter on the London wharfs,[47] he died a wealthy man. Announcing his death (in 1832), a London newspaper reported that he left £25,000 invested in the Funds, and went on to ask the obvious question: 'If that be true, how could he have got it?'[48] The answer seems to be that he had substantial income from several sources to add to his base pay of a pound a week as a runner. These included the £200 a year as a leader of the security detail at the royal palaces, and a steady 40 guineas a year from the Bank of England, for providing, with Sayer, a form of security on the dividend days on which the Bank handled large amounts of cash.[49] They also included significant sums from the 'extraordinary' payments reported in the office accounts every quarter, almost certainly for additional work on behalf of the royal family—for travelling and other duties beyond regular attendance at weekly drawing rooms and levees, and on the major celebratory occasions of birthdays and anniversaries.[50] In addition, Townsend and Sayer received gifts for attending to the comfort and well-being of the aristocratic families who were in frequent attendance at court—for which they were well rewarded, as Sayer disclosed before the parliamentary committee in 1816.[51]

The other six runners were less favoured financially, but they continued to earn a great deal more than their counterparts in the police offices because they got more

---

to a duel by a clerk in a lead mill and wanted a warrant to have the challenger arrested. His request was granted. When Birnie asked Townsend to serve the warrant, he got this response:

'What!', said the veteran . . . 'is it after a public service of 46 years, in which I have had to do with Dukes, Marquisses, and Earls, and even with Royalty itself, that I am to be sent after such rif-raf as clerks and bakers? Things would be coming to a pretty pass indeed, Sir Richard, if John Townsend, your oldest, I will not say your best, officer, for I am getting into years now, should disgrace his name and service by running after the tag-rag [sic] and bobtail of society. Remember, Sir Richard, I have been employed before now to prevent men of the first rank in the country from breaking the King's peace.'

And he followed with a long catalogue of intended duels among men of the upper class, including peers of the realm, that he claimed to have prevented, concluding with the assertion that 'it would degrade a man of my service and experience to be scouring the country, over hedges and ditches, to prevent a meeting between a clerk and a baker?' Birnie (who had himself begun life as a saddler) agreed. 'We respect your long services too well,' he said, 'to degrade you by any such commission.' (*The Times*, 1 November 1827).

[47] According to the *Morning Chronicle*'s notice of his death, 11 July 1832.

[48] *Examiner*, 22 July 1832.Cox notes that no such sum is included in Townsend's will, but also that it is a brief document in which he leaves all his worldly goods to his wife, without mentioning 'any monetary amounts.' David J. Cox, *A Certain Share of Low Cunning. A History of the Bow Street Runners, 1792–1839* (Cullompton, Devon, 2010), 48–9.

[49] Townsend revealed his and Sayer's work for the Bank and some of their other sources of income to the 1816 *Committee on the Police of the Metropolis*, 137–41.

[50] TNA: T 38/674; see above ch. 7, sect. 3(b).

[51] An example of such ingratiating attention was noted in the *The Times* on 3 October 1823 when the king and court moved to Windsor in October 1823. Chief magistrate Birnie and the Bow Street officers were present to keep order around the entrance to the castle. The paper reported sardonically that Townsend, 'the old police-attendant at Windsor, undertook the higher duty of escorting the Marquis of Conyngham and the Earl of Fife through the crowd.'

opportunities to investigate offences for which they were paid either by private clients or from the Bow Street funds. The runners continued to share what the chief magistrate called the 'general duties' of the office. These included managing the comings and goings of complainants and accused offenders before the magistrates, and the policing work for which the government had originally provided funds— the investigation of offences and apprehension of suspects. Their incomes from London crime diminished in the new century as the dominant position that Bow Street had once held as the main source of commitments of accused felons to trial at the Old Bailey continued to erode with the expansion of the patrol, and the creation of the new police offices in 1792. During the subsequent quarter century of war, the Bow Street magistrates committed only 15 per cent of accused offenders sent to trial at the Old Bailey from Middlesex. And that share fell even further in the decade after 1815, when the patrols were further enlarged, as we will see, and took on more and more of the policing across the metropolis. The Bow Street patrols became in effect a police force for the metropolis outside the City of London—a proto-Metropolitan Police—when they were authorized to take the non-capital offenders they apprehended to the nearest police office, rather than undertaking what might easily be a long journey to Bow Street.[52] By the early 1820s, Bow Street was responsible for just over 10 per cent of the accused felons in Middlesex being committed to await trial at the Old Bailey.[53]

The contribution of the runners to the policing of property offences in the metropolis was also diminished by the falling away of violent offences in the capital. They continued to investigate offences in London, but nowhere near as actively as they once had. Cox finds them giving evidence in only a scattering of trials at the Old Bailey between 1815 and 1829, a mere 53 altogether, though reports in *The Times* show them to have been a little more active than the trial accounts suggest.[54] They continued to work regularly for the Post Office, investigating thefts by letter carriers and other employees.[55] They continued to be sent to prevent duels,[56] occasionally to take part in raids on gambling houses,[57] and to help in crowd control when the king went in procession to parliament or went to the theatre or, as George IV did regularly, went to the horse races at Ascot.[58] One of the runners was generally on duty at the office overnight, along with a squad of patrolmen, to deal with emergencies; one or more managed the appearances of accused offenders

[52] *The Times*, 10 August 1824; 11 October 1824.

[53] See ch. 7, text at n. 35. There are serious gaps in the records after 1812. The figure of 10% is based on the gaol calendars of the three January sessions in 1820–22 (LMA: OB/C/P).

[54] Cox, '"A Certain Share of Low Cunning"', App. 4. Just over half were in larceny cases, 20% in forgery, almost 10% in burglaries, and the remainder divided among arson, coining, murder, and the arrest of illegally returned transportees.

[55] For examples of the cases noted in *The Times*, see 25 October 1815, 31 October 1815, 30 January 1819, 26 April 1819, 11 August 1819, 29 April 1824, 25 November 1825.

[56] Examples can be found in *The Times*, 7 August 1823, 2 June 1824; 19 July 1826; 23 June 1828; 28 July 1828, and others up to at least 1833.

[57] *The Times*, 25 January 1833.

[58] TNA: HO 61/1, 75, 123, 127, 172.

before the magistrates at their twice-daily sittings. In addition, the runners also continued occasionally to act on orders from the Home secretary to make arrests in London. George Ruthven, for example, led a large group of patrolmen to apprehend the so-called Cato Street conspirators in 1820 as they assembled above a stable before attempting to carry out their intention of assassinating the members of the cabinet. The job was botched, and one of the patrolmen, Richard Smithers, was killed. But Ruthven was praised for his work, as was James Ellis, a captain of the patrol who was to become a runner: they were rewarded with gifts of £100 and £50 respectively.[59]

The runners' most regular employment after 1815 was to respond to requests for help from prosecutors outside London. When Sir Robert Peel came to the Home Office in 1822 and wanted to understand the work each of the police offices was doing, he asked the magistrates to send in the number of warrants they had issued over the previous five years and the populations of the districts they served. Birnie replied that since Bow Street 'had no prescribed district, we receive informations and act on them almost in every part of the kingdom.'[60] John Stafford, the chief clerk, explained what that meant for the runners when he was asked by a select committee of the house of commons a few months later what their recent employment had been. He said that Townsend and Sayer were in Brighton, attending the king, and as for the other six: Salmon and Ruthven 'have been upon the Continent in pursuit of persons who have absconded with property belonging to their employers in the city'; Bishop has been 'at a variety of places in the country . . . on business'; Taunton had recently followed some suspected offenders to Scotland and had brought them back, before going to Exeter assizes and Maidstone assizes to give evidence; Vickery had been employed by the Post Office to investigate thefts; Smith had been employed in a variety of matters in Kent, Essex, Hertfordshire, and Norwich.[61]

David Cox has found a sample of 146 cases (out of a larger unknown total) between 1815 and 1829 in which one or more of the runners were sent by the Bow Street magistrates or the Home Office to investigate offences in the provinces.[62] As in previous years, these were likely to have been cases in which the runners' skill and experience was thought to be useful, or in which their courage in conducting investigations and making arrests in situations that could easily have been dangerous was perhaps even more valued.[63] Their fees and expenses were mainly paid in this period by the clients for whom they worked, rather, that is, than the Bow Street magistrates or the Home Office. It is impossible to learn if their overall incomes

---

[59] TNA: HO 59/1, 39.

[60] TNA: HO 59/1/41.

[61] *Parliamentary Papers*, 1822, vol. 4 (440): *Report from the Committee on the State of the Police of the Metropolis*, 21–2.

[62] Cox, '"A Certain Share of Low Cunning"', App. 4. They were distributed as follows: murder or attempted murder – 21.9%; larceny – 16.4%; burglary – 9.6%; arson or damage to property – 8.9%; smuggling – 6.8%; forgery – 5.5%.

[63] See above, ch. 7, text at nn. 55–6.

Table 8.2. Runners in receipt of 'extraordinary' payments, 1819–1829[1]

Officer	Number of quarters in receipt of funds	Total	Average/ quarter
		£	£
Townsend	17	1139	67
Sayer	16	977	61
Taunton	11	501	46
Vickery	5	188	38
Bishop	8	176	22
Ellis	7	107	14
Salmon	8	92	12
Ruthven	13	107	8

[1] Source: TNA: T 38/674 (based on a sample of 17 of the 44 quarterly accounts for the years 1819–29).

were reduced as a result, but the runners drew less in these years from the office funds. Townsend and Sayer continued to receive large 'extraordinary payments' because their work for the royal family required their attendance at various palaces and frequent travel. In a sample of seventeen accounts in the 1820s, Townsend put in bills that averaged £67 a quarter, and Sayer £61. Together they accounted for about 30 per cent of all payments made to the runners and patrolmen. The other runners put in bills much more erratically, and, while Taunton, Vickery, and Bishop averaged sums that suggest they continued to undertake work under orders from the magistrates at about the same level as they had before 1819, others received much less (Table 8.2).

In sum, then, the runners remained active in several areas of criminal investigation and prosecution after 1815, but particularly in the provinces. With the changing character of crime in London, they were no longer as centrally engaged as they once had been with the issues that dominated the news and troubled the authorities. What in the past had been relatively high levels of highway robbery and street muggings had given way to an insistent expansion in the number of less threatening offences and of young offenders coming before the courts, offending that was not going to be deterred by the detection and arrest of a few more suspects. What was required, it became clear in this post-war world, was a more effective preventive strategy, and a refocusing of the ancient tasks of the parochial forces of watchmen and constables. What that would entail was entirely unclear in 1815. But, as offences mounted alarmingly in London and in many other parts of the country, the need for some sort of intervention gave rise to a more sustained discussion of policing issues than had ever been held before. The outcome was to have fundamental consequences for the future of the police offices, including Bow Street.

3. THE LIMITS OF POLICE REFORM, 1815–1822

Discussion of policing matters had been largely in abeyance during the quarter century of warfare that followed the creation of the new police offices in 1792. The most obvious exception to that was the work of Patrick Colquhoun, whose *Treatise on the Police of the Metropolis*, the first extended discussion of English policing, was published in 1795. Colquhoun, a successful Glasgow merchant who had come to London some years earlier, had been appointed a stipendiary magistrate at the Shadwell police office in 1792 through the patronage of his fellow Scot, Henry Dundas, secretary of state for the Home Department. He published his analysis of London crime and policing as a way of making himself useful to the government and thus advancing his career in the way he thought his talents deserved.[64] Colquhoun expanded his views on crime and policing in London through six subsequent editions of his *Treatise* over the next decade, setting out in doing so a great deal of information about the criminal law, the structure of policing, and other aspects of criminal administration in the metropolis. The central matter of these volumes was an account of the nature and extent of metropolitan crime, by far the most detailed analysis of the whole range of criminal offences that had ever been attempted, and the first to attempt to bring some precision to the subject by providing statistical evidence for his claims about the number of offenders of various kinds, receivers, the total value of goods stolen, and so on.

Much of this quantitative evidence was quite clearly guesswork. But it was essential to the argument he wanted to put forward about how the problems of largely petty crime should be dealt with. Colquhoun shared the common view that crime in the metropolis was the product of vice and immorality. But he particularly emphasized the importance of receivers and receiving—and not merely by pawn-brokers and other large dealers, but most especially by the large number of petty traders, shopkeepers, artisans and others whose willingness to take in purloined goods encouraged in his view widespread fraud, pilfering, and larceny. Crime would only be reduced, Colquhoun argued, if controls were imposed upon men in trades who dealt in small amounts of metals and textiles and lumber and other saleable and easily transported goods.

Colquhoun was given a platform for his ideas when the house of commons committee on finance, instituted by prime minister William Pitt in 1797 and chaired by Charles Abbott, took up as one of its many lines of enquiry the state of

---

[64] *A Treatise on the Police of the Metropolis*, (London, 1795); six subsequent revised and enlarged editions were published in the following five years, and a seventh in 1806. The latter has been reprinted by Patterson Smith (New Jersey, 1969). On Colquhoun's career and writings, see Sir Leon Radzinowicz, *A History of the English Criminal Law and its Administration from 1750*, 4 vols., (London, 1948–68), vol. 3, chs. 9–10; Ruth Paley, 'The Middlesex Justices Act of 1792: its origins and effects', Ph.D. thesis (University of Reading, 1983), 345–56; *idem*, 'Patrick Colquhoun (1745–1820),' *Oxford Dictionary of National Biography*; David Philips, 'Three "moral entrepreneurs" and the creation of a "criminal class" in England, c. 1790s–1840s', *Crime, Histoire & Sociétés/Crime, History & Societies* (7, 2003), 82–8.

the police and prisons in London. Colquhoun was the only witness the committee consulted with respect to policing, and his ideas were incorporated into the report issued by the committee in the following year. The main plank of his plan was a proposal to centralize the policing function in the hands of officials best placed to exercise control over the large number of tradesmen in the capital. To this end, his principal suggestion was that two institutions currently charged with the licencing of street sellers and of men offering means of public conveyance—the Offices of Hawkers and Pedlars and of Hackney Coaches and Chairs—should be consolidated and form a central Board of Police, led by five 'commissioners' appointed by the Home Secretary. They would be charged with requiring not only hackney coachmen and chairmen, hawkers and pedlars to take out licences, but also a wide range of people who exercised the trades that Colquhoun regarded as 'dangerous and suspicious' in that they could easily shield receiving and thus contribute to 'the Encouragement and Multiplication of Crimes.' Licencing would require inspection, and thus the possibility of control. It would also raise a revenue that would be sufficient, by Colquhoun's calculation, to pay the costs of policing. That was obviously an attractive element of his plan. But Colquhoun's main objective in creating a central Board of Police would be to bring a wide range of trades 'under a regular Mode of Inspection and Control' and make it possible to limit the activities of the receivers who now made petty crime profitable.[65]

Colquhoun's proposed changes in the structure of the London police followed in part from his view (a point that had been implicit in Reeves's doomed 1785 bill, though little understood at the time) that the two principal functions performed by magistrates with respect to the prosecution of crime should be separated. Magistrates should concentrate on judicial matters, he argued, leaving their ministerial role as leaders of the policing forces to others—in this case, to the commissioners of police. He also thought that the existing forces of constables and watchmen should be bolstered by the addition of a number of salaried officers in every parish. And he made a number of other striking suggestions about the policing and criminal administration in the capital, including a proposal that the government should provide funds for a public prosecutor so as not to leave victims of serious offences entirely on their own to carry the burden of prosecutions, and (following Reeves) that the City of London should have stipendiary magistrates and be part of the centralized system he proposed under the new Police Board.[66]

As a magistrate at Shadwell, Colquhoun made a particular study of the problem of crime on the river and the docks, and he played an important part in the creation

---

[65] *The Twenty-eighth Report of the Select Committee of the House of Commons on Finance: Police and Convict Establishments: Parliamentary Papers* (1798, 348). It is included in Sheila Lambert (ed.), *House of Commons Sessional Papers of the Eighteenth Century*, vol. 112. Colquhoun published a version of the report in the following year to highlight the proposals he had laid before the committee for a reform of the police: *The Report of the Select Committee of the House of Commons relative to the Establishment of a New Police in the Metropolis* (1799). For an account of the committee and its report, see Radzinowicz, *History of English Criminal Law*, III, 298–311.

[66] *The Twenty-eighth Report of the Select Committee of the House of Commons on Finance* (1798); *The Report of the Select Committee of the House of Commons* (1799), 1–4; Radzinowicz, *History of English Criminal Law*, vol. 3, 222–3, 301–12.

of a new office in Wapping in 1800—the Thames River Police—with responsibility for dealing with those issues.[67] But his hopes for much wider reform were unfulfilled. The plan he had proposed in 1798 was sketchy at best on the matter of how the leadership of his Police Board would be exercised, what the relationship would be between the new paid policemen in each parish and the existing forces, and indeed how other aspects of the plan would be implemented. Some of those issues might have been clarified if the bills that he went on to prepare in 1799 in anticipation of the government's willingness to take action on policing matters had been introduced and debated in parliament.[68] But in fact all of this was still-born. The parliamentary committee concerned with financial issues in every area of central administration had appeared to welcome his initiatives, but in 1798 and 1799 the government itself was deeply engaged in other matters, in particular with rebellion in Ireland, the threat of insurrection at home, and the prospect of invasion by a French army in its support.[69] A restructuring of London policing was not on the cabinet's agenda in the middle of a war and in the midst of a serious crisis. Colquhoun's policing plan was never to receive serious consideration by the government or parliament, then or later. He submitted his plan, as we shall see, to another parliamentary committee looking into the police of the metropolis in 1816. That committee was entirely out of sympathy with such centralizing ideas and simply ignored his submission. That was indeed to be his fate in the future. In the discussion of police reform after 1815, and in the decision-making around the making of the new Metropolitan Police in 1829, there is little evidence that Colquhoun's writings were consulted by anyone or that his proposals were revisited.

With the important exception of the creation of the mounted police unit in 1805—an unusual expenditure of money during a war, achieved almost certainly by the influence of the chief magistrate at Bow Street, Richard Ford, at a time when highway robbery was thought to be on the increase—few changes were made in the structure of London policing in the early years of the nineteenth century. But the nature of that policing was to come under scrutiny as the long wars against France came to an end in 1815 and rising levels of reported and prosecuted property crime were met by another investigation into the police of the metropolis undertaken by a select committee of the commons. This was a committee created in 1816 against the government's advice and preferences on the initiative of Samuel Romilly, who had led for some time a campaign to eliminate capital punishment for minor property offences and who now encouraged Henry Grey Bennet, another reform-minded member of parliament, to propose this committee and to act as chairman.[70] The committee was established to report on the state of the police of the metropolis. It took a great deal of evidence concerning Bow Street and the police offices in 1816, which it published, but without issuing a full report. The

[67] Radzinowicz, *History of English Criminal Law*, vol. 2, ch. 13.
[68] Ibid, vol. 3, 308–9.
[69] See above, ch. 7, text at nn. 83–4.
[70] *Memoirs of the Life of Sir Samuel Romilly... Edited by his Sons,* 2 vols. (London, 1841), 2, 414.

committee requested instead that it be reconstituted in the following session to examine other issues it considered relevant to the subject of policing: the licencing of alehouses; the effect of paying state rewards for the conviction of felons; and the state of gaols in the metropolis. On these matters it issued two reports in 1817 and one in 1818, along with transcripts of the evidence gathered.[71]

It is at first sight surprising that Romilly should have wanted a committee to investigate the police of the metropolis. Like many whigs, he had opposed the Westminster Police bill in 1785 and the 1792 act that created the stipendiary magistrates—opposing them as enhancements of the government's influence and patronage and as threats to the parochial bases of peace-keeping, the local control that he believed to be crucial to the preservation of the freedom and liberties of the king's subjects.[72] The defence of local control may, indeed, have been the main reason why he proposed the 1816 committee—anticipating that the post-war increase in prosecutions would be likely to raise questions about the policing of the metropolis, and that an enquiry conducted by a commons committee would almost certainly propose centralizing measures that would weaken the capacity of local authorities to manage their own affairs. Such moves had indeed been threatened four years earlier, partly as a result of the increase in prosecutions revealed by the criminal returns now being laid before parliament, partly because of horrendous attacks in December 1811 on families living on the Ratcliffe Highway. Two houses had been invaded at night and several members of each family had been brutally murdered, including an infant battered to death and other victims seriously mutilated. Horror and alarm had been nationwide. Letters flowed into the Home Office demanding better policing, with the result that a select committee of the house of commons had been established to examine the night watch and the police of the metropolis more broadly—the first such investigation since 1774, when a parliamentary enquiry had resulted in a statute that made significant changes in the night watch of the City of Westminster.[73] The report of the 1812 committee resulted in a bill that, had it been passed, would have required all parishes within the metropolis (outside the City of London) to bring their watch forces up to the standard established for Westminster in 1774, and in addition would have increased centralized control over parochial policing by giving supervisory authority to the magistrates in the police offices. That threat had been vigorously opposed by the local authorities in many of the affected parishes who resented the implication that their night watches were not capable of protecting their own communities and who objected in addition to the increased costs such a

---

[71] Parliamentary Papers: *Report from the Committee on the State of the Police of the Metropolis* 1816, vol. 5 (510); 1817, vol. 7 (233); 1817, vol. 7 (484); 1818, vol. 8 (423).

[72] For the continuing strength of the view that a police consisting of unpaid citizens taking their turns to serve as constables and watchmen under local control was essential to the freedom and the liberties enjoyed by Englishmen, see Francis M. Dodsworth, '"Civic" police and the condition of liberty: the rationality of governance in eighteenth-century England', *Social History*, 29 (2, 2004), 199–216.

[73] Elaine A. Reynolds, *Before the Bobbies: the night watch and police reform in metropolitan London, 1720–1830* (Basingstoke, 1998), 50–7; *idem* 'Sir John Fielding, Sir Charles Whitworth, and the Westminster Night Watch Act, 1770–1775', *Criminal Justice History*, XVI (2002, 1–22).

plan would impose on them. It was also vigorously opposed by the whig opposition in the house of commons, led by Romilly, and by radicals like Sir Francis Burdett, who espoused an antique version of the view that the responsibility for policing should lie with householders.[74]

It seems likely that it was out of a concern that the post-war increase in criminal prosecutions would lead to another committee of enquiry into policing and another threat to the local control of the watch and constabulary that encouraged Romilly to take a lead in this area and to propose a committee that would include members supportive of his ideas, not only about policing but also criminal law reform and prison reform—men like Sir James Mackintosh and Thomas Fowell Buxton—and a committee whose agenda he and Bennet could control. He may have had other objectives in mind too, judging by some of the matters the committee pursued. One was to deny the argument—made vigorously by the judges in the house of lords—that the removal of capital punishment from minor property offences would result in an increase in crime. Another was to play down the seriousness of the apparent increase in crime after 1815 in order to remove a potential impediment to further reform of the criminal law, while making the point that *if* policing needed to be improved, the institutions that should come under scrutiny were the police offices, including Bow Street, about which they found a great deal to criticize.[75]

In its first sessions, the 1816 committee collected evidence about the working of Bow Street and the police offices from a large number of witnesses, including two Bow Street magistrates, Conant and Nares, the chief clerk, Stafford, the runners, Townsend, Sayer and Vickery, and numerous stipendiary magistrates. They interviewed Patrick Colquhoun at length, providing him with another opportunity to present his ideas about the need for a Board of Police that would supervise the licensing and control of the numerous trades in London that he thought were responsible for much of the crime in the capital. The committee made their opposition to such centralizing ideas clear in their final report. In their examination of the Bow Street magistrates and the stipendiaries they revealed that their main interest was in finding ways to eliminate what they considered to be the harmful aspects of detective and prosecutorial policing. They were concerned, for one thing, about the corrupting effects of rewards—all rewards, private as well as public, but particularly the sums paid by statutory authority for the conviction of certain offenders. They probed witnesses on the effects that rewards had on officers' behaviour, on the temptation they faced, for example, to ignore petty offences and make arrests only when it was worth their while. Questions were asked about

---

[74] Reynolds, *Before the Bobbies*, 95–102; Ruth Paley and Elaine A. Reynolds, 'Politicians, Parishes, and Police: The Failure of the 1812 Night Watch Bill', *Parliamentary History*, 28 (3, 2009), 375–91. For the Ratcliffe Highway murders and the bill, see Radzinowicz, *History of English Criminal Law*, vol. 3, 315–47; P. D. James and T. A. Critchley, *The Maul and the Peal Tree: the Ratcliffe Highway Murders, 1811* (London, 1971).

[75] In the course of their lengthy enquiries they also found much that was wrong with the lack of control over the licensing of public houses, the extent and toleration of prostitution in London, and—a matter of particular interest to several members of the committee—the very poor condition of prisons in the metropolis. These issues were taken up mainly in the two reports issued in 1817 (see above, n. 72).

other corrupt activities, like the officers' willingness to accept bribes to turn a blind eye, or worse, actually to encourage certain kinds of offences—activities that had been all too clearly revealed by charges brought in 1816 against George Vaughan, a Bow Street patrolman, for conspiring with others to encourage burglaries by men they could then arrest and prosecute in the expectation of collecting handsome reward money.[76] The officers were being tempted to act in these ways, the committee concluded, by weekly pay that was too low, and they pursued with the Bow Street and other magistrates the possible advantages of increasing that pay while at the same time abolishing fixed rewards and enabling magistrates to award payments to deserving officers at their discretion. They found a lot of agreement among the magistrates and from the Bow Street runners, who had never received more than a few pounds reward money in a year and who now found their main source of parliamentary rewards—robbery convictions—shrinking rapidly away. They agreed that such fixed rewards were no longer useful. This evidence, and a great deal more collected by the committee in later sessions, encouraged Bennet to introduce the legislation that abolished parliamentary rewards in 1818.[77]

Members of the committee explored other weaknesses in the policing carried out by the Bow Street officers, including their willingness not only to tolerate, but to make use of 'flash houses,' where suspected thieves and robbers were known to congregate and which members of the committee thought were obvious encouragements of crime. Conant demonstrated that the age of John Fielding was well and truly over by denying all knowledge of the runners' policing techniques and activities: their visits to flash houses, he said, were 'a part of the mystery, or of the art, or of the policy [of being a police officer] which I can neither understand or explain.'[78] The runners, on the other hand, were happy to admit that knowing where offenders gathered was essential to detective work, confirming in doing so the committee's conviction that there was a good deal that needed to be put right with the policing being conducted by Bow Street and the police offices.[79]

The committee also probed the lack of communication among the police offices and Bow Street's failure to take a lead to help coordinate their work. Conant was dismissive of the importance of regular contact among the police offices and denied that Bow Street had any duty to act as a central clearing house for information about offences and offenders—fending off a series of increasingly testy questions about this. He finally agreed that the sharing of criminal information might help with respect to serious offences. But he insisted that it would make no difference to the management of the vast majority of offences they dealt with; information 'flying around' the metropolis about the large number of petty offences would only, he said, 'cloud' matters. And even in the case of serious offences, he thought it

---

[76] Radzinowicz, *History of English Criminal Law*, vol. 2, 334. For later charges of corruption against Bow Street officers, see below, text at nn. 176–81.

[77] *Committee on the Police of the Metropolis* (1816), 7–9, 138, 212–13. Bennet's statute abolishing rewards is 58 Geo III, c. 70 (1818), on which see Radzinowicz, *History of English Criminal Law*, vol. 2, 74–82.

[78] *Committee on the Police of the Metropolis* (1816), 21.

[79] Ibid, 142, 178–80, 213.

unnecessary, since all the offices already have knowledge of important offences 'from the parties, or from the Police officers, or from the public newspapers, which last mode of communication is the most universal way of any, and in some measure supersedes any other system.'[80]

The committee accepted without comment the chief magistrate's complacent view that the police offices learned as much as they needed to about serious offences in the metropolis from the press. They did so perhaps because they were anxious to underplay the seriousness of crime. One can see this in their questioning of the Bow Street runners, particularly leading them to agree that the 'manners' of the working population of the capital were much improved over what they had been 30 years ago and that crime was much less violent than it once had been.[81] Romilly was particularly anxious to promote his campaign to remove capital punishment from minor property crimes by diminishing the widespread concern about the apparent post-war increase of crime—an increase that the high court judges had pointed to in their opposition to further reforms of the capital laws beyond that enacted with respect to pocket picking. He appeared as a witness before the committee to refute the recorder of London, Sir John Silvester's argument that the removal of capital punishment for pocket picking was responsible for the sharp increase in the offence in recent years.[82]

The committee's views of crime shaped their final report in 1818. It included assertions about crime not frequently heard from the propertied class that were clearly designed to deny the need for serious policing reform and to reinforce Romilly's contention that the reform of the criminal law would not result in a massive increase in property offences. Although there had been a recent 'alarming augmentation of criminals,' the committee wrote, the evidence of numerous witnesses was that 'the character of offences [had been] more mild than heretofore, and the general manners and morals of the people [had] been on a course of gradual improvement.' In any case, the increase was the result of a period of 'poverty and distress among the people', and it would thus diminish when prosperity returned. With respect to police, the final report declared that the committee had been persuaded by Conant's arguments that a central 'board of police' was not necessary. Conant had said no such thing in declining to act as a clearing house for police office criminal information, but what he had said provided the committee with a useful answer to Colquhoun.[83]

The committee also concluded that the prevention of crime should be pursued as an issue of fundamental importance, but that they found the means that had been proposed (with Colquhoun very much in mind), 'odious and repulsive.' The system that had been suggested would make 'every servant of every house a spy on the actions of his master, and all classes of society spies on each other.'[84] In place

[80] *Committee on the Police of the Metropolis* (1816), 12–13, 15.
[81] Ibid, 143, 173–4.
[82] Romilly, *Memoirs*, 430; *Committee on the Police of the Metropolis* (1816), 222–5, 245–7.
[83] *Parliamentary Papers*, 1818, vol. 8 (423): *Report from the Committee on the State of the Police of the Metropolis*, 22–3.
[84] Ibid, 32.

of police reform, they offered the vision of the law-reformers who had led this enquiry. 'The police of a free country,' the final report asserted, 'is to be found in rational and humane laws, in an effective and enlightened magistracy, and in the judicious and proper selection of those [parochial] officers of justice, in whose hands, as conservators of the peace, executive duties are legally placed.'[85]

None of this provided guidance to Lord Sidmouth at the Home Office who had been facing the consequences of increasing numbers of property offenders while this committee had been sitting. His principal response after 1818 was to bolster preventive measures by introducing minor improvements in the Bow Street patrol that intensified the effects of patrolling.[86] He appointed John Stafford, the chief clerk at Bow Street, as inspector of the patrol with the duty to coordinate the activities of the 13 parties currently working under their conductor/captains.[87] In the harsh winter of 1820–21 he intervened more decisively when a further rash of complaints poured into the Home Office about the state of crime in the metropolis. Some of his correspondents were willing to acknowledge that much of the crime was the result of the severity of the weather and the lack of employment which were putting so many of the poor in serious difficulties, as, for example, in a riverside parish in which the 'depression of trade' meant that many families were having difficulty finding food and shelter.'[88] But mainly they complained about the sharp increase in offences, particularly the 'constant street robbery', the 'numerous Robberies and other Crimes . . . daily committed in the metropolis', and 'the swarmings of pedestrians by gangs, some of them very young.'[89] Such offences, the chairman of the vestry of St Giles in the Fields said, were increasing 'daily, hourly'.[90] A resident of Brook Street in Lambeth, wrote in December 1820 to say that a third of the hundred houses in his street had been attacked in some way during the previous year.[91] Whatever the reality of the state of crime, the complaints were frequent and loud enough to persuade Sidmouth that 'the system established in the Metropolis for the prevention of robberies is inadequate to the urgency of the public service,' and that *something* needed to be done to change and improve it.[92]

---

[85] Ibid, 32–3. In this final report they also disclose a revealing change in the parliamentary class's knowledge of the Bow Street runners' work and personnel. In introducing the Middlesex Justices Bill in 1792, Dundas said that he had spoken that morning to Macmanus to get his views on a point in the bill. Lord North in reply referred to Townsend and Jealous. Neither thought it necessary to identify them as runners (above, ch. 6, text at n. 126). In 1818, the final report refers to one of the runners as 'a person of the name of Vickery' (at 27)—a small point, but perhaps a revealing consequence of the reduction in the danger faced by the wealthy in traveling to and in London, and the consequent loss of their familiarity with the Bow Street office and men.

[86] Radzinowicz, *History of English Criminal Law*, vol. 2, 423–4.

[87] TNA: HO 65/2, letters of 28 September and 10 October 1818.

[88] TNA: HO 42/203, 105.

[89] TNA: HO 61/1, 25, 31, 55–6; HO 59/1, 30.

[90] TNA: HO 42/184, f. 105; HO 61/1, ff. 25, 31, 55; HO 59/1, 5 December 1820.

[91] TNA: HO 61/1, 25.

[92] TNA: HO 36/19, 298.

Seeking guidance as to what that something might be, Sidmouth sought the views of the men closest to the problem—the police magistrates.[93] He also got unsolicited advice when it became known through the press that, as one correspondent said, it was 'in contemplation to adopt a more extended organization of the police.'[94] Sidmouth received a variety of suggestions, virtually all of them focussed on the problem of street crime and on ways in which patrolling and surveillance could be strengthened. Several proposed an increase in the number of constables attached to the police offices to be employed in patrolling during the day as well as at night. Some offered plans to establish a body of men who could be held in reserve to be called upon as needed, and from whom regular officers could be recruited. Other schemes were less ambitious, but they all had in common a focus on the police offices themselves, and an ambition to prevent offences by increasing the number of officers under the magistrates' control.[95]

Advice was also forthcoming from a man with considerable experience (though a chequered reputation) as a magistrate of Middlesex, George Boulton Mainwaring.[96] He wrote his *Observations on the Present State of the Police of the Metropolis* over the winter of 1820–21, when, as he said, high prices and want of work made for difficult times for the poor who 'must either live by plunder or die from starvation.'[97] The policing issue was how to control crime 'without violating the constitution,' and the solution was to bring 'the principle of preventive police' into action by close communication among the police magistrates and by establishing a system of 'incessant observation.'[98] The parochial constables and night watch could not be relied on. Nor, in his view, could the officers in the present police establishments, because they had no inducements to do anything but respond to offences committed. Their salaries of a guinea a week were too mean; and the magistrates—unlike those at Bow Street—had no funds with which to reward them for the 'incessant vigilance' the times required. If these constables were given more authority to arrest on suspicion, and if their numbers were augmented at each office, they might emulate the success of the Bow Street mounted patrol, which, he claimed, eliminated highway robbery not by being everywhere at every minute, but by creating a credible threat to be anywhere at any time.[99] 'The question,' Mainwaring concluded, 'is punishment, or prevention.'[100]

---

[93] TNA: HO 65/2 (for the text, see Reynolds, *Before the Bobbies*, 112).

[94] TNA: HO 61/1, 47.

[95] TNA: HO 59/1, 12 December 1820 (two letters); 26 December 1820, 28 August 1821; HO 61/1, ff. 47, 55. For these plans, see Radzinowicz *History of English Criminal Law*, vol 3, 405–13.

[96] He was the son of William Mainwaring, chairman of the Middlesex quarter sessions for 36 years before being forced out by scandals connected with his business dealings and the failure of his bank. The younger Mainwaring was also forced to resign as Treasurer of the county in 1822 over irregularities in his accounts. Radzinowicz, *History of English Criminal Law*, vol. 3, 377, n. 9.

[97] George Boulton Mainwaring, *Observations on the Present State of the Police of the Metropolis* (1821), 8.

[98] Ibid, 24–8.

[99] Ibid, 69.

[100] Ibid, 140. For other pamphlets recommending police reform in this period, see *A Letter to A Member of Parliament on the Police of the Metropolis* (1821); L. B. Allen, *Brief Considerations on the*

The advice coming into the Home Office in 1820 and 1821 was that the answer lay in building up the police offices to create a more intensive system of patrolling (and a police less vulnerable to temptations to act corruptly) by recruiting more constables and paying them a better salary. Sidmouth did indeed move to intensify patrolling, but he did so not by increasing the number of officers under the police magistrates, but by reorganizing and augmenting the existing Bow Street patrols. In January 1821, he wrote to the Treasury, and under-secretary Hobhouse wrote to the police offices, to announce that he had decided to expand and reorganize the Bow Street patrols. The Metropolis was to be divided into 16 districts (outside the City of London), in each of which a conductor and four foot-patrolmen would carry out surveillance duties from 5 or 6 p.m. to midnight. Beyond that, another conductor and 18 patrolmen were to attend at Bow Street to be available as emergency support to any of the patrols, or to carry out other duties required by the magistrates. Further, to intensify policing at the centre of the metropolis, the foot patrols were to be given shorter routes. They would no longer be asked to guard streets in the suburbs—suburbs which had expanded extensively since 1791, when the Bow Street foot patrol were first given responsibility to patrol there. The foot patrol were now to concentrate on the inner streets of the city—on the 'stones', as was said—and not beyond. To take their place, a new force of patrolmen was to be created to protect the suburbs, consisting of 90 patrolmen, eight sub-inspectors and four inspectors. They were to patrol the roads beyond the routes covered by the foot patrol and up to five miles from London. Beyond that point responsibility moved to the mounted patrol who were responsible for a jurisdiction five to 25 miles from the city centre.[101]

The new body of a hundred men was to be known as the 'dismounted patrol' because, although they walked their beats, they were conceived as a branch of the horse patrol. Like the horsemen, they were to be veterans of cavalry regiments and under 40 years of age, available to serve as a source of recruits to fill vacancies among the mounted men. They were paid and controlled by the conductor of the horse patrol, William Day. This was a useful administrative arrangement, but its main value was that it placed the policing of the suburban roads directly under the Home Office, since Day, as the keeper of the criminal registers in the office, was based there in regular contact with the under-secretary. It also perhaps better ensured that the men of the dismounted patrol would be well suited to the job. Like the mounted men, the new patrolmen were stationed near the areas they were expected to guard. It was no doubt their remoteness from the office, and lack of daily contact with the magistrates or with their conductor in the Home Office, that explains why it was thought necessary (as it had been for the mounted patrol from its inception) that each of them was given a printed pocket-sized booklet setting out the rules and orders governing their conduct, along with their stations and the roads for which they were

---

Police of the Metropolis: with a few suggestions towards its improvement (1821), discussed by Radzinowicz, *History of English Criminal Law*, vol. 3, 410–11.

[101] TNA: HO 36/19, p. 298; HO 61/1, 27 January 1821.

responsible.[102] The dismounted patrol of a hundred men was a considerable addition to the Bow Street forces, aimed at providing a modicum of policing for parishes and villages on the outskirts of the capital that were being incorporated in effect into the metropolis by the relentless expansion of its population.

4. SIR ROBERT PEEL AT THE HOME OFFICE

Thus things stood when Robert Peel succeeded Sidmouth at the Home Office in January 1822. The need for a more effective, a more preventive, police in London was very much on the agenda, and after several years in which police reform had been the subject of a more focussed discussion than had ever taken place before, several points were clear. Any talk of reform or improvement was limited to the Bow Street office and the police offices. The latter were given permanent life in 1821, after 30 years during which their founding statute had had to be renewed at regular intervals. The new statute transferred the Shadwell office to Marylebone and amalgamated the police offices and the river police establishment at Wapping. It also slightly increased the magistrates' authority over the parish night watchmen and patrols by making it possible for them to dismiss men for cause, and appoint replacements. And it increased the authority of magistrates to use the Vagrancy Act of 1744 to convict suspicious persons and 'reputed thieves' taken into custody by the constables of the police offices.[103] The magistrates' suggestions for the improvement of the police in 1820–21 had not included serious scrutiny of the local peace-keeping forces, from whom it seems to have been widely believed that little could be expected. There was general agreement that better policing would only come from an increase in 'trained and disciplined' officers. It might not be possible to eradicate crime entirely, *The Times* conceded in its comment on Mainwaring's pamphlet, but it might be 'controlled by an extension and reformation of the police establishment' under the stipendiary magistrates, whose job 'is to prevent crimes.'[104] After a few months at the Home Office, Peel set out to make Bow Street and the police offices—the two branches of the police—as effective as possible.

Peel came into office having served as chief secretary in the Irish administration for six years, 1812–18, during which he had become familiar with the working of the police of Dublin, a unified and centralized force originally established in 1786 on the model of Reeves's failed London police bill of the previous year. The Dublin police had gone through several transformations since then, but in Peel's day it had regained its character as a unified force under a chief magistrate, dispersed through the six divisions into which the city was divided, and made up of armed constables and night patrols to a total of close to 800 men.[105] Peel had also been responsible

---

[102] TNA: HO 61/1, 27 January 1821.
[103] 1 & 2 Geo IV, c. 118 (1821).
[104] *The Times*, 2, 5, 9 November 1821.
[105] Stanley H. Palmer, *Police and Protest in England and Ireland 1780–1850* (Cambridge, 1988), 99–100, 117–20, 133–6, 149–57; Norman Gash, *Mr. Secretary Peel. The Life of Sir Robert Peel to 1830* (London, 1961), chs. 4–5.

for the construction of a Peace Preservation Force in 1814, a form of national police that was intended to reduce the reliance of the Dublin government on military force in dealing with uprisings and discontent throughout the country.[106] When he accepted the secretaryship of the Home Office in January 1822 he was better prepared than any of his predecessors to take up the questions surrounding the policing of the metropolis that had been at the forefront of the department's concerns for some time. Peel built on the work that Sidmouth had been doing in his final years at the Home Office and made it clear that the government had taken firm possession of the policing debate.

With the help of his hard-working and knowledgeable under-secretary, Henry Hobhouse, Peel engaged from the beginning in a much tighter management of Bow Street and the police offices than any of his predecessors had attempted—no doubt another consequence of his days in Dublin. He requested immediately an account of the history, structure, duties, and costs of the mounted patrol, including an account of the number of suspected offenders apprehended by the dismounted section since their inception in the previous year.[107] He wanted to know the ages of persons connected to the police in receipt of superannuation allowances or pensions—including retired chief magistrate Sir Nathaniel Conant and the widow of Sir Richard Ford.[108] Peel further required the Bow Street and police office magistrates to report the size of the populations in the districts they served, how many warrants they had granted over the previous five years, and an account of the number of accused offenders they had committed to trial, separating felons from those charged with misdemeanours.[109]

Peel made it clear from the beginning that he was going to manage metropolitan policing in a way never previously attempted. Receiving a complaint that two police magistrates had refused to deal with a case brought before them by a Bow Street patrolman on the grounds that they were obliged only to examine offenders brought in by their own constables, Peel gave them a dressing down, making it clear he expected them to pay more attention to the public's business than to their own convenience.[110] He criticized other magistrates for finding fault with a patrolman who had arrested a man on suspicion.[111] He scrutinized lists of police office constables before approving their appointment.[112] In general, he made it clear to the stipendiary magistrates that he wanted to be kept informed about their work, not just in the monthly report he required them to send to the Home Office, but whenever anything 'of an extraordinary nature' came to their attention.[113] There could be no doubt that, as someone had said of Sidmouth in the previous year, Peel made himself 'the head of the police' in London.[114]

---

[106] Palmer, *Police and Protest*, 195–217.
[107] TNA: HO 61/1, ff. 101–7, 246.
[108] TNA: HO 44/11, 27 March 1822.
[109] TNA: HO 60/1, 53, 58–9; HO 59/1/41;. HO 60/1, 53; HO 59/1/109.
[110] TNA: HO 61/1, 59–60.
[111] Ibid, 107.
[112] Ibid, 72.
[113] Ibid, 74.
[114] TNA: HO 59/1/47. For evidence of Peel's attention to the financial side of Bow Street and the police offices, and other examples of his more general management, see TNA: HO 59/1/106, HO 44/11 (27 March 1822), HO 60/1, 72, 84, 85, 88, 95, 179–80.

In furtherance of his information-gathering, and perhaps to see what might or might not be accomplished in improving the police in London, he persuaded parliament soon after he came into office to create another select committee to enquire into the state of the police of the metropolis which he himself chaired. He wanted members with knowledge of the issues, but not necessarily men of like minds. The committee he named included several members who had served on the 1816–18 enquiries, including Buxton, Bennet, Mackintosh, and other law- and prison-reformers, and they clearly had some influence on its final report. But Peel made sure that this body would have a much sharper focus that its predecessors. The only witnesses called were men directly involved with the police, beginning with Sir Richard Birnie, the chief magistrate at Bow Street, and the two men in charge of the patrols—John Stafford and William Day. They were followed by eight magistrates from the police offices, and then three men familiar with policing in the City.[115]

The Bow Street witnesses were asked about the patrols, their routes and hours of work. Peel—at least I assume it was the new secretary of state—also wanted to know in some detail whether the Bow Street runners continued to conduct investigations in London or if they were entirely occupied in responding to requests from provincial magistrates and victims of serious offences outside London. The answers led the committee to recommend in its report what was essentially already the case in practice—that the constables at the police offices concentrate exclusively on patrolling their own districts, and leave work outside the capital entirely to the Bow Street men.[116] The police magistrates were closely questioned about patrolling, in particular whether it would be helpful to establish a day patrol across the metropolis, and about ways in which their constables might be better controlled and encouraged to show more commitment to the work of the office. The committee—led here perhaps by the whig members and law-reformers whose support for local control of policing remained undiminished—also asked some of the police magistrates about the effectiveness of the parochial forces in their districts with respect to the prevention of crime and got what must have been seen as a mixed response. Some of the richer parishes were reported as having satisfactory night watches. But the dominant answer from police magistrates was that the parochial forces were on the whole unable to cope with the increasing levels of offences. 'What do you think of the state of the watch generally in the metropolis?' a magistrate from the Queen's Square office in Westminster was asked. 'I think it is very bad,' was his answer. Would it be improved if the police magistrates had the power to appoint watchmen and controlled their work? 'Undoubtedly,' was his reply. He spoke so disdainfully about the parish constables, that he was asked if he 'would regret it if you heard tomorrow that it was not

---

[115] *Committee on the Police of the Metropolis* (1822).

[116] Ibid, 11. Birnie and particularly Stafford, who continued in the early nineteenth century to fill the role that John Fielding's 'register clerks' had performed as a form of captain of detectives, made it clear that the runners were almost entirely occupied by the 1820s responding to calls from outside the metropolis.

intended to appoint parish constables any more?' 'I should be very glad to hear it,' he said, though he was not willing to answer when asked if he saw any objection to the parishes paying a rate for providing constables if the appointment of those constables was in the hands of the magistrates or the secretary of state.[117]

The report is usually cited as a continuing rebuff to those who wanted extensive changes in the structure of metropolitan policing. Virtually every historian who mentions it reproduces the following passage as representing the committee's central conclusion:

> It is difficult to reconcile an effective system of police, with that perfect freedom of action and exemption from interference, which are the great privileges and blessings of society in this country; and Your Committee think that the forfeiture or curtailment of such advantages would be too great a sacrifice for improvements in police, or facilities in detection of crime however desirable in themselves if abstractedly considered.[118]

David Philips quotes this 'classic statement of the old doctrine of the necessary balance between freedom and order' as evidence that Peel had been 'unable to induce [the committee] to come out with a recommendation in favour of a preventive police.'[119] Norman Gash similarly sees what he also calls a 'classic' statement as a rebuff to Peel—on the assumption, presumably, that the Home Secretary wanted the committee to endorse a more ambitious plan for police reform. '[O]n the only issue that counted,' Gash declared, the committee 'recorded a flat negative.'[120] This conclusion is so common that it makes one think historians have paid more attention to the views of their predecessors than to the report itself. In fact, the statement of attachment to the ancient parochial basis of peace-keeping was in answer to an isolated suggestion made to the committee for the creation of new powers 'for the repression of particular abuses.'[121] In the context of the whole report, it was essentially an aside. There is not the slightest evidence that the committee stood in the way of an ambitious plan that Peel had hoped to have endorsed. Indeed, it seems clear that he had formed no such plan, that he had no ambition at this point to overturn the current structure. If anything of that kind had been in his mind, it is odd that he chose to include men on the committee who had made their negative positions on these issues perfectly clear just a few years earlier. Peel may well have wanted more than the committee was prepared to give, and he may have been testing the waters. But principally he seems to have been looking for ways to improve the performance of the police then in being—the Bow Street and police office constables. He had prepared the way by meeting with the

---

[117] Ibid, 45.

[118] Ibid, 11.

[119] David Philips, '"A New Engine of Power and Authority"': The Institutionalization of Law-Enforcement in England, 1780–1830', in V. A. C. Gatrell, Bruce Lenman, and Geoffrey Parker (eds.), *Crime and the Law. The Social History of Crime in Western Europe since 1500* (London, 1980), 181.

[120] Gash, *Mr. Secretary Peel*, 313.

[121] *Committee on the Police of the Metropolis* (1822), 11.

police magistrates in advance of their testimony ('to confer with them respecting the Committee which is about to be appointed'),[122] and they provided support for the improvements he had begun to make in the management of Bow Street and the police offices. Beyond that, the committee introduced ideas and suggestions for further change in London policing, themes that occupied a more prominent place in its report than the defence of the established structure.

Two such ideas were particularly important. One was the advantage of a unified system of policing. The subject was opened for discussion by the evidence of the three men from the City of London who could speak most knowledgeably about its policing arrangements—the chief clerk of the Guildhall magistrates court, the City marshal, and the City solicitor—witnesses who, it seems reasonable to think, were there at Peel's request in order to underline a point that had been made a decade earlier by the house of commons committee that had enquired into the state of the night watch in the metropolis.[123] This was that the City's unified and coherent governing structure under the lord mayor and aldermen had helped to produce a system of police in which there were 'gradations and subordinations of the different officers' and a 'subdivision of districts' that together produced a 'unity of action.'[124] The contrast with the City of Westminster, which the 1822 committee went on to make in its report, could not have been clearer. The fact that Westminster had never been incorporated meant that it contained competing centres of authority in the dean of Westminster and high steward and court of burgesses, on the one hand, and the parish vestries on the other. The result was a continuing muddle and weakness in its peace-keeping arrangements. Although the committee went on to conclude that the 'the obstruction to public justice' that existed in Westminster was not sufficiently serious to 'warrant them in recommending any fundamental change,' the point about the value of a unified system under clear leadership had been put on the table.[125] And in some furtherance of central control over the vestries, the committee endorsed the magistrates' authority to replace incompetent watchmen that had been included in the revised Police Act of 1821, and raised the possibility of that authority being extended.[126] They also recommended the creation of the office of head constable at Bow Street and the police offices—a post to be filled by one of the officers being raised above the others in salary and authority and with the duty to direct and manage their work.[127]

A second element in the 1822 committee's report was an emphasis on the value of patrolling as a preventive policing strategy. Several of the stipendiary magistrates wanted to see an increase in the number of constables at their offices so as to make

[122] TNA: HO 60/1, 49.

[123] *Parliamentary Papers*, 1812, vol. 2 (127): Report *from the Committee on the Nightly Watch of the Metropolis*, 23–4. The testimony of the City of London witnesses is at *Committee on the Police of the Metropolis*, 1822, 72–95. On the City police in this period, see Andrew Harris, *Policing the City: crime and legal authority in London, 1780–1840* (Columbus, 2004).

[124] *Committee on the Police of the Metropolis* (1822), 6.

[125] Ibid, 9.

[126] Above, text at n. 103.

[127] *Committee on the Police of the Metropolis* (1822), 10.

patrolling possible in their districts during the daylight hours—their argument being that the worst kind of swarming robberies no longer happened after dark, but during the day, and with the perpetrators having little fear of being confronted and pursued. The 1822 committee endorsed the idea of daytime patrolling, but rather than increasing the number of police constables, it recommended—no doubt under Peel's guidance—that a new patrol be established at Bow Street, since the administrative structure was in place and the existing Bow Street patrols were managed effectively.[128] The argument in favour of a day patrol caught the tone and central message of the report much more truly than the statement quoted above in defence of the established parochial basis of London policing. 'Your Committee,' the report concluded,

> are so strongly impressed with a conviction of the advantages which have resulted from the establishment of the horse and dismounted Patrol, and the increase of the Bow-street foot patrol, that they earnestly recommend the further extension of the principle on which they are founded, and the application of a system of patrol by day. . . .
>
> They are satisfied, that no check so effectual can be devised upon those who gain their livelihood by habitual plunder, as an impression that they are under the vigilant inspection of persons who are acquainted with their persons and characters, and are at hand to defeat their purposes, or to assist in their apprehension.
>
> Your Committee consider that the chief recommendation of a patrol consists in its tendency to harass and banish the offender, by a persevering and annoying scrutiny, and thus to prevent the commission of crime.[129]

It was typical of Peel's approach to changes of this kind that the committee proposed 'to make the experiment on a limited scale' in the first instance, with the idea that it could be extended if it proved to be successful. It was indeed a limited day patrol that was deployed in August 1822. It consisted of three groups of eight men, each headed by an inspector, who were to patrol the principal streets of the metropolis from 9 a.m. until the night patrol came on duty. Like the horse- and dismounted- patrols, the new men were mainly ex-soldiers, and like them, they wore a uniform of blue coat and trousers with a red waistcoat—to foster pride in the establishment, Peel said. Like all Bow Street patrolmen, they were armed with cutlasses and truncheons, some with pistols, and they carried handcuffs.[130]

The committee's recommendations were embodied in a statute revising the Police Act of the previous year.[131] Peel sent a copy to the magistrates at Bow Street and the police offices, along with a stream of requirements arising from the new elements in the legislation: that the magistrates send him an account of the relative merits of the constables in their offices so that he could select one to be the 'head constable' approved by the Act; that they forbear to send police office constables to the provinces, but leave that duty entirely to Bow Street; that they allow the various

---

[128] Ibid, 9.

[129] Ibid, 9.

[130] For the day patrol establishment, and the rules and regulations that were to govern all the foot patrolmen, see Radzinowicz, *History of English Criminal Law*, vol. 2, 521–8.

[131] 3 Geo IV, c. 55 (1822).

patrols to take cases to the police offices in the districts in which they arose in order to promote good understanding between Bow Street and the police offices—'the two branches of police'; that magistrates reside in their districts or at least at a convenient distance from their offices; that they inspect the nightly watch in their districts and to use their new authority to dismiss negligent and inefficient watchmen.[132]

It is clear that Peel thought the committee's recommendations were important, and that the policing of London was going to be improved if the magistrates and their officers paid constant and vigilant attention to their duties. He seems to have particularly wanted improved vigilance on the streets, where he expected the police constables to exercise the powers conferred on them in the Police Act of 1792 (and reinforced in the Act of 1821) that authorized them to stop, search, and arrest people whom they 'knew' to be habitual offenders or who they 'suspected' of having committed an offence. When, on entering office, he had asked magistrates to report the number of accused felons they had sent for trial over a five-year period, he also wanted to know how many had been committed under that clause.[133] And when he found resistance from magistrates in carrying out their role in the administration of the 'sus' laws—that is to treat those so arrested as vagrants if they failed to give satisfactory accounts of themselves—he responded vigorously. Two magistrates who criticized a patrolman for arresting a porter on suspicion whom they subsequently found innocent received a stern note from Hobhouse conveying Peel's view that they were wrong to criticize the patrolman since 'a large proportion of convicted thieves in London are detected by having been arrested in the first instance on suspicion.'[134]

It is difficult to know if this kind of management of the policing forces in the interests of making a more effective preventive force represented the limits of Peel's ambition for the policing of London at the end of 1823 when this letter was written. He had turned his attention to other matters closely related to crime and the criminal law once the 1822 committee had reported and the statute authorizing the changes it recommended had passed. Whether he intended that the work he undertook on consolidating the criminal law and clarifying penal practices would lead back to police reform is unclear. That seems likely, given his belief in the intimate connection among crime, police, and penal reform, a point he made in moving the establishment of the committee of 1822 and that, as Norman Gash has said, he never tired of reiterating in the house of commons.[135] Whether, however, he anticipated that within six years he would be proposing as major a restructuring of the police of the metropolis as his 1829 legislation would turn out to be is another matter. A new surge of prosecutions in the second half of the decade—the evidence coming not only in the annual prosecution data presented to parliament but also in the monthly reports received from the police offices—may have been the

---

[132] TNA: HO 60/1, 68–71.
[133] Above, text at n. 109.
[134] TNA: HO 61/1, 107.
[135] *Parl. Debates*, new series, 5 (1821), 1165; Gash, *Mr. Secretary Peel*, 342.

trigger for further discussions in the Home Office about policing issues. There were also by then new elements at play that seem to have had a bearing on the form the legislation would take—a form that was clearly not anticipated by anyone in 1826, including Secretary Peel.

5. THE METROPOLITAN POLICE ACT, 1829

The criminal law and policing were closely related aspects of the administration of justice in Peel's mind, but he might not have become deeply involved in reforming the law if that subject had not been vigorously pursued by an active group of parliamentarians, led by Sir James Mackintosh and Thomas Fowell Buxton, who had carried on the campaign following Romilly's suicide in 1818. They had managed to establish a commons committee of enquiry into the state of the criminal law in 1819 which had recommended the repeal of numerous obsolete statutes, the consolidation of dozens of others relating to forgery, and the removal of capital punishment from several property offences that had been the target of reformers for some time, including shoplifting and theft from dwelling houses.[136]

With Peel in office, Mackintosh sought the implementation of these proposals by presenting nine resolutions to the house of commons in 1822 as a prelude to the introduction of legislation. While agreeing with much of Mackintosh's programme, Peel was unwilling to leave criminal law reform in his hands, and he committed the Home Office to taking the lead. The result was the passage of several statutes in 1823 and 1824 that, among other things, consolidated a host of statutes relating to imprisonment and transportation, repealed the Black Act, and abolished capital punishment for shoplifting and theft from ships.[137] In subsequent years Peel introduced legislation that consolidated the multiplicity of criminal statutes that had built up over several centuries relating to malicious injury to property, larceny and related offences, and offences against the person. This major work of consolidation removed capital punishment from some minor offences and eliminated antiquated aspects of the criminal law, including benefit of clergy and the distinction between grand and petty larceny.[138] It did not go as far as Mackintosh and other reformers wanted—and indeed Peel's major statutes were replaced in the much more fundamental attack on capital punishment in the 1830s. But his work may have persuaded them that reform of the police was at least not inimical to their ambitions when he returned to policing issues in the last years of the decade.

Peel took up once again the search for a more preventive police in London in 1826. He did so, he said, because of his dismay at the evidence in the criminal

---

[136] Radzinowicz, *History of English Criminal Law*, vol. 1, ch. 17; Randall McGowen, 'The Image of Justice and Reform of the Criminal law in Early Nineteenth-Century England', *Buffalo Law Review*, 32 (1, 1983), 89–125; Phil Handler, 'Forging the Agenda: The 1819 Select Committee on the Criminal Laws Revisited', *The Journal of Legal History*, 25 (3, 2004), 249–68.

[137] Radzinowicz, *History of English Criminal Law*, vol. 1, ch. 18.

[138] Ibid, ch. 18; Gash, *Mr. Secretary Peel*, 326–43; Richard R. Follett, *Evangelicalism, Penal Theory and the Politics of Criminal Law Reform in England, 1808–30* (Basingstoke, 2001), 171–83.

statistics collected by the Home Office that, after six years of relative stability, criminal prosecutions were once again on the rise.[139] Committals to gaols to await trial in London increased from just over 2,500 in 1823 to 3,450 in 1826, an increase of almost 40 per cent in three years.[140] Like most of his contemporaries, Peel was certain that such a surge in prosecutions could not be entirely explained by the undoubted increase in the population of the metropolis—though he was conscious of that as a factor.[141] More immediately, it signalled the failure of Bow Street and the police offices to prevent crime by providing the constant surveillance he required of them. He had had 'great hope,' he told Sydney Smith in March 1826, that his law reforms and the efforts that he had also been engaged in to make non-capital punishments more certain and more effective would result in a 'diminution of crime.'[142] By the end of the year during which committals rose by 20 per cent these hopes were fading, and he had decided on a new course. He informed his under-secretary, Henry Hobhouse, in December that he intended to establish a committee of enquiry to examine the state of the police in the metropolis and in the districts surrounding it. He thought it necessary, he said, because

> [t]he continued increase of crime in London and its neighbourhood appears to me to call for some decisive measure, and I feel satisfied that I can make a better arrangement after a searching enquiry and a thorough exposure of the defects of the present system, in regard to the administration of justice by county magistrates, and state of the police by night and day, than in any other mode.
>
> I am strongly inclined to think that there is but one effectual remedy.
>
> My plan would be to take a radius of ten miles, St. Paul's being the centre. I consider the whole of the district included within the range of the circumference (excepting the City of London, with which I should be afraid to meddle) as one great city, the laws of which ought to be administered by paid and responsible functionaries, and the police to be managed on a uniform plan. I would make six Police Divisions . . . .
>
> In each division I would have a police office about seven miles from London, but I doubt whether I would have the police of the district under the exclusive control of the divisional justices.
>
> . . . . Perhaps my plan is too extensive, and I shall never be able to overcome the combined opposition of vestries and all other parish authorities. I think, however, I can succeed in showing that the present system is thoroughly defective, which is the first step towards a remedy.[143]

Peel concluded with a sentence that confirms how heavily the level of prosecutions weighed on his mind as he moved towards a significant alteration in London police:

---

[139] *Parliamentary Papers*, 1828, vol. 6 (533): *Report from the Committee on the State of the Police of the Metropolis*, Appendix.

[140] Ibid, Appendix.

[141] *Parl. Debates*, new series, 21 (1829), 869–70.

[142] Charles Stuart Parker (ed.), *Sir Robert Peel from his Private Papers*, 3 vols. (London 1891), vol. 1, 403. For Peel's engagement in penal reform, see Gash, *Mr. Secretary Peel*, chs. 9, 14.

[143] Parker, *Peel from his Private Papers*, vol.1, 432–3.

'46 Capital Convicts at one Sessions—what further proof can be requisite that the present system is defective.'[144]

In the event, Peel's plan for police reform was interrupted by political events precipitated by Lord Liverpool's stroke in February 1827. The prime minister's resignation in the following month led to two short-lived administrations in which Peel refused to serve because of his unwillingness to support Catholic Emancipation, the great political issue of the day. He did come back into office, however, early in 1828, when his friend, the duke of Wellington formed a new government.[145] Restored to the Home Office, he immediately took up the issue of police reform in London and put in train the committee of enquiry whose report provided the evidence and the recommendations Peel needed to bring forward legislation to create the 'better arrangement' of police he thought necessary for the metropolis.[146] Much has been written about the rapidity of the process that in a matter of months made possible the passage of legislation that produced a major change in the nature of the policing forces of the metropolis, sweeping away an ancient institution and substituting an entirely new structure that was essentially under the control of the government. What made this possible, when there had been such resistance to just such a police a mere seven years earlier, has been the subject of some debate. But before we explore that, let us examine exactly what the Metropolitan Police Act established.

An Act for improving the Police in and near the Metropolis was required, the preamble declared, because offences against property had increased and the local establishments of nightly watch had been found inadequate to its 'prevention and detection.'[147] The watch was thus to be eliminated. Under a new 'system of police' the City of Westminster and the parishes and parts of the counties of Middlesex, Surrey, and Kent set out in a schedule to the Act were to form a single police district that was to be governed from a central office by two magistrates, soon to be known as commissioners. Under the loose supervision of the Home Office, the commissioners would control a new force of constables, who would have the same powers to arrest on suspicion as the constables of the police offices had been granted under successive Police Acts. No details were provided in the legislation about how many constables would be hired, how much they would be paid, and, crucially, what their duties would be, beyond acting to prevent crime within the new metropolitan police district. The watch rate was abolished and in its place the overseers of the

---

[144] Add Mss 40390, ff. 190–2. Peel included a sketch to illustrate his ideas, which Parker did not reproduce—a circle divided into six segments, each with a square labelled 'Police Office,' and a smaller circle at the centre to represent London and Westminster. The division boundaries, he made clear, would follow parochial lines rather than the straight lines of his sketch. Nor did Parker include Peel's final sentence about the level of recent capital convictions. Simon Devereaux identifies the session at the Old Bailey that Peel refers to as September 1826 ('Peel, Pardon and Punishment: the Recorder's Report Revisited' in Simon Devereaux and Paul Griffiths (eds.), *Penal Practice and Culture, 1500–1900: Punishing the English* (Basingstoke, 2004), 275.)

[145] Gash, *Mr. Secretary Peel*, chs. 12–13.

[146] Peel moved the establishment of the committee in February 1828. Its report was tabled at the end of the parliamentary session in July: *Report from the Committee on the Police of the Metropolis*, 1828.

[147] 10 Geo. IV, c. 44 (1829).

poor were required to collect an additional rate of no more than eight pence in the pound for the purposes of the police and to transfer those funds to a receiver to be appointed to manage the financial affairs of the new force. It was left to the commissioners, in consultation with the Home Secretary, to set out the structure of the force. The first appointees—Charles Rowan and Richard Mayne—did this immediately, dividing the district into eight divisions, the divisions into sections and beats, and creating a hierarchy of inspectors, sergeants and constables under a superintendent in each division. Equal numbers were to patrol at night and during the day. Men were hired immediately, and the first patrols began at the end of September 1829, when the force stood at about 1,000 officers. By May of the following year it reached its full complement of 3,000.[148]

As Ruth Paley and John Styles have argued, not everything about the New Police was in fact new.[149] But many of its central features were indeed major innovations: the abolition of the night watch; the creation of a single police district with a unified force under the command of commissioners who were not working magistrates; a hierarchical structure much more elaborate than anything that had gone before; a new pattern of patrolling which perhaps resulted in less intensive surveillance in some parts of the metropolis after dark than the old watch had in theory been expected to manage,[150] but which now covered a much wider area than had been guarded in the past, during the day as much as at night, and an area that could for the first time be easily expanded.[151] Replacing the local night watch with outsiders led by men who would be accountable not to their local communities but to the Home Office also involved a transfer of authority of the kind that had been resisted for decades. These were bold strokes that had been accepted by both houses of parliament after very little debate, virtually no opposition, and without divisions.[152]

Historians have offered a variety of explanations of Peel's motivation in introducing the Metropolitan Police Act, and a variety of speculations about why it was passed so easily. Peel's own reason for promoting what he saw as a fundamental change in London policing centred on the problems posed by mounting criminal offences in the metropolis and its outskirts, and on the weaknesses of existing police arrangements. Those issues were at the heart of his speeches moving the establishment of the 1828 committee and introducing the Metropolitan Police bill a year later. The long sections devoted to rehearsing the evidence of the criminal returns have been seen as a deliberate effort to lull the commons into accepting the bill without a great deal of enquiry about what its very general propositions would

---

[148] Palmer, *Police and Protest*, 296–7.

[149] Ruth Paley, '"An Imperfect, Inadequate, and Wretched System"? Policing London before Peel', *Criminal Justice History*, X, (1989), 95–130; John Styles, 'The emergence of the police—explaining police reform in eighteenth and nineteenth century England', *British Journal of Criminology*, 27 (1, 1987), 15–22.

[150] Paley, '"An Imperfect, Inadequate and Wretched System"', 115–16.

[151] Section 34 of the Act (10 Geo IV, c. 44) gave the cabinet authority to add further parishes to the Metropolitan Police district as it became necessary in the future in the counties of Middlesex, Hertfordshire, Essex, Kent, and Surrey that were within the 12-mile circle.

[152] *Parl. Debates*, new series, 21 (1829), 867–83. For the brief debate in the house of lords, see ibid, 1750–3.

actually mean in practice.[153] On the other hand, they could equally be seen as evidence of his own conviction that crime was a serious problem when committals to trial in London had increased by more than 50 per cent in the matter of a few years, and, as he said, less than a third of that increase could be explained by the growth of the population.[154]

That explanation of his motives satisfied an earlier generation of historians for whom the establishment of a 'modern' police was simply a long-overdue mark of progress. The past four decades have seen more complex and competing explanations of the forces behind the transformation of the police, more recognition of the class interests at work and of the opposition to, as well as support for, the new force.[155] In this broader context, the New Police have been seen as intended principally to bring order to society, to correct the worst consequences of immorality in the working population, to oppose riotous crowds without recourse to the military—in general to impose 'higher standards of social discipline' in the metropolis and across the country.[156] And certainly historians have found evidence to support such a judgement in the aggressive behaviour of new forces of police established across England in subsequent decades.[157]

As a consequence in part of an emphasis on a need for more discipline in society and more control over the working population as the underlying motive for police reform, the crime data on which Peel relied in making a case for the necessity of a new force have been viewed with a good deal of scepticism. The commitment figures have been taken not so much as reflecting a change in criminal behaviour, as a change in the behaviour of victims. Gatrell, for example, has argued that an increased willingness to prosecute—much of it owing to a statute of 1826 that provided more generous financial support to victims of felonies and some misdemeanours—largely explains the increase in committals to trial in London in the late 1820s.[158] A greater willingness to prosecute, encouraged by the financial support of the state, was indeed accepted by the 1828 committee (along with the growth in population) as part of the explanation of the apparent increase in crime in the capital. But not as the whole explanation. Contemporaries *believed* they were experiencing a serious crime problem in the late 1820s. Peel spoke to an audience that did not have to be persuaded on that score.

---

[153] Gash, *Mr. Secretary Peel*, 493.

[154] *Parl. Debates*, new series, 21 (1829), 871.

[155] What is now a large body of literature has been usefully examined by Robert Reiner, *The Politics of the Police* (Hemel Hempstead, 1992; 4th. edn., Oxford, 2010), 39–66.

[156] Paley, '"An Imperfect. Inadequate, and Wretched System?"', 124–6. For analyses of recent work, see David Taylor, *The new police in nineteenth-century England: crime, conflict and control* (Manchester, 1997), 14–24; Haia Shpayer-Makov, *The Ascent of the Detective: Police Sleuths in Victorian and Edwardian England* (Oxford, 2011), ch. 1.

[157] See Robert Storch, 'The Plague of Blue Locusts: Police Reform and Popular Resistance in Northern England, 1840–57', *International Review of Social History*, 20 (1975), 61–90; *idem*, 'The Policeman as Domestic Missionary', *Journal of Social History*, 9 (1976), 489–509.

[158] V. A. C. Gatrell, *The Hanging Tree. Execution and the English People 1770–1868* (Oxford, 1994), 575. On the relationship between indictment levels of juvenile defendants, the changing attitudes of committing magistrates and victims, and other changes in criminal administration in the early nineteenth century, see King, *Crime and Law in England*, ch. 2.

But Peel was also conscious, as I have suggested, of another aspect of the crime problem of the metropolis that had emerged strongly in the 1820s and that played a large part in his own thinking—and that has not in my view been sufficiently taken into account in explanations of the timing and the character of the 1829 Act. That is, the evidence that offences were increasing in areas in the vicinity of the metropolis that had virtually no policing beyond that provided by a parish constable or two. The problem of how to extend the new police into such areas shaped the way the force was conceived and how its financing was arranged. It also helps to account for the flexibility contained within the Act with respect to the possible future expansion of the police district. The question of how to bring policing to areas that had never raised a rate to sustain a night watch had troubled Peel for some time, and helps to explain his motivation in establishing the 1828 committee and bringing in the bill in April 1829. Taking these matters into account does not eliminate deeper ambitions at work in the construction of the Act, but it does suggest that Peel's concern with crime cannot be simply written off.

From at least 1826, it was Peel's intention to improve the police not just 'in', but also 'near' the metropolis. Parishes, villages, and small towns that had not required anything more than the rudimentary policing typical of rural parishes—a resident magistrate (if they were lucky), and a constable doing his annual turn—were themselves increasing in population by the 1820s and at the same time being drawn within the orbit of the expanding built-up area. They were also coming to experience a strong increase in crime by the 1820s, in part perhaps because of a displacement of offences from the centre of the metropolis. Whatever the reason, there was, as *The Times* reported, 'an astonishing increase in the crime of burglary' and other offences in areas on the outskirts of the metropolis that had virtually no policing.[159]

It is unclear when Peel became sufficiently aware of the problem of the unpoliced areas in the vicinity of the metropolis to think seriously about possible solutions. He was certainly being informed about the increase in offences towards the end of 1826 in letters from inhabitants. An Irish peer living in Twickenham wrote in November, for example, about the weakness of 'the police of this and the neighbouring parishes,' asking for something to be done by act of parliament or otherwise, 'for we are all in a very loose and unprotected state.'[160] It also became clearer if it had not been before that Bow Street patrolling would not solve this problem. The mounted patrol might be able to extend its range, but there was a natural limit to the ground the foot patrols were able to cover. Nor were the runners numerous enough to make a difference, even in the case of serious offences. At the end of December 1828, when *The Times* reported that 'there has been scarcely a day for the past two months that informations have not been received at Bow-street-office of two or three burglaries on the previous night' in the 'villages and places round about the metropolis,' and complained that the magistrates were unwilling to help, the response from magistrate Halls was that there was not manpower enough to

---

[159] *The Times*, 27 December 1828.
[160] BL: Add Mss 40390, f. 46.

meet the size of the problem with the suburbs 'spreading almost daily'. How could Bow Street, he asked, 'prevent burglaries 10 or 15 miles in the country?'[161] The problems faced by parishes on the outskirts of the metropolis were made all the worse when the Metropolitan Roads Commission, a body established in 1826 to consolidate turnpike trusts north of the Thames, reduced the number of watch-men on the roads.[162]

As we have seen, Peel was ready to act by December 1826 when he had informed Hobhouse of his call for a committee of the house of commons to gather evidence on the state of crime and policing 'in the district that surrounds the metropolis.'[163] When he spoke in that letter about 'the defects of the present system, in regard to the administration of justice by county magistrates, and state of police by night and day,' it was with respect to the parishes surrounding London, places that had never had any police other than that provided by a constable serving his year in office.[164] It was with that continuing rural pattern of police in mind that Peel was later to say that 'the country has entirely outgrown its policing institutions.'[165] It was as much for the parishes on the outskirts as for the metropolis itself that he sought a unified police in a single policing district that was large enough to include them. That consideration determined some of the main provisions of the Act that would be passed in 1829. The replacement of the existing night watch by a new form of police was undoubtedly the central matter. But the second strand—bringing police to new areas—explains a good deal about the substance of the Act.

In his speech moving the establishment of the committee in 1828, Peel made it clear that he wanted attention to be paid to 'the districts which border on the metropolis' where 'the security for property, is not what it ought to be in every well-regulated society.'[166] The environs of the metropolis have grown in late years 'to an extraordinary extent', he said later in this speech, 'yet no adequate provision has been made for the safety of property, or the administration of criminal justice within their limits.'[167] The committee took these matters seriously, interviewed witnesses from outlying parishes, and commented on their evidence as a major aspect of the report. An inhabitant from Deptford said that the population of the parish had reached more than 20,000 and yet there was not a single watchman or other policeman on duty during the night. Edgeware, had 'no police men, no regular patrol.' In Acton, the 'principal inhabitants' had agreed to support a watch force, but their willingness to go on paying was waning. A subscription in the parish of Chelsea had similarly supported a private, voluntarily-supported watch, but there were so many robberies that the subscriptions had been withdrawn. The clerk to

---

161 *The Times*, 27 December 1828.
162 Reynolds, *Before the Bobbies*, 125, 137–8.
163 BL: Add Mss 40390, f. 190.
164 Parker, *Peel from his Private Papers*, vol. 1, 432–3.
165 Ibid, vol. 2, 37.
166 *Parl. Debates*, new series, vol. 18, 786.
167 Ibid, 794.

the magistrates of the Kensington Division reported on the parishes in the Division: 'We have no regular police,' he said, only a total of six constables, some of whom are active because, though they are unpaid, they can put in bills for their work. 'That is all the police you have for these fifteen miles circumference?' he was asked. 'That is all we have,' he replied. The committee received similar evidence from Tottenham and other parishes. A few places reported having a decent watch supported by private subscriptions, but in none was there a sizeable contingent of publicly-funded police.[168] Asked by the committee about the character of the policing on the outskirts of the metropolis, the Bow Street chief magistrate, Birnie, said that he had an 'abundance of letters from gentlemen resident in different parishes, from eight to twelve and fourteen miles from London, asking for assistance, always concluding by saying that our force is of no use.'[169]

Such evidence was important in the making of the bill. Peel made much of it in introducing the legislation, and all of the places he mentioned as lacking adequate police in the face of increasing crime—Kensington, Fulham, Chiswick, Ealing, Acton, Putney, Deptford, and several other places named in a schedule to the Act—were included in the police district that was to stretch in a 12-mile radius from Charing Cross.[170] Naming such places to be included in the new police district was easily done. But how their incorporation would be managed was not at all clear to Peel as late as December 1828, when on 12 December he sought the advice of the man he had long depended on—Henry Hobhouse, by then no longer under-secretary, but still willing to give counsel. Peel's ideas at that point were far from clear. For example, he told Hobhouse in December 1828 that he thought it would be necessary to create unions of parishes on the outskirts of the metropolis under local boards of commissioners who could seek parliamentary approval to raise a watch rate; with respect to the metropolis itself, he thought that his new force could replace the night watch, but that the Bow Street day patrols and the mounted patrol attached to the Home Office could be retained—with both bodies being governed by new leadership. Indeed, he confessed to Hobhouse that he had 'difficulty with the details' of how the new force could be instituted and paid for.[171]

In the event, Peel left the details and the drafting of the bill to his officials in the Home Office—to Samuel March Phillipps, who had replaced Hobhouse as under-secretary, and to William Gregson, a barrister whom Peel had employed for some time to draft legislation,[172] and who may have been its main architect. Peel's difficulty in 'determining how the expense shall be provided for, how it shall be justly appropriated among the several·parishes,'[173] was solved by Hobhouse or Gregson by raising funds in the rural parishes through the existing structure of collections in support of the Poor Law, requiring the overseers of the poor to collect

---

[168] *Committee on the Police of the Metropolis*, 1828, 26–30.

[169] Ibid, 37.

[170] *Parl. Debates*, new series, vol. 21, 874–5.

[171] BL: Add Mss 40397, ff. 376–82. Largely, though not entirely, printed in Parker, *Peel from his Private Papers*, vol. 2, 39–41.

[172] Gash, *Mr Secretary Peel*, 330, 495.

[173] Parker, *Peel from his Private Papers*, vol. 2, 41.

an additional rate of up to eight pence in the pound to be turned over to the new receiver of the police. It was presumably to establish a uniform system through the whole district that that same method of financing the police was applied to the central parishes where the watch rate was abolished and the police funds were collected with the poor rate. This provided a common means of payment across the new police district, but it also may have meant that more people would become liable to pay for the new police in the metropolitan parishes than had paid for the watch. One of the problems that led several parishes to complain once the new system was in place was that the costs went up significantly while the level of patrolling they had come to expect was diminished.[174]

It may have been the case that Peel's determination to create a unitary force under new leadership was strengthened in the months before the bill was introduced by revelations of corrupt practices by the runners with the tacit approval of the Bow Street magistrates. They had not fallen into the kind of corruption that notorious eighteenth-century thief-takers like Jonathan Wild or the McDaniel gang had practised—persuading men to commit offences in order to convict them and earn substantial rewards.[175] But it was revealed in the late 1820s that the runners had been prepared to compound felonies by agreeing to negotiate with receivers and indirectly with offenders on behalf of banks and wealthy merchants to obtain the return of stolen bank notes, jewellery and other valuables. The victims in these arrangements paid a large ransom, the runners received a fee (which might or might not have been larger than the rewards they could have earned from a conviction), and the offenders received a promise that they would not be prosecuted.

There had been suspicions of this for some time,[176] before evidence emerged in 1827 and 1828 that made it certain, and—what was worse from Peel's point of view—also made it clear that the magistrates had known and approved. At Peel's request, the matter was taken up by the 1828 committee who discovered that it had been a common enough practice—particularly engaged in by country bankers who lost bank notes in transit—that they spoke of it as a system. At any event, they judged the evidence they gathered or the names of the witnesses too sensitive to be

---

[174] For complaints about and difficulties in the new system of financing police under the Act, see Reynolds, *Before the Bobbies*, 153–8.

[175] For thief-takers, including Jonathan Wild and the McDaniel gang, see above, ch. 1, n. 17. No runner was ever charged with facilitating offences in order to earn rewards, but a Bow Street patrolman, George Vaughan, had indeed been convicted of just such an offence in 1816. Along with another patrolman and a constable from the City, Vaughan had enticed a group of five men into carrying out a burglary and had arrested them in the hope and expectation of earning five £40 rewards. He was charged and convicted under a statute that had been passed to put a stop to Wild's elaborate thief-taking scheme and that had been little used since. Radzinowicz, *History of English Criminal Law*, vol. 2, 333–7. The case caused a great stir. *The Times*, *Morning Chronicle* and other papers carried the story in virtually every edition from 10 July 1716 well into August. His trial at the Old Bailey is at: OBP, September 1816 (John Donnelly and George Vaughan) t18160918-6. In the course of its extensive reporting of this affair, *The Times* remarked that Vaughan 'must not be confused with the Bow street officers, who are respectable persons'—naming the eight runners (*The Times*, 11 July 1816).

[176] It was raised in the 1822 committee, e.g., but not pursued when Birnie denied that compounding was taking place (*Committee on the Police of the Metropolis* (1822), 20).

printed. But the subject formed a significant element in their report.[177] The Bow Street magistrates, Birnie and Halls, denied all knowledge of compounding, but the runners who gave evidence, Bishop and Salmon, made it clear that they thought they had 'the sanction of higher persons of their establishment for engaging in such negotiations.'[178]

Peel was outraged by the Bow Street magistrates' attempts to explain themselves before the committee—outraged by their apparent indifference, and what was worse, their lack of leadership. When the report was published in July, Peel did no more than chastise the magistrates for their 'laxity of practice', and to reinstate Bishop, whose suspension he had ordered when the evidence of his involvement in compounding had first emerged, and who Peel now said should not carry the burden of guilt on his own.[179] It seems likely, however, that the revelations of the magistrates confirmed for Peel the difficulties that could arise when the supposed leaders of the police were working magistrates. In conducting their committal hearings, magistrates were obliged by the early nineteenth century—in practice if not in law—to make a judgement about the sufficiency of the evidence upon which an accused felon would be sent to trial. That in itself tended to distance them from the policing work of the runners and the patrolmen, but that separation was made all the more certain by the number of men conducting policing activities from the Bow Street office. When asked about the work of the runners by the committees of the house of commons, the magistrates were always vague about the way they went about their business, either out of prudence or genuine ignorance. In any case, they were clearly not good managers of policing work. Nor, as judges, did they want to be. All of this was brought home decisively by the revelation of the systematic compounding of felonies by the late 1820s. It may have been in any case Peel's inclination to put his new police under the control of a non-working magistrate. He said as much when he outlined his ideas about a new structure for the police in 1826.[180] But the report of the 1828 committee must surely have confirmed that intention.

Those revelations, which were widely reported in the press as well as by the committee, may have persuaded some members of parliament that some form of police reform was essential, but they are not likely to explain why, in view of the strong decades-long opposition to a large police force under government control, the Metropolitan Police bill passed both houses of parliament without serious opposition. Peel's political ability may have been important, as historians have said—his management of the committee of 1828, and his skill in not raising the rhetorical level in his speeches calling for the committee and introducing the bill in

---

[177] 'Your committee have deemed it advisable, for obvious reasons, not to annex the Evidence relating to this subject; but they are very desirous, by stating the general result, to impress upon the Government and the Legislature the necessity of some effectual stop to this increasing evil.' *Committee on the Police of the Metropolis* (1828), 9. Their discussion of the issue follows at 9–15.

[178] Ibid, 12. That Bishop and Salmon gave evidence about their part in some of these negotiations was disclosed by *The Times* on 29 April 1828.

[179] TNA: HO 60/1, 397–8.

[180] Parker, *Peel from his Private Papers*, vol. 1, 432–3. See above, text at n. 144.

parliament. It has also often been noted that the bill was introduced just after the long, deeply contested, emotionally-draining debates over Catholic Emancipation, which may have distracted attention from police issues.[181]

It was also clearly important that Peel avoided raising a storm by deliberately excluding the City of London. The main surprise might be that two other sources of opposition that had been decisive in the past were not in evidence on this occasion. One had been constitutional objections of whig and radical members of parliament who from the 1780s had taken the line that a police force under the Home Office would inevitably encroach upon the freedom and liberty of citizens. Protection against property offences, to this way of thinking, would not be worth the threat of tyranny posed by such an addition to executive power and to the patronage resources of the crown. Surprisingly, no such opposition was offered to the police bill in either house of parliament. Among the leading opponents of a police controlled by the government had been men anxious to reduce the scope of capital punishment who had resisted proposals for police reform out of fear that they would focus attention on increases in crime, and make it more difficult to moderate the penal law. That anxiety had dissolved by 1829, either because their certainty that crime was not a problem had been undermined by levels of commit-tals that were alarmingly high, even for them, or because Peel's own reforms of the criminal law satisfied them that, as Peel always argued, police reform would make further penal law reform possible, not stand in its way.

The second group that might have opposed the Metropolitan Police Act, indeed the group from whom Peel expected opposition,[182] were the local authorities in London. In their case, the overwhelming and unprecedented number of offenders they had to deal with seems to have undermined their determination to go on managing local policing. Elaine Reynolds has shown that many of the men who for years had jealously guarded control of their own parish watches were much more amenable by 1829 to turning over their duties to a central authority if the cost did not increase hugely. Unlike the 1822 committee, which had confined the gathering of evidence and opinion largely to the magistrates at Bow Street and the police offices, the 1828 enquiry had sought the views of a much wider sample of men involved in peace-keeping, including many involved in the maintenance and control of parish watchmen, and who were being overwhelmed by then by the sheer number of offences that had to be dealt with. Reynolds' conclusion in her fine analysis of their struggles in these years was that they were worn down by 'the daily grind of providing basic police protection for their neighbours' and had come to favour the efficiency that centralization promised.[183]

My sense, then, is that the 1829 Act was passed by the house of commons without objection because of long-term changes, on the one hand, in the attitudes of the governing class towards the meaning of crime and the threat that crime and disorder posed to social stability, and on the other—and most

[181] Gash, *Mr Secretary Peel*, 496.
[182] Parker, *Peel from his Private Papers*, vol. 1, 432–3.
[183] Reynolds, *Before the Bobbies*, 135–7.

immediately—because opposition to a centralized police force under the Home Office had been eroded by the experience of crime over the previous four years. There were to be subsequent objections about the way the force was deployed, about the behaviour of the new police, about their failure to provide the quality of protection that some parishes had enjoyed under the night watch, and from many places about the mounting costs.[184] But anxieties on these scores, if they existed, had not impeded the passage of the bill. One cannot rule out entirely the importance of Peel's political skill, the dulling effect of the long struggle over the Catholic question, the exclusion of the City of London, and a concern about political radicalism, as Palmer has argued.[185] But the absence of constitutional objections to the new police or concerns about the loss of local control, suggests that the principal force at work in both the making of the bill and its acceptance, was the evidence in the press, in the Old Bailey printed *Proceedings*, and in the committal data in the returns laid before parliament, that crime was a serious and growing problem both in the metropolis and perhaps especially in the unpoliced areas on its borders.[186]

6. BOW STREET AND THE METROPOLITAN POLICE

The policing responsibilities of the Bow Street magistrates were very considerably diminished by the establishment of the Metropolitan Police. The first instructions issued by the commissioners began with the ringing declaration that

> the principal object to be attained is '*the Prevention of Crime.*' To this great end every effort of the Police is to be directed. The security of the person and property, the preservation of the public tranquillity, and all the other objects of a Police Establishment, will thus be better effected, than by the detection and punishment of the offender, after he has succeeded in committing the crime.[187]

By means of an 'incessant watch' and constant surveillance, the crime that was assumed to be the greatest problem—the petty property offences that filled the

---

[184] Phillip Thurmond Smith, *Policing Victorian London: political policing, public order, and the London Metropolitan Police* (Westport CT, 1985); Palmer, *Police and Protest*, 303–13; Philip Rawlings, *Policing: A Short History* (Cullompton, 2002), 119–24.

[185] Palmer, *Police and Protest*, 289.

[186] It might be said that, in response to a question from a member of the 1828 committee about the reality of crime behind the committal numbers, chief justice Birnie was confident that crime had risen even more quickly over the past three years than the crime returns suggested because Bow Street received many more reports of offences than they could respond to. In addition, a large proportion of accused offenders examined by the magistrates were discharged because, he said, although there might be some evidence against them, it was insufficient to support trial at the Old Bailey (*Committee on the Police of the Metropolis* (1828), 40). He also told the committee that he thought distress and unemployment (as a consequence of the collapse of a building boom) was responsible for the increase in reported crime, along with the increase in the population, larger numbers of juvenile offenders, and 'cheap spirits' (ibid, 34, 38, 40, 45).

[187] TNA: MEPO 8/1.

court calendars—would be prevented or at least its perpetrators would be caught and prosecuted.[188] The patrol forces at Bow Street could be fitted into this model, and they were gradually absorbed into the new force.[189] The transfer of the foot patrols began in November 1829 and was completed just over a year later.[190] The mounted patrol followed in October 1836.[191] Those transfers removed a large proportion of the men who had been attached to the office, and considerably reduced the office budget.

Bow Street was left with the runners—more or less the force that John Fielding had managed. There was no suggestion in 1829 that they would be a useful addition to the new force, or indeed that a detective department of any kind would be necessary. The Home Secretary who followed Peel, Viscount Melbourne, clearly thought that such work was of little value. He was mainly concerned to bring Bow Street's finances under control. Melbourne reduced the regular costs of the office, taking the opportunity of the transfer of the patrol to reconstruct the basic establishment in February 1831. Among other things, he ordered that when Townsend and Sayer were 'removed' from the list of officers, their lavish grants of £200 a year each for organizing security at the royal palaces were not to be continued. He also reduced the salaries of the door keeper and gaoler, and forbade runners from holding as sinecures the posts of office keeper and messenger (which John Fielding had allowed in the early days in his effort to bind men to the policing work). Although the number of officers was increased to nine, Melbourne made it clear that he expected the magistrates to manage the pubic business on a reduced, though in his view 'amply sufficient' budget.[192]

With respect to the runners, Melbourne declared that the payments they had hitherto received for work 'out of town' were 'much higher than are necessary' and issued new limits to the amounts they could charge for board and lodging and for their own fees when on such duty.[193] The runners continued to respond to calls for

---

[188] Edwin Chadwick, published an essay just before the passage of the 1829 Act that expresses many of the assumptions and ambitions that the commissioners brought to the creation of the New Police. Most property crime, he was certain, was committed not out of necessity or poverty, but out of an aversion to work. What was required was a repressive police regime that by effective guarding and surveillance would preserve order, and make theft, receiving, and escape from justice impossible. 'Preventive Police', *London Review* (I, 1829), 252–305.

[189] Peel thought the mounted patrol that had been managed by William Day at the Home Office over the past quarter century provided a model for what he had in mind. In introducing the bill in April 1829, he had praised the horse patrol, not only for bringing about 'a cessation of robberies,' but because it provided a good example of preventive policing under strong leadership. They had been successful, he said, because attention had been paid in their recruitment to their ages, general fitness, and 'previous character;' and because 'their promotion was made to depend upon their good conduct; and they were always under the surveillance and control of one establishment.' These were the principles, he said, upon which 'he would propose to establish the patrol contemplated by this bill.' *Parl. Debates*, n.s. 21 (1829), 878.

[190] TNA: HO 60/1, 7 November 1829; MEPO 1/50, 16. The transfer was authorized by 10 Geo 4, c. 45 (1829).

[191] TNA: HO 60/3, 11.

[192] TNA: HO 1/50, 10 February 1831.

[193] TNA: HO 1/50, 5 January 1831; and see HO 60/2, 110; HO 60/3, 31; MEPO 1/50, January 1832, 29 October 1836, 13 December 1836.

their help from provincial authorities and private prosecutors; indeed, Cox has found that they were even more actively involved in cases outside London in the 1830s than ever before, just as they continued to take on cases in the metropolis, though there on a diminished scale.[194] Their activities were now carried out very much more under the authority of the Home Office, and, when costs were not borne by the parties being helped, more directly at the government's expense. The Bow Street magistrates' effective loss of control over the runners' work and the government's concern to control expenditures meant that the office fund for 'extraordinary' charges was much diminished in the 1830s. Where Bow Street had regularly expended several hundred pounds every quarter in support of the investigation and prosecution of criminal offences as well as the provision of security services for the royal family, those charges diminished after the establishment of the Metropolitan Police and ended altogether in 1834.[195]

These were efforts to limit extravagance, not to eliminate the runners and their work. There was no immediate indication when the New Police was created that the runners' future as policemen of national importance was under threat. Most of the men who had been in office in 1829 retired soon thereafter—within a few years only George Ruthven remained of the pre-1829 group—but replacements were hired and the post clearly continued to offer prestige and decent rewards: the runners' basic weekly rate of pay was 25 shillings against the 21 shillings of the Met, and they continued to have opportunities to add to it. Constables from the other police offices sought transfers to Bow Street: two long-serving men from Marlborough Street and one from the Marylebone Street office did so in 1833 and 1834, including Henry Goddard, the only runner to leave an account of his life as a Bow Street constable.[196] And, significantly, three Metropolitan Police officers were also transferred to Bow Street in the 1830s, promoted on the basis of merit, as Melbourne said.[197]

The creation of the New Police nonetheless did put the future of Bow Street as a policing office in doubt because of difficulties in the working relationships of the new and the old policemen, and the anomalous position of the police magistrates that these difficulties exposed. Problems that arose from a lack of cooperation between the runners and the Met constables were made all the more evident when a Metropolitan Police station was opened in Bow Street in 1832, immediately across

---

[194] Cox, *A Certain Share of Low Cunning*, 218–22.

[195] In the third quarter of the 1831, six runners shared a total of £139; a year later that had been reduced to £84. The final account was for the second quarter of 1834 (TNA: T 38/674).

[196] Cox, *A Certain Share of Low Cunning*, 218–22. Goddard had been a patrolman at Bow Street, 1824–27, and a constable at Marlborough Street Police Office, 1827–34, before rejoining Bow Street (ibid, 16). He became chief constable of Northamptonshire when the runners were disbanded in 1839 (ibid, 44). He wrote his memoirs—a record of some of his cases—late in life. Patrick Pringle published a selection of these cases in *Memoirs of a Bow Street Runner* (London, 1956). The manuscript, in four volumes, is in the Police Museum.

[197] TNA: HO 60/2, 186, 290, 540–1. One of those transferred to Bow Street, Joseph Shackell, had been a sergeant in the Metropolitan Police. He returned to the Met as an inspector when the runners were disbanded in 1839 and subsequently became the second head of the group of detectives, established, as we will see, in 1842. See below, Epilogue, and Cox, *A Certain Share of Low Cunning*, 224.

from the magistrates' office. The problems that arose from this uneasy relationship were brought into the open when a parliamentary committee was established in 1833 to enquire into the state of the police when the Act under which the 1792 police offices had been created once again came up for renewal. One source of irritation that the committee looked into arose from the Bow Street magistrates' insistence on preserving their independence from the new commissioners in Whitehall. If this had been mere form, it might not have caused difficulties. But it had annoying consequences. When a Metropolitan police constable—a man from across the street—presented evidence at Bow Street that a felony had been committed, the magistrates insisted on issuing a search or arrest warrant, if one were needed, to one of their own officers, one of the runners. The constable from the Met, whose case it was, would be obliged to go along with the Bow Street officer if he was going to meet his responsibility to carry out an investigation. This obviously gave rise to bad feelings.

In his evidence before the parliamentary committee in 1833, Sir Frederick Roe, who had succeeded Birnie in 1832 as the chief magistrate of Bow Street after serving at Marlborough Street for a decade, defended this practice on the grounds that magistrates needed to have their own constables, men they could trust to act with discretion. His men were skilful and experienced, he said; they knew how to act in situations that required delicacy and restraint. The constables from the new force, on the other hand, were bound into a hierarchical structure which (he asserted) made it difficult for them to adjust their behaviour as circumstances required. Besides, they would inevitably report to their immediate superiors everything the magistrates said and did, information that would just as inevitably reach the commissioners in Whitehall. Roe was unconvincing in his answers to a stream of questions about why this mattered, and why more generally Bow Street needed its own constables, and why a gradual infusion of constables from the Met would not make for a more integrated, unified, and effective policing system than the present unreformed arrangement. Roe denied that there was jealousy and difficulty between the old and new police officers, or that problems arose from a lack of cooperation between them. His testimony in fact exemplified the problems in the clearest way.[198]

The committee largely ignored these arguments, and in their report (issued in 1834) they recommended that the Bow Street men and the constables at the police offices 'should be incorporated with as little delay as possible with the Metropolitan Police.' For the future, they suggested, a group of Met constables should be assigned to the stipendiaries to serve warrants and manage the comings and going of prosecutors, suspects, witnesses and other office business. They conceded that while they were on office business these constables would be under the control of the magistrates, while being ultimately responsible to the commissioners.[199] This was not, however, implemented, and it took another committee three years later,

---

[198] *Parliamentary Papers: Report from the Select Committee on the Police of the Metropolis*, 1834 (600) vol. 16. Roe's evidence is at 73–5, 83–105.
[199] Ibid, 16.

sitting again to take evidence ahead of another renewal of the police act to bring the discussion to an end. This committee reported that the jealousy that had existed between the constables of the 'police establishments' and those of the new metropolitan force 'has gradually subsided.'[200] Their concern was now much broader. In the interests of arriving at a truly unified police for the whole metropolis they recommended that all the 'constabulary forces' of the metropolis be consolidated under the new commissioners of the Metropolitan Police—that is, the constables at the police offices, the river police, and the City of London police. This may or may not have included the Bow Street men even if it had been carried out. But a second major recommendation of the committee certainly did, and it essentially brought about their disbandment: that was a proposal concerning the powers and authority of magistrates.

The heart of the matter was a question that had been in the air for a generation by then, that is, whether it was proper for a magistrate to be a policeman and a judge at the same time, to wield what were usually described as administrative or executive powers on the one hand and judicial powers on the other. Was it right, for example, for a magistrate to commit a suspect to trial at the quarter sessions and then sit on the bench that presided over his trial? In the case of felonies in London, should a magistrate who committed an accused to trial have influence over the way evidence was collected? Patrick Colquhoun, a magistrate himself, had been in favour of separating magistrates' powers, and limiting them to their judicial role. Opinion had broadly been moving in that direction in the early decades of the nineteenth century.[201] Predictably, Roe saw no way to distinguish these two functions. He insisted on what was by then a fanciful view of pretrial hearings when he argued that if a felony charge was weakly supported, the magistrate should have the ability to bring it 'to that state of perfection that it is fit to be sent before the court.'[202] The committee ignored that, and recommended that police magistrates exercise for the future only judicial powers, leaving 'duties of an executive nature' in the hands of the commissioners of the Metropolitan Police.[203] This was enacted into law as part of a further renewal of the Police Act in August 1839. Two clauses of the Act ordered that 'a sufficient number of constables belonging to the Metropolitan Police Force' be in attendance at each of the police offices to execute summonses and warrants, and that all such magistrates' orders be executed by a Met constable 'and none other.'[204] Bow Street and the police offices were named as police *courts* in legislation passed at the same time.[205]

These two statutes, which, along with the Metropolitan Police Act of 1829, were to be 'construed together as One Act,'[206] eliminated the magistrates' ministerial or

---

[200] *Parliamentary Papers: Report from the Select Committee on the Metropolis Police Offices,* 1838 (578) vol. 15, 5.
[201] See ch. 7, text at n. 62.
[202] *Committee on the Police of the Metropolis* (1834), 102, question 1535.
[203] Ibid, 14.
[204] 2&3 Vic., c. 47 (1839), ss. 11–12.
[205] The Police Courts Act: 2&3 Vic., c. 71 (1839).
[206] Ibid, s. 55.

administrative authority, and in doing so made the constables at the police offices and the runners at Bow Street redundant. The disbanded men were to be offered employment as ushers (£100 and £90 a year), door keeper and office keeper at £80 a year, gaoler (£80), and messenger (£70) in the offices in which they had served as constables. Or, as an option, they could make a claim for a level of compensation based on their years of service. Six of the runners did so. Ruthven, the most senior, was in the end awarded a pension of £230 a year, a sum that confirms how well rewarded some of the runners had been; four others—Gardner, Ballard, Goddard, and Keys—received pensions of £100 a year each; Fletcher had to be content with a single payment of £150; and Shackell, who had just recently joined the office, was made an inspector in the New Police, with a promise of promotion, another indication of the regard in which the runners were held, even as they were disbanded.[207]

In announcing this result of their claim for allowances in December 1839, *The Times* recalled that they had been 'superseded in their duties when the New Police Act came into operation' earlier that year. That seems to have been the full extent of the press coverage of the closing down of an institution that had been an active force in London for close to a century.[208] The runners left the public stage as quietly as they had entered.

---

[207] *The Times*, 18 December 1839.

[208] Cox and Pringle confirm that this was the only notice in the London press of the disbandment of the runners: Cox, *A Certain Share of Low Cunning*, 225; Henry Goddard, *Memoirs of a Bow Street Runner*, ed. Patrick Pringle (London, 1956), xx.

Epilogue

In his testimony before the committees of the house of commons that sat in 1833–34 and 1837–38 to make recommendations with respect to the renewal of the Police Act, Sir Frederick Roe, the Bow Street chief magistrate, argued for the continuance of the Bow Street office, including the runners. Roe emphasized the value of policemen who were sufficiently independent that they could follow a trail of evidence wherever it led. The excessively tight hierarchy of the New Police, he argued, would stifle that freedom. He also made a case for maintaining the executive authority of the police magistrates. The occasional engagement of committing magistrates in the investigation of offences, he insisted, worked to strengthen sound prosecution cases without compromising their judicial role.[1]

None of this was any longer persuasive. The world had changed since John Fielding and Sampson Wright had directed the policing efforts of their officers against violent offenders on the highways around London and on the streets of the city. Gathering information in those years, wherever it could be found and by whatever means, was crucial to the investigation of serious offences, the apprehension of dangerous men, and the collection of the evidence that would convict them. The crime problem of the 1830s was entirely different—and a very different attitude towards the role of magistrates had been forming since the last decade of the eighteenth century. The reports of the commons committees on the police in the 1830s made it clear that the assumptions and practices of the Fielding years were no longer acceptable, and that the Bow Street officers had no place in what was intended to be a more strictly controlled and a more moral police force. With the exception of Edward Gibbon Wakefield, who had strong personal reasons to dislike them,[2] witnesses before the police committees in the 1830s were not highly critical of the runners personally. But they were critical of what were thought to be

---

[1] *Parliamentary Papers*, 1834, vol. 16 (600): *Report from the Select Committee on the Police of the Metropolis*, 13–18, 88–9; *Parliamentary Papers*, 1837–8, vol. 15 (578): *Report from the Select Committee on the Metropolis Police Offices*, 20–4.

[2] The runners were so corrupt, Wakefield said, that it was difficult to distinguish them from thieves; detection under the old police 'was a mockery.' (*Committee on the Police Offices*, 1837–38, 121). None of this was reflected in the committee report, no doubt because the members recognized the personal experience and prejudice that lay behind it. Ten years earlier Wakefield (then 30 years old) had been arrested in Calais by Bow Street officers (Taunton and Ellis) for abducting a 15-year-old heiress, and had served a three-year sentence in Newgate gaol as a consequence. (*The Times*, 22, 23, 28, 30 March 1826). This had been Wakefield's second attempt to acquire a fortune through marriage. He had eloped with another young heiress in 1816 who had died in childbirth five years later. David J. Moss, 'Edward Gibbon Wakefield', *Oxford Dictionary of National Biography* (Oxford, 2004).

the old policing methods—the runners' familiarity with flash houses, their use of informers, their dealings with receivers, and what appeared to be their unwillingness to act unless money was offered.[3]

The intentions behind the New Police were that it would prevent crimes against property taking place, not by catching and punishing a few offenders while ignoring the rest, but by making it difficult for all offenders to carry out their plans by maintaining order on the streets and an effective surveillance over the community. Of course, commissioners Rowan and Mayne conceded in their testimony before the committees of the 1830s, not all offences could be prevented by surveillance. Detection might be necessary on occasion. But it would not involve the practices the runners had employed at Bow Street. Nor, more to the point, would it need a special group of detective policemen. Investigating offences, following offenders, and making arrests, took no particular skill beyond the intelligence many of the new policemen would bring to the job. Rowan and Mayne were asked if their men would be as capable as the constables in the police offices if they were sent to investigate 'a case that requires some skill to detect'—robbery in a shop, for example. Many of the Met policemen are 'as fully competent . . . as the old police officers,' they replied. Still, the questioner continued, 'is that a duty so different in its nature from the general duty of police constables, that it would be advisable to attach certain men, in order that they might become skilful in it'—that is, should there not be a detective department? 'No,' one of the commissioners replied, 'I think there is not so great a difference in that respect.'[4] In their determination to avoid what they considered the mistakes of the runners, the commissioners failed to recognize the positive qualities that had made them successful in dealing with difficult cases—an immediate and coordinated response to news of a serious offence (in many cases with the costs paid from office funds), expertise in gathering evidence, coordination of effort, and the mutual support that developed among men working together over a long period.

The commissioners' complaisance was a product in part of the powerful belief in preventive measures, and in the quality of at least the upper ranks of the New Police. But it was made possible by the particular character of post-1815 London crime—in particular the dominance of property offences of relatively low value and the historically low levels of violence. It is difficult to imagine that the leaders of London policing would have been able to take the view that surveillance by an unarmed police would have been all that was needed if eighteenth-century experience had continued—if cabinet ministers, members of parliament, the social elite, and London merchants and bankers were being regularly held up and threatened by armed, mounted men in the 1830s as they came and went from London on business or for pleasure, or if they were being attacked in the streets by violent gangs. So long as there were few complaints about personal safety from people whose opinions mattered, the makers of the Metropolitan Police could shape the force as they saw fit.

[3] *Committee on the Police of the Metropolis* (1834), 21–2.
[4] *Ibid*, 13.

It did not take many years after the disbandment of the runners, however, for the limited detective capacities of the Metropolitan Police to be exposed. In his testimony before the 1837 commons committee, Edward Gibbon Wakefield was critical of the commissioners' failure to establish a group of men capable of rooting out nurseries of crime and tracking down professional offenders—burglars and receivers, for example. Ordinary constables, he said, would not have the skill or experience necessary.[5] But the need for such a group became clear in practice, not from problems arising from failures to prosecute property offences—which were not perhaps likely to arouse sustained public anxiety—but from murder, which was a different matter, particularly cases that became subject to intense newspaper scrutiny because of the prominence of the victim or the ghoulishness of the killing. This had never been an issue for the runners, who, as we have seen, had only rarely been called upon to deal with murder cases in the metropolis. It became a problem for the Metropolitan Police, though not because the commissioners went out of their way to act in such cases. For the most part homicide charges continued to reach the Old Bailey through the coroners' inquests. But the establishment of police stations in each division and the regular presence of the Met constables on the streets, day and night, meant that from time to time unexplained deaths would be reported to them, opening the possibility that divisional sergeants and inspectors might be drawn into their own investigations, even as the coroner was conducting his. This did not happen often: only about 18 murder cases at the Old Bailey in the 1830s seem to have involved the Metropolitan Police at any stage.[6] But it needed only a few cases that attracted sustained newspaper attention to expose the limitations of a police dedicated entirely to the prevention of crime. Several such cases, soon after the disbandment of the runners, damaged the reputation of the New Police in ways that forced the commissioners to recognize that prevention alone could not solve all the problems of crime, and that the ability to find offenders and support their prosecution were essential attributes of effective policing.

The new force was cast in a bad light by their conduct in the investigation into the murder of the 73–year-old Lord William Russell by his Swiss valet, Benjamin-François Courvoisier, in 1840. Inevitably, the killing of such a socially prominent man—he was the brother of the duke of Bedford—by a foreign servant, recently hired, drew a great deal of public interest. The officers from the Metropolitan Police called in to examine the murder scene and to interrogate the other servants in the household were obviously anxious to gather the evidence that would convict Courvoisier—perhaps too anxious, as it turned out, since there was a strong suspicion in some quarters that they planted some of the evidence that supported the jury's guilty verdict.[7] *The Times*, which was broadly supportive of the new force, was critical of its failure in this case, and more generally of its inadequacy in

---

[5] *Parliamentary* Papers, 1834, vol. 12 (451): *Report from the Select Committee on Metropolis Police Offices*, 121–2, 125, questions 1192–4, 1206.

[6] Based on a survey of trials at the Old Bailey (⟨http://www.oldbaileyonline.org⟩).

[7] Allyson N. May, *The Bar and the Old Bailey, 1750–1850* (Chapel Hill, 2003), 212–19; Judith Flanders, *The Invention of Murder. How the Victorians Revelled in Death and Detection and Created Modern Crime* (London, 2011), 200–9.

detection that the paper blamed on its tight hierarchical structure and concentration on prevention. In contrast, the paper conceded that whatever the faults of the Bow Street men and the constables of the old police offices, they 'had acquired great experience, and were in every respect qualified for the discharge of the important duties entrusted to them.... [A]s a detective police they seldom failed and we are satisfied that to ensure the apprehension of offenders recourse must be had to them.'[8]

The Times noted several other examples of the Met's failures in detection in this same article. But the most decisive case to draw attention to the limitations of the new force with respect to the investigation and prosecution of serious offences was almost certainly that of Daniel Good, a coachman, who murdered his common-law wife, Jane Jones, in April 1842 after meeting and taking up with another woman. Good invited Jones to visit him at the stable at which he worked where he killed her and dismembered her body. This might not have been discovered for some time had he not also stolen a pair of trousers from a pawnbroker, an offence that earned him a visit from a constable of the Metropolitan Police, stationed in Wandsworth. Searching Good's stable for the trousers, the constable came upon Jane Jones's dismembered torso, only slightly hidden under some hay. Good took to his heels, locking the stable door behind him. The constable decided that his best course was to continue to search the stable and to alert his superiors in Wandsworth. A sergeant and an inspector arrived later that day and all three then returned to their station. By this time Good was long gone. That was the essence of the problem. The constable had essentially had him in custody, allowed him to escape, and decided not to pursue him. Nor were the police able to find him over the coming days. Only when he was recognized by an ex-policeman and caught by the railway police was Good brought before a magistrate and committed to trial. In the intervening 10 days, the press had had a field day with such a rich story of betrayal and butchery, and, increasingly, of police incompetence.[9]

The bad press that accompanied the police effort to catch Good was the final piece of accumulating criticism that persuaded the commissioners that it would be necessary after all to establish a specialized detective section of the Metropolitan Police. They may have been forming such a group in practice, using a number of Whitehall Division officers in plain clothes to conduct some enquiries.[10] The experience of the Good case pressed them to make this public and to admit in effect that detection required experience and some skill. They must have taken it as a painful rebuke that *The Times* again explicitly compared the bungling of the Met to the more skillful work of the Bow Street runners. On 28 April, when Good had finally been caught and committed for trial, the paper expressed the view that the

---

[8] *The Times*, 8 May 1840, quoted by R. M. Morris, '"Crime Does Not Pay": Thinking again about detectives in the first century of the Metropolitan Police' in Clive Emsley and Haia Shpayer-Makov (eds.), *Police Detectives in History, 1750–1950* (Aldershot, 2006), 80.

[9] Ibid, 141–7; Rachael Griffin, 'Detective Policing and the State in Nineteenth-Century England: The Detective Department of the London Metropolitan Police, 1842–1878', Ph.D. thesis (University of Western Ontario, in progress).

[10] Morris, 'Crime Does Not Pay,' 81.

case raised the question 'whether the metropolitan police force are at all effective as a detective police.' Several recent examples of failure could be pointed to, the paper continued, but the absence of the 'tact and ability as a detective force displayed on all occasions by the old Bow-Street officers has been more fully demonstrated in the present case of Daniel Good.'[11]

The press criticism had an effect. In June 1842, Richard Mayne submitted a memorandum to the Home Office setting out a plan for a detective department. It was necessary he said, because the perpetrator of the recent barbaric murder was able to remain at large and undetected for such a long time and this has been 'assumed to show want of skill in the Metropolitan Police, and a defect of general organization applicable to detective duties.'[12] His recommendation was accepted that such a department be established directly under the commissioners to consist of two superintendents and six sergeants—about the same number of men that the Fieldings had thought adequate almost a century earlier.[13] They remained a small group until the 1860s when their numbers were increased at headquarters and detectives were also attached to the police stations in the divisions. A further reorganization took place in 1878 with the creation of the Criminal Investigation Department.

The creation of the detective group at Scotland Yard and the involvement of its officers especially in murder cases not only in London, but throughout the country, emphasized and enlarged an emerging picture of the police detective as a man of particular and individualistic skills. It was accompanied by an interest in detection more generally, an interest that grew across the nineteenth century in the wide-spread reports of leading cases, in the memoirs of retired Scotland Yard policemen, and above all in stories and novels that created a new genre of detective fiction.[14] It was this interest in crime writing and in the work of detectives, amplified by stories and novels by Edgar Allen Poe and Wilkie Collins in the middle decades of the century and especially a little later by Conan Doyle's adventures of Sherlock Holmes, and that has continued to grow since, that helps to answer a question that is otherwise inexplicable: why were the runners not only remembered in the years after they were disbanded, unremarked and unlamented, but continue to be remembered today?

The runners did not feature much in novels in their own time, but a large part of the anonymous *Richmond: Scenes in the Life of a Bow Street Runner, Drawn Up from His Private Memoranda* (1827) is devoted to a novelistic account of investigations

---

[11] *The Times*, 28 April 1842.
[12] TNA: HO 45/292, 1. I am grateful to Rachael Griffin for providing me with a copy of this document and, more generally, for generously sharing with me the fruits of her extensive research into the creation of the Detective Department at Scotland Yard, including newspaper evidence concerning the Good trial.
[13] For the creation of the detective department, see Haia Shpayer-Makov, *The Ascent of the Detective: Police Sleuths in Victorian and Edwardian England* (Oxford, 2011); Morris, '"Crime Does Not Pay"', 79–102; and Griffen, 'Detective Policing and the State'.
[14] Philip Rawlings, *Policing: A Short History* (Cullompton, Devon, 2002), 170–1; Shpayer-Makov, *The Ascent of the Detective*; idem, 'Explaining the Rise and Success of Detective Memoirs in Britain,' in Emsley and Shpayer-Makov, *Police Detectives in History*, 103–33.

carried out by a supposed runner into a number of offences, including an abduction case, a body-snatching, and smuggling. Despite its title, it was not written by a runner, but was based on cases reported in the press. It was not a publishing success.[15] The runners appeared in other novels thereafter and in numerous magazine articles, though not always in a favourable light. Dickens introduced them in two novels. In *Oliver Twist*, published in serial and then book form in 1837–38 while the runners were still active, two runners by the not very promising names of Blathers and Duff, are called to the burglary committed in Chertsey by Bill Sikes and his gang. At this stage, Dickens had no commitment to any other group of detectives, and his account of their work is, as Collins says, only 'mildly satirical'. They do become distracted in the middle of their investigation when they fall to arguing about another entirely unrelated case, but Dickens also seems to concede them a certain professionalism.[16] His attitude towards the runners changed sharply once the Metropolitan detective department was created and Dickens came to know and to associate with those officers. Indeed he became so enamoured of them that his memory of the runners became obviously distorted. When he brought them into his much later novel, *Great Expectations* (1860–61), he painted them as incompetent and corrupt.[17]

It seems clear that what drove Dickens to adopt such harsh opinions about the runners, while knowing in truth very little about them, was his admiration for the Scotland Yard detectives on the one hand, and, on the other, the gathering reputation that Bow Street was acquiring in retrospect as skilful investigators who always got their man. In his weekly magazine, *Household Words*, in 1850, Dickens was surely admitting to this widely held view of the runners when he said that 'there was a vast amount of humbug about these worthies.' Though they were ineffectual as a preventive police, he continued, and 'as a Detective Police were very loose and uncertain in their operations, they remain with some people, a superstition to the present day.'[18]

This superstition—in the sense of misdirected reverence—has remained and grown. As Gary Kelly has said, the Bow Street runners 'continued to circulate in fact and fiction' after 1839. He has found numerous references to them over the past century and a half in novels, films, and television programmes. American and British rock bands have taken the name, as have pubs and blogs on the internet.[19] A few years ago, Britain's Channel 4 commissioned an online 'Flash Mystery Game' called 'Bow Street Runner', in which the player pretends to be one of the Fieldings' new recruits. Without a doubt, the Bow Street runners are well remembered in popular culture. It is my hope that they may also now be a little better understood.

---

[15] It was republished by Dover Books, New York, in 1976 (ed. E. F. Bleier) and it has been recently included as vol. 2 in Gary Kelly (ed.), *Newgate Narratives*, 5 vols. (London, 2008), with an excellent introduction and notes.

[16] Charles Dickens, *Oliver Twist, or, the Parish Boy's Progress*, ed. Philip Horne (London, Penguin Books, 2002), Bk. 2, ch. 8; Philip Collins, *Dickens and Crime* (2nd. edn., London 1962), 201–2.

[17] Charles Dickens, *Great Expectations*, ed. Charlotte Mitchell (London, Penguin Books, 2003), ch. 16; Collins, *Dickens and Crime*, 201.

[18] *Household Words*, 27 July 1850, 409.

[19] Kelly, *Newgate Narratives*, vol. 2, xl–xlii.

Bibliography of Manuscript Sources

THE NATIONAL ARCHIVES

Home Office
HO 26   Criminal Registers
HO 35   Correspondence Treasury to Home Office (1790–1810 placed in HO 42 in error)
HO 36   Correspondence with the Treasury, Entry Books
HO 40   Correspondence and papers re disturbances, 1812–55
HO 41   Outletters and warrants, Entry Books
HO 42   Correspondence and Papers, 1782–1820
HO 43   Domestic Entry Books, 1782–1820
HO 44   Correspondence, 1820–30
HO 45   Registered Correspondence and Papers, 1841–1909
HO 47   Judges' reports 1784–1829
HO 59   Police courts and magistrates, in-letters, 1820–59
HO 60   Police courts correspondence, Entry Books, 1821–65
HO 61   Metropolitan Police correspondence, 1820–40
HO 62   Police offices daily reports, 1828–39
HO 64   Correspondence relating to rewards and pardons, 1820–40
HO 65   Entry Books of correspondence relating to police 1795–1921
HO 75   *Hue and Cry* and *Police Gazette*, 1828–45
HO 82   Home Office accounts—contingent payments

Metropolitan Police
MEPO 1   Correspondence and Letter Books, 1829–60
MEPO 2   Correspondence and Papers, 1799–1988
MEPO 3   Correspondence and Papers, 1830–74
MEPO 4   Miscellaneous Books and Papers, 1818–1987
MEPO 5   Receivers' correspondence, 1829–74
MEPO 6   Habitual criminals, 1834–1959
MEPO 8   Confidential Books and Instructions, 1829–1984

The Royal Mint
MINT 1   Record Books, 1572–1910
MINT 15   Prosecutions for coinage offences, 1686–1884

Privy Council Papers
PC 1   Unbound papers

Secretary of State Papers
SP 36   State Papers, Domestic, George II (1727–60)
SP 37   State Papers, Domestic, George III (1760–82)
SP 44   Entry Books

Treasury Papers
T 1   Treasury Board Papers
T 27   Out-letters, 1668–1820
T 38   Departmental Accounts, 1558–1937

Gifts and Deposits
PRO 30/8   Chatham Papers

LONDON METROPOLITAN ARCHIVES

OB/SP   Old Bailey, Sessions Papers
MJ/OC   Middlesex Justices, orders of the court of quarter sessions

BRITISH LIBRARY

Althorp Papers	Add Mss 75899–900
Astle Historical Collections	Add Mss 34712
Auckland Papers	Add Mss 34412–3
Birch Mss	Add Mss 4307
Grenville Papers	Add Mss 57809, 57821
Hardwicke Papers	Add Mss 35590, 35604, 35621
Leeds Papers	Egerton Mss 3438
Liverpool Papers	Add Mss 38201–2, 38211, 38334
Newcastle Papers	Add Mss 33055
North [Sheffield Park] Mss	Add Mss 61861
Peel Papers	Add Mss 40390–99

DEVON COUNTY RECORD OFFICE

Sidmouth Mss 152M: Correspondence

BANK OF ENGLAND

Roehampton F48   Correspondence relating to prosecutions

NATIONAL LIBRARY OF IRELAND

Bolton Mss 15929(3)   Account of Bow Street, 1777
Bolton Mss 15930(1)   Account of Bow Street, n.d., (1783?)

Index